Housing Design for an Increasingly Older Population:
Redefining Assisted Living for the Mentally and Physically Frail

"Longer lifespans and the needs of the oldest old are challenging the senior living industry to find bold and compassionate solutions to combine programs and services with housing. Victor Regnier's latest research provides a thoughtful and insightful roadmap that arrays new ways of thinking from small-scale settings to community based options. International case studies offer possible solutions with the best thinking from around the globe . . . all with Vic's unique perspective of extracting themes and concepts that are broadly applicable and essential to addressing the needs of those that live on life's fragile edge."

—J. David Hoglund, FAIA, LEED AP
President and Chief Operating Officer
Perkins Eastman Architects
New York, New York

"In his latest book, Victor Regnier relies on best practices from northern Europe to identify a three-prong approach to housing our most vulnerable elders. First, provide comprehensive home care services in an "apartment for life" setting. Second, reform the conventional nursing home by developing small-group accommodations. Third, combine new technology with community based services. He illustrates these ideas using case-studies from the U.S. and abroad. The rapid growth of the 90+ and 100+ population expected in the next 50 years make it clear how important it is to address this concern today."

—Edward Steinfeld, ArchD, AIA
SUNY Distinguished Professor of Architecture
ACSA Distinguished Professor, SUNY Buffalo
Buffalo, New York

"Healthcare for the aged is transitioning from institution to home, across North America. Regnier carefully examines this movement in the context of the increasing number of the oldest-old in need of humane care environments. The humanization of technology, and optimization of the impact of nature as a therapeutic modality are examined in relation to health policies in support of the aged. This book is timely insofar as this societal cohort is having a significant impact in both the public and private sector of the healthcare industry, and will do so for the foreseeable future."

—Stephen Verderber, PhD
ACSA Distinguished Professor
Professor/Architect, University of Toronto
Toronto, Ontario

"A goal of gerontologists is to increase health-span, how well we live, to the same degree that we have advanced life span, how long we live. In this book, Victor Regnier explores the increasingly clear connection between our homes and our health. He offers valuable insights into how to design dwellings that increase our access to care and community, safety, and security. He also identifies best practices that can help us to continue to improve our quality of life to the oldest possible age."

—Pinchas Cohen, MD
Dean, Leonard Davis School of Gerontology
University of Southern California
Los Angeles, California

"Victor Regnier has, once again, provided important insights into some of the most important issues facing those who plan, design, develop, operate, and regulate senior living. His own senior living design experience combined with his extensive international research give him a unique perspective on this important part of the built environment and its role in the lives of a rapidly growing cohort of the world's population. I strongly recommend this book to anyone with an interest in the needs of the cognitively impaired and physically frail."

—Bradford Perkins, FAIA, MRAIC, AICP
Chairman and CEO
Perkins Eastman Architects
New York, New York

"Victor Regnier demonstrates once again why he is America's most perceptive commentator on housing for older adults. In this book he surveys the continuum of senior housing and long-term services and supports, drawing on best practices in northern Europe and the United States. Regnier is first and foremost an architect, which is obvious from the exciting and illuminating case studies he describes, but he is also a student of the sociology and physiology of aging. With this multifaceted expertise Regnier has been challenging the status quo in senior housing for decades, while pointing the way to more humane and beautiful living environments. In the process, he has become our most influential critic of housing design for older frail adults."

—Len Fishman, JD
Director, Gerontology Institute
McCormack Graduate School of Policy and Global Studies
University of Massachusetts, Boston

"The ultimate goal of assisted living is to support the needs and preferences of each resident and enhance their quality of life. While this can be more challenging for an older, frailer, and many times cognitively impaired resident, Victor Regnier's latest book demonstrates that it is achievable. Through his extensive exploration of a variety of settings that offer housing with services, Victor identifies the impact building design and use of indoor and outdoor space can have in stimulating social interaction and improving quality of life. His book is an excellent resource for senior living providers and will inspire a new generation of creative and meaningful housing options for the elderly."

—Maribeth Bersani, MS Gerontology
Chief Operating Officer, Argentum
Expanding Senior Living
Washington, DC

"The older we get, the more important—exploring and discussing new directions for housing, care, and quality of life becomes. Regnier's book does just that—raising significant questions that deserve attention. Does living longer mean more life quality, or more time with chronic conditions? Is housing part of healthcare, or is healthcare just a construct? Can those living with dementia experience a satisfying life, or does a dementia diagnosis mean despair and loss? The difference he addresses between nursing homes and alternative housing options reflects a fundamental conflict between an age-stigmatizing narrative of despair and a hopeful You-Can-Make-a-Difference (YCAMAD) approach."

—John Zeisel, PhD, Hon DSc,
Author, I'm Still Here: A New Philosophy of Alzheimer's Care
Boston, Massachusetts

"This is the best book about how to meet the needs of a growing population of older persons for a range of housing choices that are enriching, supportive, and linked with services. It is well written, beautifully illustrated, and full of wonderful examples drawn from Victor Regnier's vast experience around the world. What makes it so special is the ability to identify ideas and concepts that can make a difference (e.g., stimulating social interaction) and then provide examples of places that have done it well. It is an indispensable resource for architects, planners, developers, providers, gerontologists, and policymakers who care about providing the best possible environments for older persons who are physically frail or have dementia."

—Jon Pynoos, PhD
UPS Foundation Professor of Gerontology, Policy and Planning
Leonard Davis School of Gerontology
University of Southern California
Los Angeles, California

Housing Design for an Increasingly Older Population

Housing Design for an Increasingly Older Population

Redefining Assisted Living for the Mentally and Physically Frail

Victor Regnier, FAIA

WILEY

Copyright © 2018 by John Wiley & Sons, Inc. All rights reserved.

Published by John Wiley & Sons, Inc., Hoboken, New Jersey.

Published simultaneously in Canada.

For general information about our other products and services, please contact our Customer Care Department within the United States at (800) 762-2974, outside the United States at (317) 572-3993 or fax (317) 572-4002.

Wiley publishes in a variety of print and electronic formats and by print-on-demand. Some material included with standard print versions of this book may not be included in e-books or in print-on-demand. If this book refers to media such as a CD or DVD that is not included in the version you purchased, you may download this material at http://booksupport.wiley.com. For more information about Wiley products, visit www.wiley.com.

Library of Congress Cataloging-in-Publication Data

Names: Regnier, Victor, 1947- author.
Title: Housing design for an increasingly older population : redefining assisted living for the mentally and
   physically frail / by Victor Regnier.
Description: Hoboken, New Jersey : John Wiley & Sons, 2018. | Includes index. | Description based on print version record
   and CIP data provided by publisher; resource not viewed.
Identifiers: LCCN 2018008635 (print) | LCCN 2018032060 (ebook) | ISBN 9781119180074 (pdf) | ISBN 9781119180067 (epub) |
   ISBN 9781119180036 (cloth)
Subjects: LCSH: Older people—Dwellings—Planning. | Older people—Dwellings—Design and construction.
Classification: LCC NA7195.A4 (ebook) | LCC NA7195.A4 R44 2018 (print) | DDC 720.84/6—dc23
LC record available at https://lccn.loc.gov/2018008635

Cover Design: Wiley
Cover Image: Top left: © Robert Benson Photography; Top right: Victor Regnier; Bottom: Courtesy of Lars Bo Lindblad;
   Back cover: Courtesy of L&M Sievänen Architects.

Printed in the United States of America

V10006669_120418

A special thank you to my wife, Judy Gonda; my children, Jennifer and Heather; my siblings (Robert and Cathy); my parents (Victor and Helen); and my grandmother Katie. We have taught one another the realities of aging and the virtues of family.

Contents

Acknowledgments   xix

Foreword   xxiii

About the Companion Website   xxxiii

1 What Do Older People Want?   1

What Possibilities Would Frail Older People Prefer in a Housing
Solution?   1

How We Age Is Often Unpredictable   1

Strategy One: Stay in the House and See What Happens   2

Strategy Two: Plan the Move and Explore Other Scenarios   5

What Aspects of Housing and Services Best Serve the Older
Frail?   9

Endnotes   10

2 What Are the Major Aging Changes that Affect Independence?   13

Changes in Sensory Modalities   13

Chronic Conditions and Disability that Limit Independence   17

Will Chronic Disease Continue to Decrease?   18

Endnotes   22

3 Demographics and Living Arrangements   25

Mortality and Fertility on the World Stage   25

Longevity Is a Primary Driver of Aging Population Growth   26

World Population Growth: 65+, 85+, 100+   26

China Is the Most Rapidly Aging Country in the World   27

European Aging Experience: Been There, Done That   28

The Triple Whammy of the Aging of Japan: Longevity, Low
Fertility, and Low In-migration   29

What About the Growth Rate of the 65+ and 85+ Population in
the US?   29

The Centenarians and Near Centenarians: 100- and 90-Year-Olds in the US   31

Impacts of Demographic Growth   31

What Other Demographic Issues Will Affect the Future?   33

Endnotes   34

4 How Is Long-Term Care Defined? What Are the Choices?   37

What Are the Major LTC Alternatives?   37

Nursing Home Facts and Figures   38

What Are the Problems of Traditional Nursing Homes?   38

Will Green House© and Small House Models Replace Traditional Nursing Homes?   41

What Attributes Should We Strive to Include in New Nursing Homes?   42

How Do Assisted Living (AL) and Residential Care Settings Differ?   43

Assisted Living, Problem One: Care for More Dependent Residents   44

Assisted Living, Problem Two: Cost of Care and Lack of Reimbursement   44

How Do Assisted Living Residents Differ from Nursing Home Residents?   45

What Can We Learn from Hospice Models?   45

Home Care Through Family Members and Formal Sources   47

Reformulating Home Care to Work at the Margin of Need   48

Endnotes   50

5 Concepts and Objectives for Housing the Frail   53

First-Order Concepts   53

Second-Order Concepts   53

Environmental Docility Hypothesis   54

Endnotes   55

6   20 Design Ideas and Concepts that Can Make a Difference   57

The Neighborhood, Site Issues, and Outdoor Space   57

ONE: Defining a Good Accessible Site   57

TWO: Orientation to the Outdoors and the Natural World   58

THREE: Courtyards for Density, Views, and Social Exchange   60

FOUR: Interstitial Spaces on the Building's Edge   60

FIVE: Atriums for Social Interaction and Exercise   62

Refining Design Attributes and Considerations   64

SIX: Making the Building Approachable, Friendly, and Noninstitutional   64

SEVEN: Create a Building that Is Accommodating and Adaptable   65

EIGHT: The Building Design Should Encourage Walking   66

NINE: Invite Natural Light   68

TEN: Embrace the Open Plan   69

ELEVEN: The Impact of Interior Design on the Senses   70

TWELVE: Special Considerations for Designing for Dementia   72

Stimulating Social Interaction   74

THIRTEEN: Places that Welcome Family and Friends   74

FOURTEEN: The 100% Corner or Community Table   76

FIFTEEN: Places for Unobtrusive Observation and Previewing   78

SIXTEEN: The Retreat   80

SEVENTEEN: The Primary Path   81

EIGHTEEN: Triangulation   82

Planning the Dwelling Unit   83

NINETEEN: Personalization that Makes the Unit Your Own   83

TWENTY: Dwelling Unit Design   85

Endnotes   88

7   12 Caregiving and Management Practices that Avoid an Institutional Lifestyle   91

Effective Caregiving Strategies   91

ONE: Accommodating Independence Through a Home Care Model   91

TWO: Primary, Secondary, and Designated Caregivers and the Computer   93

THREE: Activity of Daily Living (ADL) Therapy   94

FOUR: Maintain a Commitment to Serve the Surrounding Neighborhood   97

Full Participation in the Life of the Place   99

FIVE: Use It or Lose It   99

SIX: Commitment to Physical Therapy and Exercise   100

SEVEN: Clubs, Entertainment, and Purposeful Activity   101

EIGHT: The Dining Experience and Nutrition   101

Creating Affect and Joy   104

NINE: Encouraging Cheerfulness and Positive Affect   104

TEN: Avoid an Institutional Lifestyle   106

ELEVEN: Plants, Pets, Kids, and the Creative Arts   107

TWELVE: Treating the Staff with Respect and Dignity   109

Endnotes   110

8   21 Building Case Studies   111

European History of Home-care Serviced Buildings   111

Service House Model Emerges   112

AFLs, Humanitas Style   113

The Continuing Care Retirement Community (CCRC) or Life Plan Community (LPC): A US Invention   118

CS ONE: Humanitas Bergweg, Rotterdam, the Netherlands   120

CS TWO: Rundgraafpark, Veldhoven, the Netherlands   125

CS THREE: La Valance, Maastricht, the Netherlands   129

CS FOUR: Neptuna, Malmö, Sweden   134

CS FIVE: De Plussenburgh, Rotterdam, the Netherlands   138

CS SIX: De Kristal (Crystal), Rotterdam, the Netherlands   144

CS SEVEN: Woodlands Condo for Life Prototype, Woodlands, Texas   146

CS EIGHT: NewBridge on the Charles, Dedham, Massachusetts   151

Small Group Living Cluster Case Studies   157

CS NINE: Mount San Antonio Gardens Green House©, Claremont, California   161

CS TEN: Leonard Florence Center for Living, Chelsea, Massachusetts   165

CS ELEVEN: The New Jewish Lifecare Manhattan Living Center, Manhattan, New York   170

CS TWELVE: Hogeweyk Dementia Village, Weesp, the Netherlands   175

CS THIRTEEN: Ærtebjerghaven, Odense, Denmark   184

CS FOURTEEN: Herluf Trolle, Odense, Denmark   190

Smaller-scale Assisted Living Buildings (25 to 40 Units) and Other Options   195

CS FIFTEEN: Vigs Ängar Assisted Living, Köpingebro, Sweden   195

CS SIXTEEN: Ulrika Eleonora Service House, Louviisa, Finland   201

CS SEVENTEEN: Irismarken Nursing Center, Virum, Denmark   205

CS EIGHTEEN: Sunrise of Beverly Hills Dementia Cluster, Beverly Hills, California   210

CS NINETEEN: Egebakken Co-Housing, Nobedo, Denmark   214

CS TWENTY: Willson Hospice, Albany, Georgia   219

CS TWENTY-ONE: Musholm Bugt Feriecenter, Korsør, Denmark   223

Endnotes   227

9 Programs that Encourage Staying at Home with Service Assistance   229

One: Home Modification Programs   229

Two: Danish Home Care System   232

Three: PACE (Program for All-inclusive Care for the Elderly)   235

Four: Home– and Community–Based Care: The 1915c and 1115 Waiver Programs and Long-term Care Insurance   238

Five: Beacon Hill Village (BHV)   240

Six: Age-Friendly Cities   243
Seven: Accessory Dwelling Units (ADU)   245
Eight: GenSmart House and Next Gen House   247
Nine: Naturally Occurring Retirement
    Communities (NORC's)   249

Endnotes   251

10 Therapeutic Use of Outdoor Spaces and Plant Materials   253

How Does the Landscape Make a Difference?   253
Biophilia   253
Physical Health Benefits   254
Mental Health Benefits   255
Design Considerations for Gardens and Outdoor Spaces   256
Dementia Gardens   260
European Atrium Buildings   261
Endnotes   265

11 How Will Technology Help People Stay Independent and Avoid Institutionalization?   267

Transportation Is a Major Barrier Today   267
Internet Service Utilization   268
Home-Delivered Services   269
Driverless Cars   271
Social Robots   271
Functional Electro-mechanical Robots   273
Transfer and Lifting Devices   274
Exoskeletons   275
Protective Clothing   276
Scooters (Personal Operating Vehicles) and Mobility Aides   276
Virtual Reality   277
Replaceable Body Parts   278
DNA-based Medicines and Therapies   278
Endnotes   279

12 Primary Themes, Takeaways, and Conclusions   281

The US and the World Will Experience a Much Older Population   281

Home Care Models and Integrated Health Care Models Are Needed   281

Assisted Living (AL) Is a Viable Alternative but Comes with Restrictions in the US   282

The Apartment for Life (AFL) Model Provides Personal and Medical Care in Independent Housing   282

Small Group Housing Clusters for the Extremely Mentally and Physically Frail Is Likely to Continue, Even with Other Options Available   283

Most Existing US Nursing Homes Are of Poor Quality and Need to Be Phased Out or Upgraded   283

How Can We Help Those with Dementia Live a More Satisfying and Meaningful Life?   284

Baby Boomers Have High Expectations for Quality Long-term Care Services but Lack the Means to Purchase Them   285

Supporting Friendships and Increasing Affect Make Places to Live Happier   285

How Will Advances in Technology Make a Difference?   286

An Emphasis on Exercise and Connections to Outdoor Spaces   286

More Comprehensive Approaches at the City and Neighborhood Scale   287

Conclusions   287

Index   289

Acknowledgments

In 25 years we will be shocked that older people were moved from independent housing to a nursing home—when their care needs could have been better provided with less money and risk using advanced technology and peripatetic support in their own housing unit.

Victor Regnier

This book was influenced by a lot of personal and professional experiences. The problem of how to help older frail people maintain their independence through better housing with services is something I have thought about a lot. It is a complicated issue because many of the models that exist are imperfect and inventing a system that benefits everyone seems difficult to achieve. Many of my ideas come from northern Europe, which comes closest (in my mind) to providing the most comprehensive and compassionate solutions.

But housing is complicated and highly individualistic—just like older people. There is no one-size-fits-all solution, especially as we enter a period of increased longevity with more age peers and fewer younger people. To understand it better, it took me a lot of conversations with a lot of people—both old and young. The following are some of the most important people who helped me and influenced my thinking.

USC and the School of Architecture made it possible for me to have the time available to write and assemble this work. Thank you, former USC Dean Qingyun Ma and Associate Dean Gail Borden (now at the University of Houston). I have great friends and colleagues at USC who were both supportive and helpful. I started this book while I was on a Fulbright in Lisbon, Portugal, which allowed me to experience the major differences in housing for the frail between northern and southern Europe. My Fulbright sponsor in Lisbon, Antonio Carvalho, a scholar in this area, helped me understand the strength of the family structure in supporting older people in the community in southern Europe. A special thank you to Helen Castle at Wiley, who saw the promise of this topic and offered me a contract to write about it.

My family (immediate and extended) is important to me. My spouse (and love of my life), Judy Gonda, and my children, Jennifer and Heather, have always been there, supportive and patient. As my daughters have matured they have become important touchstones for me. They can always be counted on for frank and insightful commentary. My brother and sister became closer as we struggled to help our own parents. The last years spent with my mother and father inspired me to think more realistically about this topic.

David Hoglund, FAIA, through our many discussions and interactions has his fingerprints all over this book. It is impossible to have a discussion with David and not learn something new. Wu Ji, my former graduate student, was incredibly helpful throughout the whole process. Her drawings and illustrations are used throughout this book. She was a great student and has turned out to be an even better budding professional. Ashley Mangus, who joined me late as a graduate assistant, did a wonderful job reading the draft manuscript and making editing suggestions to clarify the content.

The dozens of people I met and the discussions I had regarding many of the buildings I visited helped me amass the data and the hundreds of photos I have shared in this book. During my travels, friends and colleagues in Europe provided places to stay, many fine meals, and great insights about the best buildings to visit as well as the flaws we need to resolve. In this regard, Jacques Smit always provided support and accompanied me to buildings throughout the Netherlands. Architectural firms and facility sponsors agreed to let me use drawings and photos of their buildings, which have made them much easily to envision and understand.

I teach studios and seminar classes in the School of Architecture where students are always asking questions. In the last several years the Apartment for Life building type was a favorite studio topic and I had a chance to watch dozens of students create their own versions of an AFL. A special tribute to Shen Zhuojun, who helped organize two previous studio monographs (available on Amazon). Michael and Mia Lehrer participated in these studios and brought with them their sensitivities to architecture and landscape architecture. Those studios also included dozens of consultants and reviewers who helped me think out how this building type might transform in a US context.

My friend Tom Safran provided insights, friendship, and financial support for this book. He is committed to affordable senior housing and learning about how it can help residents stay happy, healthy, and independent.

I have a joint appointment at the USC Andrus Gerontology Center, where I have many supportive colleagues like Jon Pynoos. Phoebe Liebig helped by providing a careful and thorough review of an early draft. Also, Eileen Crimmens and her assistant read through the demography chapter to crosscheck statistics and trends.

My Wiley editors, Vishnu Narayanen, and Kumudhavalli Narasimhan and their US-based Wiley colleagues Kalli Schultea and Margaret Cummins were patient and helpful in leading me through the publication process. Special thanks to Amy Handy, my Wiley copy editor for her thoughtful comments on the manuscript toward the end of the process.

Others who spent time talking out issues included Keren Brown Wilson, Bob Newcomer, Bob Kane, and Maribeth Bersani. The work of Bill Thomas in creating the small-scale group home model of the Green House© was very inspirational, as was the writing of Atul Gawande. I am hoping this publication will get architects to think more about their overall responsibility to the well being of older frail people, the way Gawande's book has influenced medical practitioners to think about the importance of housing.

I am a lucky guy who was mentored and influenced by many great colleagues, including Powell Lawton, Jim Birren, and Bob Harris. All three of them were life-long supporters who encouraged me at every step. Hans Becker, the creator of the AFL building type, was a major source of inspiration and knowledge. His work introduced me to a way of viewing housing for the frail as more independence-inducing and joyful.

Other influential colleagues introduced me over the years to specific aspects associated with many of the issues discussed in this publication. They include David Allison, Jonas Andersson, Hans van Beek, Betsy Brawley, Margaret Calkins, Martha Child, Gary Coates, Dean Hassy Cohen, Uriel Cohen, Jodi Cohn, Harley Cook, Neal Cutler, Alexis Denton, Frank DiMella, Dick Eribes, Len Fishmen, Steve Golant,

Armando Gonzalez, Tom Grape, Chuck Heath, Maria Henke, Brian Hofland, Lillemor Husberg, Hakan Jossefsson, Hal Kendig, Paul and Terry Klaassen, Emi Kiyota, Heli Kotilanen, Chuck Lagreco, Claire Cooper Marcus, John Mutlow, Doug Noble, Jorma Ohman, Julie Overton, Susanne Palsig, John Paulsson, Brad Perkins, Joyce Polhamus, Eka Rehardjo, Susan Rodiek, Graham Rowles, Rick Scheidt, Benyamin Schwartz, Judith Sheine, Susanna Siepel-Coates, Billy Shields, Jim Steele, Rob Steinberg, Edward Steinfeld, Chris Tatum, Steve Verderber, David Walsh, John Walker, Jerry Weisman, Bob Wiswell, and John Zeisel.

Last but not least are the people who helped me most recently in this publication to secure materials, clarify intentions, and discuss the state of the art of housing with services for the frail. These include Eva Algreen-Petersen, Y. E. van Amerongen-Heijer, Floor Arons, Mereme Aslani, John Becker, Hans van Beek, Gonçalo Byrne, Carol Berg, Kathryn Bloomfield, A.N.A. Michael Bol, Roland van Bussel, Lis Cabral, Habib Chaudhury, Andy Coelho, Carlos Coelho, Mat Cremers, Matt Dines, Henny De Wee, Diane Dooley, Knud Ebbesen, Anne Marie Eijkelenboom, Connie Engelund, Doug Ewing, Jesper Hallstrom Eriksen, Molly Forest, Lise M. Francker, Arnoud Gelauff, Peter Gordon, Dan Gorham, Wolfgang Hack, Aaron Hagedorn, Willemineke Hammer, Karina Hartwig, Maartin Heeffer, Jim Hempel, Mark Hendrickson, Anette Hjorth, Matthias Hollwich, Andre Jager, Mette Lykke Jeppesen, Louise Kanne, Will Keers, Karen Kensak, Evald Krog, Jackie Lauder, Jerry McDivett, Susanne Maganja, Jason Malon, Rita Meldonian, Lori Miller, Bianca van Mook-eerhart, Keith Diaz Moore, Stina Moller Nielsen, Susanne Nilsson, Toinen van Oirschot, Niklas Olsson, John Paris, Pia Parrot, Michael Petersen, Liduine van Proosdij, Santos Rodriguez, Erik de Rooij, Niek Roozen, Martin Rubow, Steve Ruiz, Frida Rungren, Edward Schneider, Markku Sievanen, Jillian Simon, Ruud van Splunder, Jerry Staley, Ruth Stark, Jennifer Stevens, Heidi Tange, Mette Thoms, Tiffany Tomasso, Andrea Tyck, Anders Tyrrestrup, and Sandra Winkels.

Thank you all!

Victor Regnier FAIA
ACSA Distinguished Professor
Professor of Architecture and Gerontology
University of Southern California
Los Angeles, CA
regnier@usc.edu

Foreword

"It is often said that the value and meaning of a civilization can be determined from the record it leaves in the form of architecture, and that the true measure of the compassion and civility of a society lies in how well it treats its frail older people"[1]

Back in the late 1980s, it was easy to be negatively influenced by the mindless proliferation of nursing homes for older frail people who could not live independently in the community. When I was a student two decades before, visiting some of the best convalescent facilities in southern California, it was not hard to ask the question—why can't we do better than this?

It was not only the failure of the architecture, but the dismal lifestyle, the sense of isolation, and the joylessness of the whole enterprise that you felt. But the reality, at least back then, was that if you were chronically impaired and could not stay with family members, you had little choice but to live in a place like this.

Figure 1 **Northern European models of housing and services for the frail have inspired gerontologists and providers for decades:** These systems, in addition to being affordable, have also involved careful attention to the physical design of the building and the care giving approach to residents.
This is Gyngemosegaard in Copenhagen, Denmark. Courtesy of Rubow Arkitekter

These were the oldest-old, usually around the age of 85. Today, with the growth of the 90+ and 100+ population, the average lifespan at birth for US women is around 81.2 years and that is expected to increase to 86.6 years by 2050.[2] The vast majority of the oldest-old are in better mental and physical condition today but unfortunately we still have those same nursing homes.

In the early '90s, after a Fulbright study of northern European care facilities, I experienced an epiphany.[3] In northern Europe, their nursing homes were more like what was emerging under the label of assisted living in the US. In northern Europe, most dwelling units were larger, single occupied, and arranged in small group clusters. Their approach to caregiving was focused on care over cure. In other words, helping older people to deal with impediments to independence was primary, while diagnosing disease was considered important but not the highest priority. Caregiving supplemented what older people couldn't do for themselves. In nursing homes and care settings, exercise was stressed and leading a normal life with help was considered the primary goal. Because all forms of long-term care (LTC) in northern Europe were partially or fully entitled, home care–based help was also available because it was often preferred over moving into an institution.

What About Assisted Living?

In the US over the last 20 years, the evolution of **assisted living** has provided a useful alternative for the cognitively and physically frail. By providing customer-centered models of housing and care, assisted living has carved out a most needed niche.

In the US, however, there are two major problems with assisted living. The first issue is the "rules" that govern the provision of enhanced medical care. These are established by states and often require residents to leave assisted living when their medical care needs increase. The second is the cost, which even though it is about half the cost ($3,750) of a private nursing home room, is still expensive. A single-occupied private-pay nursing bed averages $8,121 per month.[4] Typically, assisted living is paid privately. Another bothersome problem is that assisted living often requires meals and services that can erode competence by helping too much. This book is not against the assisted living option; it simply argues for more choices and examines ideas from northern Europe caregiving systems and new innovations in the US, which can support the evolution of LTC in this country.

Shortcomings of the Conventional Nursing Home

The vast majority of conventional US nursing homes haven't changed much in the last 50 years—they are still terrible places to live for longer than a couple of weeks. Designed as a cheaper alternative to hospitals, the original nursing home was never considered a good setting for lengthy stays. Today short-term "rehabilitation" residents cycle in and out of nursing homes, with an average length of stay of 23 days. However, about half of the residents in nursing homes use them as a permanent place to live. The official average length of stay for residents who die in a nursing home is about 2.25 years (835 days).[5] Most residents are there because they have run out of other alternatives and they have no other choice. More than two-thirds are women and Medicaid supports about half of the total cost of nursing care, which is primarily provided to the financially indigent.

No one feels good about this building type. Physicians see them as dreary clinical settings for people who are losing an inevitable battle; families see them as an inescapable and undesirable final stop; residents see them as places where they get little respect, have less control, and experience no privacy; and nursing home administrators see them as a difficult business with narrow margins that require extreme efficiency.[6,7,8]

Let's face it—they are institutions, just like prisons and hospitals. The work of Erving Goffman appropriately named **Asylums**[9] describes institutions that sound a lot like nursing homes where life is regimented, cut off from outside influences, and dominated by a central authority. In these places we lose track of ourselves and our humanness. Visiting a colleague at home and two weeks later in a nursing home was an eye-opening experience. During the nursing home visit, he seemed like an entirely different person. The environment (both physical and operational) created a context that made him appear older, frailer, and less competent.

How Could Nursing Homes Be Improved?

It is easy to beat up on traditional US nursing homes but it is more fruitful to examine the northern European examples in Chapter 8. These case studies describe in drawings, photographs, and short narratives how the building has been designed and managed to optimize resident satisfaction. Chapter 6 and 7 contain a list of 32 caregiving and environmental attributes associated with good practice that come primarily from northern European models. Chapter 8 also introduces three US Green House© Case Studies (CS 9, 10, and 11) and four northern European nursing homes (CS 13, 14, 16, and 17) that provide insights into the use of smaller-scale resident clusters and their innovative operational philosophy. Providers here and abroad that embrace these attributes are committed to making the life of the older resident more meaningful. Using smaller-scale clusters, residential design treatments, and innovative care approaches, they have successfully reduced the institutional attributes of this building type.

Housing and Service Alternatives for the Oldest-Old

Writing in 2018 there are some noteworthy alternatives to traditional nursing homes and assisted living. Unfortunately, these settings and choices are not universally available. Some of the buildings in this book are older than typical new case study examples. The reason for this is to examine buildings that are successful in supporting frail populations and have a proven track record. It is also important for me to fully disclose that I served as a consultant to the planning and design teams for three of these buildings: Case Study Seven Woodlands Condo for Life Prototype, Case Study Eight LPC: NewBridge on the Charles, and Case Study Eighteen Sunrise of Beverly Hills.

An additional problem with many architecture case study books addressing housing for the elderly is their focus on large buildings with a strong formal presence. These are sometimes very interesting architecturally and urbanistically, but are not necessarily the best places for older frail people to live. Having said that, several of the Apartment for Life buildings are large buildings. What makes them different is that scale is used to offer discretionary services (like meals) and they are open to the public. Also, their unique caregiving philosophy is very personal and the larger 50+ mixed-age populations they attract embrace both frail and younger-older residents.

Figure 3 **Home care–based personnel (nurses and helpers) visit older frail residents in their dwelling units at home and/or in purpose-built housing:** Home helpers can make as many as five to seven trips per day to provide personal care assistance. This nurse visits on an "as needed" basis to make ongoing assessments and "fine tune" the medical plan for each recipient.

The bulk of this book is focused on three housing and service arrangements I believe are worth pursuing as we wrestle with the problem of how to care for the increasing number of the oldest-old in the next 30 to 50 years.

The three options are:

ONE: The Dutch Apartment for Life model

TWO: Smaller-scale, decentralized, nursing and dementia settings (often referred to as small houses or Green Houses© in the US)

THREE: Enhanced personal and health care provided to people at home to allow them to live longer in their own apartment or single-family home

These alternatives will be presented in depth and detail throughout this book but especially in Chapter 8, which includes cases studies from projects in the US and northern Europe, and Chapter 9, which showcases new programs to help people stay independent in the community.

The nursing home models referred to as **Small Houses or Green Houses©**[10] have reduced the size of unit clusters and flattened the caregiver hierarchy, making these settings more user-friendly. These decentralized models, which have been common in northern Europe for decades, are new to the US and are redefining the nursing home in many positive ways.

The most inventive European option underscored throughout this book is the **Dutch Apartment/Condo for Life (AFL)** model with its adaptive physical design, digitally supported care information system, and home care–based service delivery approach.[11, 12] For 20 years it has been successful keeping frail people out of institutions and within purpose-built independent housing. The tacit commitment has been to support older residents until the end of life, avoiding the move to a nursing home. Recent models have created small group clusters for people with dementia to provide better protection and more customized support for those who become severely cognitively impaired as they age in place.

The AFL is a hybrid housing and care option offered to both the younger-old (70s) as well as to the oldest-old (85+). Like most northern European models, community-based services such as meals and home care are also delivered to residents in the surrounding neighborhood. Neighbors are invited to participate in programs or utilize adult day care in the AFL building. It is quite different than the US system, where most housing is private and self-contained with little community connectivity.

Finally, evolving new technologies and portable delivery systems portend a creative **expansion of home care services** in age-restricted, purpose-built independent housing to help people stay in their neighborhood longer. This seems unrealistic to many US service providers but that is due to the self-inflicted blinders they impose. In acute health care, the military has explored for decades moving surgery suites and care units to field operations. The idea that someone can be treated in a residential environment (especially today) seems easily doable. Furthermore, the strategy of providing in-depth care services delivered on an as-needed basis to people in their own homes has been available for decades in northern Europe.

Figure 4 The Iris Marken is a nursing center with two 9-unit clusters of nursing home residents and two 9-unit clusters of dementia residents: The long, thin building is sandwiched between two great views. One side has a pond with ducks and the other side overlooks an active sports playing field.

It has been viewed as a way to "stay at home and receive care as needed." Northern European programs are designed to be ramped up so even a very frail person can be supported in the community with services such as food, bathing, and toileting. When the older person feels the need for greater security, a "service house" or a nursing home unit (single occupied with a separate bedroom) is usually recommended. Here the older person can live in a group situation (similar to assisted living) but with medical services typical of a nursing home. But in most cases, initial efforts center on keeping the older person in the community as a first priority.

Nine other programs, including **PACE, Friendly Cities, NORC,** and the "**Village to Village Network**" are described in Chapter 9. These demonstrate the progress being made to help older frail people stay in their own homes for as long as possible. It is encouraging to know that in 2013 more than 50% of funding for Medicaid long-term services and supports (LTSS) was devoted to home- and community-based care services (HCBS) through the 1915c and other waiver programs.[13, 14] In the past this money would have gone directly to care in nursing homes.

To be more strategic and focused, this book has selected examples of many housing and service solutions to stimulate thinking about the possibilities of community service models. The selection of northern European (Sweden, Denmark, Finland, and the Netherlands) case studies is a result of their experience with innovative, high-quality settings of proven value. The innovations we recognize today in the US often share components of these systems. The northern Europeans have in-depth experience with housing that offers home care–based services. These housing and service combinations have kept many of the oldest frail in the least restrictive, choice-oriented settings.

Another aspect that must be mentioned is the financing system in these countries. These community-based systems allow older people to have free or graduated-cost access to LTC. Higher income taxes throughout their lifetime have financed these

Figure 5 The Hogeweyk Dementia Village contains 23 small 6–7 unit group clusters of individuals with severe memory loss: The secure plan allows residents to walk freely around the "village." The boulevard, which links seven courtyards, contains services and activities that residents can visit by themselves or with a care worker.

care subsidies. In the US, private LTC insurance is available but most older people use savings and home equity to finance care. In northern Europe, innovations include caregiving strategies, design practices, and community service systems. There is also evidence that these home care–based systems are less expensive than placement in a care facility. We have much to learn from their experience. Demographically, these countries have traditionally had higher percentages of 65+ and 85+ populations. In the US, our ability to examine how they have dealt with increasing numbers of the oldest-old is also useful in contemplating our own future.

What Is Driving the Oldest-Old Population Numbers?

In one word: **longevity**.

The Stanford Center of Longevity, in describing US trends, states in more contemporary language: "75 is the new 68." In other words, the 75-year-old US male in 2010 faced the same mortality risk as a 68-year-old man in 1970.[15] If you reached 65 in 1950, you could expect to live 13 more years to age 78. That same 65-year-old in 2010 could expect to live 17 more years to age 82. That is a net gain of 48 months within 60 years.

Will this trend continue? In the last year or so there has been a slight hiccup in life expectancy, which has seen a slight decrease.[16] That could be the result of growing obesity or other societal impacts (like the opiod crisis). But most suspect with new medical technology, longevity will continue to grow. Some researchers believe that age 125 is the maximum human lifespan—even after we discover cures to the major chronic diseases of the world.[17] Given the potential for life-enhancing medical breakthroughs and the role of technology in improving health status, the chances are we will be seeing many more very old people in the future. However, many of them, even with enhanced technology (or because of it), will likely continue to experience 5 to 10 years of chronic impairment. It is this group that will benefit most from these care and housing innovations.

Figure 6 In a typical PACE program, different professionals diagnose and treat a range of symptoms: These include mental health, physical therapy, neurological concerns, behavioral issues, medication interactions, and dental care. This on-site gym provides a comprehensive array of physical therapy and exercise equipment.

More Emphasis on Chronic Disease and Less on Acute Care

How to best support healthy aging has long been the subject of much debate. Unfortunately, our current health system focuses on acute care and is less prepared to deal with chronic disease.[18, 19] Simply stated, to understand how disability affects health status, we need to know more about the day-to-day life of the person. The current emphasis of the health care system on identifying and treating diseases can overlook the importance of safety, movement, and lifestyle considerations. Geriatricians have complained for years about the need to aid older people in adapting healthy lifestyles, including exercise and nutrition. These can have important impacts on mobility and may delay the onset of chronic diseases like arthritis and problems with balance control that often lead to falls. The current medical system that relies on a once-a-year check-up for shots and medications misses many opportunities for discussion about everyday impediments and healthful activities. This is why housing (especially housing combined with personal care assistance) is so important. Older people often spend more time in their housing unit, where considerate design, the fellowship of others, and the possibility of leading a more active lifestyle can lead to a longer and better life. Monitoring the older person's health and lifestyle is a very different approach to medical care.

Gawande[20] describes a successful geriatric assessment/treatment team approach in Minneapolis that meets periodically with patients to 1) simplify medications, 2) control/monitor arthritis, 3) keep toenails trimmed, and 4) focus on food and nutrition. These are hardly big-time medical interventions but they are often what is **really needed** to keep older people independent in the community. Our medical care system has not done a very good job carrying out these simple but very important tasks. The PACE program described in Chapter 9 presents a much more effective model to monitor these important factors.

Gawande's treatise that outlines the broader responsibilities of the physician in maintaining the health of the older person was an inspiration to me in writing this book. I believe that architects, policy makers, housing sponsors, and caregivers need to recognize the importance of the housing environment in leading us to a long and healthy life. How can the building design and its caregiving philosophy best respond to the needs of the older person? What housing choices will make sense for you—as you become older, more frail, and at risk?

Endnotes

1 Regnier, V. (2002), *Assisted Living Housing for the Elderly: Design Innovations from the United States and Europe,* John Wiley & Sons, Hoboken, NJ.

2 US Census International Programs, World Population by Age and Sex (2010–2050), https://www.census.gov/population/international/data/idb/informationGateway .php (accessed 9/26/17).

3 Regnier, *Assisted Living Housing for the Elderly*.

4 Genworth Financial, Compare Long Term Care Costs Across the Country, https://www.genworth.com/about-us/industry-expertise/cost-of-care.html (accessed 10/1/17).

5 Jones, A., Dwyer, L., Bercovitz, A., and Strahan, G. (2009), *The National Nursing Home Survey: 2004 Overview*. National Center for Health Statistics, Vital Health Statistics 13(167).

6 Gawande, A. (2014), *Being Mortal: Medicine and What Matters in the End*, Metropolitan Books, New York.

7 Kane, R., and West, J. (2005), *It Shouldn't Be This Way: The Failure of Long-Term Care*, Vanderbilt University Press, Nashville.

8 Thomas, W. (2007), *What Are Older People For?* VanderWyk and Burnham, Acton, MA.

9 Goffman, E. (1961), *Asylums: Essays on the Social Situation of Mental Patients and Other Inmates*, Doubleday and Company, Garden City.

10 Thomas, W. (2007), *What Are Older People For?* VanderWyk and Burnham, Acton, MA.

11 Becker, H. (2003), *Levenskunst op leeftijd: Geluk Bevorderends Zorg in enn Vergrijzende Wereld*, Eburon Academic Press, Rotterdam.

12 Becker, H. (2011), *Hands Off Not an Option! The Reminiscence Museum Mirror of a Humanistic Care Philosophy*, Eburon Academic Press, Rotterdam.

13 Golant, S. (2015), *Aging in the Right Place,* Health Professionals Press, Baltimore, 190.

14 Ng, T., Harrington, C., Musumeci, M., and Reaves, E. (2015), *Medicaid Home and Community-Based Services Programs: 2012 Data Update,* Henry J Kaiser Family Foundation, #88, Menlo Park.

15 Hayutin, A., Dietz, M., and Mitchell. L. (2010), *New Realities of an Older America: Challenges, Changes and Questions*, Stanford Center on Longevity, Stanford, CA, 5.

16 Stein, R. (2016), Life Expectancy Drops for the First Time in Decades, National Public Radio, December 8, http://www.npr.org/sections/health-shots/2016/12/08/504667607/life-expectancy-in-u-s-drops-for-first-time-in-decades-report-finds (accessed 10/1/17).

17 Weon, B.M., and Je, J. (2009), Theoretical Estimation of Maximum Human Lifespan, *Biogerontology* 10, 65–71.

18 NIA/NIH, (2011), *Global Health and Aging*, GPO Publication #11-7737, Washington DC.

19 Butler, R. (2006), *The Longevity Revolution: The Benefits and Challenges of Living a Long Life*, Public Affairs, New York.

20 Gawande, *Being Mortal*, 49.

ABOUT THE COMPANION WEBSITE

This book is accompanied by a companion website:

www.wiley.com/go/hdop

The website includes an instructor's manual.

Housing Design for an Increasingly Older Population

CHAPTER ONE

What Do Older People Want?

What Possibilities Would Frail Older People Prefer in a Housing Solution?

If we were starting over and wanted to design the best housing for older frail people in this country, what would it be like? How large would the dwelling unit be? How connected would it be to the surrounding community and to friends? Would it be part of a normal age-mixed community or would it be better if the people were the same age with a similar outlook on life?

Would it have high-tech gadgets that increase safety, security, and communication, or just an old fashioned lock on the door? Would there be an area to display prized possessions and a place for a favorite piece of furniture? Would it be important to have a pet?

How would support be provided if there was a need for help with meal preparation or taking a shower? Would children or relatives volunteer to help? If confusion or memory loss occurred, then what would be the solution? What if driving the car to the store was too difficult or risky? How can safety be increased without giving up too much autonomy? How important is it to do things yourself?

Finally, would it be affordable, so you could live there until you die?

THE OVERWHELMING ANSWER APPEARS TO BE "AGING IN PLACE"

When we ask adults about the future, they tell us they would prefer to stay at home with everything the way it has always been rather than move to a smaller house or apartment, independent senior housing, assisted living, or (heaven forbid) a nursing home. An often quoted AARP survey states that 73% (of their over-age-45 sample) **strongly agree** with the statement "What I'd really like to do is stay in my current residence for as long as possible."[1] Let's also keep in mind that more than 75% of the over-age-80 households are homeowners.[2]

The overwhelming preference to age in place also coincides with the easiest thing to do, which is nothing. The fact that we have no idea what will happen in the future fuels our confidence about the status quo. But thinking about the problem does make it easier to understand and allows more and better solutions to materialize.

But does that work for everybody? What are the issues that govern our choices and thinking about the future? Does one size fit all? Or is one size okay for a while but needs refitting over time? Also, how does aging, disability, and family support fit into this picture?

How We Age Is Often Unpredictable

If we were all the same and life was predictable, it would be easier to answer these questions. Today we have more choices than a decade ago, but that hasn't made it easier to figure it out. One aspect that makes it difficult (but also interesting) is the level of unpredictability associated with growing old. Aging is inevitable but *how* you age is anything but easy to foresee. One of the fascinating aspects of aging is how different older people are from one another.

Figure 1-1 **The shopping choices, transportation options, and neighborhood safety within blocks of the Kristal Case Study (CS) make it convenient:** Moving is an important choice to consider when faced with a neighborhood or dwelling unit that will cause difficulties as you become older. Staying in the general vicinity may minimize the disruption of losing friends.

The words **mentally and physically frail** and **oldest-old** are used to describe this constituency, but there is tremendous variability among individuals. We also know that differential aging starts early in life. Belsky and his colleagues[3] found in a sample of nearly a thousand 38-year-olds that the "functional age" of that group ranged from under 30 to slightly less than 60, which is amazing just 20 years after high school graduation.

We start at birth with a unique DNA genetic profile, and every day after is a step in a direction that makes us more "different" than others. Our behaviors, habits, lifestyle choices, and experiences lead us to be totally unique by the time we reach retirement age. We all know our birthday but have no idea about our **death day** – or how we are going to get there. It is no surprise that the choice for one person's "ideal" setting would have different components from another person's.

Lifespan is just one issue. Pinchas Cohen[4] reminds us that health span and wealth span also need to be considered. Living to age 95 sounds great, but will the last 5 to 7 years be active or highly constrained? Without proper planning it is easy to run short of financial resources and those last 5 years could be even drearier. In most cases it is important to pay attention to the control one has over lifestyle. **Housing for older people is not just about what it looks like**. This book examines housing from the perspective of the older person. Not just the "formal" appearance of the building, but how

it supports everyone's very unique life. What impact does location have? How much of an impediment is a two-story dwelling? Is it handicapped accessible?

For many of the oldest-old in this country, looming in the distance is the ultimate default move to a Medicaid nursing home. There are 1.4 million nursing home residents in the US,[5] the majority of which are Medicaid supported. It is the option of last resort, especially for older women living alone in poverty.

There appear to be two major strategies that the oldest-old and their families employ when thinking about their future housing situation.

> **One of the fascinating aspects of aging is how different older people of the same age are from one another.**

Strategy One: Stay in the House and See What Happens

The most common strategy is to do nothing and continue without thinking about it. You could call it the "batten down the hatches" scenario. Home modifications are often

Figure 1-2 **Age-restricted or age-targeted active adult communities are purpose designed to meet the needs and expectations of an older constituent:** Most designs are one story with two bedrooms. Frequently, as in this illustration, the kitchen, living room, and dining are combined into a single "great room."

made along with adjustments in lifestyle. Couples often rely on one another like they always have. This is advantageous for men because if they have married someone about the same age, they will likely die before their spouse (because of gender-based differences in longevity). Also, as men decline in competency they will have a built-in caregiver often willing and able to care for them. However, the remaining spouse is left in limbo and is often exhausted from caregiving duties. In the end, the surviving spouse often stays at home and waits to see what will happen next. But without the friendship or security of a spouse, survivors often feel the need to move to a more supportive arrangement or, if they have children, to rely more on family help.

THE PREDICTABILITY OF A CONVENIENT AND SUPPORTIVE NEIGHBORHOOD

Another emotional factor is the neighborhood. In the same AARP research that reported a strong preference for aging in place, 67% also strongly agreed they would like to stay in their communities as long as possible.[6] Connections with familiar merchants, neighbors, stores, and services in the local community represent more than access to goods and services. The mailman, the local hardware store handyman, and the beauty salon stylist/barber can be important confidants. These are often people you have come to know in places that are familiar.

Roots to community infrastructure like churches, libraries, parks, grocery stores, and pharmacies are also deep. So losing the house also involves losing a connection to community resources or a neighbor who is always willing to do you a favor. Predictability is also another factor. Knowing what to expect in your neighborhood such as personal security, traffic, or proximity to important resources is assuring. The nursing home and assisted living residence by their nature are self-contained. Staff members provide all of your needs, including food, personal assistance, a beauty shop, and transportation. They replace neighborhood ties with services they provide.

WHY DO SO MANY PEOPLE WANT TO AGE IN PLACE AND NOT MOVE?

For many the house is like a museum of life experiences. Everything valuable seems to be on display or easily accessible. Books, photos, furniture, and gifts from family members may be the most salient. The objects and the place itself evoke memories of noteworthy occasions and special people.[7] Even the views to the outside remind us that we are located within a rich context of plant materials and sunlight.

Many older people describe their abode as providing a "sense of place" or as architects sometimes call it, a "genius loci."[8] It is not just the uniqueness of the physical environment but the emotional attachment to place that makes it intimate and authentic. Layers of time connect with emotionally significant events, and the physical environment acts as a powerful mnemonic that allows many to relive the past. Sometimes the most commonplace item – like a stuffed animal – can recall a deep or cherished memory. The house can even become like another layer of skin that encompasses the self and protects from negative outside influences.

For many of the oldest-old, the home or apartment represents a life well lived. The size can accommodate friends and family members for an overnight stay or provide the setting for a traditional family event. For homeowners, it can represent social class and success. For many it is also their most important financial investment, which is often used to secure their retirement.[9]

MOVING IS DISRUPTIVE

Although maintenance is a hassle, moving is even a bigger physical and psychological burden. Compared to people in middle age or younger, the aged are very residentially stabile. According to the 2011 American Housing Survey, 60% of the 80+ population have lived in their houses for 20 years or more[10] and an additional 18% have lived in the same dwelling for 10–19 years. When they move, it is often to a smaller apartment or house. Of all population age groups, older people have the lowest rate of moves and the highest rate of local (same county) moves, when they do move.[11]

Because rooms in rental housing are often smaller, new smaller pieces of furniture may need to be purchased. Sorting through decades of acquisitions is time consuming and sometimes disconcerting. The oldest-old have additional constraints, but their participation is important in a successful move. One undeniable aspect is that parting with objects that elicit important memories takes a lot of emotional and psychic energy.

> ## We all know our birthday but have no idea about our death day – or how we will get there.

MANAGING AN INDEPENDENT HOUSEHOLD CAN PROVIDE A SENSE OF MASTERY

One of the worst aspects of housing with services is that much of the day-to-day work that keeps an older frail person engaged is often eliminated because someone else does it. Most licensed supportive care settings provide services that eliminate the habitual, familiar tasks that give the day meaning. Some of those tasks, like

Figure 1-3 **This Erickson community of approximately 2000 units is a CCRC located on a 120-acre campus:** Erickson communities are targeted to middle-income seniors. The scale of the development allows it to support several restaurants, a comprehensive exercise venue, a large auditorium for special events, and many individual clubs.

housekeeping, not only fill the day but can give the older person a sense of accomplishment along with a light workout. Incremental home care support and the "use it or lose it" philosophy associated with the Apartment for Life solves this problem by making household tasks more of a benefit than a burden.

FOR MANY OLDER FRAIL PEOPLE, LIVING INDEPENDENTLY MEANS LIVING ALONE

Those who choose to stay at home are likely to find themselves isolated in the community. Nearly 6% of the 65+ who are living in the community are homebound, a number that is 1.5 times larger than the number of residents in nursing homes. Many of these individuals rarely or ever get out. Some have severe impairments while others have barriers like steps that are difficult to navigate. Unless you have neighbors or family willing to visit and take you out, this can be a lonely and depressing lifestyle.[12] Residents in group living situations like senior housing or assisted living get out much more frequently than people living alone, because they often have access to transportation and travel companions. Isolation is even more severe in rural areas and small towns.[13]

MOVES ARE OFTEN TRIGGERED BY AN EMERGENCY WITH LITTLE TIME TO REFLECT

Some people avoid thinking about their situation and how to position themselves to deal with an emergency. That event could be a fall, a stroke, a heart attack, or a traffic accident. If it requires clinical attention, everyone, including family, gets into the picture. With doctors, paramedics, social workers, and discharge nurses involved, placement in a formal clinical setting is usually the default solution. With no advanced discussion or plan to follow in response to a traumatic event, there is little time to reflect and respond creatively. If an assisted living or nursing facility is involved, the decision is made without much discussion. Because of this the older person can feel marginalized when not directly involved in decisions. Testing out a family support solution with home care assistance should be explored, until a more permanent solution can be devised. If the older person breaks a hip or has a major cognitive episode, it is harder to avoid an institutional solution but at least it is not a forgone conclusion.

Figure 1-4 **This affordable senior co-housing project in Brabend, Denmark, reduces monthly costs by creating resident committees that take on maintenance tasks:** Although residents don't provide direct personal care assistance to one another, they are a tight-knit community who help one another.

Strategy Two: Plan the Move and Explore Other Scenarios

The second strategy examines the situation realistically and considers the choices that make sense and the ones to avoid. These types of individuals are often referred to as "contingent" movers.[14] If individuals have enough financial resources, they may look at a Continuing Care Retirement Community (CCRC) or Life Plan Community (LPC) because these settings have contracts that cover assisted living, dementia, and nursing care in addition to independent living. Another approach might be multiple moves, which occur as the individual becomes less

Figure 1-5 For some, the ideal is a cottage affiliated with a larger community building that provides meals and activities: This is one of the fifty cottages at the NewBridge CS. People that move to a CCRC/LPC often come from larger single-family homes and even though they downsize they still select relatively large units.
Copyright Chris Cooper ©, Courtesy of Perkins Eastman.

capable and the need for services becomes more frequent or medically complex.

First moves should be to places with convenient stores and services, near family members, and with good access to parks, houses of worship, libraries, and other valued destinations. The analysis should also consider home safety, wheelchair adaptability, transportation options, and home care delivery possibilities. These can be apartments, condominiums, single-family houses, or age-restricted housing, but should be carefully analyzed with regard to how they will support the individual as they age in place. A person can move in with their family or could secure home care services in the community. These options are easy to implement when research is done in advance and the outcomes of various alternatives have been considered and studied.

WHY NOT JUST MOVE TO A BETTER PLACE AND LOCATION?

This is a rational position that is often overlooked. It is a relatively easy task to list out the qualities and characteristics of a housing choice that could optimize today's situation and work for tomorrow's contingencies. Age-friendly, affordable apartments or condominiums located near commercial districts with good access to transportation, family help, and

home care support are often available. Furthermore, if this choice is altered by a future event that reorders priorities, moving again is usually not as disruptive. The process of listing important features and thinking about future contingencies can make it easier to deal with an ambiguous future.

This approach is very American. Since World War II the strategy has been to buy the newest-model home, hold it for appreciation, and then leverage the sale for an even higher-value investment with greater profit potential. There is less affection for the house as a place and more reliance on its ability to appreciate in value over time, providing a nest egg for the future or a going-away present to offspring.

In fact, the US tax code makes it advantageous for older people to sell their house and exclude up to $250,000 ($500,000 per couple) of the capital gain difference between the original cost of their property and the current sale value. The money can be used tax free for reinvestment or for savings.[15]

ADAPTABILITY AND RESILIENCE ARE IMPORTANT

Adaptability is central in this scenario. People can change their habits, their lifestyle, and their use patterns. They can change the environment by making safety modifications,

Figure 1-6 **The kitchen at the Rundgraafpark CS is a galley configuration with a window overlooking an atrium:** One- and two-bedroom units here are larger, ranging from 800 to 1100 SF. The possibility of staying here with additional home care service reduces worry about having to move again.

installing new equipment, or moving to a better, more supportive setting. Earlier in life, that is how most people respond to problems that limit options or make it impossible to continue as they have in the past. But older people are often very cautious and can't imagine moving from where they have raised their family or put down roots in the community.

Resilience is also a successful reaction to adversity and is commonly recognized today as one of the most powerful coping mechanisms of the oldest-old.[16] Being able to deal with disruptive change by rebounding with the capacity to move forward is an effective strength to nurture. "Seeing the glass half full" encourages optimism and self-efficacy. More importantly, this attitude can be taught or encouraged through behavioral therapy. One of the best ways to think out dilemmas is through peer discussions with friends, confidants, and family members.

THE HOME IS OFTEN TOO BIG AND MAINTENANCE IS A BURDEN

Another motivation to move is an oversized dwelling unit that made sense 50 years ago but doesn't today. The home designed to fit the family of yesteryear with five people sharing it is larger today than what is needed. As a home reaches the half-century mark, maintenance expenses can become costlier. Routine tasks such as raking leaves, shoveling snow, cutting the grass, and fixing a roof leak are more difficult responsibilities to shoulder in old age. It is somewhat surprising that an enterprising online hospitality service hasn't figured out how to market this extra space to others. The National Shared Housing Resource Center[17] has over 60 agencies in 24 states involved with brokering house share matches. But their efforts are meager when compared to the millions of underutilized houses available.

> **The house can become like another layer of skin that encompasses the self and protects from negative outside influences.**

SAFETY AND HOME CARE SERVICES ARE NECESSARY FOR THE FRAIL

Older frail people often suffer disabilities that limit self-care or require supplemental personal care assistance. For example, more than 40% of the age 80+ population has trouble walking.[18] In the US, help usually comes from family, friends, or paid personnel. The family often provides a great deal of help in these situations. The more intense the assistance, the more likely the individual will need to move in with a family member or rely on help from a part-time, paid worker. Today's Medicaid waiver program, which has been growing in popularity, also helps older people stay with family help in their own dwelling unit.

Electronic safety systems are evolving from emergency response to more comprehensive online monitoring devices. Cameras and voice transmission are being integrated as part of the "internet of things." As they grow in sophistication and networking capability they will provide more help to families through service providers that monitor the older person. Designed to improve comprehensive monitoring, these new technologies will improve safety and provide assurance that someone will be available to respond.

HOW DOES DEMENTIA CHANGE THINGS?

The most difficult individuals to manage are those with memory impairments. They are erratic, behaviorally complex, and may be unable to recognize family members and paid caregivers. Northern European systems have their greatest advantage here because they have invested heavily in a system of home health care and high-quality nursing homes that provide dementia training as well as comprehensive solutions. Their goal is to keep the older person at home for as long as possible. They are driven by the preferences of the older person (and family) and the desire to avoid the higher cost of institutional care. In Holland, for those who must move, there are small dementia group homes located nearby to keep the cognitively impaired close to their spouse and friends. In northern Europe today only the most severely impaired eventually end up moving to nursing homes because these countries do such a good job of supporting people independently in the community.

SHARING YOUR LIFE WITH OTHERS HAS MANY ADVANTAGES

Living in senior housing with services provides the possibility of increased peer interactions and encourages new friendship formation. This is an issue for many of

Figure 1-7 **Access to well-designed exercise options is important to many older people:** This swimming pool in Denmark is shared with the community and features a recessed edge to facilitate discussion and feedback to individuals seeking aquatic exercise. Water resistance exercises are an effective and benevolent medium for aerobic workouts and strength training.

the oldest-old because over time they lose many close friends. A well-designed "purpose-built" environment also increases safety, accessibility, and independence. Most unit layouts are designed to be adaptable and flexible in response to a range of potential future outcomes. Living with a group of peers can also facilitate shared activities. Exercise can include shared equipment configured for the unique physiology of the older body. Living with others can also make it easier to find an exercise partner, which can have important motivational value.

Active adult communities targeted toward residents over age 50 or 55 are very successful in cultivating new friendships at an earlier age.[19] Aging in place in an active adult community also seems advantageous. When the project is sold out and the developer exits, an elected resident council representing homeowners usually works with a professional management company to oversee the operation of the community.[20] Even though these settings are not marketed toward the oldest-old, as the population ages the community responds to the need for supportive services like transportation and home-delivered meals. Because these are owner-occupied developments, residents have more flexibility because they are less regulated than a typical continuing care retirement community or assisted living facility.

> **Given all the underutilized space in the housing stock owned by older people, it is surprising an online hospitality service hasn't figured out a way to market it to others.**

CONSIDER DRIVING, WALKING, AND OTHER MOBILITY OPTIONS

Another major dilemma is dealing with transportation when you can no longer drive a car. Moving to a location where you can walk, bike, or take a scooter to stores and services gives you more freedom and flexibility. If you stay at home and are one of the 50% of older households located in the suburbs,[21] then you may need to rely on family, friends, and taxis to get around. Surprisingly, only 24% of the over 80 are carless,[22] while 90% of the 65–69 have access to an automobile (presumably through friends and relatives).

Bus transit is rarely reported as a primary source of mobility for the oldest-old. The second most common form of transportation is riding with a friend or family member and following that is walking,[23] Para-transit, which involves vans that pick you up at home and deliver you to your destination, have well-trained drivers and rolling stock configured for the special needs of the handicapped. Today, the use of vehicles from the "access" inventory of online providers also makes it easier. Taxicabs work especially well in small towns or cities that lack formal para-transit or online providers.

MOVING CLOSER TO A FAMILY MEMBER IS HELPFUL

Moving near the primary family member taking overall responsibility for the older person is also a good idea. In fact, two-thirds of the frail who receive services at home get them from family members (primarily wives and adult daughters).[24] The burden for caregivers is often overwhelming. Much is sacrificed to keep mom and dad at home and out of a nursing home. Given smaller families, the dispersed nature of living arrangements, and the increased economic pressure on middle-aged couples still supporting children, this resource will be less available in the future.

In order to respond to this trend, the northern Europeans and the Japanese have heavily subsidized day care services to reduce this burden and provide well-deserved respite for family caregivers. Day care in the US is much more available today than it was 10 years ago but is still out of reach for those with moderate incomes who are not poor enough to qualify for subsidies. Also, remodeling the home to accommodate an accessory apartment or moving a prefabricated unit to the site are other possibilities described further in Chapter 9.

What Aspects of Housing and Services Best Serve the Older Frail?

Creating optimal housing and service satisfaction requires a constellation of factors. Figure 1.8 identifies four important influences: **Nutrition, physical exercise, social interaction, and managing injury and chronic conditions.**

Exercise is frequently described as almost a magical elixir to the problems of aging. "Physical fitness (is) perhaps the single most important thing an older person can do to remain healthy," according to Rowe and Kahn.[25] It is inexpensive, under your control, and directly benefits your physical and mental competency. Furthermore, the evidence appears to have grown even more compelling over time. Designing the building to encourage and optimize walking inside and outside is vital. The use of physical therapy and exercise equipment in common spaces

Figure 1-8 Optimizing Housing and Service Satisfaction: Four important components should be satisfied to create an optimal environment: 1) a physical design and friendly relationships that encourage social inclusion, 2) opportunities for exercise and strength building, 3) nutritious and flavorful food, and 4) careful attention to safety and well-being.

and corridors is common in Denmark, where for decades programs have been in place to carefully monitor and build physical competency.

Social interaction may be the most compelling reason to create group housing for older people. Looking beyond the financial benefit of sharing a nurse, administrator, or cook, making it possible to interact with others is the best reason to bring together a group of people in an age-restricted setting. But the idea of creating a "friendly building" by layering the circulation and activity spaces is often overlooked or not considered in design decision making. Social exchange and friendship formation is important for a successful and happy life. Creating the conditions that encourage this to happen is an important design goal.

Managing injury and chronic conditions requires careful thinking about how to monitor the unique problems each person experiences. Whether those conditions are physical or cognitive, the approach must optimize the individual's ability and independence, while challenging them to do as much as they can for themselves. It is important to focus on care over cure and encourage experiences that can have the greatest positive impact on the

individual. Safety, accessibility, and adaptability are within the control of the designer and are central to success.

There are 1.5 times more homebound elderly living alone than the number of residents in nursing homes.

Nutrition involves food choices and the transactional aspects of taking a meal. This is a process that is both pleasurable and one that supports social camaraderie as well as sustenance. Like medications, we are learning more about how nutrition affects each individual in unique ways based on their DNA profile. This will become someday as important, if not more important, than medications. Given the fact that smell and taste decreases in acuity over time and that food quality, variety, and flavor is often an important and controversial issue in senior housing, it requires more attention. The physical setting for taking meals and snacks also requires better design attention to noise, lighting, floor covering, and furniture design (including well-designed comfortable chairs).

Identifying choices for future housing and exploring those options in advance is important. Whether you decide to "age in place," move to a service-supportive housing arrangement, or look for ways to gain more direct assistance from family members, planning is required to reach the best outcome. Keep in mind the unpredictability of the future may require more than one plan and sometimes more than one move. Flexibility and resilience is necessary in exploring the many possibilities that exist.

The next chapter outlines changes that often occur with normal aging and conditions the oldest-old frequently experience. An excellent method to easily sensitize yourself to design decisions and caregiving priorities is to think like you are a frail 85-year old female.

Endnotes

1 Keenan, T. A. (2010), *Home and Community Preferences of the 45+ Population,* AARP, Washington DC, 3.

2 Joint Center for Housing Studies of Harvard University (2014), *Housing America's Older Adults: Meeting the Needs of an Aging Population*, Cambridge, MA, 9.

3 Belsky, D., Caspi, A., Houts, R. et al. (2015), Quantification of Biological Aging in Young Adults, *Proceedings of the National Academy of Sciences (PNAS),* 112(30), 4104–10.

4 Cohen, P. (2014), Personalized Aging: One Size Doesn't Fit All, in *The Upside of Aging* (ed. Paul Irving), John Wiley & Sons, Hoboken, NJ, 19–32.

5 CDC National Center for Health Statistics (2014), Nursing Home Care, https://www.cdc.gov/nchs/fastats/nursing-home-care.htm (accessed 10/1/17).

6 Keenan, *Home and Community Preferences of the 45+ Population,* AARP, Washington DC, 4.

7 Rowles, G., and Bernard, M. (2013), *Environmental Gerontology: Making Meaningful Places in Old Age,* Springer Publishing, New York City.

8 Free Dictionary, http://www.thefreedictionary.com/genius+loci (accessed 10/1/17).

9 Joint Center for Housing Studies, *Housing America's Older Adults,* 9.

10 Ibid.

11 Ihrke, D., and Faber, C. (2012), *Geographical Mobility: 2005 to 2010,* US Census P20-567. GPO, Washington DC.

12 Span, P. (2015), At Home, Many Seniors Are Imprisoned by Their Independence, *New York Times,* June 19, https://www.nytimes.com/2015/06/23/health/at-home-many-seniors-are-imprisoned-by-their-independence.html.

13 Ganguli, M., Fox, A., Gilby, J., et al. (1996), Characteristics of Rural Homebound Older Adults: A Community-Based Study, *Journal of the American Geriatrics Society, 44(4), 363–370.*

14 Koss, C., and Ekerdt, D. (2016), Residential Reasoning and the Tug of the Fourth Age, *The Gerontologist,* 57(5), 921–929.

15 Fishman, S. Top Seven Tax Deductions for Seniors and Retirees, http://www.nolo.com/legal-encyclopedia/top-tax-deductions-seniors-retirees-29591.html (tax consequences of selling house; accessed 10/1/17).

16 Resnick, B. (2014), Resilience in Older Adults, *Topics in Geriatric Rehabilitation,* 30(3), 155–163.

17 National Shared Housing Resource Center. http://nationalsharedhousing.org (accessed 10/1/17).

18 Joint Center for Housing Studies, *Housing America's Older Adults,* 11.

19 Simpson, D. (2015), *Young-Old Urban Utopias of an Aging Society,* Lars Muller Publishers, Zurich.

20 Suchman, D. (2001), *Developing Active Adult Retirement Communities,* Urban Land Institute, Washington DC.

21 Hayutin, A., Dietz, M., and Mitchell. L. (2010), *New Realities of an Older America: Challenges, Changes and Questions,* Stanford Center on Longevity, Stanford, CA, 2010.

22 Joint Center for Housing Studies, 25.

23 Ibid.

24 Ibid.

25 Rowe, J., and Kahn, R. (1998), *Successful Aging,* Pantheon Books, New York.

What Are the Major Aging Changes that Affect Independence?

DESIGNING an environment for a physically and/or mentally impaired person requires some knowledge of the changes that occur in people as they age. Some of these changes are considered "normal aging," which means they are a byproduct of getting older. Other ailments are more specific to the individual and result from a chronic disease or injuries. Knowing the competency status and mobility problems of a typical older person is necessary when designing a setting for optimum functionality. Knowing that a person is "elderly" is often not much help. An older person can range from 65 to 100+ years of age. One might be capable of running a marathon while another might not be able to walk. Many architects and design decision makers are unaware of the range of resident abilities that coexist in housing with services.

In most instances we are measuring the fit between the individual and the environment. Lawton's Competence-Press theory helps to visualize this. When applied to housing, his theory states that an individual's ability (competence) should be matched to the supportiveness of the environment. In fact, creating a situation that is slightly "challenging" to the individual can cause a positive stimulus. Housing can vary in its supportive quality. A walk-up apartment is one example of a potential environmental stressor. For some this can be overwhelming but for others with greater competence it might encourage fitness. The theory suggests that for every individual there is an optimum environmental fit.

Older people often need assistance, but when we do things for them they can do for themselves, we do not help them build strength and resiliency but instead are subjecting them to "learned helplessness."[2] We need to allow frail older people to do as much as they can for themselves, while monitoring and supporting them when they are faced with tasks that are beyond their capability.

> **An excellent way to discover what matters most in the environment is to imagine yourself as a frail 85-year-old female.**

Changes in Sensory Modalities

Our five senses are paramount in decoding, understanding, and appreciating the environment. Part of normal aging is the experience of losing sensory acuity, which

Figure 2-1 **Lawton's Environment-Press Model**[1]:
This diagram (also known as the Ecological Model) provides a way of matching an individual's competency with the level of difficulty associated with an environmental context. It demonstrates that when the environment slightly challenges the individual, it is usually more satisfying to that person.
Source: Lawton 1973. Reproduced with permission of American Psychological Association.

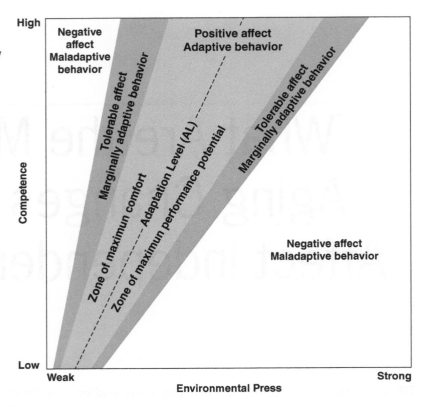

can put older people at risk. Ninety-four percent of the 65+ population experience a sensory deficit in at least one modality and 28% have experienced loses in three or more senses.[3] Losses in ability can vary from inconvenience to total incapacitation. The following outlines the major effects of these losses and how designers can mitigate them.

VISION LOSS

Vision loss begins to be noticeable after age 40. Seven out of 10 older adults find it necessary to wear glasses or contact lenses.[4] The main problems appear to be a decreased ability to 1) see objects clearly, 2) focus on objects at different distances, 3) see at low light levels, and 4) distinguish colors. However, only a small percentage of the 70+ population is blind.[5]

With age, the lens of the eye thickens and yellows, causing loss in visual acuity. Glare is more of a problem especially when driving at night. Also the ability to adapt from low to high light situations is hampered (like exiting a dark movie theater in the afternoon). Peripheral vision and depth perception may also suffer. Presbyopia, or the

inability to focus on near objects, is a common complaint and often causes eye strain.[6] The big diseases that affect vision are cataracts, diabetic retinopathy, glaucoma, and macular degeneration. Slightly more than 11% report serious impaired vision in their seventies (70–79), but this doubles after age 80. People with visual impairments are twice as likely to report difficulty walking as well as preparing meals and managing medications.[7]

Responses: Glare can be avoided by using indirect fixtures or pendant lighting that block a direct view of the lighting source. Because of the yellowing of the cornea, colors like blue and green appear gray and can run together. The 60-year-old eye needs twice as much light to see as well as a younger adult and for those over 80 three times the amount of light is necessary. So higher light levels, simplified lettering, and more brightly lighted public spaces can help.[8]

HEARING LOSS

The onset of hearing loss can be gradual and take 25–30 years to become noticeable. A loss of 1% in hearing ability is common for every year beyond your 40th birthday.

Figure 2-2 **Trading Ages is a simulation exercise that allows younger people to experience old age:** Bandages simulate arthritis and ear plugs reduce hearing capacity. These students are wearing colored glasses that mimic the yellowing of the cornea, while given the task of separating different-colored pastel pills that all look alike.

Although 10% of the population has hearing impairment that affects communication, that jumps to 34% for men and 21% for women after age 70.[9] After age 85, it is closer to 50%. Although hearing loss is common, deafness and profound hearing loss affects only 7.3% of people over 70.[10]

A major limitation is the inability to hear high-frequency sounds (above 4000 vibrations per second) that are common in language transmission. Low-frequency sounds are often unaffected. Many older people complain about hearing in noisy places with hard surfaces like restaurants or the inability to understand what is being said. Sometimes the origin is difficult to pinpoint. It is especially difficult to discern words that sound alike such as tea/pea/key. Hearing loss can have social consequences and has been linked to depression, withdrawal, and reduced functional health.[11]

Responses: Noise reverberation can be reduced with sound absorptive materials. Carpeting the floor and using fabric-covered padded furniture are very cost effective, but porous wall or ceiling panels also help. Lowering the ceiling in areas where conversation takes place helps to direct sound more effectively. Sometimes adding light allows a conversation partner to read lips. When speaking to a person with hearing loss it is effective to reframe the question in different words or direct your voice to the older person's face rather than speak louder.

LOSS OF TASTE

Losing your sense of taste can start in the mid-50s but accelerates during the 60s. Because the loss is slow, most people don't notice it. Taste is difficult to discuss without mentioning the sense of smell. Both of them interact to create the sensation of flavor, which also includes texture, spiciness, temperature, and aroma. Two-thirds of our ability to taste depends on our sense of smell. For example, if you hold your nose and eat chocolate, you can taste sweet but not chocolate. Although there are approximately 10,000 taste buds embedded in the tongue, by age 70 they are greatly reduced.[12] Less saliva can also affect taste. In a University of Chicago study, taste was identified as the most prevalent sensory loss, with a total of 74% rating taste as either fair (26%) or poor (48%).[13]

Five distinct tastes are relegated to different parts of the tongue: sweet, salty, sour, bitter, and savory (umami). With aging, sweet and salty sensations are affected first, followed by bitter and sour. Sometimes to overcome losses older people

Figure 2-3 **The eyes of an older person need twice as much light to see at the same level of visual acuity as a younger person:** The easiest way to solve this problem is to increase the wattage of a light bulb. However, this may not work if the fixture cannot safely accept a higher-wattage bulb.

it becomes difficult to differentiate between smells like lemon and orange. By age 80, most report major impairments. The sense of smell and taste work together but are separate systems.[14] The sense of smell is triggered by nerve endings in the olfactory bulb located deep in the nasal cavity. Smelling losses typically result from impairment in the olfactory bulb or the nerves that transmit the signal to the brain. The loss of smell that occurs with age is called presbyosmia. Although there is no official measurement system for smells, good, foul, and fruity are often used. The loss of smell is very personal. Evidence suggests it declines more slowly in women.[15]

Responses: Smell is used to identify dangerous situations like gas leaks, smoke, and food that has spoiled. A 2006 study found that 45% of subjects over age 65 could not detect the warning odor in natural gas.[16] Loss of smell has been shown to lead to depression and weight loss. Smoking also affects a person's sense of smell. Odors have strong emotional impacts on the individual and, like music, can evoke both good and bad experiences. Scent emitters and aroma therapy is frequently used to help people with dementia recall time and place.

> **When speaking to a person with hearing loss, it is more effective to reframe the question in different words rather than just speak louder.**

will add additional sugar and salt, which can exacerbate medical conditions like hypertension and diabetes.

Responses: Older people often compensate for a loss in taste by adding herbs and spices to their food. Other strategies involve a focus on texture, temperature, and flavor. Losing your sense of taste can also result from smoking, disease, and medications. When older people refuse food because it is unpleasant, they can lose weight. Savory tastes are especially helpful in the diets of older people.

LOSS OF SMELL

The nose can recognize up to 10,000 different scents. Sense of smell diminishes gradually after age 60, when

HAPTIC (TOUCH) LOSS

The sense of touch (often called haptics) is the first sense to develop and the last to go. There is generally a 1% decrease per year from age 20 to 80 in the acuity of touch, which is caused by changes in the nervous system. Older people use their sense of touch to learn, protect themselves, relate to others, and experience pleasure. The organ responsible for touch is skin – all 18 square feet of it.[17] Because touch accounts for basic pleasure and pain it can have powerful impacts on safety and emotional well-being. A decrease in pain sensation starts around age 50. Losing pain sensitivity makes us more susceptible to burns, hypo- and hyperthermia, frostbite, and cuts/bruises/blisters. Losses

Chronic Conditions and Disability that Limit Independence

Disability is an important consideration because it differentiates the self-reliant oldest-old from those who are struggling to maintain their independence. There are many ways to measure chronic disease and disability. These are often used to establish the level of impairment a person experiences, along with the help needed to restore greater independence. Disability is often defined as a result of three factors.

Three Causes of Disability

ONE: **Disease: specific diseases such as diabetes or arthritis**

TWO: **Lifestyle injuries or bad habits**

THREE: **Normal aging changes: such as changes in muscle mass, vision, hearing, etc.**

With chronic illness comes disability.[19] Eight chronic conditions that affect older people include the following. The number of people with more than five of these chronic conditions increases from 20% to 30% between ages of 65 and 74 and 85+.[20]

Eight Chronic Conditions[21]

1. **Heart disease**
2. **Hypertension**
3. **Stroke**
4. **Asthma**
5. **Bronchitis/emphysema**
6. **Cancer**
7. **Diabetes**
8. **Arthritis**

> **Disability results from three factors: 1) disease, 2) lifestyle, and 3) normal aging changes.**

Another way to measure disability is through Activities of Daily Living (ADLs). The six ADLs are what we

Figure 2-4 **This meeting room in the DePlussenburgh CS uses pendant fixtures for better light coverage and a carpet to absorb unwanted sounds:** A pendant fixture is an excellent solution to the problem of glare. Light bounces off the ceiling as well as being spread evenly by the translucent suspended lens.

are most acute in the feet and hands where blood flow is impaired and nerve damage occurs. As skin ages, it also thins, loses elasticity, and is more susceptible to bruises and tears.[18]

Responses: Touch sensation is very useful for people who have lost other sensory modalities as a compensatory sense. A lack of compassionate touch can also lead to depression, memory deficits, and illness. Fine motor skills that require dexterity, like writing, can also be affected. The relationship between the brain and a loss of kinesthetic function can cause falls and unsteadiness. Massage therapy involving the hands and feet is used for people with dementia or those with impaired functionality. Wood furniture and the feel of other natural materials are also known to trigger emotional responses.

need to live independently at home. We might expect a 5-year-old to be capable of carrying out these tasks. These measures are often used to establish the level of care necessary for a frail older person.

Six Activities of Daily Living (ADLs)[22]

1. **Feeding ourselves**

2. **Bathing**

3. **Dressing**

4. **Toileting**

5. **Walking**

6. **Getting in and out of a chair**

IADLs are more difficult and are necessary to live independently in the community. We might expect a 16- to 18-year-old to be capable of carrying out these six tasks. They include complex activities that are necessary for communication and independent living.

Six Instrumental Activities of Daily Living (IADLs)[23]

1. **Cooking**

2. **Heavy housework**

3. **Using a telephone**

4. **Shopping**

5. **Light housework**

6. **Keeping track of finances**

Generally, we can get outside help to support instrumental activities (IADLs) but ADLs require personal help and support. Only 8% of the 65+ living in the community had three or more ADL limitations, while 68% of the 65+ living in a nursing home had three or more limitations. Increased disability also pushes us toward institutionalization.[24] Although the need for ADL help increases with age, 77.8% of older people over age 85 are still living in a traditional household in the community while 14.2% are in a nursing home. For many, family support is essential, with adult children (42%) providing the largest amount of help with ADL/IADL needs, followed by spouses at 25%. Of the 70+ population, women report higher ADL/IADL functional limitations than men.

Figure 2-5 **The restaurant in the La Valance CS has employed 48" planters that break up the dining room spatially and absorb noise:** There are also soft fabric panels suspended from the ceiling to create additional acoustic absorption. The hard floor and the surrounding glass window wall reflect rather than absorb sound.

Will Chronic Disease Continue to Decrease?

One encouraging sign is that between 1982 and 2001 severe disability in the 65+ US population dropped by 25%.[25] In 2012, an amazing 67% of the 85+ also rated their health as good, very good, or excellent.[26] The main reasons for this uptick appear to be improved medical treatments, positive behavioral changes, widespread use of assistive technologies, rising education levels, and improvements in socio-economic status.

Figure 2-6 **The bay window in this assisted living dining room is configured to avoid uncontrolled noise:** The U-shaped alcove isolates the space from the open plan of the surrounding dining room. Also sound reflected from the lower ceiling makes it easier to understand conversations around the table.
Source: Martha Child Interiors and Jerry Staley Photography.

Excessive weight gain is the only countervailing influence, which could reduce mobility and lead to more chronic illness like an increase in Type 2 diabetes. In 2009–10, 38% of the 65+ were considered obese.[27] One of the contributing factors is sedentary behavior.[28]

SARCOPENIA

Also known as muscle wasting, this condition involves the loss of muscle mass, strength, and function. Being inactive after age 30 can amount to a 3–5% loss of muscle mass every decade. Sarcopenia has become more of an issue as the number of oldest-old has grown.

The term, often associated with the concept of frailty, affects 10 percent of those over 60, but increases to 53 percent of men and 43 percent of women by age 80. By age 90 older people have lost over 50 percent of muscle mass. Lean muscle mass is 50% percent of total body weight in young adults but after 75, that percentage reduces to 25 percent. Even though you may weigh more, the extra weight is fat not muscle.[29]

Responses: The loss of muscle strength leads to mobility limitations, weak bones (osteoporosis), falls, fractures, and decreased activity levels. Inflammation, decreased hormone levels, chronic disease, and inactivity can exacerbate Sarcopenia. Resistance or weight training can partially reverse the disease by increasing strength

capacity. It is important to avoid being sedentary, which is common among the oldest-old.[30] For example, age 65–74 individuals in 2010 spent approximately 26 hours a week as couch potatoes, which increased to 30 hours a week for those over age 75. Nutritional therapies center around eating more protein, which is necessary for repair.

ARTHRITIS AND STRENGTH CAPACITY

Arthritis is the leading cause of disability affecting 52.5 million, or a quarter of the total US population. Approximately, half of the 65+ population has arthritis (45% men and 56% women).[31] The three most common types of arthritis affecting older people are osteoarthritis (affecting 75% of sufferers), rheumatoid arthritis, and gout. However, more than 100 different types of arthritis exist. Acuity varies from annoying periodic aches to chronic disabling pain and 20 million people report severe limitations. There is no way to prevent it or cure it and it has plagued society for thousands of years.

By age 90 older people have lost over 50% of muscle mass.

Rheumatoid arthritis is an autoimmune disease that causes swelling and stiffness. Arthritis starts when cartilage wears away in joints. The symptoms are pain in the hands, neck, lower back, and larger weight-bearing joints (knees and hips). The main impact is inactivity, with 22.7 million sufferers reporting activity limitations such as problems walking or carrying out social activities. Severity increases with age and by age 85, 25% have developed painful arthritis in their hip. In terms of co-morbidity, 53% of those with arthritis have high blood pressure and 47% have diabetes. Cigarette smoking can also affect the production of the joint lubricant collagen. For many the pain and disability is so great they choose surgery. Yearly more than 600,000 knee replacements and 300,000 hip replacement surgeries are reported.[32]

Responses: The best way to treat arthritis is with rest, exercise, a healthy diet, cold/hot packs, weight loss, and medications (NSAIDs). Joint-friendly exercises like swimming, bike riding, and walking are highly recommended. Some sources claim that regular exercise three times a week can reduce the risk of arthritis by half.[33] Environmental modifications can be made that allow people with severe arthritis to function effectively. Single-lever faucet controls and lever door handles (in place of round doorknobs) are helpful. Chairs and sofas with arms, well-placed grab bars in the bathroom, elevated toilet seats, and nonslip flooring are additional considerations. Arthritis also makes it hard to manipulate small objects

like buttons, shoelaces, toothbrushes, and flatware. Many redesigned household items are available that mitigate the weakened grip capacity caused by arthritis.

BALANCE CONTROL AND FALLS

One-third of the 65+ population falls each year. One in five falls result in a broken bone or head injury, making falls the leading cause of death due to injury. Every 20 minutes an older person dies as a result of a fall. In fact, 87% of all fractures in the elderly are due to falls, which account for 25% of hospital admissions of older people and 40% of all nursing home admissions. When older people are admitted to nursing homes because of a hip injury, 40% do not return to an independent life and 25% die within a year.[34] Falls are tragic for the oldest-old, who fall frequently and because of general frailty are likely to sustain severe injuries.[35] Falls are the most common cause of traumatic brain injury in the older population. Although falls are common in nursing homes, 6 out of 10 falls occur around the house.[36]

The biggest risk factor for falling is having fallen in the past. Because of this the older person is more cautious and may exercise less, thus increasing future risk. The most common problems are balance and gait impairment, decreased muscle strength in the legs, visual

Figure 2-7 **The walking club at the Rundgraafpark CS offers regular exercise along with good conversations:** One of the great advantages of group housing is the possibility of meeting others and creating new friendships. Making a social experience out of exercise provides an incentive to continue it.

impairment, walking difficulty, dizziness, and cognitive impairment. Other factors include vitamin D deficiency, unsafe footwear, and low blood pressure. The risk of falls doubles or triples with cognitive impairment. Those who have suffered a stroke have a 40% chance of a serious fall within the next year, as do those returning from a sedentary hospital stay. Between one-half and three-quarters of nursing home residents fall each year.

Responses: Muscle and gait problems account for 24% of fall incidents, while environmental hazards such as wet floors, poor lighting, and bed height account for between 16 and 27%.[37] The best way to understand the problem is through a physical health evaluation that assesses risks. The best treatment is an exercise program that addresses muscle strength, gait, and balance. The worst thing is to reduce activity in response to a fall. Prevention care also involves knowing how to get up after a fall and call for help. About half of those who fall cannot get up even if they are not injured. Older people live in older houses with few safety features. A home assessment can identify potential hazards. Some modifications are expensive to make but many involve minor changes or behavioral adjustments. For example, the stairs in a multistory house can be a dangerous feature. Adding handrails to both sides and increasing the light level or moving to a ground-floor bedroom are good ways to mitigate these dangers.[38]

> # When older people are admitted to nursing homes because of a hip injury, 40% do not return to an independent life and 25% die within a year.

MEMORY LOSS AND DEMENTIA

Dementia is a disease caused by a decline in memory, language, and problem-solving skills. It affects 10% of people over the age of 65 but is more prevalent in the oldest-old cohorts. Of those diagnosed with dementia, 17% are between the ages of 75 and 84 and 32% are over the age of 85.[39] More women (17%) are afflicted than men (11%) in the over-age-71 population. Older African Americans are two times and Latinos are 1.5 times more

likely to have dementia.[40] In 2017 the estimated US population with dementia was 5.5 million but that number will increase 2.5 times by 2050, when an estimated 13.8 million Americans (16% of 65+) could have the disease.[41] One in three people who die were suffering from dementia (700,000 in 2017) and it is one of the leading causes of death for those over age 65 in the US. Worldwide, projections are more dramatic. The 35.6 million people with dementia in 2009 is anticipated to grow more than 3.2X to 115.4 million by 2050.[42]

Memory loss is caused by a buildup in beta-amyloid proteins and tau tangles in the brain. Six drugs are currently approved that temporarily improve the symptoms by increasing neurotransmission in the brain, but there is no cure.[43] The major symptoms are an inability to plan/problem solve, difficulty with familiar tasks, confusion with time and place, trouble understanding visual images and spatial relationships, speaking impediments, misplacing items, poor judgment, withdrawal from work, and changes in mood and personality.

As the disease progresses, people lose track of time and live a 24/7 life. They can be behaviorally difficult. Fifty-eight percent of the 65+ population with dementia live in the community and are taken care of by their children or spouse.[44] Of the care provided to older adults in the US, 83% comes from family and other unpaid caregivers. Older people typically live 4–8 years after diagnosis but

Figure 2-8 **This Shaker-style plate shelf and peg design for the Woodside Dementia building near Pittsburgh, Pennsylvania, helps people with memory loss:** The narrow shelf allows objects and photos to be displayed while the pegs are convenient for hanging clothing items. This feature is used on two walls of each dwelling unit.

can live as long as 20 years. Ronald Reagan lived approximately 11 years from diagnosis to death. Severe dementia can rob individuals of the ability to recognize people, eat, swallow, and speak. This severe stage currently afflicts half of those who are currently diagnosed.

One encouraging recent trend is a decrease in the incidence of the disease.[45, 46] New promising approaches to treatment are continually being tested but the increasing numbers of the oldest-old are a problem. Without a cure or better medications to extend competency and delay institutionalization, the cost of care is likely to rise. Total payments in 2017 for all individuals with Alzheimer's disease and other dementias was estimated at $259 billion. The estimate for 2050 costs is expected to be as much as $1.1 trillion (in 2017 dollars).[47] The average amount of time needed to care for someone with dementia is 2.5 times more than caring for an impaired person without dementia (171 hours/month vs. 66 hours/month).[48]

Responses: Given these problems it's not surprising that large numbers of dementia residents live in long-term care facilities. In assisted living, 42% of residents have dementia and in nursing homes the number is closer to 61%.[49] We know surprisingly little about how to develop building designs that meet the needs of older people who are afflicted with memory loss. Design guidebooks by Cohen and Weisman,[50] Cohen and Day,[51] and Brawley[52] have helped to identify important design principles but there is much to be learned. Twenty years ago people with dementia were routinely sent to a nursing home and placed in a "locked ward." In these settings they paced up and down a corridor having little idea where they were and limited access to the outdoors. Some of the case study examples in Chapter 8 like the Hogeweyk Dementia Village, Green House© and Sunrise of Beverly Hills Dementia Cluster explore ways to provide more freedom and better access to a normal life.

Endnotes

1 Lawton, M.P., and Nahemow, L. (1973), Ecology and Aging Process, In *Psychology of Adult Development and Aging* (eds. C. Eisdorfer and M.P. Lawton), American Psychological Association, Washington. (Copyright 1973 by American Psychological Association. Reprinted with permission).

2 Martin Seligman, M. (1972), Learned Helplessness, *Annual Review of Medicine*, (23) 407–412.

3 U Chicago Medicine (2016), Sensory Loss Affects 94 Percent of Older Adults, http://www.uchospitals.edu/news/2016/20160218-sensory-loss.html (accessed 10/2/17).

4 Fisk, A.D., Rogers, W.A., Charness, N., Czaja, C.J., and Sharit, J. (2009), *Designing for Older Adults: Principles and Creative Human Factors Approaches* (2nd ed.), CRC Press, Boca Raton.

5 Dillon, C., Gu, Q., Hoffman, H., and Ko, C. (2010), Vision, Hearing, Balance and Sensory Impairment in Americans Age 70 Years and Over, *NCHS Data Brief, No 31*, GPO, Washington DC.

6 CDC (2011), The State of Vision, Aging and Public Health in America, http://www.cdc.gov/visionhealth/pdf/vision_brief.pdf (accessed 10/2/17).

7 Campbell, V., Crews, J., Morierty, D., Zack, M., and Blackman, D. (1999), Surveillance for Sensory Impairment, Activity Limitation, and Health-Related Quality of Life Among Older Adults: United States, 1993–1997, *CDC #48(SS08)*, 131.

8 Fisk, A.D., Rogers, W.A., Charness, N., Czaja, C.J., and Sharit, J. (2009), *Designing for Older Adults: Principles and Creative Human Factors Approaches* (2nd ed.), CRC Press, Boca Raton.

9 Ibid.

10 NIH (NIDCD) (2016), Age-Related Hearing Loss, https://www.nidcd.nih.gov/health/age-related-hearing-loss (accessed 10/2/17).

11 Dillon, C., Gu, Q., Hoffman, H., and Ko, C. (2010), Vision, Hearing, Balance and Sensory Impairment in Americans Age 70 Years and Over, *NCHS Data Brief, No 31*, GPO, Washington DC.

12 NIH/NIA (2015), How Smell and Taste Change as You Age, https://www.nia.nih.gov/health/publication/smell-and-taste (accessed 10/2/17).

13 Chicago News (2016), Losses in Smell, Taste Common with Age, U of C Researcher Finds, *Chicago Sun-Times*, April 2, http://chicago.suntimes.com/news/health-smell-taste-losses-common-with-age-university-chicago-doctor-finds (accessed 10/2/17).

14 NIH/MedlinePlus (2017), Aging Changes in the Senses, https://www.nlm.nih.gov/medlineplus/ency/article/004013.htm (accessed 10/3/17).

15 NIA/NIH AgingCare.com (2017), Problems with Sense of Smell in the Elderly, https://www.agingcare.com/Articles/When-elderly-lose-sense-of-smell-133880.htm (accessed 10/2/17).

16 Nagourney, E. (2012), Why Does My Food Have Less Flavor? *New York Times,* December 6, http://www.nytimes.com/2012/12/06/booming/sense-of-taste-changes-with-age.html?_r=0 (accessed 10/2/17).

17 Wickremaratchi, M.W., and Llewelyn, J.G. (2006), Effects of Aging on Touch, *Post Graduate Medical Journal,* 82(967), 301–304, http://www.ncbi.nlm.nih.gov/pmc/articles/PMC2563781 (accessed 10/2/17).

18 University of Maryland Medical Center (2014), Aging Changes in the Senses, http://umm.edu/health/medical/ency/articles/aging-changes-in-the-senses (accessed 10/2/17).

19 Wiener, J., and Tilly, J. (2002), Population Aging in the United States of America: Implications for Public Programs, *International Journal of Epidemiology,* 31, 776–781.

20 Federal Interagency Forum on Aging Related Statistics (2012), *Older Americans 2012: Key Indicators of Well Being,* GPO, Washington DC.

21 Ibid.

22 Ibid.

23 Ibid.

24 Ibid.

25 NIA/NIH, (2011), *Global Health and Aging,* Publication # 11-7737, GPO, Washington DC.

26 Federal Interagency Forum on Aging Related Statistics (2012), *Older Americans 2012: Key Indicators of Well Being,* GPO, Washington DC.

27 Ibid.

28 Ibid.

29 Vella, C., and Kravitz, L. (n.d.), Sarcopenia: The Mystery of Muscle Loss, University of New Mexico, http://www.unm.edu/~lkravitz/Article%20folder/sarcopenia.html (accessed 10/17/17).

30 Waters, D.L., Baumgartner, R.N., and Garry, P.J. (2000), Sarcopenia: Current Perspectives, *Journal of Nutrition, Health & Aging,* 4(3), 133–139.

31 CDC (2017), Arthritis-Related Statistics, https://www.cdc.gov/arthritis/data_statistics/arthritis-related-stats.htm (accessed 10/17/17).

32 NIH/NIAMSD (2016), Hip Replacement Surgery, https://www.niams.nih.gov/health_info/hip_replacement (accessed 10/2/17).

33 CDC, Chronic Disease Prevention and Health Promotion, Arthritis (2017), Improving the Quality of Life for People with Arthritis, http://www.cdc.gov/chronicdisease/resources/publications/aag/arthritis.htm (accessed 10/2/17).

34 CDC, Home and Recreational Safety (2017), Important Facts about Falls, http://www.cdc.gov/Home and RecreationalSafety/Falls/adultfalls.html (accessed 10/2/17).

35 Scott, J.C. (1990), Osteoporosis and Hip Fractures, *Rheumatic Diseases Clinics of North America* 16(3), 717–40.

36 Fall Prevention Center of Excellence, USC Leonard David School of Gerontology (2017), Basics of Fall Prevention, http://stopfalls.org/what-is-fall-prevention/fp-basics (accessed 10/2/17).

37 Al-Aama, T. (2011), Falls in the Elderly: Spectrum and Prevention, *Canada Family Physician,* 67(7), 771–776, http://www.ncbi.nlm.nih.gov/pmc/articles/PMC3135440 (accessed 10/2/17).

38 National Center for Injury Prevention and Control (2006), Falls Among the Elderly: An Overview, http://www.menshealthnetwork.org/library/fallsfacts.pdf (accessed 10/2/17).

39 Alzheimer's Association (2017), *2017 Alzheimer's Disease Facts and Figures,* Alzheimer's Association, Chicago, 18.

40 Ibid, 20.

41 Ibid, 18.

42 Mebane-Sims, I. (2009), *2009 Alzheimer's Disease Facts and Figures,* Alzheimer's Association, Chicago, 234–270.

43 Alzheimer's Association (2017), *2017 Alzheimer's Disease Facts and Figures,* Alzheimer's Association, Chicago, 71.

44 Ibid, 33.

45 Landhuis, E. (2016), Is Dementia Risk Falling? *Scientific American*, January 25.

46 NIA Demography of Aging Centers (2016), Eileen Crimmens says Recent Research Suggests the Likelihood of Getting Dementia in Old Age Is Decreasing, https://agingcenters.org/news/detail/2243 (accessed 10/2/17).

47 Alzheimer's Association (2017), *2017 Alzheimer's Disease Facts and Figures*, Alzheimer's Association, Chicago, 60.

48 Ibid, 37.

49 Ibid, 55.

50 Cohen, U., and Weisman, G. (1991), *Holding on to Home*, Johns Hopkins Press, Baltimore.

51 Cohen, U., and Day, K. (1993), *Contemporary Environments for People with Dementia*, Johns Hopkins Press, Baltimore.

52 Brawley, E. (2006), *Design Innovations for Aging and Alzheimer's: Creating Caring Environments*, Wiley and Sons, Hoboken, NJ.

CHAPTER THREE

Demographics and Living Arrangements

Mortality and Fertility on the World Stage

For the first time in history (sometime during 2018) the number of children in the world under the age of 5 will equal the number of people over the age of 65.[1] This sounds amazing, but if we examine the "most developed" countries of the world we find this benchmark was passed decades ago. In fact, as early as 2030 those in the US under age 15 will equal those over 65. Why is this happening? What is the root cause?

This epidemiological transition, also referred to as the "crossing," started gaining momentum 100 years ago with the conquering of infectious and acute diseases and the emerging of chronic and degenerative diseases.[3] Public health improvements reduced premature death, especially in developing countries, while continuing

urbanization of the population reduced the need for large families.

Two major demographic forces are driving this transition: 1) increasing **life expectancy** and 2) decreasing **fertility.** As they grow in opposite directions, we will experience a world with fewer children and more older people. Since both of these groups combine (along with the population of ages 5 to 64) to define the total population, the lessening of one creates a proportional increase in the other.

> **Amazingly, longevity is like an escalator. Since 1840 we have increased life expectancy at birth by 3 months for every calendar year.**

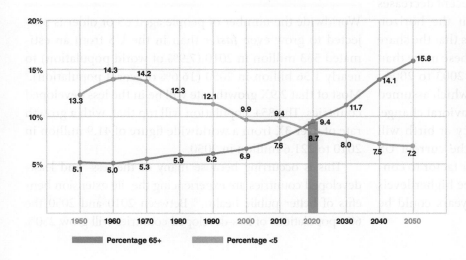

Figure 3-1 **Young children and older people as a percentage of the world population, 1950–2050:** It's not just that we are growing older; an even bigger concern is that there will be fewer children to support the aged through transfer payments and family support in the future.[2]
Source: Reprinted with permission of the United Nations.

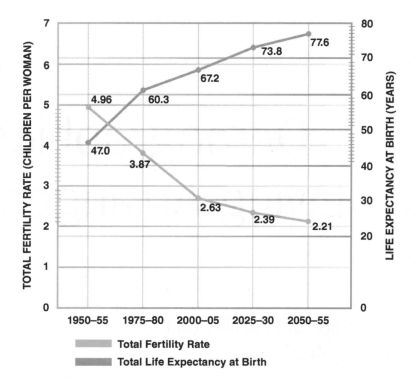

Figure 3-2 Total fertility rate and life expectancy at birth in the world, 1950–2050[4]: This diagram is the result of life expectancy and fertility moving in opposite directions. Life expectancy has experienced unprecedented growth for more than 100 years, while urbanization has reduced the need for children.
Source: Reprinted with permission of the United Nations.

Longevity Is a Primary Driver of Aging Population Growth

Longevity has been increasing for a long time. From 1840 until 2000, female life expectancy increased an amazing 40 years.[5] This is based on the fact that in 1840 the longest life expectancy was for females in Sweden at 45 years old. By 2000 life expectancy had for females reached 85 in Japan. **That is a lifetime bonus of 3 months for every calendar year, or nearly 6 more hours for every day.** It is not quite as dramatic today because the growth curve started to flatten in 1950. But growth in the aging cohort still continues.

What could mitigate this trend? With recent decreases in chronic disability[6] the only cloud on the horizon appears to be **obesity**. What we do know is that the share of 20- to 74-year-olds in the US who are obese more than doubled from 15% in 1971 to 34% from 2003 to 2006.[7] However, the MacArthur Network study, which assumed advances in technologies and further behavioral change, still estimates that in 2050 life expectancy at birth will be between 86 and 90 years, still above the current US Census Bureau figure of 83 years.[8] Another factor to consider is that with increased age we may see higher levels of impairment. So some of those extra years could be spent struggling with chronic conditions.

> **Why do we have more older frail people? 1) Longevity is driving the growth rate of the oldest-old and 2) A low birth rate (fertility) is resulting in a higher percentage of the oldest-old in the general population.**

World Population Growth: 65+, 85+, 100+

Worldwide the number of people aged 65 or older is projected to grow even *faster* than in the US from an estimated 533 million in 2010 (7.9% of world population) to nearly 1.56 billion in 2050 (16.6% of world population).[9] Most of that 2.9X growth rate will be in the less developed countries. The 85+ population will top that, with a growth rate of over 3X from a worldwide figure of 41.9 million in 2010 to 221.6 million in 2050.

This is occurring because many of the less- and least-developed countries are experiencing the life extension benefits of better public health.[10] Between 2010 and 2050 the 60+ populations of less-developed countries will grow 250%

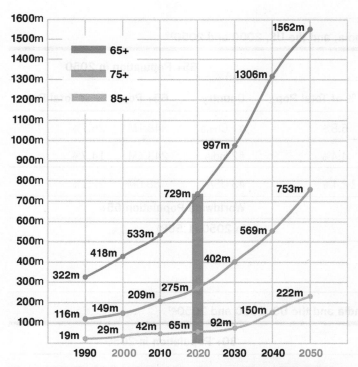

Figure 3-3 World population 65, 75, and 85+, 1990–2050 (millions)[12]: The population 65+ will grow by a factor of 4.8 from 1990 to 2050, but the 75+ growth rate (6.5X) and the 85+ growth rate (11.6X) are even higher. Most of this growth will occur in less-developed countries.

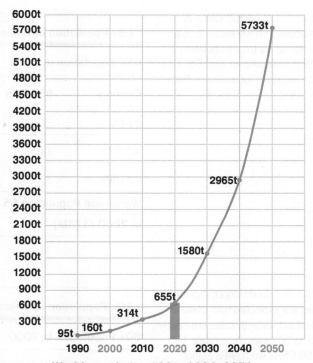

Figure 3-4 World population 100+, 1990–2050 (thousands)[13]: Centenarians, the fastest-growing age, cohort will be more than 60X greater in 2050 than in 1990. The growth rate is exponential, almost doubling every 10 years. The largest increase in numbers will begin around 2020 and by 2050 (30 years) they will be almost nine times greater.

compared to 71% for developed countries. These projected growth rates are so high that by 2050, 80% of the 60+ worldwide population could be located in less developed countries. The aging of the population is truly a worldwide phenomenon.

Theoretically we could live to 122 – Jeanne Calment did that in 1997.

One of the most interesting aspects of this change is its rapid pace. It took France 100 years to move from 7% to 14% of its population over age 65, but that same growth rate has taken only 20 years in Brazil.[11.]

The number of persons worldwide over age 80 is projected to increase more than fourfold, from 106 million in 2010 to 446 million in 2050.[14] This is amazing, considering that fewer than 14 million people over the age of 80 were on the entire planet just a century ago.[15] By 2050, it is projected that the six countries with more than half of the 80+ worldwide population will be China (114M),

India (53M), the US (33M), Japan (20M), Brazil (13M), and Germany (10M).[16]

Examining the 100+ worldwide population is breathtaking. In 2010 there were 314,000 people over the age of 100 in the world (16% of whom were in the US).[17] By 2050 that number will grow 18 times to 5.7M and the US percentage of that total will shrink to 7%. Today more than three-quarters of the 100+ population live in the most developed countries, but by 2050 it will be more like two-thirds.

China Is the Most Rapidly Aging Country in the World

Due in part to public health improvements and the "single child rule," China's 65+ population is anticipated to grow by a factor of *four* between 2000 and 2050, from 86M to 348M. This is in contrast to a 2.5X growth rate of the 65+ in the US during that same time period, from 35M to 88M. The 80+ Chinese population will grow at an even

Table 3-1 By 2050 China is predicted to have more than a quarter of its total population (348.1 Million) over age 65. This is an amazing 4X increase from the 2000 figure of 86.4 million.

65+ Population in China, India, and the US, 2000 and 2050[19]					
65+ Population in 2000			**65+ Population in 2050**		
Country	65+ Pop	% of Total Pop	Country	65+ Pop	% of Total Pop
#1 China	86.4M	6.8%	#1 China	348.1M	26.7%
#2 India	44.5M	4.4%	#2 India	243.4M	14.7%
#3 USA	35.1M	12.4%	#3 USA	88.0M	22.1%
Worldwide Population 65+ in 2000 (373M)			**Worldwide Population 65+ in 2050 (1.56B)**		

Table 3-2 Even larger growth rates are expected with China's oldest-old. Growth rates are nearly 10X in 50 years. Amazingly, by 2050 China will have a higher percentage of 80+ population than the US.

80+ Population in China, India and the US, 2000 and 2050[20]					
80+ Population in 2000			**80+ Population in 2050**		
Country	80+ Pop	% of Total Pop	Country	80+ Pop	% of Total Pop
#1 China	10.9M	.9%	#1 China	113.7M	8.7%
#2 USA	9.2M	3.3%	#2 India	52.8M	3.2%
#3 India	4.8M	0.5%	#3 USA	32.6M	8.2%
Worldwide Population 80+ in 2000 (71M)			**Worldwide Population 80+ in 2050 (446M)**		

fasterer clip during that same 50-year period, from about 11M in 2000 to 114M in 2050.[18]

This is a growth factor of more than 10 times the 80+ population in the year 2000. In 2000, China had less than 1% of its population 80+ while the US had approximately 3.3% of its population 80+. The amazing statistic is that in 2050 the US and China are projected to have close to the **same percentage** of the population over 80. The US 80+ projected growth rate from 2000 (9.2M) to 2050 (32.6M) is a factor of 3.5.[21] That growth rate has everyone in the US concerned. Imagine if the US had to contend with a factor of change – like China's 10.4X – which is nearly three times larger than our projected growth rate?

European Aging Experience: Been There, Done That

What about Europe? Many of the western and northern European countries have already experienced the gains we are projecting in the next 40 years. In 2007, the 65+ average for the 27 EU countries was 17.0% (compared to a US percentage in 2010 of 13.0%). In 2030, the projected 80+ population of the EU 27 will be 7.3% compared to a projected 80+ population in the US of 5.1%.[22] In general, European numbers of the 65+ population are 20%–25% higher than US averages.

Because of that, Europe is a great model for the US to study. They have been struggling for decades with an aging demographic that will soon be our reality. In Europe, for example, there is a far stronger commitment to the "age-friendly" cities movement. This may reflect the realization that making it easier for older people to shop, walk, ride public transit, exercise, and use existing public services might be the most effective investment a city can make in helping its older population maintain independence in the community. From a public policy and economics perspective, everyone wins. The northern European commitment to housing with services is designed to avoid institutionalizing their aging population.

REDUCED FERTILITY RATES PROVIDE FEWER REPLACEMENTS

One of the biggest problems in Europe is the dearth of new babies. When the fertility rate is low and there is low in-migration or high out-migration, the overall population generally drops. The most critical example in Western Europe is **Germany**, which until recently was projected to lose 12% of its total population from 2010 to 2050 (82M to approximately 72M).[23] Germany's fertility rate of 1.3 is one of the lowest in the EU. Their recent effort in welcoming immigrants (albeit causing other side effects) has helped their demographic circumstances. Germany is not alone. The southern European counties of Portugal, Italy, Greece, and Spain are also aging rapidly, again due to low fertility rates.

In the US and Canada in-migration and higher fertility has kept the population relatively young. In 2016, the US fertility rate was estimated to be around 1.87 but the 2050 future estimate is pegged closer to 2.0.[24] In terms of annual immigration, the US may continue to be the world leader. Receiving 1.4 million immigrants in 2010, it is predicted to increase by 1% per year, reaching 2.1M in 2050 unless political changes adjust overall policies.[25] Fertility in the less-developed countries has been traditionally high but is also dropping. It went from 6.2 in 1950–55 to 2.9 by 2000–05. Future predictions place world fertility in the less-developed countries at 2.2 by 2045–50 – close to the zero population growth rate of 2.1.

The Triple Whammy of the Aging of Japan: Longevity, Low Fertility, and Low In-migration

The most robust aging scenario is in Japan, which is experiencing gains in the oldest-old through increasing longevity while suffering from low fertility (1.4 in 2014) and policies that severely limit immigration. Japan is expected to lose 16% of its total population from 2010 (128M) to 2050 (107M).[26] So by 2050, the 65+ population is likely to represent a third of their total population. Imagine a typical Japanese neighborhood where in 2050 only five of six current houses will be needed to shelter the population and every third house will accommodate an older person. Life expectancy in Japan also holds the world record of 84.3 years. Projections expect it to reach 88.4 by 2050 and 94.2 by 2100 – within striking distance of 100. Aging in place in Japan is difficult because the existing housing stock has narrow corridors, small bathrooms, and frequent level changes.[27] Japan also has the highest number of centenarians per capita of any country in the world (4.1 per thousand population).[28] In 50 years (2000–2050) the 100+ population in Japan will grow from 12,500 to 1.3 million – or more than 100 times the 2000 census.[29]

> **The US population of 85+ individuals in 1940 appears to be very close to the number of the 100+ population we expect to see in 2050.**

What About the Growth Rate of the 65+ and 85+ Population in the US?

The over age 65 and age 85 population has been growing at a far faster pace than those under the age of 65 for decades. In fact, between 2010 and 2050 the over-65 population in the US will double, compared with a meager 12.2% growth rate in the population under age 65.

Figure 3-5 US population growth 65, 75, 85+, 1950–2050 (millions)[33]:
The 65+ population will double every 40 years between 1970 and 2050. In 2015 the onset of the baby boomer cohort begins with major increases in the 65+ population. The growth rates in all aged cohorts are high between 2020 and 2040.

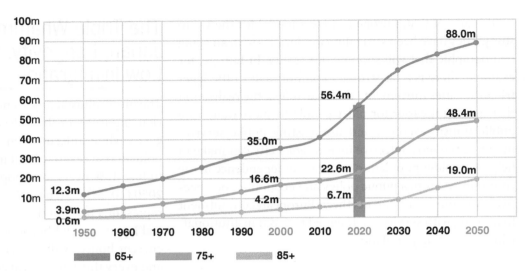

Figure 3-6 US population growth 100+ (thousands)[34]: Major increases in the 100+ population are occurring today and are set to continue until 2050 and beyond. With 65+ population numbers doubling every 40 years, the 2010–2050 rate of increase in the 100+ population will be 7.3X.

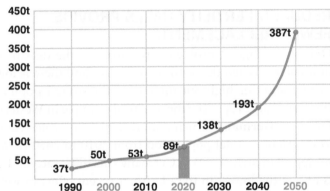

Table 3-3 Simply put, the US population doubles every 80 years, the 65+ population doubles every 40 years, the 75+ population doubles every 30 years, the 85+ population triples every 40 years, and the 100+ will grow 7–10 times in 40 years.

US population 65+, 75+ 85+ and 100+ (1950–2050)[35]

US POPULATION GROWTH (1950–2050)

YEAR (Total Pop)	65+	%65+	75+	%75+	85+	%85+	100+	%100+
1950 (150,697,000)	12,270,000	8.1%	3,875,000	2.6%	577,000	.4%	2,000	.01%
1960 (179,323,000)	16,560,000	9.2%	5,539,000	3.1%	939,000	.5%	3,000	.02%
1970 (203,212,000)	20,066,000	9.9%	7,611,000	3.8%	1,511,000	.7%	5,000	.02%
1980 (226,546,000)	25,549,000	11.3%	9,940,000	4.9%	2,240,000	1.0%	15,000	.07%
1990 (248,710,000)	31,242,000	12.6%	13,180,000	5.3%	3,080,000	1.2%	37,000	.15%
2000 (281,422,000)	34,991,000	12.4%	16,640,000	5.9%	4,240,000	1.4%	50,000	.18%
2010 (308,746,000)	40,268,000	13.0%	18,509,000	6.0%	5,494.000	1.8%	53,000	.17%
2020 (334,503,000)	56,441,000	16.9%	22,622,000	6.8%	6,727,000	2.0%	89,000	.27%
2030 (359,402,000)	74,107,000	20.6%	33,833,000	9.4%	9,132,000	2.5%	138,000	.38%
2040 (380,219,000)	82,344,000	21.6%	44,973,000	11.8%	14,634,000	3.8%	193,000	.50%
2050 (398,328,000)	87,996,000	22.2%	48,365,000	12.1%	18,972,000	4.8%	387,000	.97%

Doubles every 80 yrs	Doubles every 40 yrs	Doubles every 30 yrs	Triples every 40 yrs	7–10 times every 40 yrs
1970–2050 = 2.0X	1970–2010 = 2.0X	1950–1980 = 2.6X	1970–2010 = 3.6X	1970–2010 = 10.6X
	2010–2050 = 2.2X	1980–2010 = 1.9X	2010–2050 = 3.5X	2010–2050 = 7.3X
		2010–2040 = 2.4X		

In simple terms, the US 65+ population doubled in the 40 years between 1970 (20.0M) and 2010 (40.3M) and is projected to more than double again in the 40 years between 2010 (40.3M) and 2050 (88.0M). During that same 40-year period, the 85+ population more than tripled (3.6X), going from 1.5M in 1970 to 5.5M in 2010. It will more than triple again (3.2X) from 2010 (5.5M) to 2050 (18.9M). This faster growth rate of the oldest-old means the 85+ population is doubling every 25 years rather than every 40 years.[30, 31, 32]

Where the percentage of 65+ was 1 in 8 (12.4%) in 2000, it will be 1 in 5 (22.2%) in 2050.[36] In Europe the 65+ percentage will be even higher – 1 in 4 (25%) by 2050.

The Centenarians and Near Centenarians: 100- and 90-Year-Olds in the US

Although the 85+ growth rates are amazing, those over 90 and 100 years (the extremely old) are growing at an even *faster* rate. Hearing about a one-hundred-year-old person used to be very rare. There were so few before 1950, the US Census had trouble counting them. In a retrospective analysis of those early counts, the US Census[37] estimated there were approximately 2300 100+ people in the US in 1950. Out of a total 1950 US population of slightly more than 150 million, that amounts to only one in **65,000** people. For example, if you were in metropolitan Kansas City back then, you might expect to find seven 100-year-olds around town. Britain counted only 24 centenarians in 1917. Today, 100 years later, it has 15,000.[38]

Children born today have a 30% chance of living to 100!

By 1980 we estimated there were about 15,000 centenarians in the US and in 2010 we counted more than 53,000.[39] But in 2050, we project there will be 387,000 centenarians. That growth amounts to more than **seven times** the 2010 population. But this is really a best guess. What happens if we find a cure for dementia or cancer? Those numbers may appear low. Consistently, we have underestimated the growth of the oldest population in the past.[40]

The Department of Work and Pensions in the United Kingdom carried out an analysis in 2011 to understand more about the probability of living to be 100.

They concluded that 30% of the children born in 2011 could expect to live to 100 or beyond. That is quite a bit more than the 8% of males (like myself) born around 1950 who are expected to reach their 100th birthday.[41]

Another amazing statistic is that the number of 85+ older people in the US in 1940[42] (365,000) appears to be very close to the number of 100+ we expect to see in 2050[43] (387,000). Given how common it is to know an 85-year-old today, it will be interesting to see how our expectations towards centenarians evolve in the next 30 years. Cover stories in *National Geographic* in May 2013 and *Time* magazine in March 2015 showed pictures of babies with the headline "This Baby Will Live to be 120"[44] and "This Baby Could Live to Be 142 Years Old."[45] Although both statements seem a bit extreme, they are nonetheless within the realm of possibility given the changes we have experienced in the last 160 years.

Impacts of Demographic Growth

We know that the oldest-old population (85+, 90+, 100+) is growing very fast here and abroad. Will those extra years be filled with opportunity or disability? There are two main theories that predict the relationship between life expectancy and competency and they are diametrically opposed to one another. One is called **compression of morbidity,** which predicts that people will continue at a high-functioning level before experiencing a short disability period preceding death. The second theory is called **expansion of morbidity.**[46] It takes the opposite perspective, predicting a slow decline with worsening disability over a long period of time that eventually ends with death. Both situations

Table 3-4 Although women outlive men by 4.9 years at birth, that margin decreases to 2.6 years at age 65. Male life expectancy rates are unlikely to catch up with females in the foreseeable future.

Current US life expectancy at birth and at age 65 by gender[48]		
Males	**Females**	
76.3 years	81.2 years	@ birth
		women outlive men by 4.9 years
83.0 years	85.6 years	@ age 65
		women outlive men by 2.6 years

are common today in individual circumstances. But what will be the trend? New medications and gene editing protocols like CRISPR (Clustered Regularly Interspaced Short Palindronic Repeats) could lead in either direction, so we will have to wait and see. What we do know is that centenarians today experience about half of the morbidity period (about 9 years) we associate with a person of average life span – which is more like 19 years.[47] What else can we say about how the increase in the oldest-old will affect housing options in US society?

WOMEN OUTLIVE MEN BUT THAT IS NOT ALWAYS AN ADVANTAGE

Examining the characteristics of the oldest-old (85+ and 100+) in the US, two conditions are apparent. This population is **overwhelmingly female** and in **poor financial condition**. Women continue to outlive men, but have generally poorer health status. In the US at birth, females hold a 4.9 year longevity margin over males. At age 65, according to Social Security data, that margin decreases by 50% but is still around 2.6 years. Some projections show men's longevity making some progress against women especially toward the mid-twenty-first century, but the guys need to face the fact that women are biologically superior (at least in terms of longevity).

In 2010 at age 65, 57% of the US population was female but at age 85 that percentage rises to 67% (2 out of 3).[50] At age 65 a female is four times more likely to be widowed than a male. In fact, at age 85+ only 17% of women are married compared to 59% of men. Put another way, men marry their caregivers and when they die, their wives are left alone with less money because pensions and Social Security are often reduced. This could change in the future with more upper-income women in powerful positions but today it is a clear weakness in the system.

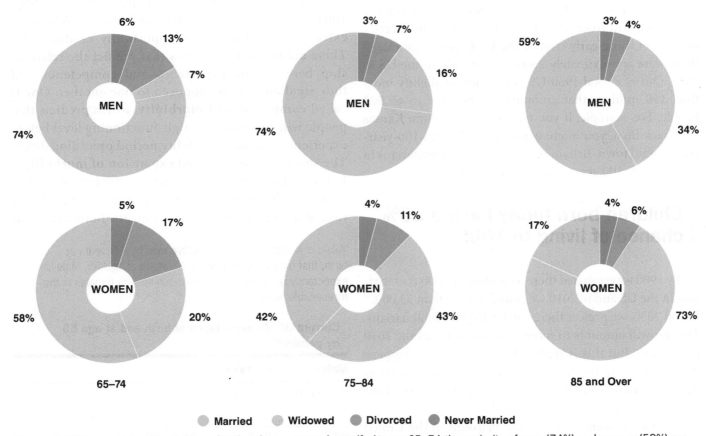

● Married ● Widowed ● Divorced ● Never Married

Figure 3-7 **US marital status by gender for three age cohorts**[49]: At age 65–74 the majority of men (74%) and women (58%) are married. But by age 85+ the majority of women (73%) have become widows while the majority of men (59%) are still married.

In fact, this is one of the most shameful aspects associated with the equitable treatment of women. Men often do not worry about moving to a nursing home because they are less likely to end up there.[51, 52] When you visit nursing homes or assisted living facilities in the US, 70% or more of the residents are female. This is often because they are the last ones left standing. As a society we have come to accept the nursing home as the last resort – even for those who have spent a lifetime caring for others. It makes you think, what if men lived longer than women? Would it be the same?

> ## The majority of men 75+ are married while the majority of women in that same age group are widowed.

What Other Demographic Issues Will Affect the Future?

A drop in the fertility rate is also likely to affect the number of children available to provide informal help and support to the oldest-old. Chapter 4 describes how important family members (especially first-born female offspring) are to the informal care system that supports most older people in their homes (or the home of a family member). The number of family members located nearby is predicted to decrease in the next 20–25 years. This change is also worldwide. Along with that is the bigger picture measured by the **Potential Support Ratio.**[53] This is a simple calculation of the number of individuals in the 15–64 age cohort who are available to support each person over age 65. Worldwide, in 1950 there were 12 people for each person over age 65.[54] In 2015, that number was 4.48 in the US. In Europe, it currently ranges from 3 to 4, but at mid-century it will be closer to 2. This not only affects family support but also impacts the transfer payment system that support the economics of healthcare and social security for the oldest-old.

OLDER ETHNIC MINORITIES WILL GROW WHILE THE WHITE POPULATION CONTRACTS

Finally, another anticipated future change in the US population is the ethnic and cultural identity of the elderly. In 2014 78% of the 65+ population was white, 9% black, 8% Hispanic, and 4% Asian.[55] By 2060, we anticipate a dramatic reduction in whites to 55% and a nearly three-fold expansion of the Hispanic population to 22%. The number of African Americans is also expected to increase to 12% and Asians to 9% of the 65+ population. Today about a third of Hispanic, Black, and Asian older people live with extended family members, compared to 13% of the white population.[56] This cultural phenomena of living in an extended family may also influence the choice of living arrangements in the future with more age-blended families.

> ## Older working adults are delaying retirement. In 1945 almost half of 65+ males were working. In 1990 that had dipped to 16%. But in 2050 it will boomerang back to 17–20%.

LOW INCOMES ALSO EXACERBATE THE SITUATION

Another depressing statistic is the average income of the oldest-old population. While the median income of 65+ households was a low but respectable $31,410/year in 2010,[57] those over age 90 have to get by with half of that ($14,760). Extending the inequality argument is the fact that even at age 90, older men made 50% more than women ($20,133 vs. $13,580).[58] This makes it easier for women to slide into a Medicaid-subsidized nursing home. Longevity pushes them half of the way and their limited financial resources finish them off. Oldest-old women have fewer options available to them.

One of the trends that has responded to an increased lifespan is the option of retiring later in life. This statistic, called the **Labor Force Participation Rate,** measures the percentage of the population that is employed. For 65+ men it has gone from a high in 1950[59] of 45.8% to a low in 1990 of 16.4%. Projections to 2050 show that it will likely stay at the 17–20% level. Older women who in 1950 experienced a rate of around 10% will likely see that stay relatively constant through 2050. Working longer and delaying retirement is one of the few options that the 65+ have within their control.

With regard to living arrangements, another side effect of aging in a relatively affluent society is that older people often live alone. This trend is also projected for developing countries in the future.[60] Among the 65+ population in 2008, 29% lived alone, but that varied a great deal by gender; 39% of women lived alone while only 19% of men lived alone.[61] Among the 85+ population in 2008, a total of 41% lived alone, the vast majority of them women. As the population ages, fewer older people live with spouses and more live by themselves or with family members or in institutions.

The longevity bonus is collected by women who find themselves in poorer financial condition and more likely to be isolated and in danger of institutionalization. That doesn't seem like a very fair payoff.

Endnotes

1 NIA/NIH (2011), *Global Health and Aging,* Publication #11-7737, GPO, Washington, DC, 2.

2 United Nations, Department of Economic and Social Affairs, Population Division, World Population Prospects (2017), https://esa.un.org/unpd/wpp/DataQuery (accessed 9/26/17).

3 Easterbrook, G. (2014), What Happens When We All Live to Be 100? *Atlantic,* October, 60–72.

4 United Nations, Department of Economic and Social Affairs, Population Division, World Population Prospects, (2017), https://esa.un.org/unpd/wpp/DataQuery (accessed 9/26/17).

5 Oeppen, J., and Vaupel, J. (2002), Broken Limits to Life Expectancy, *Science,* 296, May 10, 1029.

6 NIA/NIH (2011), *Global Health and Aging,* Publication #11-7737, GPO, Washington, DC 12.

7 Hayutin, A., Dietz, M., and Mitchell, L. (2010), *New Realities of an Older America: Challenges, Changes and Questions,* Stanford Center on Longevity, Stanford, CA, 56.

8 Olshansky, S. J., Goldman, D. P., Zheng, Y., and Rowe, J.W. (2009), Aging in America in the Twenty-first Century: Demographic Forecasts from the MacArthur Research Network on an Aging Society, *Milbank Quarterly* 87, 842–862.

9 US Census International Programs (2017), World Population by Age and Sex (2010–2050), https://www.census.gov/population/international/data/idb/informationGateway.php (accessed 9/26/17).

10 NIA/NIH (2011), *Global Health and Aging,* Publication #11-7737, GPO, Washington DC, 4.

11 Ibid.

12 US Census International Programs, World Population.

13 Ibid.

14 Ibid.

15 NIA/NIH, *Global Health,* 5.

16 US Census International Programs, World Population.

17 Ibid.

18 Ibid.

19 Ibid.

20 Ibid.

21 Ibid.

22 Mamolo, M., and Scherbov, S. (2009), *Population Projections for Forty-four European Countries: The Ongoing Population Ageing,* Vienna Institute of Demography, Vienna, 2.

23 Statistiaches Bundesamt (2006), *Germany's Population by 2050,* Federal Statistics Office, Weisbaden, Germany, 5.

24 United Nations, Department of Economic and Social Affairs, Population Division, World Population Prospects (2017), https://esa.un.org/unpd/wpp/DataQuery (accessed 9/26/17).

25 Wiener, J., and Tilly, J. (2002), Population Aging in the United States of America: Implications for Public Programs, *International Journal of Epidemiology,* 31, 776–781.

26 US Census International Programs, World Population.

27 Kose, S. (1997), Housing Elderly People in Japan, *Ageing* International, 23(3–4) 148–164.

28 Pew Research Center (2016), World's Centenarian Population Projected to Grow Eightfold by 2050, http://www.pewresearch.org/fact-tank/2016/04/21/worlds-centenarian-population-projected-to-grow-eightfold-by-2050 (accessed 10/17/17).

29 US Census International Programs, World Population.

30 Hobbs, F., and Stoops, N. (2002), Demographic Trends in the 20th Century, Census 2000 Special Reports, *U.S. Census Bureau Report # CENSR-4*, Washington DC.

31 Werner, C. (2011), The Older Population: 2010: Census Briefs, *US Census Bureau, Report C2010BR-09*, Washington DC.

32 Ortman, J., Velkoff, V., and Hogan, H. (2014), An Aging Nation: The Older Population in the United States: Population Estimates and Projections, US Census Bureau, *Current Population Reports*, Washington, DC 25.

33 US Census International Programs, World Population.

34 Ibid.

35 Ibid.

36 Hetzel, L., and Smith, A. (1999), The 65 Years and Over Population: 2000, U.S. Census Bureau. *Report #C2KBR/01-10*, Washington DC.

37 Krach, C., and Velkoff, V. (1999), Centenarians in the United States 1990, US Census Bureau, *Report # P23-199RV*, Washington DC.

38 Anonymous (2017), The New Old, *Economist,* July 8, 3.

39 Werner, C. (2011), The Older Population: 2010: Census Briefs, *US Census Bureau, Report C2010BR-09.*

40 NIA/NIH (2011), *Global Health and Aging,* Publication #11-7737, GPO, Washington DC.

41 Office for National Statistics (2017), Estimates of the Very Old Including Centenarians, 2002–2016, People, Population and Community, ONS, London, UK. https://www.ons.gov.uk/peoplepopulationandcommunity/birthsdeathsandmarriages/ageing/bulletins/estimatesoftheveryoldincludingcentenarians/2002to2016 (accessed October 1, 2017).

42 Boscoe, F., (2008), Subdividing the Age Group 85 and Older to Improve US Disease Reporting, *American Journal of Public Health*, July 98(7), 1167–1170.

43 Ortman, J., Velkoff, V., and Hogan, H. (2014), An Aging Nation: The Older Population in the United States: Population Estimates and Projections, US Census Bureau, Current Population Reports, Washington DC, 25.

44 Hall, S. (2013), New Clues to a Long Life, *National Geographic*, 223(5), 28–49.

45 Anonymous, (2015), The Longevity Report, *Time* magazine, 185(6–7), 68–97.

46 Fries, J. (1983), The Compression of Morbidity, Milbank Quarterly 61(3), 397–419.

47 Hall, S. (2013), New Clues to a Long Life, *National Geographic*, 223(5), 28–49.

48 National Center for Health Statistics, (2017) Health, United States, 2016, With Chartbook on Long-term Trends in Health, Hyattsville, MD. http://www.cdc.gov/nchs/hus/content2016.htm#015, (Accessed May 15, 2018).

49 Federal Interagency Forum on Aging Related Statistics (2012), *Older Americans 2012: Key Indicators of Well-Being,* GPO, Washington DC, 88.

50 Ibid.

51 Jones, A., Dwyer, L., Bercovitz, A., and Strahan, G. (2009), The National Nursing Home Survey: 2004 Overview, National Center for Health Statistics. *Vital Health Statistics* 13(167).

52 Kemper, P., and Murtaugh, C. (1991), Lifetime Use of Nursing Home Care, *New England Journal of Medicine,* 324, 595–600.

53 Jacobsen, L., Kent, M., Lee, M., and Mather, M. (2011), America's Aging Population, *Population Reference Bureau* 66(1), 12–14.

54 United Nations, DESA, (2001), World Population Ageing 1950–2050, *Report #ST/ESA/SER.A/207*, New York.

55 Federal Interagency Forum on Aging Related Statistics (2016), *Older Americans 2016: Key Indicators of Well-Being*, GPO, Washington DC.

56 Ibid.

57 Ibid.

58 Wan, H., and Muenchrath, M. (2011), *American Community Survey Reports, ACS-17, 90+ in the United States: 2006–2008*, U.S. Census Bureau, Washington, DC.

59 Toosi, M. (2002), A Century of Change: The U.S. Labor Force, 1950–2050, *Monthly Labor Review*, 22, https://www.bls.gov/opub/mlr/2002/05/art2full.pdf (accessed 9/10/17).

60 NIA/NIH (2011), *Global Health and Aging,* Publication #11-7737, GPO, Washington DC, 22.

61 Hayutin, A., Dietz, M., and Mitchell. L. (2010), *New Realities of an Older America: Challenges, Changes and Questions*, Stanford Center on Longevity, Stanford, CA, 5.

How Is Long-Term Care Defined? What Are the Choices?

TWENTY years ago the words "long-term care" (LTC) meant skilled care in a nursing home. Today LTC is viewed as a bigger concept describing a range of possible alternatives, including home help and home health care. LTC also includes assisted living, small group homes in the community, dementia care settings, end-of-life care, and adult day care in the community. Nowadays, new alternatives assist people to stay more independent in the community, like PACE or home- and community-based personal care alternatives. These are ALL considered long-term care choices.

The words "assisted living" connote a building type but should refer more broadly to how we can assist people with impairments and disabilities to live a better, more independent life. Unfortunately, when people become extremely frail, the nursing home is often the default solution. Although only 1% of those ages 65–69 live in nursing homes, this number jumps to 3% for ages 70–79 and 11.2% for ages 85–89. At ages 90–94 the percentage is 19.8%, 31% for ages 95–99, and finally 38% for those over 100.[1]

Although only 15% of the 85+ population in 2013 were in nursing homes,[2] more than 40% of the nursing home population is over 85.[3] Among those who reach age 65, more than two-thirds will need LTC services during their lifetime.[4] There is a 46% chance that everyone will spend some time in a nursing home.[5] So if you avoid it, probably your spouse or your sibling will not. The "oldest-old" population has the highest disability rate as well as the highest need for LTC services. Along with advanced age is the probability that you are more likely widowed, living alone, and unable to count on anyone to provide daily assistance.[6,7] We all have a stake in replacing nursing homes with something better or reforming them because if you live long enough and are disabled enough you are likely to end up there.

What Are the Major LTC Alternatives?

In terms of scale and ubiquity, there are 67,000 regulated LTC service providers in the US serving 9 million people.[8] This includes 15,600 nursing homes, 30,200 assisted living residences, 12,400 home health care agencies, 4800 adult day care centers, and 4000 hospices. LTC is also a major expense. Recent estimates peg yearly LTC costs between $210.9 billion and $317.1 billion.[9] The increase in the number of older frail people using nursing homes, residential care, and home care services is estimated to grow from 15M in 2000 to 27M in 2050.[10]

Figure 4-1 **Adult day care in northern European transports residents from their home to a community setting for the day:** Because housing and service buildings are community care partners, adult day care often meets in the common space of age-restricted housing. A typical adult day care program serves 10–15 participants who visit 2–4 times/week.

Figure 4-2 **Often the assisted living, dementia, or skilled nursing components of a CCRC have a more clinical look than independent living:** In the Fox Hill CCRC the same corridor and common space interior treatments used in independent living were carried through to assisted living and dementia care, giving the building a seamless look.
Courtesy of John Becker, DiMella Shafer.

The average size of a nursing home in the US is 108 beds.[12] Nearly 70% are managed under proprietary ownership. Although 15% of the nursing home population is under age 65, the residents over age 65 are similar in age and gender to assisted living residents. The average age is approximately 80, of which two-thirds are female. Today 7.7% of the nursing home population is over age 95.[13] Cost is also a problem for many. Medicaid pays for nursing care but you must "spend down" to be eligible. A growing number of older people have LTC insurance, but it rarely covers the entire amount. Otherwise, older residents are expected to pay these costs from their savings.

Nursing Home Facts and Figures

The residents in nursing homes represent only 2.8% of the 65+ population, and that number has been steadily declining in the last 10 years.[11] During the same time the number of 85+ residents has increased by more than 20%. What accounts for the shift away from nursing homes appears to be the availability of assisted living and the expansion of home care in the community. Nonetheless, nursing homes continue to be the last resort for the isolated, frail, and indigent older person in this country.

> **Although only 15% of the 85+ population in 2013 were in nursing homes, more than 40% of the nursing home population is over 85.**

What Are the Problems of Traditional Nursing Homes?

The nursing home began to proliferate in the 1950s[14] when the growth of the older frail population and the rising costs of hospital care led to the creation of the

Figure 4-3 Snoezelen therapies often involve colorful projections, soothing music, and affect-laden objects to relax individuals with severe dementia: These methods are used with people who have lost their ability to communicate and they serve as a method for rekindling emotional responsiveness. Snoezelen methods are also used in conjunction with bathing and music.

building type. As a hospital-like environment, the standard was set at 100 SF/person in a communal sleeping room that could accommodate two to four people. It was a low standard, but that was 70 years ago. Since then, hospital environments as a result of increased quality and infection control standards have moved to single-occupancy rooms. Almost all new hospitals in the US have 100% single-occupancy rooms and extra space for an overnight stay.[15]

When we think about the 1950s we are reminded of cars with fins, mimeographs, typewriters, and bulky leased phones. Traditional nursing homes are still locked into this decade and require that you share a bedroom and bathroom.

THE LIVING SITUATION IS BLEAK

In a traditional nursing home the patient room is not only small but is usually occupied by two unrelated people. Unless the bed configuration is "toe to toe," you control either the window or access to the bathroom and entry door. A thin fabric privacy curtain separates the two beds, which does not stop noise or odors. Furthermore,

the large 42" entry door (designed to move beds) is often left open as a matter of convenience for staff. This means noise from the corridor, which is often uncontrolled, can reach residents even in the middle of the night. Sharing a toilet and sink is also problematic. Your roommate, who has a 50% chance of being cognitively impaired, could inadvertently use your toothbrush or comb.[16] Although US nursing homes have been the subject of a great deal of criticism, most studies contain little information about the physical environment. We know little about the ratio of single- to double-occupied rooms or how many share a toilet, sink, or shower. These characteristics can have as much impact on privacy, autonomy, and mood as many of the current quality-of-care indicators used to rate nursing homes.

Nursing home scandals that report on terrible conditions and neglectful caregiving situations[17, 18] fill the literature. Even the best nursing homes often value efficiency over choice.[19] Efficiency usually means residents adapt to an institution's rules and schedules. Nursing homes are apt to be even less attractive to the upcoming boomer cohort, who have higher expectations and a greater need for control.

NURSING HOMES ARE INSTITUTIONS, NOT HOUSING WITH SERVICES

An institutional schedule can reduce choice for residents. Northern European and Green House© projects have implemented "Op Maat" or "customization" programs.[20] These allow the resident to set the parameters for when they get up, eat, sleep, shower, and what they do during the day. It vests the control of decisions with the resident and not the institution.

An additional concern is the critical issue of workforce continuity. Taking care of older people is a hard job that requires strenuous physical labor. Unfortunately care workers are also paid poorly and the stigma of the job makes retention and recruitment difficult.[21] In northern Europe, workforce shortages are also an issue, but have been avoided by paying the staff more and insisting that the job of taking care of "everyone's mother" is one that demands dignity and respect.

WHAT CAN BE DONE ABOUT OLD-STYLE NURSING HOMES?

How do we avoid a future where the predominant choice for the most frail is an overpriced, old-style nursing home? The strategy the Danes used in 1987 was to place a moratorium on nursing home construction.[22] This resulted from concerns about rising operational costs and the assumption that home care could better serve frail people in the community. After 2000, they restarted a limited nursing home construction program. The Aertebjerghaven and Herluf Trolle CS's are examples of projects from the post-moratorium period. The northern Europeans have made improvements by creating new buildings or remodeling existing buildings that are subdivided into smaller clusters with 100% single-occupied units. This was possible because most buildings were owned and operated by a local municipality. Most citizens saw them as part of the cradle-to-grave continuum for families. Civic pride and genuine self-interest made them as good as they could be for the oldest-old.

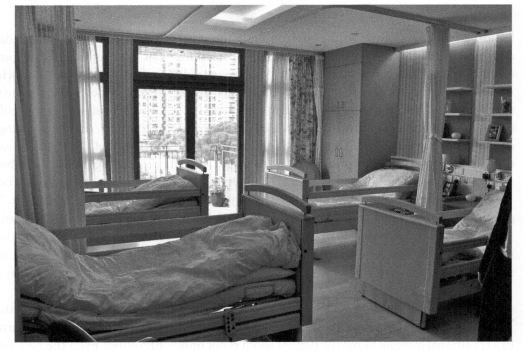

Figure 4-4 **Even though single-occupancy rooms are the standard in northern Europe, many LTC settings in Hong Kong and China continue to use three- and four-bed wards:** In the US a shared (two-bed) room has been the standard for decades. Before that multi-bed wards were also common in both hospitals and nursing homes in the US.

Figure 4-5 The Aertebjerghaven CS in Odense, Denmark, houses 45 nursing home residents in 5 small group clusters: A centrally located courtyard daylights the middle of the building and appears in this photo as an extension of a covered patio. Projects at this scale are common in northern Europe.

US nursing home owners claim to have slim margins and not enough reinvestment capital for even minor improvements.[23] Without a concerted effort, they are likely never to be replaced or substantially remodeled. The sad fact is that these outmoded institutions are a significant component of our nursing home stock and will not get better on their own.

There is a 46% chance that everyone will spend some time in a nursing home.

Institutional interiors, stifling rules, and less than optimum care[24] are not the only problems. Many buildings constructed between 1960 and 1980 are worn out or outmoded. The majority are low- to moderate-quality one-story wood buildings that average 36 years of age, are energy inefficient, monotonous in appearance, and shopworn.[25] Some policy makers even believe there is a conspiracy to keep nursing homes looking and feeling dreadful. The phenomenon is referred to as the "woodwork effect,"[26] the presumption being that if nursing homes were better, more people would be attracted to move there.

Will Green House© and Small House Models Replace Traditional Nursing Homes?

One of the most encouraging replacements for traditional nursing homes on the horizon is the Green House© or small house model. Chapter 8 contains a good introduction to this building type. The Green House© uses ideas that have been popular in northern Europe for decades. The physical environment is conceptualized as a collection of small group clusters of 10–12 residents. The management strategy is non-bureaucratic and rests primarily on the caregiving staff of nursing assistants, who typically provide 80–90% of contact time with residents. In a short time it has become the preferred model for nursing home design in the US. The big problem is that it has taken 15 years for the Green House© movement to produce 200 Green House© homes (approximately 2200 units).[27] Even with an estimated 1500 units in production and a hugely optimistic pace of 5000 units/year it would take almost 300 years to just replace the current nursing home stock in the US.

What Attributes Should We Strive to Include in New Nursing Homes?

Using US Green House© and northern European nursing homes as examples, Table 4-1 introduces 45 attributes we should be following in new nursing homes and assisted living environments to make them more independence inducing and less institutional. Both physical and operational attributes are important in these care settings. There are 10 attributes dealing with general policies and 13 items with environmental attributes. The remaining 22 items deal with program, activity, lifestyle, and operation.

Table 4-1 Forty-five environmental and caregiving attributes that are more effectively addressed in northern European and US Green House© nursing home environments: Old-style nursing homes in the US have many shortcomings that have been overcome by newer designs and caregiving strategies. This is a helpful checklist for any nursing home or LTC setting.

General Policies (10)

1. Freedom and choice should be optimized.
2. Personal resident preferences should rarely be overridden by rigid rules.
3. Individuality and variety should be encouraged.
4. Empathy and respect should be valued.
5. Control and subjugation should be minimized.
6. The overall institutional priority is care over cure.
7. High efficiency and uniformity should not occur at the expense of personalized care.
8. Noise should be effectively controlled making it easier to sleep at night.
9. Long-term care in northern Europe is paid as an entitlement for everyone regardless of income.
10. Regulations should focus on quality-of-life issues rather than easy-to-measure items.

Environmental Attributes (13)

1. Care settings should be noninstitutional with fewer restrictions.
2. The environment should be residential, lively – not like a hospital.
3. Double-occupied rooms sacrifice privacy and should rarely be employed.
4. The average resident room should be large enough for furniture and meaningful objects.
5. Single-loaded corridors and skylights should be used to introduce natural light.
6. Small group clusters of residents should minimize travel distances to dining and activity spaces.
7. Large windows with low sill heights will allow outside views from the bed.
8. Private and accessible outdoor spaces are valuable and should be provided.
9. Overhead lifts should be used to reduce the back injuries of staff.
10. Noise, glare, and odors should be identified and mitigated.
11. Interiors should be upbeat rather than lifeless and depressing.
12. A tub bath should be accompanied by low light levels and aromatherapy.
13. More emphasis should be placed on a joy-filled day than on disease treatment.

Caregiving and Lifestyle Attributes (22)

1. Chemical restraints for people with dementia should be minimized.
2. Communication therapies for dementia residents (like Snoezelen) should be available.
3. Happiness, mirth, joy, laughter, optimism, and playfulness should characterize the place.
4. More emphasis should be focused on reconciling life and preparing for the end of life.
5. Activity of Daily Living (ADL) therapies should be commonly employed.
6. Exercise, muscle mass development, and physical therapy should be a priority for the most frail.
7. Explore taking "vacations" and overnight outings even for the most frail – a northern European tradition.
8. Nursing homes should provide a high-quality, end-of-life experience.
9. Resident activities should embrace purpose rather than just fill time.
10. Residents should be encouraged to carry out tasks and do as much as they can for themselves.
11. Family visitation and overnight stays should be encouraged.
12. Family members and friends should be made to feel welcome.
13. Families should be counseled about how to make their visit a good experience.
14. Peer group sharing between family members should be emphasized.
15. Dangerous and awkward two-person manual lifts should not be attempted.
16. Spousal visitation should be facilitated and encouraged.
17. Activities should operate on the resident's schedule, not the institution's.
18. Staff turnover should be minimized.
19. Nurses/caregivers should be encouraged to make friends with residents.
20. Nursing assistants caring for residents should be given more respect by family members.
21. Training for nursing assistants should be rigorous with salaries that reflect their training.
22. Designated/primary caregivers should be regularly assigned to residents.

How Do Assisted Living (AL) and Residential Care Settings Differ?

The terms "assisted living" and "residential care" are often used interchangeably. But assisted living buildings usually have more than 25 units and are more like apartments than a single bedroom. AL dwelling units typically have private bathrooms, lockable doors, and some limited food storage.[28] In states with licensure requirements, buildings with more than 25 residents are held to a higher technical standard (fire safety and building code considerations) than smaller buildings. Of the 31,100 residential care/assisted living communities in the US, it is estimated that 50% are small (4 to 10 residents) and another 16% are medium in size (11 to 25 residents). There are some regional differences. Smaller buildings are more common in the west than the northeast.[29] Small residential care buildings are often the size of a large single-family house and can fit into most residential neighborhoods. Small buildings are relatively easy to create. A family seeking a placement for an older relative can transform a house and recruit other residents. These buildings of four to six residents are generally intimate and personal. Although smaller residential care buildings are usually licensed, the standards are minimum. These usually have an attendant who does everything, including fixing meals and providing personal care, but employees often have little formal training. Unlike the Green House©, which benefits from economies of scale when 6 to 10 of these buildings are clustered together, these accommodations are often isolated in the community. They can be less expensive depending on their location and accommodations.

> **The number of people using nursing homes, residential care, and home care services is estimated to grow from 15M in 2000 to 27M in 2050.**

ASSISTED LIVING BUILDINGS ARE LARGER AND MORE PROFESSIONALLY MANAGED

Four characteristics are the basis for the Argentum (Assisted Living Federation of America) resident-centered philosophy[30]: 1) enabling choice, 2) preserving dignity, 3) encouraging independence, and 4) promoting quality of life. Personal care assistance and memory care are usually available in AL, but medical services that require more sophisticated equipment or expertise are usually only provided by exception.

The most recent industry survey[31] found the average size of an AL community was 54 units. Fifty-four percent of residents were over the age of 85. Around 70% were females and 63% were widowed. About 40% of elderly residents needed help with more than three ADLs. In caregiving terms, the most common needs were bathing (75%), dressing (54%), toileting (37%), and assistance in eating (22%). Around 40% of the residents need help with incontinence,[32] and most residents take seven to eight medications that must be monitored.[33] In terms of chronic ailments 59% had hypertension, 37% heart disease, 26% depression, 29% arthritis, and 22% osteoporosis.[34] About a quarter of the population in these communities can walk on their own, with half needing a cane or walker and the final quarter in need of a wheelchair.

Forty-six percent of residents have a dementia diagnosis but 40% have no cognitive impairment symptoms.

Figure 4-6 Thought-provoking activities like card playing stimulate memory and recall: In general, activities with genuine purpose have useful benefits. In small Danish towns, residents are often involved in helping to create decorations for special events. Usually everyone participates, even if it involves only watching the activity.

Slightly more than a quarter of the communities provide separate personal care and dementia services.[35] Dementia is often treated like other chronic conditions. When memory-impaired residents can function with other assisted living residents, they are often mainstreamed. But if behaviors become problematic, they are often moved to a secured area of the building. These are usually small group clusters of 12 to 20 residents where the care, activities, and food program are centered on their unique needs. Clusters on the smaller end of the scale are easier to manage when one or more residents become agitated.

In terms of nursing and caregiving personal, Certified Nursing Assistants (CNAs) provide 80% of the 2.32 hours

Figure 4-7 **Furniture clusters in dementia housing can be focused on activities and themes like grooming, putting on makeup, and playing with life-like baby dolls:** These so-called "life stations" not only serve to decorate corners and alcoves but are often a popular source of activity. This vanity table is used for putting on makeup as well as, trying on hats and jewelry.
Courtesy of Martha Child Interiors and Jerry Staley, photography.

of daily contact time provided to residents. Many communities (37%) have a registered nurse.[36] Because family members want to visit, building locations near a close relative (34%) are preferred. Forty-two percent of residents are visited daily or several times/week and 26% see visitors weekly, while only 9% have no visitors.[37]

Two frequent concerns when a family member moves to assisted living are 1) What happens when your medical and personal care needs can no longer be cared for in Assisted Living? and 2) What happens if you run out of financial support?

Assisted Living, Problem One: Care for More Dependent Residents

Two-thirds of AL communities have policies that discharge residents to nursing homes when they need higher levels of care. Although state requirements provide some flexibility, generally conditions like tube feeding, ventilator support, and complex medical interventions are not sanctioned. There has been some effort to create "negotiated risk agreements" for residents who have aged in place and become medically dependent. These agreements usually require AL community, family, older resident, and physician approval. The other approach is to receive a hospice diagnosis that provides end-of-life services. Both provide enhanced support often through home-care-based assistance. Argentum has supported this through their "informed choice initiative." Several larger states have agreed in principle to the idea but it remains difficult to implement because liability insurance providers often believe these agreements result in lawsuits. This is unfortunate as it doesn't seem to be the case in northern Europe.

Assisted Living, Problem Two: Cost of Care and Lack of Reimbursement

Running out of money is equally unpredictable because no one knows how long one will live and under what circumstances. The majority of AL communities are proprietary (72%) and offer private pay services. Although 43% of facilities participate in Medicaid, only 19% of residents use Medicaid to pay for services.[38] Costs vary based on the location of the community, the size of the units, and the intensity of the caregiving. The average cost in 2017 of AL was $3,750 a month.[39] Although about half the cost of a nursing home, it is still expensive. Typically as older people become more impaired they need more help, which can also increase their costs. Residents leave AL because they die (33%), they need more health care (47%), or they have financial problems (6%).[40] Those who leave move either to a nursing home (59%), to another assisted living building (11%), back to their home (9%), or to a relative's home (5%).

> **Nursing home buildings are often low- to moderate-quality one-story wood buildings that average 36 years of age.**

How Do Assisted Living Residents Differ from Nursing Home Residents?

The physical and cognitive health status of nursing home residents is lower than that of assisted living residents. Sixty-one percent of nursing home residents suffer from dementia, compared to approximately 42% in assisted living.[41] Twice as many nursing home residents (48.7%) are clinically depressed,[42] compared with 23.2% in assisted living.[43] Because so many residents have moderate to severe dementia, nursing homes rarely treat those with memory loss as a unique population, as is the case in most AL settings.

The biggest contrast is in ADL measurements. Nursing home residents[44] are 50% more likely to have needs for bathing and dressing assistance and they are twice as likely to require walking and eating assistance than AL residents.[45] Medicaid supports 62.9% of nursing home residents. About a third are bowel and/or bladder incontinent and 5.7% receive nourishment through a feeding tube.[46] The average length of stay for nursing home residents[47] is approximately 2.25 years as compared to 2.7 years for AL.

It is clear from this data that assisted living cares for a much less impaired population with fewer medically oriented needs, which, given what we know about northern European settings, could easily be extended.

Figure 4-8 Domestic animals are often an object of affection as well as a source of activity: Having a shared pet or contact with a visiting pet program is the high point in the day for many residents. For the more independent individual, walking or caring for a pet can be a healthy outlet.
Courtesy of Hans Becker.

What Can We Learn from Hospice Models?

Inpatient hospice care entitled by Medicare or supported by private insurance or private pay are great models to study. Hospice care is flexible and can take place in various settings, including AL, nursing homes, hospitals, and the home. Because dying at home is considered preferable, the best purpose-built hospice buildings have been highly influenced by residential environments rather than hospitals or nursing homes. In addition, with hospice care the individual is encouraged to exit life with dignity and control. This avoids the effort of lifesaving medical care treatment and creates an environment more conducive to care and comfort than a miracle cure.[48] Although some believe all efforts at fighting infections are not allowed while under hospice care, that is usually not the case. Hospice is a service that seeks to satisfy the resident and the family. Most residents are older and many have a cancer diagnosis.

Figure 4-9 **For older people with limited mobility, a lockbox with an entry key nearby can make it easy for a home care worker to check on a client:** These can be unlocked with a code that can be changed to maintain security.

To qualify for hospice, most participants must have a physician certification that declares they have only six months to live. Hospice has many purposes, but a major one is reconciling emotional and spiritual issues with the help of family members. The main participants are family members, a hospice nurse, and the older person. Hospice care is most valuable for pain management and reconciling fears and uncertainty. The process is often personal and contemplative. Thus the environment often instills calmness, comfort, and serenity. Important, emotionally charged conversations take place in a way that promotes forgiveness and gratification. Family interaction is often of paramount importance as is the ability to experience nature.

The staff is trained to deal with the physical and emotional stress created by the dying process. Given how many older frail people experience end-of-life circumstances, it is strange the same level of sensitivity and closure is not a standard aspect of the AL and SNF operating culture. Maybe, in the future if the length of stay in formal LTC is reduced to 6 months or less, all nursing homes will be more like hospice environments, with a focus on quality and comfort rather than an obsession with efficiency and control.

WHAT CAN WE LEARN FROM PURPOSE-BUILT HOSPICE ENVIRONMENTS?

Visiting a well-designed hospice is always an eye-opening experience. A common reaction is how much better designed it is than a nursing home or assisted living residence. Often the unit is larger than a nursing home room and is usually single occupied. The larger size is used to accommodate additional equipment, as well as making it easier for family members or friends to spend the night. Even if space for an overnight stay is meager, solutions like the convertible window seat discussed in the Willson Hospice case study in Chapter 8 demonstrate sensitivity toward family participation. Places for families to socialize and grandchildren to play make it clear everyone is welcome.

The interior design responds to personalization, making it easy to display photos and meaningful objects. Wood is often a predominant natural material in floor, ceiling, and furniture treatments. It has special philosophical meaning because it was once alive but continues to be a soothing material. Light earth tones promote relaxation and are used in place of bold colors.[49]

Given the disability many residents experience, all spaces should embrace accessibility needs. Building scale can vary but a range of 24–30 residents is optimum. This is large enough to stand alone or to be connected to another care-providing entity, like assisted living.

Direct sunlight, darkness, view orientation, window size, and light control are important factors. Sleep disturbance is an issue, so exterior windows and doors must be soundproof but operable for fresh air. Landscaped outdoor space should be viewable from the bed or a chair near the window. Ground cover and multicolored plant species are especially valuable on overcast, cold, or windy days. On good days, an outdoor patio or balcony with a south or partial south orientation makes sitting outside enjoyable. Grounds with accessible pathways encourage walking and wheelchair jaunts. Watching wildlife, listening to nature, or relaxing in a natural habitat are also stress reducers.

A small shared residential kitchen for guests encourages them to bring a favorite dish, which can make the visit more personal and memorable. There should be places for interaction with others, as well as privacy. Shared spaces for playing cards, talking, watching TV, and taking a meal should be available. Pets are often meaningful companions for the dying because they demonstrate unconditional affection. A shared dog or cat may be best if individual pets are not practical.

Even with a hugely optimistic pace of 5000 Green House© units/year, it would take almost 300 years to replace the current nursing home stock.

Home Care Through Family Members and Formal Sources

A 2013 national study of long-term care providers reported that home health agencies served approximately 4.9 million of the 9 million recipients of long-term services and supports.[50] Much of this was Medicare-covered post-acute care in the person's dwelling unit, but there is great potential to utilize ongoing home care in combination with family support to help older people stay independent in the community.

Traditional nursing homes are losing popularity, and more older people are staying in the community with the help of family, friends, and home health providers. Looking at the 85+ population, 14% are living in nursing homes, 8% in community housing with services (including assisted living), and 78% in traditional housing in the community.[51]

Figure 4-10 **This afternoon the dining room table at the Aertebjerghaven CS has been transformed into a workshop so residents can participate in making decorations for a local celebration:** Purposeful activities that have a positive impact on others is a priority for how residents choose to spend their spare time.

Figure 4-11 **Easy access to gardens with sunny and shaded sitting areas at the La Valence CS is valued by dementia residents:** Installations often include raised gardens, a fountain, whimsical sculptures, and looped pathways so individuals can benefit from activities and exercise.

For those living outside of group accommodations, 90% of informal care comes from family members and friends. Two out of three older people get help exclusively from unpaid individuals such as family members, friends, and neighbors.[52] Many who advocate for community-based health care point out that home health care can be 35–40% cheaper than a nursing home placement,[53] but that can still amount to as much as $30,000/year.

An additional 25% get a combination of help from family and from formal sources, while only 9% rely solely on formal help.[54] The most active informal caregivers are spouses providing 31% of the help, while children provide another 50%. A daughter typically provides twice as much help as a son.[55] Tasks in the beginning involve shopping, transportation, laundry, and medical appointments. Later medication management, meal provision, and personal care support absorb more time. Formal caregivers, in addition to providing direct assistance, can also provide information about products and practices that save time or solve difficult problems.

Finding time to help is a challenge for many family members. Seven out of 10 caregivers have outside jobs.[56] Even though it requires splitting time between their children and their parents, two out of three family members report caregiving to be a generally positive experience. Psychological rather than physical stress often causes more unhappiness. The future for family caregiving will be challenging. Higher divorce rates and greater mobility mean the number of typical 75-year-olds without a spouse or child nearby will double from 875,000 in 2010 to 1.8 million in 2030.[57]

Reformulating Home Care to Work at the Margin of Need

The US needs a version of the peripatetic home care delivery system that is built into the AFL building type and has operated successfully in northern Europe. Home-care-based services allow all kinds of housing choices like co-housing, independent living, and "village-type" community organizations to support the frail. Home care in the US has not evolved the way it has in northern Europe, where it is available with generous subsidies. Rather than managing care at the margin of need, it is still common to find private home care in the US insisting on 24/7 caregivers when this level of care is often not necessary. With systems like PACE and community-based care, there is a move toward broadening home care options. We need access to this type of help for ALL older frail people, not just dual-eligible Medicaid/Medicare recipients.

WHAT ABOUT DEMENTIA CARE AT HOME OR A FACILITY?

Dementia is the most costly and time-intensive home care health condition. An average home care recipient with dementia needs two and a half times more help

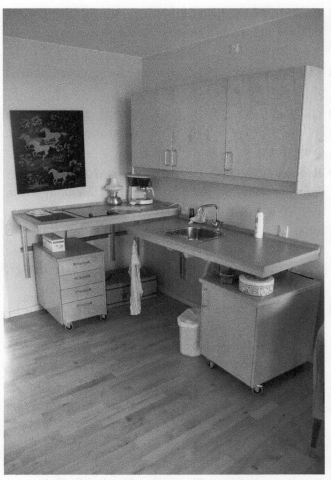

Figure 4-12 Scandinavian designs for wheelchair-dependent individuals are brilliant in their flexibility, beauty, and simplicity: This L-shaped kitchen design is modular and can be height adjusted to match the anthropometric characteristics of the user. The rolling cabinets below the counter are flexible and easily accessible.

than a resident with just chronic ailments.[58] Furthermore, the longer the battle with dementia goes on, the more difficult it becomes. It is particularly hard on female family members, who are physically and mentally exhausted by the struggle. In terms of ADLs, a 2009 study found nearly 30% of patients needed to be toileted, bathed, and fed. In the last year of life, 59% of caregivers reported they were on-duty 24 hours/day. Although the majority of support for those with dementia comes from the family, one study found that two-thirds of people 65+ who develop dementia ultimately die in a nursing home.[59] Moving the person to a nursing home minimizes physical stress but emotional costs often increase.

Families need respite support and adult day care in the community. These types of resources allow adult children and spouses to take important time off while balancing the responsibility of caring for family members. In northern Europe nursing home providers often manage day care, respite care, and home health care as a system of community supports. This makes it easier to manage the needs of an older frail person by selecting the resources needed. Home care in Scandinavia is successful in maintaining older people through the middle stages of dementia at home. Because of the long onset of dementia, a combination of home care with a placement in a dementia facility or nursing home is often the most common outcome.

THE FUTURE

We need to develop support systems that help those who are impaired to live independently in the community and avoid moving into an institution. This should include adult day care, an expanded home health care delivery system, and respite care for families. Finally, we must recognize that keeping older people out of an institution and in normal community housing is one of the best investments we can make. Medical science is likely to have a profound impact on mortality, but if the systems are not in place to support this burgeoning frail population, those extra years will end up more problematic than joy filled.

Endnotes

1 He, W., and Muenchrath, M. (2016), *90+ in the United States: 2006–2008*, GPO, Washington, DC.

2 Federal Interagency Forum on Aging Related Statistics (2012), *Older Americans 2012: Key Indicators of Well-Being*, GPO, Washington, DC.

3 Harris-Kojetin, L., Sengupta, M., Park-Lee, E., and Valverde, R. (2013), Long-term Care Services in the United States: 2013 Overview, National Center for Health Statistics, *Vital Health Statistics* 3(37).

4 Kemper, P., Komisar, H.L., and Alecxih, L. (2006), Long-term Care Over an Uncertain Future: What Can Current Retirees Expect? *Inquiry* 42(4), 335–50.

5 Spillman, B.C., and Lubitz, J. (2002), New Estimates of Lifetime Nursing Home Use: Have Patterns of Use Changed? *Med Care,* 40(10), 965-75.

6 Feder, J., and Komisar, H. (2012), *The Importance of Federal Financing to the Nations Long-term Care Safety Net*, Georgetown University, Washington, DC.

7 Houser, A., Fox-Grage, W., and Ujvari, K. (2012), *Across the States: Profiles of Long-term Services and Supports*, 9th ed., AARP, Washington, DC.

8 Harris-Kojetin, L., Sengupta, M., Park-Lee E., et al. (2016), Long-term Care Providers and Services Users in the United States: Data from the National Study of Long Term Care Providers 2013–2014, National Center for Health Statistics, *Vital Health Stat* 3(38).

9 O'Shaughnessy, C. (2014), The Basics: National Spending for Long-term Services and Supports (LTSS) in 2012, http://www.nhpf.org/library/the-basics/Basics_LTSS_03-27-14.pdf (accessed on 10/4/17).

10 United States Congressional Budget Office (CBO) (2013), *Rising Demand for Long Term Care Services and Supports for Elderly People,* GPO, Washington DC.

11 Centers for Medicare and Medicaid Services (2013), *Nursing Home Data Compendium 2013 Edition,* DHHS, Washington, DC.

12 Jones, A.L., Dwyer, L.L., Bercovitzm, A.R., and Strahan, G.W. (2009), The National Nursing Home Survey: 2004 Overview, National Center for Health Statistics, *Vital Health Statistics* 13(167).

13 Centers for Medicare and Medicaid Services, *Nursing Home Data Compendium 2013 Edition.*

14 Verderber, S., and Fine, D. (2000), *Healthcare Architecture in an Era of Radical Transformation,* Yale University Press, New Haven, CT.

15 Ibid.

16 Hiatt, L. (1991), *Nursing Home Renovation Designed for Reform*, Butterworth Architecture, Boston.

17 Institute of Medicine (1986), *Improving the Quality of Care in Nursing Homes*, National Academy Press, Washington, DC.

18 Mendelson, M. (1974), *Tender Loving Greed,* Alfred A. Knopf, New York.

19 Gawande, A. (2014), *Being Mortal: Medicine and What Matters in the End,* Metropolitan Books, New York.

20 Regnier, V. (2002), *Design for Assisted Living: Guidelines for Housing the Physically and Mentally Frail,* John Wiley & Sons, Hoboken, NJ.

21 Wiener, J., and Tilly, J. (2002), Population Aging in the United States of America: Implications for Public Programs, *International Journal of Epidemiology,* 31, 776–781.

22 Lelyveld, J. (1986), Denmark Seeks a Better Life for Its Elderly, *New York Times,* May 1, http://www.nytimes.com/1986/05/01/garden/denmark-seeks-a-better-life-for-its-elderly.html (accessed 10/4/17).

23 Joint Center for Housing Studies of Harvard University (2014), *Housing America's Older Adults: Meeting the Needs of an Aging Population*, Joint Center, Cambridge, MA.

24 Kane, R., and West, J. (2005), *It Shouldn't Be This Way: The Failure of Long-Term Care,* Vanderbilt University Press, Nashville.

25 Joint Center for Housing Studies, *Housing America's Older Adults,* 49.

26 LaPlante, M. (2013). The Woodwork Effect in Medicaid Long-Term Services and Supports, *Journal of Aging & Social Policy*, 25:2, 161–80.

27 The Green House Project (2016), The Green House Project Reaches Important Milestone, http://blog .thegreenhouseproject.org/the-green-house-project-reaches-important-milestone 2016 (accessed 10/4/17).

28 Khatutsky, G., Ormond, C., Wiener, J.M., et al. (2016), *Residential Care Communities and Their Residents in 2010: A National Portrait.* DHHS Publication No. 2016-1041, National Center for Health Statistics, Hyattsville, MD.

29 Ibid.

30 Argentum (2017), Learn More About Our Mission and Values, https://www.argentum.org (website accessed 10/4/17).

31 AASHA, AHSA, ALFA, NCAL, and NIC (2009), *Overview of Assisted Living,* American Association of Homes and Services for the Aging, American Seniors Housing Association, Assisted Living Federation of America, National Center for Assisted Living, National Investment Center, Washington, DC, 26.

32 Khatutsky et al., *Residential Care Communities,*

33 AASHA, AHSA, ALFA, NCAL, and NIC, *Overview of Assisted Living.*

34 Khatutsky et al., *Residential Care Communities.*

35 Ibid.

36 Ibid.

37 Ibid.

38 AASHA, AHSA, ALFA, NCAL, and NIC, *Overview of Assisted Living.*

39 Genworth Financial (2017), Compare Long Term Care Costs Across the Country, https://www.genworth .com/about-us/industry-expertise/cost-of-care.html (accessed 10/1/17).

40 AASHA, AHSA, ALFA, NCAL, and NIC, *Overview of Assisted Living.*

41 Alzheimer's Association (2017), *2017 Alzheimer's Disease Facts and Figures,* Alzheimer's Association, Chicago, 55.

42 Centers for Medicare and Medicaid Services, *Nursing Home Data Compendium 2013 Edition.*

43 AASHA, AHSA, ALFA, NCAL, and NIC, *Overview of Assisted Living,* 26.

44 Centers for Medicare and Medicaid Services, *Nursing Home Data Compendium 2013 Edition.*

45 AASHA, AHSA, ALFA, NCAL, and NIC, *Overview of Assisted Living.*

46 Centers for Medicare and Medicaid Services, *Nursing Home Data Compendium 2013 Edition.*

47 Jones, A.L., Dwyer, L.L., Bercovitzm A.R., and Strahan, G.W. (2009), The National Nursing Home Survey: 2004 Overview, National Center for Health Statistics, *Vital Health Statistics* 13(167).

48 Gawande, *Being Mortal.*

49 Verderber, S., and Refuerzo, B. (2006), *Innovations in Hospice Architecture,* Taylor and Francis, New York.

50 Harris-Kojetin et al. (2016), Long-term Care Providers and Services Users.

51 Federal Interagency Forum on Aging Related Statistics (2012), *Older Americans 2012: Key Indicators of Well Being,* GPO, Washington, DC.

52 Population Reference Bureau (2016), Today's Research on Aging: Family Caregiving, http://www.prb.org/ Publications/Reports/2016/todays-research-aging-caregiving.aspx (accessed 10/7/1).

53 Joint Center for Housing Studies, *Housing America's Older Adults.*

54 Doty, P. (2001), The Evolving Balance of Formal and Informal, Institutional and Non-institutional Long-Term Care for Older Americans: A Thirty Year Perspective, *Public Policy and Aging Report,* 20(1), 3–9.

55 Ibid.

56 Ibid.

57 Ibid.

58 Alzheimer's Association, *2017 Alzheimer's Disease Facts and Figures,* 37.

59 Hayutin, A., Dietz, M., and Mitchell. L. (2010), *New Realities of an Older America: Challenges, Changes and Questions,* Stanford Center on Longevity, Stanford, CA.

CHAPTER FIVE

Concepts and Objectives for Housing the Frail

THIS chapter starts by identifying 10 first-order concepts that articulate how the environment should support the lifestyle and the sense of well-being of older frail residents. These are words that describe attributes that have both social and psychological value to the older person. More significantly for the architect and the caregiving staff, they specify important feelings older residents should sense in supportive housing. They are followed by 15 environmental qualities and characteristics that represent attributes of the physical environment that encourage independence and a high quality of life. Collectively they provide criteria that help us to judge the importance of design decisions, as well as how the caregiving and management staff should operate to optimize residential well-being and life satisfaction.

These are outcome measures that should be kept in mind while designing approaches for small group clusters as well as purpose-built housing and service environments. A major theme of this book is to avoid institutional care by helping the oldest-old stay independent longer. For the most mentally and physically frail, settings should be available that allow these individuals to exercise as much freedom as possible. These principles can be used to test how the design of housing can provide support for independence and autonomy.

First-Order Concepts

The 10 general first-order concepts specify the quality of the social and physical environment based on how well it supports the basic needs of the older person. These words describe how older people feel, and they are selected to underscore the freedoms residents should have in supportive housing. They are **Autonomy, Independence, Dignity, Choice, Control, Privacy, Social Connection, Individuality, Comfort, and Predictability**. These are commonly accepted attributes that have been articulated in other publications (Regnier,[1, 2] Regnier and Pynoos,[3] Weisman and Calkins,[4] Wilson,[5] Cohen and Weisman,[6] Brummett,[7] Tyson,[8] Zeisel, Hyde, and Levkoff,[9] Marcus and Sachs,[10] Kellert, Heerwagen, and Mador,[11] Brawley,[12] Perkins Eastman,[13] Steinfeld and Danford[14]).

They help us to frame questions about the larger purpose of a supportive environment, as well as how older people can achieve an independent and satisfying life.

Second-Order Concepts

These 10 concepts are followed by 15 more specific qualities and characteristics representing attributes of the physical environment that make these buildings supportive and satisfying to the older resident. These words can be used to measure qualities of the physical setting that make them better for an older population: **Accessibility, Sensory Stimulation, Functional Purpose, Personalization, Familiarity, Stimulation, Homelike Appearance, Adaptability, Safety, Encourage Wellness, Purposeful Activity, Exercise, Respect for Staff, Welcoming Family and Friends,** and **Supportiveness.** These are present, in whole or in part, in the books referenced earlier as well as additional texts (Moore, Geboy, and Weisman,[15] Verderber and Refuerzo,[16] Cohen and Day,[17] Husberg and Ovesen,[18] Marcus and Barnes,[19] Steinfeld and White,[20] Story[21]).

These attributes are demonstrable and can be described with a greater degree of specificity. Together these 25 concepts, qualities, and characteristics establish a useful set of principles and targets that can test the viability of an architectural idea or a caregiving strategy. They are straightforward and in some cases self-evident, so little explanation is necessary to detail why they are important or how they can be applied. Chapters 6 and 7 outline 32 detailed descriptions of design and caregiving practices. These are considered exemplary concepts and are referenced in many of the case study buildings in Chapter 8.

Environmental Docility Hypothesis

In this chapter and the next two chapters, both design and caregiving ideas are presented to underscore how the "environment" is both social and physical. Attributes associated with management philosophy and the approach to caring for residents may actually be more important than the building design. In other words, the way something is designed and the way it is used directly influence the older resident.

When psychologists describe the environment they often refer to it at several different scale levels. Lawton[22] used three levels: **the personal, the physical, and the supra-personal** to describe the context. The personal involves relationships with family and friends. The physical is the nonsocial objective place, and the supra-personal involves social characteristics of the people in the surrounding context.

Design and caregiving ideas can operate at the physical and supra-personal levels. The social context defined by caregivers and other residents, as well as the shared physical setting, both influence resident behavior. Designers cannot control all dimensions of the supra-personal environment because this involves the behavior between residents, staff, family, and even the neighborhood. However, the physical environment is the setting within which behavior transpires and is the world of the architect and design decision maker.

First Order Person-centered Concepts

1. **Autonomy:** The sense of freedom an individual feels from the constraints of others or of a confining situation (closely aligned with self-determination)

2. **Independence:** Freedom of outside control or influence from others (with aid and support)

3. **Dignity:** Being worthy of honor and self-respect (appreciative of the formality of a situation)

4. **Choice:** The act of being selective to satisfy your own preference

5. **Control:** The power to influence or direct behavior (authority command)

6. **Privacy:** The condition of being free from observation or disturbed by others

7. **Social connection:** Incidental social interaction between individuals that could lead to a more substantial affective bond in the future

8. **Individuality:** The qualities and characteristics of a person that distinguishes them from others

9. **Comfort:** The state of physical ease and freedom from pain or distress

10. **Predictability:** The ability to reduce unhappy events by making them known in advance.

Second Order Characteristics of the Environment

1. **Accessibility:** A design consideration that makes it easy for people in wheelchairs and with reach capacity limitations to use the environment as it was intended

2. **Sensory Stimulation:** A design that takes into consideration the reductions of acuity and impairments that impact sight, hearing, smell, touch, and taste

3. **Functional Purpose:** A simple but direct way of achieving an intended outcome, often applied to tools and other universal design applications

4. Personalization: The ability for a person to make changes to their dwelling unit so it is consistent with their interests and tastes

5. Familiarity: The quality of an object or place that makes it seem known

6. Stimulation: A quality or action that makes a place lively and entertaining

7. Homelike Appearance: An aesthetic that makes a place seem comfortable and residential in character

8. Adaptability: The ability to adjust an object or setting so that it conforms to the changing needs of a resident

9. Safety: Actions or equipment that keep a place from being harmful

10. Encourage Wellness: An environment that encourages residents to exhibit behaviors that are consistent with good health

11. Purposeful Activity: Activities and projects that are centered on creating tangible benefits for others

12. Exercise: Equipment and procedures that allow people to build their physical strength and aerobic capacity

13. Respect for Staff: The affectionate and warm treatment of caregivers

14. Welcoming Family and Friends: Policies, programs, and places catering to the needs of family members that encourage them to visit relatives

15. Supportiveness: The quality of the social and physical environment that makes it easier to help people

The underlying goal associated with the environment is its ability to serve **health, longevity, and happiness.** The examples that follow in the next two chapters are split into two categories, design ideas and caregiving/management practices. These appear to be influential changes in the environment that have major social and operational influences on residents. They are not an exhaustive list but they represent important influences. I believe they capture a comprehensive inventory of design and management considerations that can stimulate our thinking about how to better create independence-inducing environments that work for the oldest-old and bring them as much joy as possible.

Endnotes

1 Regnier, V. (1994), *Assisted Living Housing for the Elderly: Design Innovations from the United States and Europe,* Van Nostrand Reinhold, New York.

2 Regnier, V. (2002), *Assisted Living Housing for the Elderly: Design Innovations from the United States and Europe,* John Wiley & Sons, Hoboken, NJ.

3 Regnier, V., and Pynoos, J. (1992), Environmental Interventions for Cognitively Impaired Older Persons, in *Handbook of Mental Health and Aging,* 2nd ed. (eds. J. Birren, B. Sloane and G. Cohen), Academic Press, New York.

4 Weisman, G., and Calkins, M. (1999), Models for Environmental Assessment, in *Aging, Autonomy and Architecture: Advances in Assisted Living* (eds. B. Schwartz and R. Brent), Johns Hopkins Press, Baltimore.

5 Wilson, K. (1990), Assisted Living: The Merger of Housing and Long Term Care Services, *Long Term Care Advances 1,* 1–8.

6 Cohen, U., and Weisman, G. (1991), *Holding on to Home,* Johns Hopkins University Press, Baltimore.

7 Brummett, W. (1997), *The Essence of Home: Design Solutions for Assisted Living Housing,* Van Nostrand Reinhold, New York.

8 Tyson, M. (1998), *The Healing Landscape,* John Wiley & Sons, New York.

9 Zeisel, J., Hyde. J., and Levkoff, S. (1994), Best Practices: An Environment-behavior (E-B) Model of Physical Design for Special Care Units, *Journal of Alzheimer's Disease,* v.9, 4–21.

10 Marcus, C.C., and Sachs, N. (2014), *Therapeutic Landscapes: An Evidence-based Approach to Designing Healing Gardens and Restorative Outdoor Spaces,* John Wiley & Sons, Hoboken, NJ.

11 Kellert, S., Heerwagen, J., and Mador, M. (2008), *Biophilic Design,* John Wiley & Sons, Hoboken, NJ.

12 Brawley, E. (2006), *Design Innovations for Aging and Alzheimer's,* John Wiley & Sons, Hoboken, NJ.

13 Perkins Eastman (2013), *Building Type Basics for Senior Living,* 2nd ed. John Wiley & Sons, Hoboken, NJ.

14 Steinfeld, E., and Danford, S. (1999), *Measuring Enabling Environments*, Kluwer Academic/Plenum, New York.

15 Moore, K.D., Geboy, L., and Weisman, G. (2006), *Designing a Better Day: Guidelines for Adult and Dementia Day Services Centers*, Johns Hopkins University Press, Baltimore.

16 Verderber, S., and Refuerzo, B. (2006), *Innovations in Hospice Architecture*, Taylor and Francis, New York.

17 Cohen, U., and Day, K. (1993), *Contemporary Environments for People with Dementia*, Johns Hopkins University Press, Baltimore.

18 Husberg, L., and Ovesen, L. (2007), *Gammal Och Fri (Om Vigs Angar)*, Vigs Angar, Simrishamn, SW.

19 Marcus C.C., and Barnes, M. (1999), *Healing Gardens*, John Wiley & Sons, Hoboken, NJ.

20 Steinfeld, E., and White, J. (2010), *Inclusive Housing: A Pattern Book*, Norton, New York.

21 Story, M. (1998), *The Universal Design File: Designing for People of All Ages and Abilities*, Center for Universal Design, NC State, Charlotte.

22 Lawton, M.P. (1983), Environment and Other Determinants of Well-being in Older People, *Gerontologist*, 23(4), 349–357.

CHAPTER SIX

20 Design Ideas and Concepts that Can Make a Difference

DIRECTING a solution to address well-identified priorities is one of the most important challenges designers face. In some cases, a site has been chosen that needs careful attention. In another, the program may dictate essential components. For this building type to be successful it must maximize the independence and autonomy of residents as they age and become mentally and physically frail. Both design and care principles are important to consider in resolving the building's plan as well as the operating philosophy.

The next two chapters outline **20 design considerations and 12 caregiving practices.** These are not meant to be comprehensive, but they establish a way of thinking about how a building should operate for the good of residents by enlisting the help of careful design thinking that facilitates better caregiving.

Covering several different building types is a challenge, but each section is written to address the universal attributes of the Apartment for Life, small group nursing cluster, and assisted living residence. Although the focus on this book is on the oldest and frailest population, the Apartment for Life (AFL) is conceptualized as a place where residents can age in place, avoid nursing home placement, and receive end-of-life care. The priorities for independence at age 65 are quite different than at 85. Addressing

this topic from the perspective of both age groups provides insights about how the building and the dwelling unit can adapt to changing needs over time.

The 20 design ideas and concepts are illustrated with photos that reveal their potential impact on creating places that respect the independence and autonomy of the oldest-old. Illustrations from the US and northern Europe are used interchangeably to illustrate similarities and differences as well as to underscore best practices.

The Neighborhood, Site Issues, and Outdoor Space

ONE: DEFINING A GOOD ACCESSIBLE SITE

Most buildings for older frail people draw residents from the surrounding nearby community. Frequent visits by family and friends, are all-important and become even more so as one ages and becomes less mobile. Visitor parking should be convenient to encourage short trips in the middle or end of the day. The site should encourage walking, whether on site or to nearby destinations. It is good to be near supportive stores, services, and activities.

Figure 6-1 The high-density, mixed-use neighborhood around the Neptuna CS is an ideal location: This redevelopment district is a strand along the beach near Malmö, Sweden. It offers convenient stores, safe places to walk, pleasant off-shore breezes, and a view of the sound. The building also contains space for cars, bicycles, and scooters.

A grocery store, drug store, bank, restaurant, as well as a place of worship and a park are considered priorities. Residents value a close connection to the nearest publically accessible hospital emergency room as well as to their own doctor's office as health care monitoring increases in frequency as an individual grows older.

In an Apartment for Life building, where residents are younger, food shopping is likely to take place and convenient access to a market is necessary. Older people, even those in their 80s, usually rely on cars to get around. Sometimes they trade favors and share a ride-with a neighbor or friend or have access to a convenient demand-response van or ride sharing vehicle. But having access to transportation

is necessary to prepare your own meals and be independent. In Europe, mixed-use buildings with grocery stores and services on the ground floor facilitate this connection. Some northern European countries subsidize Personal Operating Vehicles (Scooters) to allow people to travel longer distances than they can easily walk. AFL buildings often include stores, hair care, physical therapy services, and restaurants.

Well-designed outdoor spaces are highly appreciated for their appearance and therapeutic benefit. Assisted living is considered both a residential and an institutional use and is frequently located on sites near both multi-family housing and retail. The building should always appear residential in design with good "curb appeal" so it will attract family and friends. Finally, the site should be safe from crime and traffic conflicts.

TWO: ORIENTATION TO THE OUTDOORS AND THE NATURAL WORLD

The more we learn about the power of nature to heal, protect, and calm, the more it appears to be a significant esthetic and behavioral component of design. This is especially true for the oldest-old population with chronic conditions that appear to benefit from views and access to outdoor places. Research reveals noticeable benefits for people with dementia, individuals convalescing from an operation, and those at the end of life.

The ability to use the site in the most creative way is often an important measure of design skill. The views from inside to outside can include both near and far views. A distant view like a lake, a skyline or a mountain range provides a background context. While views of immediate off-site and nearby spaces often have higher utility because they are physically accessible. Richard Neutra[1] used large windows and floor-to-ceiling glass in the corners of a room to allow the indoor space to blend effectively with adjacent outdoor areas. This allowed rooms to be perceived as larger because views stretched effortlessly beyond the perimeter of the building.

The purpose of housing is often to protect the individual from outdoor influences such as, snow, heat, rain, and wind. For the frail, going outdoors can be difficult and fraught with danger, especially in the winter. Making the outdoors visually accessible through windows with low sill heights and greenhouse-style windows can bring the outdoors inside. Outdoor areas lack protection, but trees and plants can

Figure 6-2 **The outdoor terrace adjacent to the La Valance CS restaurant provides a powerful first impression:** The combination of high canopy green trees with bright red umbrellas is striking. Areas from complete shade to complete sun are available and the terrace wraps the restaurant perimeter, providing a lively controlled view from inside.

Figure 6-3 **The "bubblan" is an acrylic enclosure for tropical plants at the Neptuna CS:** This protected greenhouse-type space allows residents to enjoy the out-of-doors when it is cold or the wind is blowing. The location near the front of the building overlooks the restaurant plaza, a busy pedestrian pathway, and the waterfront.

provide shade and block the wind. Outside the air seems fresher, the smells stronger, and the colors more saturated.

Making visual and physical connections to outdoors is important. Other outdoor features include fauna, like birds, squirrels, insects, and animals that live in this domain. Older people value watching these activities vicariously. The Willson Hospice CS demonstrates how shade, sun, and breezes can enhance this experience. Having nearby outdoor spaces large enough to accommodate major events and small enough for intimate family get-togethers is ideal. Planning for outdoor spaces includes the possibility of food service, music, and lighting. Water features help to cool spaces in the summer and are often necessary to attract and sustain wildlife.

The ratio of hard to soft space also affects its "garden-like character." Large hard surfaces of concrete, tile, or gravel create a plaza-like space rather than a garden. The color, texture, and seasonal growth of plant materials also has an impact on the liveliness of a place. Monotonous plant selections lack visual, olfactory, or haptic variety. For people with dementia,[2] a secure fence 6 to 8 feet high is necessary, along with views into the garden for staff observation. Older people enjoy walking, so a looped pathway around the building and the grounds is often popular. Seating near entry and exit doors is used to greet others and is valued because it is accessible to facilities inside the building as well as providing a sense of security.[3] Using the site as an exercise space allows residents additional options to stretch muscles and stay fit.

THREE: COURTYARDS FOR DENSITY, VIEWS, AND SOCIAL EXCHANGE

Courtyard designs are efficient configurations that maximize density and land coverage. They create secure and rich landscaped outdoor spaces that can be seen or accessed from dwelling units. Courtyards have special value in senior housing because they can encourage social exchange and interaction. Interior common spaces designed to overlook a courtyard can extend the view as well as encourage the use of outdoor spaces. Courtyards are also used as shortcuts from one side of a building to another. They animate the space through pedestrian movement and provide another option for circulation.

Courtyards are relatively easy to use with small group clusters. In a taller, densely configured Apartment for Life building, covered courtyards can become atriums. The opportunity to bring visual and social focus to a centrally located courtyard can make the building friendlier.

When a single loaded corridor is adjacent to a courtyard, it introduces light and aids wayfinding. Significant landscape features can create visual prominence. A large tree, a special fountain, a covered sitting area, birdhouses, and bird feeders are commonly used to bring focus, scale, and activity to courtyard spaces. Depending on the shape and orientation of the courtyard, it can be light-filled while reducing exposure to unpleasant breezes.

The best courtyards should be at least twice as wide as the surrounding building height to accommodate adequate sunlight. If a courtyard becomes too large it can be subdivided into several discrete areas. Courtyards are commonly used for exercise, to stage activities, or as a sitting area. The Vigs Angar CS is an excellent example of a double courtyard design that uses both single- and double-loaded corridors to create a compact footprint while optimizing controlled views. The Hogeweyk Dementia Village CS consists of three major courtyards, a boulevard, and four minor courtyards. Residents are encouraged to walk for exercise, enjoyment, and to help with shopping. The purposeful trips residents make in this "village-like" setting appear to keep many residents more physically fit.

Courtyards can be defined by a continuous perimeter or they can be L- or U- shaped, utilizing fences, trees, or shrubs to define the perimeter. The Neptuna CS has a U-shaped configuration that visually and physically connects ground-floor spaces to a central garden and enclosed winter garden. Secured courtyards can allow residents with memory loss to have unimpeded access to an outdoor area. When a courtyard is located above a parking garage or an occupied lower floor, it is often a challenge to add plant materials in a way that gives it a lush landscaped feeling.

FOUR: INTERSTITIAL SPACES ON THE BUILDING'S EDGE

Walls usually form a barrier between indoors and outdoors. But the zones of space on both sides of a wall have great potential. Spaces that push and pull on the building's perimeter are often referred to as "interstitial spaces." They exist between the outside and inside and fuzzy the distinction between these two realms.

On the inside of the wall a window seat can provide an enhanced view of the surrounding landscape. When that feature is located on an upper floor the view becomes a perch that takes in a broader outlook. At the ground floor, the wall can be extended through an attached glass winter garden. When the glass wraps around three sides and juts out into the landscape, it captures a panoramic view that further enhances the visual connection with the outdoors from a protected inside place. The European erker is also a type of special edge condition. Like a square bay window, it extends out 18–24". It is frequently used on upper floors to expand views and enhance air circulation, as well as provide additional visual interest to the building facade.

(a)

(b)

(c)

(d)

Figure 6-4a–d These courtyards combine hard and soft surfaces in a confined space that adds security and enhances use: Courtyard designs are popular when high-density development is desired and the space can be used for social purposes and activities. Courtyards are also particularly helpful in providing a secured space for people with dementia.
Clockwise from upper left: Sunrise Senior Living of Hermosa Beach (Courtesy of HPI Architects and RMA Architectural Photography), Herluf Trolle of Odense, Denmark, Sunrise of Frognal House, London, UK (Courtesy of Martha Child Interiors and Jerry Staley Photography), and Raufosstun of Raufoss, Norway.

On the outside of the building, there are many different types of attachments, including open porches, arcades, three-season enclosed porches, screened porches, verandas, and trellis structures. These exterior spaces provide differing degrees of protection from climatic conditions. An enclosed porch provides the most protection,

Figure 6-5 This secured garden in Maryland has several places sandwiched between the inside and outside: Starting on the left is an enclosed sunspace with floor to ceiling windows and a garden view. Next to it is a covered porch and then a screened porch. Each space differs in the amount of protection and the indoor/outdoor experience it provides. *Courtesy of Martha Child Interiors and Jerry Staley Photography.*

while a covered or screened porch is less protective. Most of these attachments limit sun, rain, and wind. Residents find these edge condition spaces attractive and frequently use them.

FIVE: ATRIUMS FOR SOCIAL INTERACTION AND EXERCISE

Atriums are courtyards with a glass roof. They work well as social settings throughout the year by sheltering residents from inclement weather. Although atrium buildings are more popular as hotels in the US, in northern Europe they are commonly employed for elderly housing and are popular for many reasons.

First, they are perceived as friendly enclosures designed to encourage social interaction. Older people spend more time at home than young families and they often interact more with their neighbors. An atrium usually contains areas and equipment for common activities, as well as space for larger gatherings.

Second, the summer in northern Europe is mild with long days, low humidity, and cool nights. Air conditioning is absent in most housing, replaced by natural ventilation or fans that circulate air. Pleasant breezes are common in the summer, especially in localities close to the sea. Conversely, the winter is cold with strong winds and short days that reduce daylight exposure.

The atrium is a welcome social space in the winter that heats up during the day. Shrubs and trees give the atrium the relief of a garden in the often dreary northern European winter.

Third, the atrium allows individuals to exercise safely, especially in the winter when it is cold and icy outside. The atrium also optimizes sunlight, which is valued in the winter and celebrated in the summer.

Atriums can be classified by the nature of the floor (soft-soil or hard-concrete) and whether the atrium is air conditioned or naturally ventilated. Soft-soil atriums without air conditioning have louvers that welcome outside air on the ground floor which exits through the roof. They often provide supplementary heating for cold winter nights. These atriums frequently have a 50% allocation of hard and soft floor materials.

Hard-floor atriums are often built above a parking garage or an occupied lower floor. They may have operable roof ventilators but are more likely to have a fully functional HVAC system. They can also circulate unconditioned air during the fall or spring. These atriums usually have plants and trees in containers. One of the benefits of an atrium compared to a courtyard is that it can be much smaller than a comparable courtyard and still be pleasing. An open courtyard that is the same size as an atrium may seem constrained, crowded, and dark in comparison.

(a)   (b)   (c)

(d)   (e)   (f)

Figure 6-6a–f Atriums are a popular building type for housing older people in northern Europe: They are either conditioned or naturally ventilated and usually have a hard floor (if there is a habitable space below) or combine a soft soil base with pavement. Atriums are popular meeting places for residents and encourage exercise in the winter.
Clockwise from upper left: La Valance of Maastricht, the Netherlands; Jan van der Ploeg of Rotterdam, the Netherlands; Bergzicht of Breda, the Netherlands; Gyngemosegaard of Herlev, Denmark; Palvelutaio of Esikko, Finland; and Akropolis of Rotterdam, the Netherlands.

Refining Design Attributes and Considerations

SIX: MAKING THE BUILDING APPROACHABLE, FRIENDLY, AND NONINSTITUTIONAL

Residential buildings often exude a friendly appearance from the street, while traditional nursing homes exude an institutional aura the minute you spot them. A good first impression can establish a sense of warmth and comfort, while the opposite creates low expectations. This building type should appear residential to differentiate it from a commercial building or a hospital. When portraying a "home" in their drawings, children often use a sloping roof, an attractive entry door, and a chimney to define the essence of a residence.

Materials that lack a reference to residential housing can make a building feel cold and unfriendly. In Finland, where Alvar Aalto strongly influenced design, wood (both stained and painted) is often used for the outside cladding and interior treatments of nursing homes. In the US, many attractive buildings use shingles and large residential-style windows to overcome a lack of balconies and patio spaces. The Mount San Antonio Gardens Green House© CS uses wood siding on the outside and wood finish materials on the inside to soften its appearance.

Techniques like adding porches to the first floor and dormers to the highest floor can foreshorten the height of the building. Lowering gutter and eve lines can also make a multistory building appear smaller in scale. Creating a more complex footprint to limit the perceived length of a building can also reduce how its size is perceived. These techniques work effectively on two- to four-story buildings. Using residential windows, doors, cladding, and roof shingles reinforces the residential character of the building.

In addition to features that tame the scale and make the building more approachable, a variety of landscape materials can be employed to soften the appearance of the building from the street and to enhance views from inside. Saving mature trees on the site is an effective way to give the building a friendly, timeless look.

The first impression upon entering should be welcoming. The smiling face of a receptionist or the greeting of a resident or family member can make the place feel congenial and sociable. Lighting should be bright enough to avoid tripping, but not so bright as to make it appear institutional. Pools of light, which are common in restaurant design, are often used to add emphasis and character to a space. Large spaces like the dining room should be subdivided to make them feel smaller in scale. Common activity rooms should be scaled to residential dimensions.

Figure 6-7 **The New Bridge CS Villas contains four units on each of three floors with underground parking:** The scale is approachable and the material choices include copper, wood shingles, stone, and wood trim, which are authentic and residential in character. These larger, 2000 SF+ units are typical of what residents expect in LPC housing in the US today.
Source: Chris Cooper©, Courtesy of Perkins Eastman.

Figure 6-8 **Fine art mounted on rough-sawn wood siding gives it a residential feeling in the La Valance CS atrium:** The use of landscape materials, daylighting, art, sculpture, and antique objects creates a stimulating environment. Although the building houses very frail residents, the upbeat interiors make it appear very non-institutional.

In many projects features like doors and windows from historic buildings add uniqueness and a sense of timelessness. Antiques, crafted objects, and friendly artwork that depict scenes of people, children, and animals give the interior design a soft and familiar look. Scenes of natural landscapes (forests, beaches, mountains, waterfalls) also enhance relaxation.

Hospitals actually became sensitive to these issues decades ago and often use atriums, gardens, artwork, and residential materials (especially in resident rooms) to give the place an uplifting feeling. The Willson Hospice CS is an excellent example of how wood materials and access to outdoor views have been used to create serenity, delight, and calmness.

SEVEN: CREATE A BUILDING THAT IS ACCOMMODATING AND ADAPTABLE

Accommodating the changing physiological conditions of older people assumes that even though residents may not be in a wheelchair today, they might be in the future. Therefore, bathrooms and kitchens should be designed at the minimum to be "adaptable." This means that only a few minor adjustments are necessary to make spaces useable for an older person in a wheelchair. Universal Design (UD) is the concept commonly used to describe complete accessibility.[4] Although the concept of UD is extremely

helpful and addresses the spirit of the problem, most people have different types of disabilities, just like they have unique aging or chronic disease profiles.

Steinfeld and White[5] in their book on inclusive housing call for two standards. One, labeled "lifespan housing," meets a high standard for accessibility. The second level, labeled as "visitable," requires modest design standards for a visiting person in a wheelchair to use a toilet or gain access to the front door. Both are helpful standards to consider for a unit that is newly constructed or remodeled.

One of the best examples of unit adaptability are the 80 "considerate design" additions outlined in the Apartment for Life Woodlands CS. About three-quarters of these items can be included in the original construction at a minimal cost, compared to being added after construction. The remaining 25% have the capability of being added later as need arises. These adaptability adjustments are planned as part of the original design. For example, instead of installing grab bars near the toilet, the walls are reinforced with heavy plywood so bars can be added later in a place that benefits the specific older resident who lives there. The same strategy is used for automatic door openers that can be prewired and installed later if needed.

Although the physical environment is important, the ability to support independence through assistance with

Figure 6-9 **The dwelling unit entry door at the Ulrika CS can accommodate the width of a bed:** A normal-appearing 3'0" width door is paired with a 12" hinged side panel with a window. When both are opened, a bed can easily be accommodated.
Source: L&M Sievänen Architects.

medication coordination, bathing, dressing, meal preparation, and toileting is a far more difficult problem to solve in independent housing. In terms of accommodation, the AFL addresses both the physical and the service-related aspects of this problem.

Specifying a larger unit (AFL units are typically 750 SF or more) also allows greater adaptability for additional equipment and overnight stays. These can be important as the need for more medical supervision and monitoring increases. An important aspect of the AFL model involves caring for moderate to severely cognitively impaired residents. One possibility is to stay with your housemate at the beginning stages of the disease. Later that person can utilize dementia day care programming and eventually (if needed) move to a small group dementia home usually located nearby in the building.

The need to move residents from their bed to the bathroom or to a wheelchair is more common today. Regulations in northern Europe require mechanical assistance to avoid workplace injuries. Ceiling-mounted and wall-mounted rails with electric lifts are used throughout Europe, but this is not common in the US. Although at least a decade or two away, personal assistance devices (personal robots) will likely be developed to help with this problem in the future.

EIGHT: THE BUILDING DESIGN SHOULD ENCOURAGE WALKING

Exercise, important for maintaining competence and well-being, often requires special equipment or a space for stretching. However, encouraging walking is easy to implement and, with the exception of falling, contains few risks. Balance control, gait problems, and muscle weakness can limit walking but should be viewed as challenges rather than limitations. Walking with others in a regularly scheduled club can also be a satisfying social experience. Walking can be competitive or carried out at a pace consistent with an individual's need and ability. Walking from one floor to another rather than taking an elevator offers an additional challenge. Making certain that benches are placed on stair landings can encourage the use of stairs. Utilitarian fire stairs with sharp edges, hard materials, and abrupt transitions can be dangerous for residents with gait control problems. But stairs with windows, enhanced lighting, stimulating murals, and carpeting are attractive and safer to use. Amigo carts and scooters are a great replacement for a car, especially when stores and services are in the neighborhood, but overreliance on these devices can also erode competency.

A typical building with outdoor walking pathways that encircle the building is one of the easiest routes to plan. This allows residents to count laps as a way of judging the distance

Figure 6-10 **Locating bench seating halfway between the top and bottom of a stair encourages residents to use it:** In the Fox Hill LPC in Bethesda, MD a landing with a bench to rest and recharge overlooks the atrium below. Residents use the stairs for exercise instead of taking the elevator.
Courtesy of John Becker, Dimella Shaffer.

they have walked. Walking with family members can benefit both generations, and can lead to good conversations. Connecting a pathway to the public sidewalk system can also encourage able-bodied residents to take longer walks.

Developing the habit of walking every day with a goal of 5,000 to 10,000 steps is a self-initiated exercise regimen that can be recorded with an activity tracker. Exercise physiologists who study long-term care settings argue that keeping individuals "walking" is one of the most important activities to encourage. It is especially important to maintain the walk (accompanied by a cane, four-prong cane, or walker) from a resident's unit to the dining room or to other important daily destinations.

Placing benches every 25–40 feet in corridors and common spaces can also encourage walking. This allows individuals with limited strength capacity to rest and recharge. The same approach should also be followed outside, with benches located within 50 to 70 feet of one another. Outside, it is important to provide shade control with appropriate mature plant materials and opportunities to view a lively landscape from a resting place. For example, a birdbath, a bird feeder, or a varied landscape (color, texture, and aroma) should be close enough to be appreciated.

For people with dementia, walking has multiple benefits, including exercise, mood enhancement, and counteracting sleep disorders. Contained within a fence, residents can walk on their own in a way that is safe and beneficial. Walking offers a shared activity with family members that can be less taxing than a trip to a local neighborhood destination.

Figure 6-11 **Outdoor exercise equipment for older people is popular in northern Europe:** Often located within parks, the equipment is designed to encourage movement, gait, and balance control, which help prevent falls in older people. Exercising outdoors in the summer is clearly preferred over a windowless basement physical therapy space.

NINE: **INVITE NATURAL LIGHT**

Light has always been important in facilitating the perception of space. The trend in multistory urban housing has been to increase the amount of glass to optimize views and invite as much natural light as possible. Maximizing natural light in small rooms using tall ceilings and large windows often makes the room appear larger. Glassed-in enclosures like three-sided bay windows can also increase the amount of sunlight that enters a room as well as expand the view.

In housing for older people where the unit size may range from 400 to 800 SF, windows should be a minimum of 6 feet by 6 feet. To see the ground from a seated position,

sill heights should be 14" to 20" high. Also, clerestory windows can extend the window height to within a few inches of a minimum 9-foot high ceiling. Sometimes residents with balance control problems can find sills that stretch to the floor disconcerting. In the Irismarken CS a window panel that stretched to the floor was glazed with translucent glass to avoid this problem. The cardinal orientation of glass is important, along with the use of energy-saving Low-E glass.

Care should be taken to avoid glare, which is a problem for older people. The best way to avoid glare is to balance the light from the window with additional light in the room. Problems with glare can also occur when an object

Figure 6-12 **Full-size window walls are often used to increase natural light:** In the Ulrika CS, optimizing natural light is important because the winter sun rises late and sets early in Finland. Low-E glass has been used extensively to reduce heat and maximize the amount of light.
Source: L&M Sievänen Architects.

Figure 6-13 **In the Neptuna CS large skylights placed above the stair and elevator core allow daylight to filter down through the building:** Placing skylights in the middle of the plan, increasing artificial light, and employing aesthetic wall treatments and wood railings can make stairs more attractive and thus encourage use.

or surface is backlit with bright light. Older people also have problems with light level accommodation when moving from a dark room to a lighter room.

Skylights that introduce natural light are often most effective in areas that have the least amount of natural light, like the center of a building. Skylights with a transparent lens also allow the direct sun, the color of the sky, and cloud patterns to be visible inside. Using daylighting in northern Europe is common because of the dearth of sunlight in winter months. The control of daylighting has been found to be an important component in dementia housing, where residents are susceptible to behavioral problems, like sundowning, associated with circadian rhythms.

TEN: EMBRACE THE OPEN PLAN

The open plan is an architectural idea often credited to Frank Lloyd Wright.[6] His designs challenged the Victorian habit of creating separate, self-contained rooms. Wright enjoyed the idea of visually extending space into adjacent areas, as well as connecting interior rooms with exterior views. This idea was adapted by others and later became a major tenet of modern architecture.

This technique creates visual connections between spaces that make them appear larger and allow you to take in a broader view. The technique often uses partial-height walls (1/2, 5/8, or 3/4 height), built-in case work, dropped ceilings, furniture placements, deep portal doorways, and changes in floor and wall materials, as well as objects like closets and moveable planters to subdivide a space. These subdividing elements come in varying heights from 3 to 7 feet and are often expressed as cabinetry, closets, fireplaces, or thick walls. As casework, they can be 30–36 inches in height and 12–24 inches wide. Often the ceiling plan above these elements is kept continuous to reinforce the spatial continuity between spaces. An open plan can define a room without making it feel enclosed.

The ability to take in a comprehensive view of a space makes it more predictable. Creating a room without doors can also make it more accessible. In buildings where people use wheelchairs, scooters, canes, and walkers, it eliminates the need to open doors, making it easier to ambulate.

Furthermore, when a building is composed strictly of corridors and rooms, it often seems more formal and institutional. This pattern of corridors and doors is often a

Figure 6-14 **This cabinet creates a flexible space separator and display wall in a dining/living room at the Holmegårdsparken near Charlottenlund, Denmark:** Cabinets on wheels can be moved to reconfigure space that can take on a range of purposes. The space can be intimate for meals or larger for stretching and movement exercises.

result of fire and smoke regulations that frequently mandate solid separations between corridors and adjacent rooms. Because flat floors are often needed for accessibility, spatial hierarchy can be introduced through ceiling height changes that create alcoves or add emphasis to transitions between spaces. These techniques add to the spatial variety of a space while making it feel open and maximizing accessibility.

The open plan also works well for people with dementia because the disease often limits their ability to know what lies behind a closed door or a wall. This technique allows a dementia resident to see into other rooms and can facilitate movement. An open plan allows a room to appear intimate but also more friendly and connected at the same time. It is a useful spatial technique, especially in common spaces where it is a priority to invite social connection.

ELEVEN: THE IMPACT OF INTERIOR DESIGN ON THE SENSES

Interior design treatments include wall and ceiling materials, colors, textures, surfaces, lighting, carpets, accessories, casework, and furniture. Along with landscape features, interior details define the environment in the eyes of everyday users. When entering a building, interior features create first impressions that contribute to your understanding of the place. The room purpose, scale, and basic organization are important to the architect, but the design and decoration of interior spaces are what most people remember. Interior treatments also establish the basic visual character of the setting. If surface treatments and colors are institutional, then the building is likely to be perceived and remembered that way. If wall coverings and accessories are overly decorative, that can also trigger a reaction. There is a happy medium between starkness and overdone that is usually the target for most senior housing projects. A successful blend of a "hospitality" look with residential references is most common today.[7]

The fondness of female residents for colors, artwork, and accessories is important to consider, because they are often the majority population.

Interior design preferences are personal and can be influenced by past experience. Interior treatments are often judged as an overall impression, which considers the impact of color, texture, material, style, furniture, and lighting. There are few rules but interior design leaves both an indelible style signature that can strike one person as elegant and another as old fashioned. Sometimes words are used to capture a feeling. For the interior design of the NewBridge CS the Yiddish word *Hamish* was used to describe the feeling of being at home in a comfortable and cozy environment.

The Dutch and the Danes also have words to describe a comfortable residential feeling. In Dutch, that word is *Gezellig* and the Danish use *Hygge*. These words evoke more than hominess because they reference the social atmosphere (friendly) and the scale (coziness). In the Hogeweyk CS, a study documented the interior treatments of homes from which residents moved. Features were specified that captured the tastes of the various lifestyle groups at Hogeweyk.

Artwork can also affect the visual interest of a place. Some settings rely heavily on crafted objects like quilts. Art tends to be most appreciated in these settings when it is more tangible and less abstract. Upbeat themes in

Figure 6-15 **To establish the NewBridge interior design style, the sponsor described it as *Hamish*, a Yiddish word connoting the concept of cozy and homey:** It encouraged the sponsor to use light wood, comfortable soft seating, residential light fixtures, and a color palette that emphasized earth tones.
Courtesy of Chris Cooper© and Perkins Eastman Architects.

Figure 6-16 **This small assisted living building greets visitors with a large stone fireplace and Arts and Crafts–style furniture:** It is positioned to subdivide the room and create a strong first impression that exudes residential comfort. A large hearth, mantel, and shelves provide locations for accessories and plants. *Courtesy of Martha Child Interiors and Jerry Staley Photography.*

visual depictions (children, pets, plants, landscapes, etc.) are believed to be more calming, especially for those with dementia.

Carpets are used because they reduce noise and mitigate falls better than hard surfaces. They are also relatively inexpensive and can be cleaned or replaced on a regular schedule. Previously incontinence was an issue. Today, you can specify carpets that are bonded to a moisture-proof backing and are easy to clean and sanitize. Improvements in incontinence products and monitoring regimens eliminate the need to cover furniture with plastic. Also, positive-pressure ventilation systems in corridors and public spaces redirect odors to unit bathrooms, where they can be easily expelled.

The Role of Furniture

Furniture is a very important consideration for the older frail person. The loss of fatty tissue around the gluteus maximus can make sitting for an extended time uncomfortable. Couches that are low and wide with soft padding are a special challenge for older users. To be comfortable, a seat must have adequate padding and be resilient and elastic. If a thin cushion is placed on a solid plywood base, it can become uncomfortable within a few minutes. In addition

Figure 6-17 **A dilemma with most soft, low couches is how difficult it is to exit from them:** Having easy-to-grasp armrests and a higher seat height is often necessary. In the Irismarken CS nursing home, wood blocks were placed under one couch to raise the seat, thus making it easier for residents to stand up.

to comfort, chairs need armrests and seats that are high enough to facilitate sitting down and standing up. The most popular seating arrangement is a "dyad," which accommodates two people.[8]

Lightweight, moveable seating is ideal because it can be repositioned closer to another person. Bringing older people together around a table or an ottoman creates a natural conversation circle, which also improves communication. Tables accommodate card playing, crafts, meals, and discussion while also providing a surface for beverages, snacks, and books. Both round and square tables have advantages. Square tables can be ganged together and round tables can accommodate more people if they choose to sit closer to one another. In a dining room a variety of seating options is desirable, from 2-person to 12-person tables. In larger buildings, 36" high bar-style counters (not 42") are popular, especially when they overlook a view or a friendly demonstration kitchen. In addition to being comfortable, furniture should look residential with attractive, soft fabrics. Today the use of stain- and odor-resistant fabrics like Crypton[9] make it easy to specify noninstitutional colors, textures, and patterns.

Finally, residents spend a lot of time sitting in chairs or wheelchairs so the room should be designed from an eye-level perspective. Frank Lloyd Wright famously believed that his interiors needed to be designed and appreciated from a seated perspective[10] and Wright was right. You literally need to picture the outlook from the occupant's perspective so windows are placed correctly and horizontal mullions do not block views.

TWELVE: SPECIAL CONSIDERATIONS FOR DESIGNING FOR DEMENTIA

Residents with memory loss are a unique constituency because cognitive impairment affects each person in a slightly different way. For some, the world is confusing and upsetting. Noise and activity creates dissonance and they seek solitude and peace. Others have lost a contemporary context and live a fantasy life influenced by childhood and young adult memories. Still others are quiet, having lost their ability to communicate. Some are physically strong and combative and frequently attempt to elope because they seek a context that is familiar and reassuring. Those suffering from profound memory loss live in a state of dreamlike confusion, which can vary from one day to the next.

Although everyone is different, the disease is progressive and most seek reassurance and safety. The disease can afflict someone for as long as a decade or progress rapidly. Eventually dementia affects ambulation, lessens balance control and leads to falls and injuries.

In early stages a person can react in a benign fashion and often be mainstreamed with other physically impaired individuals. However, eventually they reach a point where a secured setting is necessary for their own protection and well-being. As the cognitively impaired age, they typically need more medical attention, which is frustrating because they can't communicate the symptoms they feel. Caring for people with memory loss requires quick thinking,

Figure 6-18 A dementia garden is a necessary component of a residential dementia cluster: In this historic Claremont, California, Arts and Crafts building an outdoor garden pavilion with a walkway was created for activities and exercise. A large live oak tree provides shade and adds character to the garden. *Courtesy of HPI Architects and RMA Architectural Photography.*

patience, and tolerance. Caregivers must be trained to respond to different challenges in different ways.

At mid-stage, therapies that involve purposeful activities of daily living (ADL) like folding laundry, setting the table, washing dishes, busing dishes, and limited food preparation are often feasible and especially popular in northern Europe. For some people these activities, well rehearsed over a lifetime, can be maintained at advanced stages. At later stages, decreases in mental and physical ability often curtail activities like reading the newspaper or playing board games. At this stage, palliative therapies such as hand massage, a soothing bath, walking outside, or family visitations are more effective.

Therapies often deal with each person's sense of reality. Short-term memory is normally affected first, leaving residents with long-term recollections. For these individuals, photos and objects from the past are often reassuring. Today's therapies do not confront residents with present realities like "Who is the current president?" Communication methods are often based on a shared reality that mainstreams a resident's thoughts within a conversational dialogue.[11] If they want to talk about their "impending

Figure 6-19 In the Akropolis AFL in Rotterdam, the Netherlands, a dementia museum showcases furniture and household objects from the past century: This is a shop installation with hand tools and equipment from a 75-year-old workspace. These displays stimulate intergenerational exchange by having older people recall and describe experiences from the past.

wedding," which could be a 50-year-old memory, it's best to do so rather than correct the person. Correcting someone can be demoralizing because it reminds them how hopeless their situation is.

The Dutch have been particularly interested in using "Snoezelen" therapies[12] to tap long-term memories and stimulate responses from individuals who have lost their ability to speak. This therapy uses objects to trigger memories but can be combined with music or bathing. Even at late stages of dementia, music can resurrect lost memories, such as the words to a song.

Access to the out-of-doors is important because depression and disturbances in the sleep/wake cycle benefit from exercise. Exercise can also reduce psychotropic drug use. Having access to an outdoor garden can offer exposure to sunlight and fresh air, as well as the soothing sounds of water and birds.

Physical Design Ideas

The cognitively impaired do better in smaller clusters of 8 to 12 people, like in the Green House© or the Dutch Hogeweyk CS. The continuity of a person's care is important and benefits when the same caregiver is maintained. Dementia clusters use references to iconic residential rooms and activities like the kitchen, the hearth, the garden, the porch, and the living room to provide a familiar context for daily activity. Conversely, a nurse's station, hospital-like finishes, and institutional furnishings can make a place seem foreign and frightening. Consolidating the nurse's station with the kitchen has made it easier to manage small groups. Today computers monitor health, medications, and food preferences and are located in quiet alcoves or in each resident's room.

Because orientation and way finding is important to well-being, an open plan allows one to see into adjacent spaces where activities take place. It also helps if the internal circulation pathway is looped and leads back to a familiar place like the kitchen or living room. Natural light and the use of phototropism can attract residents to various places and can also direct movement. Bright winter gardens and light-filled enclosed porches are especially attractive, while darker spaces are often overlooked. Thus, placing an exit/entry door in a dark, isolated alcove can "disguise" the door, keeping residents from eloping. Unique pieces of furniture, artwork, and accessories placed in visible locations can sometimes be effective landmarks for those with low to mid-level impairment. Shadow boxes with family

Figure 6-20 **This U-shaped kitchen serves a Dutch dementia cluster of 10 residents in the Kristal CS:** The space behind the counter is wide enough for several people to prepare food together. Glass-fronted cabinets and open shelving make it easier for residents to identify objects. The kitchen is compact but also spacious and accommodating.

photographs and salient objects are often placed near resident entry doors to cue them. These objects also introduce the resident to the staff, other residents, and other visitors by communicating important aspects of their life.

Furniture groupings can suggest various subjects. For example, a clothes tree and hat rack can display clothing items that reflect historic or contemporary themes. Wedding dresses, military uniforms, scarves, hats, and accessories can add color, texture, and interest. Desks for writing and reading, makeup tables for grooming, dolls, cribs, and workbenches have been used to add interest and engage residents in a range of activities.

In the unit, techniques like allowing residents to display items on shelves or hang clothing on pegs can remind them of what to wear. Woodside Place[13] did this effectively by introducing a Shaker-inspired plate shelf with pegs around the perimeter of each resident room slightly above eye level. The plate shelf displayed photos and artwork and the pegs were used to hang hats and clothing. In the closet, wire baskets for storing clothing made it easier to identify items. Dutch half doors can open the upper portion of the resident's entry door to the corridor while the closed portion provides security.

Making the toilet visible from the bed or wiring the bathroom light to turn on when you walk by the bathroom door can encourage the memory-impaired person to use the toilet. Larger shared spaces are available in dementia clusters, but it is also important to have resident rooms with enough space for personal possessions and furniture.

Stimulating Social Interaction

THIRTEEN: PLACES THAT WELCOME FAMILY AND FRIENDS

Families are one of the most important constituencies to attract to LTC settings. The emotional bond that children have with their parents is difficult if not impossible to replace by a paid staff member. Most residents have family who are interested in visiting. But visiting a building can be an alienating or unfriendly experience. Making friends and family feel welcome is the best way to encourage participation. Because staff members play a prominent role in caregiving, they often dominate the social ecology of the place. If staff are not friendly the place can appear more like an institution than a housing environment. Family-friendly attitudes, features, and events can make the place much more sociable.

Some buildings feature an oversized dining room and deeply discounted meals in order to attract family and friends. Opening the dining room (like a restaurant) to a more public audience as well as providing private "retreat"

Figure 6-21 **This three-season porch in an assisted living building in the UK has a wide-angle view of the street and parking lot:** Intimate interior spaces with expansive views are especially attractive to families because they can talk privately in a place that connects them with the landscape.

Figure 6-22 **In the Hogeweyk Dementia Village CS families have assembled scrapbooks that represent important events in a resident's life:** They are personal accounts that include both happy and sad periods of their life. When viewed with family members they become a vehicle for conversations and a method to stimulate long-term memories.

spaces for family interaction can make families and friends feel welcome. Symbolic features can change the impression of the place. For example, a playground space for children or a toy box for toddlers can be a delightful invitation to children. Creating an activity room that includes computer games provides an additional activity for younger family members and can be fun for residents who watch and even participate. Outdoor spaces in the late spring, summer, and early fall can support an impromptu picnic, which makes a routine trip more memorable. Families are busy and often schedule visits at lunchtime between other commitments. Having conveniently located visitor parking also encourages drop-by visits. It is important to recognize that the friendlier the place becomes, the more successful it will be in attracting volunteers who appreciate the setting as a community resource.

Another way to help family members is to host seminars or discussion sessions on clinical or psychological topics so they can learn more about the onset of disease and useful coping mechanisms from peer interactions. Others who have been through difficult times can provide empathy and insights. Sometimes these interactions lead to long-term friendships or a commitment to help others through volunteering. Families may choose to limit visits because they are stressful and upsetting. Probably the most disconcerting problem is the loss of intimacy with a parent who is experiencing memory loss. The inability to carry out a conversation or recognize a family member is both tragic and frightening.

Children have many reasons to spend time with their parents at the end of life. Reconciling rough times or expressing appreciation for help and support are important for both sides to hear or express. Families can be under great pressure, which includes financial and emotional strains. Some may feel guilty about participating in a placement decision, while others might believe their siblings are not doing their part. It is important to imagine what families are going through and seek ways to help them.

FOURTEEN: THE 100% CORNER OR COMMUNITY TABLE

The term "100% corner" is usually applied to the busiest intersection in a downtown metropolitan district. It can refer to either pedestrian flow or car counts associated with the place that attracts the greatest amount of use and activity. In this context, the phrase refers to the most socially active place in the building. Enhancing the use of a common space though activities and social interaction adds to the friendly nature of the building. A successful 100% corner usually requires a nexus of features to make it attractive and engaging.

The components of a typical 100% corner in LTC begins with a table that seats six to eight, positioned so residents can easily converse and interact. The table should overlook stimulating activities in adjacent rooms and outside areas. Having a proximal connection to major circulation pathways generates visitations and provides something to watch. In addition, games, cards, or reading materials support group or individual activities. Other features include comfortable seating, access to a bathroom, and proximity to snacks and beverages.

Community tables at settings like coffee houses and restaurants serve a similar purpose.

These types of spaces may occur naturally in a building, but they can also be created by assembling the necessary components in an optimal location. The 100% corner is similar to the concept of a "third place,"[14] where residents come together. This might be for card playing, or just watching vicariously the ebb and flow of circulation and activity.

Post-occupancy evaluations often find that decentralized common spaces located throughout a building are poorly used. The 100% corner philosophy is based on the concept that a nexus of activity enhances use and the greater the activity, the more compelling and popular it is. Activity begets activity. The best way to identify a 100% corner is to notice where residents congregate in the building. Usually there are a few places that are more effective at attracting groups of people or individuals.

A 100% corner is enhanced by adjacent uses and strategic placement. The following are 11 viewpoints, adjacencies, and features that can make a 100% corner more successful.

Viewpoints, Adjacencies, and Features

1. Views and direct access to a **porch or the outdoors**

2. Connection/view into **adjacent activity spaces** (library, living room, dining room)

3. View of well-traveled pedestrian pathways and **resident activities**

4. Adjacency to a **kitchenette with snacks** or drinks

5. View of the **primary path** between the entry and the elevator

6. Access to a nearby **public restroom**

7. Adjacency to the **mailroom** or a place to wait for the mail

8. **Good artificial and natural light**

9. View of **staff activities,** including office spaces and administrative functions

10. **Comfortable seating**

11. Access to storage, **supplies, puzzles, and games**.

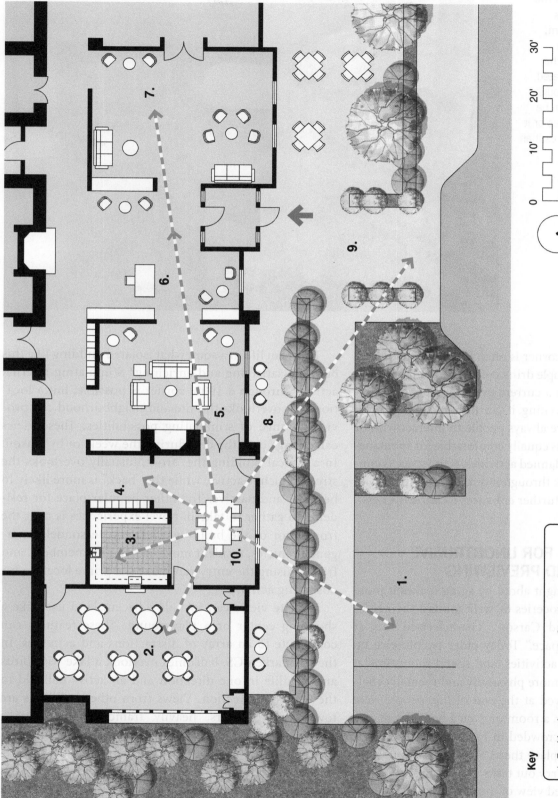

Key

1. Parking Lot
2. Activity Room
3. Country Kitchen
4. Mail Alcove
5. Library
6. Concierge
7. Dining Room
8. Porch
9. Entry
10. Table (100% Corner)

Figure 6-23 This plan demonstrates the 100% corner idea in an assisted living project near Boston: This table has 10 visual connections to surrounding common spaces, rooms, and circulation routes throughout the building and the grounds. This nexus of visual activity makes the 100% corner a stimulating place to be throughout the day and evening.
Courtesy of Dimella Shaffer Architects.

Figure 6-24 **This table in the La Valance CS overlooks the restaurant, the atrium, and the main circulation pathway that traverses the building:** It is centrally located, well lighted, and visible through clear glass partitions. It can be used for a range of activities or it can be ignored, which makes it an effective 100% corner.

A successful 100% corner is often busy throughout the day. In the morning people drink coffee and read the newspaper, in the afternoon a current events discussion might take place, and in the evening, it can attract card players. In the meantime, there are always people to interact with or watch. It is a place that is equally comfortable for spontaneous interaction or for planned activities. If the space is configured so you can walk through it or near it on the way to another destination, it further enhances its attractiveness.

FIFTEEN: PLACES FOR UNOBTRUSIVE OBSERVATION AND PREVIEWING

Reduced mobility brought about by aging makes it more difficult to shop for groceries or walk around the neighborhood. Pastalan and Carson[15] characterized this as a restriction of "life space." Today older people give up driving, reduce travel activities, and spend more time at home as they become more physically and mentally challenged. Pastalan believed at the end of life, people were restricted to a corridor, a room or even a bed. The reason a nurse's station is so crowded in most nursing homes is because activity takes place there. Staff and visitors enter the building, nurses carry out tasks, and its strategic location allows an expanded view of the surrounding context. It is a great place for observing activity in a setting that typically has very little activity to observe.

How can life in a somewhat isolated building like this be more satisfying and enriching? Stimulating internal activity through a 100% corner is possible, but a location that overlooks the site and neighborhood can provide a range of stimulating possibilities. These views can change over the day, during the week, or by season. In a typical building the "front," usually overlooks the street, which is active, while the "back" is more likely to be quiet and passive. The other popular place for residents to gather to take in novel experiences is near the front door of the building. Delivery personnel, emergency vehicles, resident move-ins, family members, and friends using the entry can make it a prime location for observing activity.

Off-site views can include adjacent land uses like a shopping center or a playground. These features can contribute to an array of distractions and activities. In the Irismarken CS, balconies overlook a lake with birds and wildlife in one direction and an active ballfield in the opposite direction. Views from other buildings are toward city centers, heavily trafficked intersections or park areas. These can be stimulating and interest provoking.

Atrium buildings are a treasure trove of activities because many people from outside of the building visit. Furthermore, atrium activity can be observed from upper floors without direct resident involvement.

Figure 6-25 **From the upper floor of the Humanitas Bergweg CS atrium you can overlook the activities below:** This unobtrusive overlook allows residents to gain the pleasure of watching an eclectic crowd made up of family members, volunteers, residents, and staff. It is also a great place to watch large group activities which are staged here.

Figure 6-26 **The Holmegårdsparken nursing center in Charlottenlund, Denmark, features a cantilevered perch in each typical room that overlooks the site and neighborhood:** This space is used by some residents as a living room, while others prefer to make it a bedroom alcove. Armoires on wheels can be moved around the unit to create different spatial configurations.

Previewing Spaces Before You Enter

The idea of previewing a space before making a commitment to enter comes from the early research of Zeisel.[16] Writing about the Captain Eldridge Congregate House in Hyannis, Massachusetts, he introduced the concept of previewing by identifying viewpoints in the building where residents could see into adjacent spaces before making a commitment to enter them. This concept gives older people better social control in a group setting.

Figure 6-27 **Porches are a great place to survey on- and off site views:** Watching deliveries, visiting families, and resident move-in activities gives this location strategic purpose. A porch is also covered and protected from the sun and can be far enough away from the front door to be unobtrusive.

In his research, the most memorable previewing spot was the landing of an open stair where residents could see into the living room below while walking downstairs. At the landing they could see in advance who was in the room before exiting the stairs. The narrative followed that if someone was living in a place with a range of unrelated individuals, there were probably people you want to see and others you would prefer to avoid.

This technique was used to avoid awkward confrontations in common rooms as well as to accommodate welcomed interactions. If a shared room was visible through a glass window from an adjacent corridor, the room could be scanned in advance to avoid an uncomfortable confrontation.

SIXTEEN: **THE RETREAT**

AFLs and care settings are group living arrangements. They are places where residents live and interact daily with other unrelated individuals, including fellow residents and caregivers. In such a setting, you share common space with many others. But getting away from everyone to read a book, meditate, or just be by yourself is important. Just as there should be places that are attractive to groups of residents (like the 100% corner and dining room), there should also be places where you can experience quiet and seclusion outside of your own room.

Retreat spaces can be located inside the building, on the edge of the building, or somewhere on the site. A retreat allows you to "get away" but still experience the protection and oversight of others. A building needs both good communal spaces and good retreat spaces. Exterior retreat spaces allow you to experience a multisensory

Figure 6-28 **A bench 100 feet from the building edge can be an attractive retreat:** On this Canadian site, sitting next to a pathway in the shade of a tree with a great view is a wonderful place to read a book. Although many residents prefer the company of others, getting away is also appreciated.
Courtesy of Martha Child Interiors and Jerry Staley Photography.

exposure to the site by communing with nature and wildlife. Gazebos are popular because they are open on all sides but covered and protected from the sun and from the elements. Sometimes a retreat can be located a short distance away in a nearby park or can overlook an interesting active or passive landscape view. Retreats can be a destination for a walk or a single bench under the shade of a tree. When coupled with an attractive landscape feature (berm, fountain, flowering plant, or birdbath) they can reward you with the scent of a flower or the chance to observe a bird or a squirrel. Retreats should be in quiet places that promote relaxation and meditation.

SEVENTEEN: THE PRIMARY PATH

Overlaps between common spaces and the circulation system of a building often stimulate social exchange. The research of Sandra Howell[17] examined the use of common

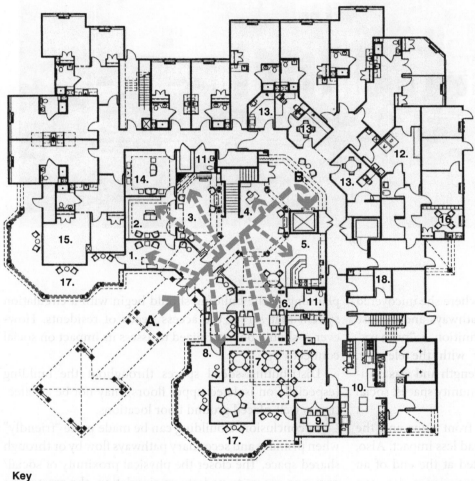

Figure 6-29a–b **The "primary path" is the main circulation route between the front door and the elevator:** In this example, eight different views into adjacent spaces are available as you proceed along the entry path. The theory posits that the more choices available, the greater the opportunity for observation and social interaction. The four-story L-shaped building in Bellevue, Washington, contains the primary path referenced in the adjacent plan. The building symmetry emphasizes the entry axis (primary path).
Courtesy of Sunrise Senior Living and Mithun Architects.

Key

A. Front Door
B. Elevator

View Corridors	Other Spaces
1. Three Season Porch	9. Private Dining Room
2. Library	10. Kitchen
3. Living Room	11. Toilet
4. Concierge Desk	12. Central Laundry
5. Bistro Bar	13. Office
6. Bistro	14. TV Room
7. Dining Room	15. Resident Unit
8. Porch	16. Staff Lounge
	17. Porch
	18. Resident Laundry

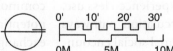

(a)

(b)

Figure 6-29a–b **(continued)**

spaces in elderly housing in Boston, where she uncovered a relationship between circulation pathways and the use patterns of common spaces. By definition a "primary" pathway connected the entry door with the elevator. When this path was 40 to 75 feet in length and was positioned to cut through or pass by community spaces, social interaction in those spaces increased.

When the distance between the front door and the elevator was too short or too long it had less impact. Also, when major social spaces were located at the end of an isolated corridor these shared spaces experienced less use. When interrelated or overlapped, circulation pathways and social spaces stimulated both informal social encounters and participation in planned events.

Further speculation about this interaction suggested that everyday trips along pathways to common "destination" spaces like the dining room, mailbox area, and resident laundry room also had the ability to activate spaces that were more dependent on spontaneous use. The

planning of the building should begin with a circulation system that serves the access needs of residents. However, it should be scrutinized to assess its impact on social connectivity.

Distributing social spaces throughout the building (especially on isolated upper floors) may not be as effective as well-placed ground floor locations.

In conclusion, a building can be made more "friendly" when primary and secondary pathways flow by or through shared space. The closer the physical proximity of social/common spaces to pedestrian circulation, the greater the potential for activation. This is important because social exchange often leads to friendships.

EIGHTEEN: TRIANGULATION

William Whyte's[18] study of small urban parks in New York City describes a concept called "triangulation." It involves a common object or activity of shared interest

Figure 6-30 Triangulation can result from any object that provokes curiosity and can be shared: The theater square in the Hogeweyk Dementia Village has several very intriguing sculptural masks and crowns supported by posts that can be "tried on" by participants. They are fanciful and fun to share with others.

that prompts strangers to talk with one another. In a park, that could be a dog or an impromptu music performance. In care settings, there is value in stimulating social exchange between residents, family members, friends, and the caregiving staff. Objects and photographs of historic value can trigger recollections and conversations. Because multigenerational perspectives are often represented, these exchanges provide a common bridge for communication about the past, present, and future. If it is historic, like the photo of a nineteenth-century kitchen, residents can be the authority on a topic of shared interest.

A historic display (or showcase) can represent a theme such as "going to the opera." This might include objects like white gloves, an embroidered program, opera glasses, and show tickets. This display can be the basis for

a multigenerational discussion about what it was like to attend an opera performance 60 years ago. In the Humanitas Bergweg CS building, extensive displays of objects that date back 60 to 100 years ago are used to stimulate the memory of residents. Antique woodworking tools or kitchen utensils can be used to tell stories about that period by explaining how these objects were used. Listening to these stories can be especially interesting to younger people. Residents have often lived interesting personal and professional lives. Tapping their knowledge about the past can intrigue caregivers and supply them with topics for ongoing conversations.[19] In dementia facilities, displays of meaningful personal objects are often mounted near a resident's entry door for wayfinding purposes. However, these displays also communicate an individual's past life, interests, and achievements.

Planning the Dwelling Unit

NINETEEN: PERSONALIZATION THAT MAKES THE UNIT YOUR OWN

Making a move to a nursing home requires that possessions assembled during a lifetime be discarded or given away. For some people, photographs are important reminders of family, friends, and salient places but objects like books, furniture, or collectibles can also have special meaning and can feel good to touch or view.

Because traditional nursing home rooms are small and often double occupied, they allow little personalization. Even if the stay is only 6 months, the lack of familiar items and the absence of display space is dysfunctional. The benefit of surrounding yourself with familiar objects is to create a place that is "yours," not a space that is anonymous.

Effective personalization requires more space and greater privacy. Northern European nursing homes, like those explored in the Herluf Trolle, Ærtebjerghaven, and Irismarken case studies, are single-occupancy units of approximately 450–500 SF. These are large enough to provide a separate sleeping area from the living room, while offering enough space for a few well-chosen personal items. A larger unit can accommodate several pieces of furniture as well as a small table. In these three referenced

Figure 6-31 **Small units require compact thinking about how to use space effectively:** In this dementia dwelling unit in the Kristal CS, shelves in conjunction with photos, an armoire, and displayed items optimize the visibility of this resident's collection. This arrangement is a treasure chest of memories.

case studies, there is also space for a bed with an overhead lift, as well as a small outdoor terrace.

In an AFL building or a CCRC/LPC, units range in size from 600 to 1200 SF. The most popular units today are two bedrooms or one bedroom with den. These units normally have balconies, a full kitchen, and enough space for a small office, study, or guest room. The Woodlands and NewBridge CSs are typical of what US unit sizes are like. These accommodations are consistent with what boomers expect and are large enough to accommodate the equipment that might be needed as an individual ages.

Personalization at the Unit Edge and Friendly Corridors

Making the unit entry more personal and unique can also make it more friendly and inviting. Because friendships between older residents are often between neighbors, having an engaging corridor and unit entry is especially effective. A common personalization treatment is to create an entry alcove that provides space for a shelf, a display board, or a piece of furniture. Alcoves often contain dropped soffits, downlights, pendant lighting, name plates, and door bells. A photo or artwork display space adjacent to the

door can offer an opportunity to share new experiences or joyful memories. These treatments also underscore the uniqueness of each individual resident. Doorbells are used to insure privacy and alert the resident to guests. In home-care-supported residential units, like the Rundgraafpark CS, a lockbox containing an entry door key is also located here.

The Captain Eldridge Congregate House in Hyannis, Massachusetts,[20] uses several different techniques for making the door alcove friendly, including an operable double-hung window, a Dutch door, a space large enough for a piece of furniture, and a sconce light. This alcove opens the unit to a corridor-atrium that also introduces natural light into the unit.

If a unit opens onto a single-loaded corridor, seating can be placed here to overlook a view or to serve as a place for reading. In some instances, sitting areas can be tucked into a bay window or widened corridor. Clustering two to four entry doors together in a corridor can lead to better informal communications between neighbors. The probability of becoming acquainted is enhanced when entry doors are next to one another. The larger space created by the clustering of doorway alcoves can also enhance the spatial variety of the corridor.

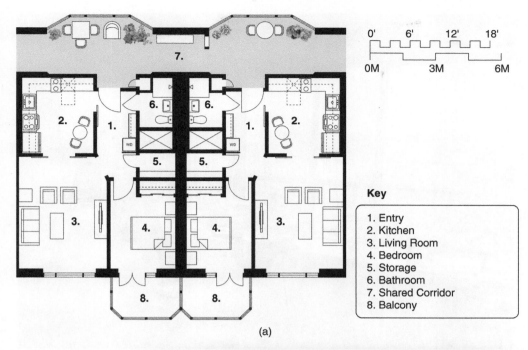

0' 6' 12' 18'

0M 3M 6M

Key

1. Entry
2. Kitchen
3. Living Room
4. Bedroom
5. Storage
6. Bathroom
7. Shared Corridor
8. Balcony

(a)

Figure 6-32a–b The bay window attached to this single-loaded corridor in Sweden has been taken over as an extension of each resident's dwelling unit: Even though every unit has a private balcony, this enclosed corridor can be used to make social contact with neighbors regardless of the weather. Residents have furnished the alcove to meet their interests, which often include a table and chair. Some have furnished the space with plants, while others have brought in a throw rug to make it cozier. *Courtesy of White Arkitekter.*

(b)

TWENTY: DWELLING UNIT DESIGN

Dwelling unit sizes and features differ from assisted living to a small group nursing home to an AFL unit. In northern Europe, dwelling units for frail people (in nursing homes or service houses) are typically single-occupied studio or one-bedroom apartments between 450 and 600 SF. Apartments for Life in northern Europe are typically targeted toward couples and widows and range in size from 600 to 1000 SF. CCRC/LPC's in the US have slightly larger units than the AFL models and can range between 850 and 1200 SF.

Figure 6-33 **The De Plussenburgh CS dwelling unit has 32 continuous feet of window wall:** A six-foot-plus sliding door separates the living room and bedroom. When closed, it rests against the exterior window mullion; when open, the wider view is visible. There are no bearing walls and thus all internal partitions can be removed.

AFLs usually contain a full kitchen and a full bathroom. Small cluster Green House-type units usually do not have any food preparation equipment in the room. They typically have a full bathroom but no mini-kitchen. The same is true of dementia units in the Hogeweyk, where individual resident rooms resemble a bedroom in a house. The smallest units are usually for people with dementia because they often spend most of their time together in shared spaces and primarily nap or sleep in their room. A typical assisted living unit usually has either a "tea kitchen" (refrigerator, cabinets, sink, and microwave) or a normal kitchen, including a stove and range. The AFL or condo for life is similar in size to a one-, two-, or three-bedroom apartment, often with a large barrier-free bathroom and a full-size kitchen. Additional square footage is often used to create an alcove or small bedroom that can accommodate a family member (or caregiver) for an overnight stay.

In general, units are small but should be accessible for the handicapped. Specifying 36" doors throughout will accommodate wheelchairs but swing doors can be awkward and bulky. Often barn doors or pocket doors are employed because they avoid circulation conflicts with furniture. Another benefit of sliding doors is how easily they can be oversized (42", for example) to accommodate a wider wheelchair, which with heavier residents is more common today. Because sliding doors can be larger, they can also be used to create more substantial connections between adjacent rooms. The De Plussenburgh CS also contains two doors into the bathroom to increase handicapped accessibility.

A distinct entry space with furniture like a mirror, coat rack, valet stand, clothes tree, or console table can create a friendly transition from the unit to the corridor. Changing the floor material and the ceiling height at the entry can also reinforce the progression from a public corridor to the private unit. Decentralized storage should be available in the kitchen, bathroom, bedroom, and living room. A walk-in closet in one of the bedrooms is also highly valued. The supporting structure for a rolling lift device should be considered in all buildings that expect someday to accommodate older frail people. In an AFL unit, some accessible features are provided from the beginning but additional items can be added as they are needed.

Outdoor balconies are popular in multistory housing. In Europe there are many systems available to "glass-in" a balcony, so it can be used in the winter. French balconies, which have been popular in space-stingy Europe, are now becoming more popular in the US.

(a)

(b)

Figure 6-34a–b **Condominium balconies in the Rundgraafpark CS can be enclosed in the winter, partially open in the fall/ spring, or completely open in the summer:** In this unit, gaps between glass panels facilitate ventilation in the summer. Differing levels of protection allow freedom in selecting furnishings for the space. These glass enclosures can be quickly opened or closed by sliding vertical glass panels to one side, where they are stored. This level of flexibility allows the space to be used throughout the year.

A Safe Bathroom and Kitchen

Bathrooms and kitchens are the most dangerous rooms in a dwelling unit. Because residents cook, chop vegetables, make coffee, and use appliances in a kitchen, they can represent a safety risk. In an AFL, dangerous appliances can be covered, disconnected, or removed. In most cases, disconnecting the stove and garbage disposal solve the biggest potential problems. For flooring, slip-resistant wood-grain sheet vinyl is useful in kitchens or bathrooms, where water is a factor.

In bathrooms, residents are at risk of slipping or falling. In northern European installations, continuous tiled bathroom floors are common. This creates excellent accessibility for a three-fixture arrangement (sink, toilet, and shower) in a smaller space. In the Herluf Trolle CS the fixtures are mounted on three walls that face the center of the room. The fourth wall is used as an access wall (door). A 5' 0" wheelchair turning diameter is available in the center of the room, equidistant from all three fixtures. The sink can be moved up and down as well as sideways for flexibility. The commode is low enough that a shower/toilet chair can be rolled over the top of it. Finally, the shower space can be expanded to wash and rinse a resident in a shower chair. Lighting is important in the bathroom because contusions and skin damage are often examined here. Higher light levels also compensate for losses in visual acuity but should be connected to a dimmer or separately switched for nighttime use. The bathroom also should be heated because older people are susceptible to cold air drafts. Sliding door access to the bathroom is preferred because a swing door that opens outward can be large and awkward.

Bathroom designs for condo/AFL units can include two or two and a half bathrooms, one of which should have a shower and the other a bathtub. Tub/shower combinations are difficult and often dangerous to use for the frail. Tubs with an access door are more popular today for those who need a place to soak. Nonslip, resilient bathroom floor finishes and grab bar locations should be carefully considered for safety. A personal emergency response system (PERS) or a voice-activated emergency call system should be available. Older people can fall at night or may feel the need to visit the bathroom when they have a heart attack or are feeling faint or dizzy.

Figure 6-35 System designs from northern Europe for bathrooms add flexibility and support: Implemented in the nursing care units of the NewBridge CS, this rail system allows lavatories to be adjusted and toilet arm supports to be lowered. The continuous waterproof floor surface accommodates a roll-in shower.

Endnotes

1 Hines, T. (1994), *Richard Neutra and the Search for Modern Architecture*, UC Press, Berkeley.

2 Rodiek, S., and Schwartz, B. (eds.) (2007), *Outdoor Environments for People with Dementia,* Haworth Press, Binghamton, NY.

3 Regnier, V. (1985), *Behavioral and Environmental Aspects of Outdoor Space Use in Housing for the Elderly,* USC School of Architecture, Los Angeles.

4 Story, M. (1998), *The Universal Design File: Designing for People of All Ages and Abilities,* Center for Universal Design, NC State University, Charlotte.

5 Steinfeld, E., and White, J. (2010), *Inclusive Housing: A Pattern Book*, Norton, New York.

6 Twombly, R. (1979), *Frank Lloyd Wright: His Life and Architecture*, John Wiley & Sons, New York.

7 Perkins Eastman (2013), *Building Type Basics for Senior Living,* 2nd ed., John Wiley & Sons, Hoboken, NJ.

8 Moos, R., Lemke, S., and David, T. (1987), Priorities for Design and Management in Residential Settings for the Elderly, in *Housing the Aged: Design Directives and Policy Considerations* (eds. V. Regnier and J. Pynoos), Elsevier, New York.

9 Brawley, E. (2006), *Design Innovations for Aging and Alzheimer's,* John Wiley & Sons, Hoboken, NJ.

10 Twombly, *Frank Lloyd Wright.*

11 Naomi Feil, N. (1993), *The Validation Breakthrough: Simple Techniques for Communicating with People with Alzheimer's-Type Dementia*, Health Professionals Press, Baltimore.

12 Snoezelen Multi-sensory Environments (2017), History and Approach, http://www.snoezelen.info/history (accessed on 10/7/17).

13 Regnier, V. (2002), *Design for Assisted Living: Guidelines for Housing the Physically and Mentally Frail,* John Wiley & Sons, Hoboken, NJ, 138–39.

14 Oldenburg, R. (1989), *The Great Good Place: Cafes, Coffee Shops, Community Centers, Beauty Parlors, General Stores, Bars, Hangouts, and How They Get You Through the Day.* Paragon House, New York.

15 Pastalan, L., and Carson, D. (1970), *Spatial Behavior in Older People*. University of Michigan, Wayne State University Press, Ann Arbor.

16 Zeisel, J. (2006), *Inquiry by Design*, W. W. Norton, New York.

17 Howell, S. (1980), *Designing for Aging: Patterns for Use*, MIT Press, Cambridge, MA.

18 Whyte, W. (1980), *The Social Life of Small Urban Spaces*, Conservation Foundation, Washington, DC.

19 Becker, H. (2008), *Hands Off Is Not an Option: The Reminiscence Museum, Mirror of a Humanistic Care Philosophy*, Eburon Academic Press, Rotterdam, the Netherlands.

20 Zeisel, J. (2006), *Inquiry by Design*, W. W. Norton, New York.

CHAPTER SEVEN

12 Caregiving and Management Practices that Avoid an Institutional Lifestyle

DESIGNING the physical environment is important, but operating the setting in a humane and empowering way is equally (if not more) important. The following 12 themes build upon design ideas by suggesting behaviors, activities, therapies, caregiving strategies, and attitudes that secure the well-being of the older resident. These methods direct the use of the environment so it operates to its highest potential. Operational philosophies such as these must be understood in conjunction with design directives to optimize the positive impact of the setting. This is comparable to the design versus the driving of a car. You can get the physical design well honed but if you drive the car without knowing how to optimize performance you are only getting half of it right.

Experience shows the best settings require **both** a great physical environment as well as enlightened operational savvy. Poor environments often keep the best caregiving from taking place, but there is nothing more frustrating than having a great environment and using it poorly. These 12 approaches are subdivided into three topic areas: **Effective Caregiving Strategies, Full Participation in the Life of the Place, and Creating Affect and Joy.**

Effective Caregiving Strategies

ONE: ACCOMMODATING INDEPENDENCE THROUGH A HOME CARE MODEL

Discovering how the home care delivery system operated in northern Europe was an epiphany. Frail people lived in independent housing served by caregivers who visited them up to 3–5 times daily, sometimes in 10–15 minute increments. Rather than living in a nursing home, they lived in normal dwellings with autonomy and it was less expensive.

Victor Regnier, USC

Figure 7-1 **Home care workers visit residents sometimes several times per day to help them with personal and medical care needs:** This home care worker has scheduled consecutive visits with different residents in this building. Nurses also make separate planned visits. Grouping visitations in one building creates efficiency.

Figure 7-2 **Home care workers visit older people in their own apartments in the neighborhood:** In northern Europe, dense urban settings make it easier to get around by bicycle or compact car. Workers typically meet in the morning and late afternoon to discuss resident cases and schedule visits in the middle of the day.

The most common approach to housing and service delivery in northern Europe is to provide normal independent housing with personal care services delivered on an as-needed basis. This system is based on each individual's ability to carry out activities that support independence. Service assistance usually starts with heavy cleaning and progresses all the way to extensive medical help. Although it is not very common, older people can live in an apartment (especially an Apartment for Life) and use a gastric tube. People receiving help and assistance can vary from those with minimal problems to those who would normally be in a nursing home if they were in the US. Home care systems vary from country to country but most are committed to the idea of helping frail older people live an independent life outside of an institution for as long as possible.

Typically, an older individual with personal care needs is visited in the morning and afternoon. Caregivers, assistant nurses, and nurses make up the caregiving team. The shortest visit is usually 15 minutes; however, a more impaired individual might require 45 to 90 minutes for dressing, toileting, showering, and breakfast preparation. What occurs over time is a ramping up of help, assistance, and care as the older person becomes less capable. Rarely does the physical environment cause major complications. But when it does, these issues are assessed and resolved. For example, an upper-story apartment in a non-elevator-supported building might require a move to the ground or first floor.

Residents do more for themselves and also volunteer to help others. When formal services are shifted to informal helpers, it saves time and money. In Scandinavia family members are not as involved, but will likely be in the future given the continuing growth of the older population.

Dementia caregiving is also causing greater concern. More people are living longer and are therefore more likely to acquire dementia. Home care has its limitations, especially when working with the cognitively impaired. They can be harder to manage and because they are often in better physical condition, they can wander, get lost, or do something that threatens themselves or others (like leaving the stove turned on). Chapter 9 outlines the positive recent experience of Danish home care providers with Skype-style technologies for those who suffer from mild cognitive impairment (MCI). In the last 5 years, northern European providers have noted an increase in the number of memory-impaired individuals who enter care facilities.

TWO: PRIMARY, SECONDARY, AND DESIGNATED CAREGIVERS AND THE COMPUTER

Someone needs to know who you are – really KNOW you! Sadly, sometimes the designated caregiver is their ONLY friend and everyone needs a friend.

Victor Regnier, USC

One of the most disconcerting aspects of traditional US nursing care settings is the lack of continuity with assigned caregivers. The amount of turnover and a focus on part-time employment all but eliminates relationships with someone who knows you well. Care homes in northern Europe, always assign a primary and secondary contact person. The primary contact person knows the resident best, and the secondary contact person is a backup for when the primary is not available. The primary contact person knows your medical and health-related conditions, family ties and personal likes and dislikes. They know if you like cream in your coffee and your favorite interests. They are individuals who you know well, that know you well. In the best US assisted living programs, having a "designated caregiver" is a standard component of quality caregiving. This person is assigned for caregiving purposes, but may not be as all-knowing as the northern European contact person. One of the duties of the designated caregiver or contact person is to advocate for the resident's preferences and needs. The best care systems today believe in *op maat,* which is Dutch for the idea of customization. This approach advocates for resident preferences over institutional practices. For example, people who want to sleep in and take their breakfast at 9:30 AM should not be roused at 6:30 AM just because it

Figure 7-3 **The op maat lifestyle is intended to serve resident preferences rather than conform to an institution's schedule:** For example, residents at the Irismarken CS can take a late breakfast or snack by themselves if they are hungry. *Op maat* literally means "cut to fit."

Figure 7-4a–b **The record of resident experiences, care activities, and challenges are transitioning from written notes to computer-based files:** This is a better system for recording daily activities but must be used in conjunction with designated caregivers who are assigned to care for a specific older resident and know them well.

(a)

(b)

is convenient for the staff. This approach, which customizes services based on individual resident preferences, is available in the best US settings but is far from standard practice here.

Today, with shorter shifts and fewer career-oriented employees, knowledge seems to increasingly belong to the computer, a universal companion in both the US and Europe. Computer systems are great for sharing information with a broader constituency, such as the doctor, the family, consulting specialists, and the staff. In Denmark, they have two systems. One system shares information with caregivers and the second system is designed for communication with doctors, nurses, and medical personnel. Caregivers communicate through the first system but they must go through nurses to communicate concerns about clients to doctors. The main problem with many computer-based systems is that **everyone** knows but **no one** has direct responsibility. Another problem is that communication is written rather than verbal when a shift changes.

For home care operations in Scandinavia, a great deal of conversation still takes place between team members. These conversations share insights, ideas, and experience so that new knowledge can be compared with past experience. Usually team meetings occur in the morning and before afternoon shifts, so the knowledge is fresh and the feedback immediate. Computers are frequently used to share written information but it complements verbal exchanges rather than replacing it.

Small group cluster programs adopt a flat hierarchy between caregiving staff, which gives each worker greater access to more information about each resident. Their burden is to communicate information to the next layer up when a change in status or a health-related problem becomes more acute. Getting caregiving staff closer to residents is an advantage in any system.

THREE: ACTIVITY OF DAILY LIVING (ADL) THERAPY

It is amazing how residents love setting the table, busing dishes and helping peel potatoes – familiar activities make it feel like home and not an institution.

Victor Regnier, USC

Helping to prepare a meal is a compelling activity of daily living, even if all you do is watch: In the Kristal CS dementia cluster, potatoes are a frequent menu item. Sharing tasks associated with meal preparation like setting the table or busing dishes is a popular activity.

Around 50 years ago, the northern Europeans started to reduce large-scale nursing homes by breaking them into smaller group clusters of 10 to 15 people. Back then, a commercial kitchen delivered pre-prepared entrees that were supplemented by soup, sandwiches, and a simple morning breakfast. As they continued to reduce the scale, the idea of having each group cluster prepare their own meals evolved. They consolidated health care monitoring and meal production into a kitchen that also served as a nurse's station for each small group. The kitchen was outfitted in the new model with medications, charts, phones, and a fax machine, as well as food preparation and serving equipment.

Along with this, a program of activities invited residents to participate in the everyday routines of cooking meals and doing laundry. This activity of daily living (ADL) program soon became common in dementia units seeking meaningful activities that residents could easily understand. Setting a table, bussing dishes, cleaning counters, washing dishes, putting away dishes, folding laundry, and helping with food preparation were tasks that residents, including those with memory impairments, could carry out. These activities were popular because they were familiar and had purpose and meaning.

Today, these ideas are being explored with a few caveats. In the US and northern Europe, the idea of allowing residents to help in the kitchen has become a victim of hygiene standards. Too many residents sampled food or were not careful washing their hands. Medications have eventually migrated to a locked box in each resident's room to control mistakes and ease distribution. Computers have replaced paper records and their locations are now on desks in a corner of the living room or attached to a wall in each unit or in a corridor on a moveable stand. Computers can still be found in the kitchen but their purpose is relegated to checking on food allergies and ordering supplies. The idea of allowing normal activities of daily living to have a role still exists in the best settings. A few well-intentioned rules have been particularly insidious in the US, keeping residents from tending gardens where the food could be shared for consumption or helping out with household choirs because it is interpreted as "work." The northern Europeans are better at seeing these activities as therapy rather than exploitation. On a recent trip to Denmark it was heartening to see two residents with an attendant leave the building for an all-day fishing trip, hoping to bring back a big enough catch for the evening meal.

The effort to live a normal lifestyle is often seen in group outings to restaurants, local cafes, or pubs. These outings connect residents with the stimulation of public places and the joy of interaction. Public service projects

Figure 7-6 **One of the most popular activity of daily living (ADL) tasks at the Hogeweyk Dementia Village CS is the daily visit to the grocery store to buy ingredients for mealtimes:** Staff members often take along residents to shop and bring groceries home. This activity allows residents to exercise as well as enjoy the outdoors.

like the making of decorations for a special event still happen. Activities with meaning and purpose continue to evolve as residents and caregivers identify situations where their help can deliver authentic benefit.

Resident Participation Is Essential

One of the most frustrating aspects of institutional life is the lack of influence residents have over decisions that control their life. In LTC you are often a passive recipient of policies and systems designed to manage you. Residents often experience having their own voice drowned out by many controlling influences that manage their health, food, activities, and lifestyle.

Because small group clusters operate on a decentralized basis, decisions about activities, food, lifestyle, and staff hiring can be more easily shared with residents. When queried about the usefulness of resident input, team leaders often believe residents ask better questions than staff. They also believe residents are often more aware of the best job applicants. Clearly allowing residents to express their preferences (and then listening) also leads to greater satisfaction with the outcome. Providing the opportunity to comment appears to provide perceived control, which is a powerful motivator. Although input

from the cognitively impaired may be less useful, everyone appreciates being involved.

When policies were being established for the Green House© model, the autonomy of each cluster and the voice of local caregivers were considered paramount. Bill Thomas, a physician, understood how rank and status could easily suppress grassroots opinion unless caregivers and residents were allowed to influence important operational decisions. In the Hogeweyk case study, the desires of seven different cultural groups influence design and lifestyle decisions. To select interior furnishings, designers visited residents from each lifestyle group in their own home. They paid close attention to the colors, patterns, and textures of fabrics and wall coverings that prospective residents had used in decorating their own dwelling unit. They also sketched layouts that showed how each cultural group dealt with the formality of entry and the relationship between indoor and outdoor spaces.

Knowing how to create a physical and cultural environment consistent with past experience allowed them to develop a comfortable and familiar context. Because so many residents were acutely demented, interviews with close family members also proved necessary.

Figure 7-7 **Danish nursing homes have a tradition of resident participation that goes back more than 40 years:** In this photo, a team leader meets with residents and staff to review events from the last two weeks while introducing them to developments expected to occur in the next two weeks.

FOUR: MAINTAIN A COMMITMENT TO SERVE THE SURROUNDING NEIGHBORHOOD

Northern Europeans see buildings for older people as community resources rather than isolated single purpose institutions. The Humanitas Bergweg dining area invites everyone including residents, neighbors, staff, family, children, grandchildren, friends and day laborers in the neighborhood – even dogs and cats are welcome.

Victor Regnier, USC

One of the historic differences between the US and northern European providers is their attitude about public access. In northern Europe decades ago, public services (like meals-on-wheels and home care) were delivered by housing providers to older people in the surrounding neighborhood—not just residents in their buildings. Even today, restaurants, activity areas, and therapy centers located within housing projects are frequently open to everyone. The purpose is to help older people age successfully either in the community or in planned housing and to eliminate the institutional stigma of a setting that might otherwise feel totally age-restricted.

Co-locating children's day care with elderly housing is also common. Both housing with services and day care for pre-kindergarten children are organized at the district

level in Scandinavia. Planners consider them compatible land uses that produce positive social benefits.

Although most home care agencies and service housing operate as separate entities, they still coordinate with one another. AFL housing continues to serve the community by renting space to retail and community service providers like physical therapists, hairdressers, podiatrists, and restaurateurs. Sometimes, as in the Neptuna CS, the building's purpose is camouflaged, allowing residents to feel completely integrated into the community. The attitude today is that housing is one of many services older people need to remain independent in the community. The De Kristal CS in Rotterdam provides 182 units of independent housing located above a three-floor platform of community-oriented uses, including parking, retail, health, and social services. Within this moderate-income, age-restricted housing, 50 residents receive home care support and a 20-unit dementia cluster is available for people with severe memory loss. The elderly housing component is a great mixed-use partner because it requires very few parking spaces and residents benefit from being close to a light rail station and within walking distance of a dozen retail stores.

In the US, there is greater interest in mixed-use urban housing than in the past. These buildings are often near transit lines and supportive retail uses that facilitate staying independent in the community. New US models

Figure 7-8 In the Humanitas Bergweg AFL CS, a call center coordinates home care visits in the neighborhood and the building: These staff members are fielding changes in appointments as well as scheduling new appointments. This type of flexibility is necessary for home care and home health services to operate efficiently.

Figure 7-9 The Humanitas Bergweg AFL CS has several adult day care programs serving people in the surrounding neighborhood: These are separated into smaller cultural and lifestyle groups that meet 3–5 times a week for several hours. Some day care participants are experiencing memory loss, while others are isolated and depressed. Many have become active as volunteers at Bergweg.

will hopefully adopt a European approach that places service housing within highly supportive neighborhoods.

Full Participation in the Life of the Place

FIVE: **USE IT OR LOSE IT**

Too much care is far worse than too little care. . . . You can kill people with kindness! Older people must do as much as they can for themselves.

Hans Becker, Humanitas,[1]

Caregivers often express how very difficult it is to watch an older person struggle to complete a task without help. It is difficult for someone in a "helping profession" to do nothing, but that is what is really required sometimes. Growing old is a struggle, and those who are successful at doing it maintain pride in their accomplishments. Doing as much as you can for yourself is always good practice. In fact, Dutch caregivers are taught to help people by "keeping their hands in their pockets or keeping their hands behind their backs." These caregiving techniques encourage residents to do as much as they can for themselves.

Normal activities of daily living keep many older people active and engaged. When they move to assisted living, there are many tasks they are no longer expected to do. For example, they no longer need to clean their apartment, do their laundry, shop for groceries, prepare meals, or take out the garbage. A lot of the responsibilities that filled their day and challenged their ability are now done by others. The same thing could be said about using a wheelchair in place of walking with the help of a cane or walker. The Humanitas AFL philosophy strongly believes you must "use it or lose it." However, they also believe that individuals should not attempt tasks beyond their capabilities that could lead to injury, such as climbing a ladder to fetch heavy items in an upper cabinet or walking without a needed support device. In the Humanitas system a care coordinator is consulted when a task appears to be beyond the capability of the individual. They believe your lifestyle should be complemented by help, not dominated by it.

Figure 7-10 **A common phase used to describe a healthy lifestyle in the Humanitas AFL program is "use it or lose it":** The saying encourages residents to take both physical and psychological control of their life. The tagline is used frequently and is painted on the side of this delivery van.
Courtesy of Hans Becker.

The context should foster independence, interdependence (people helping one another), and individuality.

SIX: COMMITMENT TO PHYSICAL THERAPY AND EXERCISE

The Danes have a moral commitment to fitness. They see it as their duty to society to keep themselves as independent as possible and they all know exercise and physical therapy is the best way to accomplish that.

Victor Regnier, USC

One important commitment we must make to ourselves, to our families, and to society is to stay as independent as possible and one of the best ways to do that is to stay physically active. Danish nursing homes and home care agencies believe in this philosophy and approach to aging. They not only have physical therapy rooms but they often place exercise equipment in visible, underutilized corridors and public spaces. They believe that a focus on competency-building activities will lead to a more active, independent, and healthier aging population.

This is also reflected in their home care program. If a client in the community is losing agility, they are enrolled in a special rehabilitation plan of action to help them gain back lost ability before they are sent to a nursing home.

The rehabilitation program is often between 5 and 14 days. It can be carried out in the person's dwelling unit, a neighborhood-based outpatient setting, or an inpatient rehabilitation setting.

Danish exercise and physical therapy settings involve occupational therapists, physical therapists, and trainers. A typical rehab room includes equipment for strength training, space for stretching, a free exercise area, and a matt table for massage (usually for the most impaired individuals). Resistance training, aerobic capacity building, and balance control are all emphasized. Training kitchens are often available for individuals who have suffered a stroke, a fall, or a heart attack to gain back lost abilities through practicing activities of daily living. In Scandinavia, a seamless connection exists between exercise and physical therapy. Physical therapy is often considered a natural extension of exercise rather than a formal clinical service. Another interesting difference is the focus on upper body strength building. Most participants are women with less muscle mass in their arms than men, so training is focused on strength building to facilitate important tasks like transferring on and off the commode.

The US is rapidly recognizing the magical properties of exercise and has made great strides in advocating age-appropriate exercise equipment and programs for older people in the community.

Figure 7-11 **The Danes are committed to keeping older residents as independent as possible:** In this dementia facility in Copenhagen, a connecting corridor has been repurposed with equipment for walking therapy. Complete with parallel bars and a lift, it was moved from an isolated room to a public location to encourage and facilitate use.

Figure 7-12 One important muscle group to exercise are upper-body arm muscles: This piece of equipment is designed to give residents in a wheelchair an opportunity to build upper body strength. This is especially important for women, who often lose the muscle strength needed for tasks like transferring to the commode.

SEVEN: CLUBS, ENTERTAINMENT, AND PURPOSEFUL ACTIVITY

Bingo can be fun – but does it help anyone? Purposeful activity can make everyone feel better. When a wife visits her husband and it makes the lives of other residents happier, it is a beautiful generous gift.

Victor Regnier, USC

Activities are important to people. Without them we face a life of boring nonstimulation. They also serve as an excellent opportunity for socializing, which we know fights loneliness, alienation, and depression. But activities should not simply consume time, especially when they can provide meaning and purpose. This is one reason why art and creative expression are satisfying to so many older people.

It is important that activities recognize the specific preferences and interests of individuals. One of the most disheartening habits in long-term care is to select activities based on the lowest common denominator for participation. For example, although bingo is a popular shared activity, it has little purpose. Activities can be used to inspire joy through singing, dancing, children's play, or helping others. Sometimes, passive entertainment like watching a funny TV program or listening to music can also be stimulating. On the other hand, walking clubs, gardening, or an impromptu picnic for lunch can create a meaningful activity out of a common pursuit. More importantly, clubs can focus on a topic for which a small group shares an interest. In the Hogeweyk, approximately 20 clubs operate on a weekly basis, attracting small groups to participate in activities like flower arranging, music appreciation, and dancing.

Helping others is enfranchising, positive, and happiness inducing. Older people with time to help others can receive a great deal of pleasure. In the Humanitas Bergweg CS, volunteers (a third of whom are residents) open the café for early breakfast, provide computer assistance, and help other residents to get around. Volunteerism like this allows residents to "play it forward" with the hope that other people like themselves will be available to help them later on. Volunteerism, especially older people helping one another, is a critical component for the future. With cost cutbacks and paid personnel increasingly expected to carry out direct care provision, volunteers will be needed to orchestrate the social life of communities. Community volunteers can work with children or organize special resident projects like creating centerpieces for an upcoming charity event. Activities that benefit others provides a strong sense of purpose and that should never be underestimated.

EIGHT: THE DINING EXPERIENCE AND NUTRITION

In the foreseeable future we will be able to select foods that benefit (like medications) our unique physiology though the science of "nutrigenomics."

Pinchas Cohen,[2] Dean, USC Gerontology Center

Figure 7-13 **This music room at the Hogeweyk Dementia Village CS is used by several different music clubs:** Residents listen to music, sing, and occasionally play instruments. They have classical music listening sessions that focus on particular composers. Music is one of the last modalities dementia residents lose, which accounts for its popularity.

Taking a meal with friends and family members is a well-honored tradition in every culture. In planned housing it has the potential to foster new acquaintances and better social connections between individuals. The design of the restaurant should encourage residents to linger, play cards, and socialize rather than just take a meal and leave. Table sizes should vary as in a good restaurant, where different choices can encourage privacy, social exchange, or people watching. Many older people enjoy small snacks rather than big meals and a good operation facilitates that choice. In an AFL the restaurant also contains an informal bar that is open much of the time.

For most people, food taste and quality is important and residents in planned housing are known to be tough-minded critics. Sometimes nutritionists are insensitive to local food traditions because they consider them unhealthy. But our relationship with food has been cultivated over a lifetime, often with deep cultural roots. Menu changes are very important, as are varied entrée choices. Tasting committees composed of residents can help refine a popular menu. Boomers with their proclivity toward variety, pre-prepared foods, and take out will also have major impacts on food consumption in the future. Another challenge is the monotony of taking a meal in the

same place 3 times a day, 7 days a week, 52 weeks a year. To remedy this, the NewBridge CS has four restaurants as well as a "grab and go" counter for sandwiches and pre-prepared salads.

The Green House© and Hogeweyk case studies underscore the desire to match food preferences to resident interests. Both places involve residents in menu choices and serve meals family style. In fact, many settings view food as an op maat choice. They cater to individuals who want only coffee at breakfast as well as those who expect a hearty serving of bacon and eggs. At Hogeweyk, seven lifestyle groups further connect the habits of various cultures with food traditions and preferences. For example, the Indonesian lifestyle house uses food familiar to their ethnic group, while the "Goois" cluster uses foods and spices common to the upper-middle class. Each house shops at the on-site grocery store and brings items back to their "home" for preparation. Food can trigger memories and other past experiences. Conversely, older people who are isolated and depressed in their own home often lose their appetite or start to rely on "tea and toast" rather than a balanced diet. The older palette also loses taste buds and scent acuity, which is why it is sometimes difficult to entice later-stage dementia residents to eat properly.

(a)

(b)

(c)

(d)

(e)

(f)

Figure 7-14a–f **Most care settings consider meal times to be important social opportunities:** This collection of images demonstrates the diversity of size and style in dining venues. All of these examples encourage visitors. These include friends, relatives, and staff, making the experience a much more inclusive one.

Clockwise from upper left: De Kristal restaurant and activity center in Rotterdam, the Netherlands; the Akropolis servery in Rotterdam, the Netherlands; the Driezorg dining room in Zwolle, the Netherlands; the Mount San Antonio Green House© dining table in Pomona, California (Courtesy of D. S. Ewing Architects, Inc.); the La Valance restaurant in Maastricht, the Netherlands; and the Akropolis dining room in Rotterdam, the Netherlands.

The science of nutrigenomics is identifying food choices that are compatible with a person's DNA makeup and are good for their health. Just like personalized medicine, food choices will soon be based on better information about how your unique body chemistry reacts to ingesting various types of foods.[3] This will likely introduce more choices, while providing better information about potential impacts. However, it is unlikely to end the struggle of choosing between things that are good for you and things that taste good.

Creating Affect and Joy

NINE: ENCOURAGING CHEERFULNESS AND POSITIVE AFFECT

Nursing homes are often sad places. But who can resist smiling at a puppy or laughing at a funny story? We have to be cheerleaders and cheer-makers committed to creating a happy and joyful place.

Victor Regnier, USC

Growing older with painful conditions and not much hope for relief is not an optimistic circumstance. For many, the move to a nursing home or assisted living facility symbolizes the end of their independent life. Most realize that once admitted, there is little chance they will return to their previous life. Optimism about a fulfilling future life is important to sustain and can be reinforced with the right actions, words, and attitude. Nurturing resiliency can also be a powerful psychological boost.[4]

Hans Becker[5] refers to nursing homes as "islands of misery" in characterizing the negative attitude and reaction they generate. Being happy, seeing joy in life, appreciating the gifts that you have, and the possibility of helping others are powerful psychological motivators. We need to identify the aspects associated with a satisfying and pleasurable life and seek ways to support and encourage those attitudes in LTC.

Cheerfulness, gaiety, amusement, lightheartedness, and playfulness are usually not associated with nursing homes, but they could be. We should be asking, "How can AFLs, nursing homes, and assisted living be more uplifting and stimulating?" not just for residents but also for family, friends, staff, and visitors. The Humanitas AFL believes in mixing populations of young and old within a well-designed and upbeat public restaurant. They also believe that furniture and accessories should be evocative and thought provoking, as well as whimsical.

Something as simple as a three-sided kiosk in a corridor can 1) announce upcoming events and opportunities, 2) display photos documenting past events, and 3) contain

Figure 7-15 A cheerful atmosphere is often hard to create in long-term care: In the Akropolis AFL, this bar is a prominent feature of the dining room. In northern Europe, areas near the entry are often created where musical events, TGIF celebrations, and alcoholic drinks can lift the mood of residents and their guests.

Figure 7-16 **The large open atrium in the Akropolis AFL has hosted concerts, political events, and contests:** However, one of the most memorable events was a mock circus that featured the administrator, Hans Becker, riding a camel through the crowd. Try not to smile when something that outrageous occurs. *Courtesy of Hans Becker.*

Meals could come from cherished family recipes, ethnic favorites, or everyday fare, but sharing it with one another is especially personal.

The northern Europeans care about bathing and how to make it pleasurable. Aromatic fragrances, message, low lighting conditions, candles, and even bath toys can make the experience a memorable one. In contrast to a shower in a cold, hard, noisy room, these alternatives are sublime.

Special holidays are also frequently etched into the minds of older people. Celebrating these not only recognizes their value but also stimulates recall. The special summer holidays of Memorial Day, 4th of July, and

funny, upbeat, and thought-provoking photos, cartoons, illustrations, and sayings. Allowing the staff, the family, and the older person to relive joyful moments can celebrate the past and establish positive future expectations.

Artwork can also be poignant, fanciful, or playful, with scenes of children, animals, and physically inspiring places (beaches, mountains, oceans, forests, overlooks). When we make a place happier and more joyful it can also attract more family members and friends. Visitors can have a profound positive impact on residents who may feel disconnected and isolated.

For many older frail people, **food and bathing** are two pleasurable experiences that are often underexplored. The Green House© has even developed the term "Convivium,"[6] which describes the emotional connection between people when they share a home-cooked meal together.

Figure 7-17 **Sometimes juxtaposition works exceedingly well at making a situation amusing:** This full-size dog toy deserves a double take, but add a hat and it seems totally absurd. Creating situations that provoke humor and whimsy are almost always welcome. Sometimes these can be accomplished more effectively through temporary decorations.

Labor Day have universal appeal and are often used as a catalyst for family get-togethers. Every week could be an excuse for celebrating something by dressing up or simple wearing a special hat. No one in a nursing home seems to complain about too many parties and celebrations.

Finally, **material choices** also have strong impacts on the perception of the place. The anthroposophic architecture illustrated in the Vigs Ängar CS uses wood and canvas as well as pastel colors under special lighting conditions to increase the richness of residential materials.[7, 8] These ideas, borrowed from the philosophical beliefs of Rudolph Steiner, also express simple pleasures with authentic materials.

TEN: AVOID AN INSTITUTIONAL LIFESTYLE

The first time I visited a nursing home as an architecture/gerontology graduate trainee, I experienced a mild anxiety attack. All I could think of was that studying how to fix prisons would have been a lot easier.

Victor Regnier, USC

Nursing homes are serious institutions. If you refer to the classic treatise of Goffman[9] regarding asylums, you quickly see how many qualities nursing homes have in common with prisons. He defines institutions as places where 1) all aspects of life are conducted in the same place, 2) daily activities are done with a group of others, 3) activities are tightly scheduled and imposed from above, and 4) a single management plan drives it all. This sounds like a prison but it also describes a nursing home.

When you imagine a typical nursing home it is usually a flat-roofed, commercial-style building with no balconies and long extruded wings in alphabet shapes (X, H, K, I). The cladding materials are usually inexpensive and undifferentiated. It lacks color and has small windows. The floor, wall, and ceiling surfaces inside are hard and bland. They are also unable to absorb noise, especially at night. The lack of spirit within can't help but reveal its true identity.

Operationally, it also has many of the same characteristics as a prison. The placement of rooms revolves around the location of a nurse's station. Old-fashioned requirements for sight lines are upheld, even though electronic monitoring replaced these antiquated communication methods decades ago. The management system is fixed,

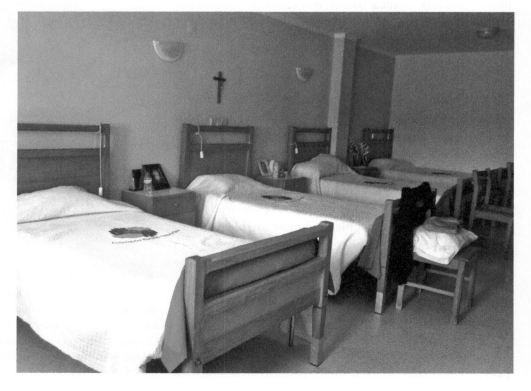

Figure 7-18 **Although northern European LTC facilities are used as models in this book, some European countries have worse conditions than the US:** In this Lar de idosos (home for elderly) located in a rural community in Portugal, four-bed rooms for indigent older people are common. In Asia, multi-bed wards are also common and are considered acceptable.

Figure 7-19 **The six-person clusters in the Hogeweyk Dementia Village CS are like small single-family houses:** Although most residents have private rooms, they all share a bathroom. Common spaces include a kitchen, dining room alcove, and living room. The Indonesian lifestyle cluster brings together roommates who share a common cultural bond.

routinized, joyless, and bureaucratic. Employees often represent authority figures. Most staff members wear a uniform that differentiates them from visitors, inmates, and workers; and are told not to become emotionally involved with residents. Activities are designed to keep the population busy, quiet, and subdued. The system is run by a central authority with little compassion or interest in how it affects residents. Food is mass-produced without much care about texture, flavor, or presentation. It may be nutritious, but it is hardly good tasting. The setting is managed to minimize expenditures and maximize social control. Most residents lose their interest in independence because the situation erodes any memory of that condition. Your small room is shared with a stranger. Thus, control and alienation are two characteristics that make both of these institutions even more deadly.

Consider the impacts it has on the family. They are often embarrassed that mom is here rather than at home. They frequently feel shame and inadequacy. They want to know what they did wrong to deserve this outcome. Was it because her income ran out? Was it her longevity and frailty that caused this to happen?

Qualities like choice, control, independence, dignity, quality of life, privacy, and personalization are absent or minimized in institutions. What do you fix first? Respect for the individual is a good place to start. Older people are generally considered to be the most unique individuals in society, in part because they have collected a lifetime of different experiences. When that is denied, so is their benefit and usefulness to society.

Creating a noninstitutional building requires revolutionary thinking. We must recognize that in creating poorly designed physical and operational settings, we are denying the value and relevance of the aged. We are creating a crime against humanity, which is a crime that will catch up with every one of us, if we live long enough.

ELEVEN: PLANTS, PETS, KIDS, AND THE CREATIVE ARTS

The great thing about pets and children is that they provide "unconditional love."

Victor Regnier, USC

The Eden Alternative popularized the notion that plants, pets, and children can add joy and affect to nursing home environments.[10] These simple, highly effective, low-cost additions have been successful in changing the culture of many nursing homes. Although the Eden movement popularized their use, these ideas have humanized LTC environments for decades.

Figure 7-20 **The Rundgraafpark CS contains a preschool for a hundred children as well as a publically accessible physical therapy center:** The preschool is on the ground floor below the two condominium buildings. Children's day care is considered a compatible land use and is a frequent tenant in 55+ housing projects.

Chapter 10 provides documentation for the positive psychological and physiological benefits that can result from views, exposure, and interaction with plant materials. The evidence from numerous studies in hospitals, nursing homes, and dementia settings describe how residents, family members, and staff benefit from stress reduction and relaxation when they have access to outdoors.

The use of animal-centered therapy and community pets also has a history of beneficial impacts. More than a hundred years ago, Florence Nightingale said that "a small pet is often an excellent companion for the sick or for those with chronic diseases."[11] We know today that stroking an animal can lower blood pressure, reduce stress, mitigate depression, and lessen loneliness. It also appears to stimulate the "feel-good" hormones oxytocin and serotonin.

AFLs welcome pets and describe them as effective distractions and opportunities for triangulation. The two big benefits of pet ownership appear to be companionship and the opportunity for exercise. As an object of affection, they provide the benefit of nurturance and responsibility. The downsides in group living arrangements are potential allergy problems and the obligation to walk, feed, and clean up after an animal. In most places the upkeep of a shared dog, cat, or bird is managed by the staff. Scheduled visits from a rescue or pet therapy organization are popular and can be extended or terminated based on their success.

Furthermore, like the evidence of benefits from plants, sometimes a proxy is good enough. The baby robotic seal,

PARO, developed in Japan 24 years ago, has proven to be an excellent device for calming dementia residents.[12] Today, toys like the Hasbro dog[13] produce a calming affect at a fraction of the cost. As AI and robotic devices evolve, enthusiasm for social robots that can communicate, entertain, and stimulate will likely grow.

Children have a way of communicating spontaneous delight. Their sweet innocence, affection, and charming mannerisms make them a joy to interact with or to watch. Numerous combinations of day care for children with senior housing exist. In Scandinavia it is common to find these building types co-located. When interaction is managed well, both groups benefit. The moments of delight and unplanned interaction that demonstrate the affection between older people and children are the basis for many positive outcomes.[14]

Optimizing the interaction on a permanent basis can be challenging. Usually children are introduced in small doses through programs that last a few hours. When both facilities are located relatively close to one another, interactions can be planned with a minimum amount of preplanning. In larger housing projects, children's day care is often offered as a benefit to employees, which can support creative resident programming.

Arts programs have also been successful in many senior housing environments. Many older people seek opportunities for self-expression in old age. Some write poetry, others pen an autobiography, and still others explore fine

Figure 7-21 Pets are more frequent additions to the households of older residents: In the film-industry-sponsored MPTF retirement community in Woodland Hills, California, a dog park called Doggywood was recently added. Not only are pets considered good companions, but they also encourage residents to walk more for exercise.

art and sculpture. One art form that seems particularly therapeutic is movement therapy to music (dancing). This can assist balance control and, because understanding music frequently persists in dementia, it has great value for these individuals.

All of these simple and effective strategies have value and can help to reduce boredom as well as add spontaneity and delight.

TWELVE: TREATING THE STAFF WITH RESPECT AND DIGNITY

How important are caregivers? Only important enough to entrust them with the care of your mother. We need to think of them in social status terms more like teachers than fast food workers.

Victor Regnier, USC

Caregivers in nursing homes, dementia units, and assisted living are often under appreciated. Many have jobs that are physically demanding and emotionally draining. The parallels with the teaching profession are clear. Caregivers work with older people by encouraging them to do their best. They often see the individual as a whole person with differing attributes. They become invested in the progress of people they care for, and they grieve when that person dies. It is a tougher job than teaching because most teachers don't have to clean up after their students or participate in decisions about treatments.

Caregivers also take responsibility for one of life's most precious gifts – your parents or grandparents. They care for the people who have spent a lifetime caring for you and helping you achieve a secure future.

Many people who care for the elderly are special individuals with great sensitivity and a "servant's heart." They carry out work for minimal compensation while remaining cheerful and positive when it is difficult to do. There are many differences between the US and northern Europe when it comes to how caregivers are treated. In northern Europe, caregivers receive more training and are paid better than in the US. Portable and fixed lift devices are common in northern Europe, where they are mandated to protect the staff from musculoskeletal injuries. In many facilities, staff are encouraged to use the building's physical therapy and exercise equipment to strengthen muscles and train for the physical demands of their job. In the US, formal protections for staff injury are minimal and lift equipment is often not required.

Staff offices should be designed to make them more approachable by older residents and family members. Using half walls, Dutch doors, and glazed windows, the staff can be visible but also protected from noise and distraction. The staff also needs private space to carry out duties without being disturbed.

The Green House©[15] model has produced an interesting reshuffle of staff influence by giving caregivers more authority consistent with their responsibilities for decision making. They have purposely flattened the management hierarchy by giving the staff the freedom to make important decisions about personal care help, meal planning, and activities.

Figure 7-22 **Inviting staff to use gardens and walking pathways promotes relaxation and exercise:** The staff have jobs that are physically and emotionally taxing and they welcome opportunities for stress reduction. Northern European providers frequently invite staff to share on-site exercise and physical therapy equipment.

Endnotes

1 Becker, H. (2003), *Levenskunst op leeftijd: Geluk Bevorderends Zorg in enn Vergrijzende Wereld*, Eburon Academic Press, Rotterdam, the Netherlands.

2 Cohen, P. (2014), Personalized Aging: One Size Doesn't Fit All, in *The Upside of Aging: How Long Life Is Changing the World of Health, Work Innovation, Policy and Purpose* (ed. P. Irving), John Wiley & Sons, Hoboken, NJ.

3 Grayson, M. (2010), Nutrigenomics, *Nature*, 468(7327), 1–22.

4 Resnick, B. (2014), Resilience in Older Adults, *Topics in Geriatric Rehabilitation*, 30(3), 155–163.

5 Birkbeck, D. (2014), Happy Meals: Finding Happiness with Hans Becker and the Humanitas Care Model, in *Designing for the Third Age: Architecture Redefined for a Generation of "Active Agers"* (ed. L. Farrelly), *Architectural Design*, March/April (228).

6 Thomas, B. (2011), Convivium: the Particular Pleasure that Accompanies Sharing Good Food with the People We Know Well, Green House Project Blog, http://blog.thegreenhouseproject.org/convivium-the-particular-pleasure-that-accompanies-sharing-good-food-with-the-people-we-know-well (accessed 10/7/17).

7 Husberg, L., and Ovesen, L. (2007), *Gammal Och Fri (Om Vigs Ängar)*, Vigs Ängar, Simrishamn, SW.

8 Coates, G. (1997), *Erik Asmussen, Architect*, Byggforlaget Stockholm.

9 Erving Goffman, E. (1961), *Asylums: Essays on the Social Situation of Mental Patients and Other Inmates*, Doubleday and Company, Garden City, NY.

10 Thomas, W. (1996), *Life Worth Living: How Someone You Love Can Still Enjoy Life in a Nursing Home*, VanderWyk and Burnham, Acton, MA.

11 Garrett, M. (2013), Pet Therapy for Older Adults, Psychology Today Blog, https://www.psychologytoday.com/blog/iage/201305/pet-therapy-older-adults (accessed 10/7/17).

12 Pedersen, I., Jøranson, N., Rokstad, A., and Ihlebæk, C. (2015), Effects on Symptoms of Agitation and Depression in Persons with Dementia Participating in Robot-Assisted Activity: A Cluster-Randomized Controlled Trial, *JAMDA*, 16(10), 867–73.

13 Liszewski, A. (2015), Gizmodo Blog, http://toyland.gizmodo.com/hasbro-now-has-a-toy-line-for-seniors-starting-with-a-l-1743122884 (accessed 7/10/17).

14 Sashin, D. (2015), Poignant Moments Unfold at a Preschool in a Retirement Home, CNN Blog, http://www.cnn.com/2015/06/19/living/preschool-nursing-home-seattle (accessed 7/10/17).

15 Thomas, W. (1996), *Life Worth Living: How Someone You Love Can Still Enjoy Life in a Nursing Home*, VanderWyk and Burnham, Acton, MA.

CHAPTER EIGHT

21 Building Case Studies

THIS chapter reviews 21 building case studies in three categories: 1) Apartments for Life (AFL), 2) small group cluster nursing homes, and 3) other LTC options, including assisted living, hospice, and co-housing. This chapter details attributes of buildings that seek to provide exemplary environments for the oldest-old. Buildings from the US, Denmark, Sweden, Finland, and the Netherlands are included.

We begin with the Dutch Apartment for Life (AFL) building type, which is illustrated by five buildings that share the same general philosophy. These purpose-built, age-restricted buildings are designed to keep people in their dwelling unit for as long as possible, tacitly until the end of life. The approach utilizes a home care–based delivery system, which includes personal and medical care services delivered to each resident's unit. The program holds onto older individuals by increasing the level of home care assistance a resident receives as they age. It ends with a description of a US-based CCRC that is actively experimenting with some of the same AFL ideas.

Next, small group, cluster nursing homes from the US, Denmark, and the Netherlands are reviewed. The examples from the United States profile three Green House© projects to demonstrate how this unique "small house" caregiving strategy works in different density circumstances. Northern European models have a long history involving this building type. Three additional case studies demonstrate how the Danes and the Dutch are exploring the idea of reducing scale and enhancing the authority and responsibility of caregivers.

The last category is an eclectic assemblage of buildings that provide different options for the frail. They include an anthroposophic-influenced care home, two small service houses, a dementia cluster within an assisted living building, a hospice, a co-housing development, and a vacation village. Each of these building types contains housing and service supports that help residents' age in place.

European History of Home-care Serviced Buildings

Northern Europe has a centuries-long history of combining home care with housing to help older people stay in their own dwelling units or in purpose-built elderly housing. Some of the earliest examples are from Germany and the Netherlands and date back to the seventeenth century.[1] In these early examples, guilds and membership societies constructed group housing for the widows of merchant marines and shopkeepers. Charitable organizations, especially the church, often provided care and assistance. Dwelling units were designed in clusters to promote informal caregiving and social exchange. They sought to integrate housing with services to keep older frail people independent. Peripatetic care workers made home visits to help residents with their needs. This tradition gained widespread popularity at the beginning of the twentieth century in northern Europe (Sweden, Denmark, Norway, and Finland) when housing with services for older people was financially entitled and considered an important part of the "cradle to grave" social contract these socially oriented societies made with their citizens.

Service House Model Emerges

After World War Two,[2] small group apartments with services were created to encourage older residents to downsize from larger independent housing. In the 1960s this building type, labeled as a service house, was encouraged throughout northern Europe with early prototypes located in Denmark and Sweden. This age-restricted housing and service option was offered to older people in towns and cities where they lived. Developments varied from large 100-unit complexes in major cities to 20–40 unit developments in smaller towns. The service house soon became a community-based, mixed-use building type that consisted of elderly housing, a restaurant, physical therapy, home-care–delivered personal care services, and social activities. The buildings were open to the neighborhood and combined age-restricted service housing with the types of activities one might find in a comprehensive senior center in the United States. Housing was physically attached to the community service component. In contrast, subsidized elderly housing in the US and senior centers had very separate and distinct development trajectories. Rarely were they co-located or coordinated with one another.

The European service house provided meals, therapy, and expertise to people from the surrounding neighborhood, as well as those in physically connected housing.[3] Home care providers helping people in the service house also visited older people in apartments in the neighborhood. This dual focus helped many physically frail

individuals age in place. Typically neighborhood residents were a decade younger[4] (70s vs. 80s) and often visited the service house for meals and activities.

Residents living in service houses were generally older with greater service needs. As the demand for housing for the frail increased, service houses found themselves serving a much frailer population. In many cases, residents were similar to those in nursing homes. The difference was that the noninstitutional philosophy of the service house supported residents in an independent residential setting using home-delivered services. Home health caregivers visited residents as often as necessary to support their needs. In the beginning, service house dwelling units were small but were almost always single occupied with a full kitchen and private bathroom.

Policies in countries like Sweden and Denmark focused on eliminating institutions and taking care of people in their own home or purpose-built apartments. For some older community dwellers, such as those in multistory buildings without elevators or in rural areas, a move to a service house was the best alternative. Still, many older frail people were supported through home care visits in their own home.

RECENT TRENDS IN SERVICE HOUSES

Over time, service house dwelling units grew, so that by the 1990s many were one-bedroom units averaging 600 to 700 SF with relatively spacious kitchens. About 15 years ago, the demand for additional housing for the frail and the increasing development costs of community service components (restaurant, physical therapy, swimming pool, and activity spaces) located within service houses became larger fiscal impediments. The current generation of service houses are models with fewer services.[5] Age-restricted housing like the Neptuna, DePlussenburgh, and De Kristal CSs provide relatively large apartments in mixed-use neighborhoods with access to home care and a small group dementia setting but do not provide services to other older people in the neighborhood.

Dwelling unit sizes have continued to grow with one-bedroom/den and two-bedroom units now common in many new projects. In addition to the traditional rental model, equity (condominium and cooperative) models have also gained popularity as the rate of homeownership has increased in these countries.

However, the commitment to providing services to older residents in their own dwellings or in fully or partially subsidized, age-restricted, independent housing is still strong. The production of new housing took a dip in the 2008 worldwide recession, but it has returned as the economy has grown. Today, there is greater interest in the creation of small-scale clusters for people with dementia and the most physically frail as explored in the second category of projects. Northern European policies continue to encourage residents to move to small group homes only when they enter the final stage of severe memory loss.

As populations in these countries grow older and the demand for housing with services increases, new housing has been increasingly targeted toward the most frail. As portable medical diagnostic and treatment technologies proliferate, there is more interest in plugging services into purpose-built housing. New housing generally meets the newest universal design standards with sensitivity toward how to adapt it, as individuals age in place.

AFLs, Humanitas Style

In the mid-1990s a new building type emerged. It was called an Apartment for Life (AFL) or in Dutch, *levensloopbestendige* (age-proof dwelling). The first prototype was initiated by the Humanitas Foundation, a large nonprofit care provider in Rotterdam established in 1945. Since then, it has grown to 33 buildings (including 1700 AFL dwelling units), 3000 staff, and 2000 volunteers.[6] The AFL was the brainchild of Hans Becker, who became the CEO of Humanitas in 1992. After an extended hospital stay, Becker had an epiphany that led him to reinvent the service house and challenge conventional thinking about how to care for older frail people. Among other things, he recognized that older people needed help and encouragement and often care settings catered to their needs but did not recognize the importance of autonomy. He also challenged the prevailing

Figure 8-2 **The Virranranta service house, located in the small Finnish town of Kiruvesi, contains a mixture of 50 housing and long-term care units for the frail:** Service houses vary in size from 20 to 200 units but most provide help to a broader constituency beyond their resident population.

idea that older people needed to move into a nursing home when they became frail. He could see ways to support even extremely frail people in a residential context with the strategies that had worked so well in service houses. The main difference was in how the building was set up to deal with the challenge of reinforcing independence rather than eroding competency. He challenged ideas about how professional care providers approached their job, how resident self-confidence and competency could be enhanced, and how the place could be more joyful. Although AFL building designs were architecturally striking, the most interesting aspect associated with the model was the philosophy about care provision and lifestyle enhancement.

AFL EIGHT CORE COMPONENTS AND CHARACTERISTICS[7]

The following eight components reflect the core beliefs and philosophies that define the Humanitas AFL lifestyle. They include physical features, operational practices, and basic freedoms. Included are also the responsibilities and pledges that residents and staff make to create an environment of positive value for all.

ONE: Be Your Own Boss: Residents in conventional settings rarely feel free to make their own choices and decisions. In most nursing homes residents are encouraged to be passive. Professionals dictate care, cure, and lifestyle decisions with little input from residents. When repeated, this treatment leads to "learned helplessness"[8] where residents become passive and stop doing things on their own. At Humanitas there is no "health fascism" or "health and diet dictatorship." Residents are encouraged to ask questions if they want an opinion, but the decision is always up to the individual. Care follows the "op maat" strategy of customization. Residents control when they get up, when they take a bath, when they eat, and when they go to sleep. They dictate their schedule rather than having the institution dictate it. Self-determination and self-management is a high priority.

TWO: Use It or Lose It: Residents are encouraged to **focus on their strengths**. They do what they can for themselves rather than worry about what they can't do. Opportunities are provided for new experiences and they are encouraged to avoid any sense of limitation. A care plan establishes guidelines for what they can do safely and how they can help others. Residents maintain a daily

routine (assisted when required) that resembles whatever they have done previously, including taking care of their apartment or making their breakfast. The Dutch care philosophy of "providing help with your hands on your back" reinforces independence and self-reliance. It may take more time to carry out a task but residents are rewarded with a sense of accomplishment. The saying "too much care is worse than too little care" underscores the belief that residents should **not get assistance if it is not needed.** Once responsibility is given to a caregiver, it is hard to reclaim. When care is needed, it doesn't seem patronizing, which boosts self-respect and dignity. An assigned care manager coordinates help from all sources, keeping residents from attempting tasks that are too dangerous.

THREE: The Extended Family: Everyone is expected to help one another and nobody is excluded. Staff, volunteers, residents, day care visitors, neighbors, friends, and family are all considered part of the Humanitas family. This extended "family" promotes social exchange especially at meal times. Good-tasting food gives residents a way to enjoy life rather than obsessing over untreatable aches and pains. This draws people into conversations and centers the place around stimulating activities. In any family, "everyone knows something interesting" and pleasure can be derived from companionship. Creating places where families can visit and areas for children to play demonstrates an appreciation of visitors. The building has stimulating spaces with art, antiques, and special events. This gives residents and visitors topics to discuss. In an AFL the staff are considered family, just like residents and volunteers.

FOUR: YES Culture: Staff start a conversation about a request by saying YES first. Nurturing a "Yes Culture" requires the staff to be creative and innovative in addressing resident needs. Any wish, suggestion, demand, complaint, or initiative is met with a sincere desire to help residents. Sometimes a request can be easily accomplished, while other times it requires creative negotiation. What is most important is the request be taken seriously. If requests cannot be granted, the next step is to discuss it and arrive at a satisfactory compromise. A request for a swimming pool was resolved by finding a nearby facility and arranging for transportation and access. In a "Yes Culture" the attitude is that enthusiasm and creativity produce results.

FIVE: Seeking Joy and Human Happiness: Perhaps the most negative aspect about living in an institution is an often joyless life. Nursing homes are sad places to

Figure 8-3 The Humanitas Bergweg CS atrium is naturally cooled with roof ventilators: Fans and moveable fabric awnings are also used to reduce the summer heat. Seating for meals and events is moveable and open to everyone including residents, staff, family members, volunteers, neighbors, and workers. Humanitas residents do as much for themselves as possible and also extend a helping hand to others.

live, work, and visit. Some of this feeling is due to the drab and depressing environment, which starts with bland double-loaded corridors with hard and shiny wall and floor surfaces. Rarely do you see an uninhibited smile or an authentic show of affection. The bureaucratic focus on efficiency and boring routine makes every day the same. The focus is on the business of care and cure and not on living life to the fullest extent. This is no way to live and certainly not a good way to die. In comparison, the AFL has lively common areas with artwork,[9] music, and animated people. It is an environment where conversations abound and unexpected events make life interesting.

SIX: Aging in Place in an Adaptable Setting: Supporting people in their own apartment by increasing services and physically adapting the unit makes the AFL a unique housing option. The tacit commitment to support residents until the end of life in their apartment fits with what most people desire. Services can be ramped up as needed or at the end of life. It is a great option for couples because they can help one another, while counting on the care system to provide supplemental support when needed. Units are large enough to accommodate furniture and meaningful objects, as well as an overnight guest. You can stay in your apartment and cook in your kitchen or take a meal when you feel like it at the restaurant. Aging in place allows social networks to stay intact and avoids moving at the end of life when it's most disruptive. Finally, an adaptable design can adjust if you require a wheelchair or walker. No wonder it is characterized as "age proof."

SEVEN: Use of a Home Care Model for Service Delivery: Residents schedule personal care and home health visits in their apartments. Some newer systems use telemedicine technology to diagnosis problems or discuss issues with specialists. A care worker might make a couple of daily visits for a medium-care resident or five to seven trips for a high-need resident. The care coordinator **creates a plan that capitalizes on a variety of helpers,** including spouses, volunteers, and family members. Home care visits are usually scheduled in advance but additional visits can be requested at the last minute if needed. Unlike a nursing home, the AFL apartment is private and care workers do not enter uninvited.

EIGHT: A Secure Place for Dementia: One of the most feared outcomes of advanced age is severe memory loss. Cognitive decline is stressful, especially on family members (particularly spouses) and frequently ends in a nursing home placement. The AFL model provides help and support during the early to mid-level stages of the disease. Adult day care services located in the building support people with severe depression or at the beginning to middle stages of dementia. As individuals become more impaired, they can move to a small group cluster (usually consisting of six to eight residents) in the building or adjacent to it. Residents move when their behaviors **become a hazard to themselves** or to others, usually at the last stage. These settings have trained workers who deal effectively with the last stages of the disease and its numerous side effects.

SEVEN ADDITIONAL AFL COMPONENTS AND FEATURES

When Humanitas set about building AFL buildings, they also established several beliefs and attributes that set them apart from the typical nursing or care home of the day.[10]

ONE: Eating a well-presented and delicious meal in a lively and aesthetically pleasing environment is an important cure for loneliness and dietary challenges. Having access to alcoholic drinks also makes the setting more convivial and adds a component of normalization. Hans Becker is fond of saying, "A good bartender can be as important as a physician."[11] Meals are offered as a discretionary purchase, meaning residents can take a meal every day or take none at all and choose to prepare food in their unit.

Figure 8-4 **The five-story atrium at the Rundgraafpark CS is a nexus for social exchange and exercise:** A café as well as tables and chairs throughout the ground floor provide places for residents to interact and space for large-scale activities. An adult day care program open to the community is also located on the ground floor.

TWO: Creating a visually stimulating and interesting environment occurs through art, sculpture, murals, photographs, and antiques (pre-1939) throughout the building. Displayed in public areas, including the restaurant, lounge, and entry, items are selected to stimulate conversations and offer visual delight. Lively colors and murals in stairwells entice residents to use the stairs for exercise. A recent addition to the Bergweg atrium involved painting the concrete columns gold to reflect light and add color to the perimeter.

THREE: Celebrating diversity and access for all people is an important principle. Ageism is just one of the barriers society faces, along with racism and cultural bias. At Humanitas, age is conceptualized not as a weakness but as a strength through wisdom and experience. Humanitas also manages its building constituency to contain a mix of younger (55–65) and older (75–80+) residents. They welcome the rich and the poor, the sick and the healthy, the migrant and the native.

FOUR: Volunteers are important to Humanitas, which has slightly more volunteers than staff in each building. Volunteers are typically recruited from residents, family members, day care recipients, and staff. In fact, the 30% of residents who are volunteers augment the staff by working in the restaurant or elsewhere in the building. Volunteering sensitizes residents to be more understanding, while challenging them to help others. Purposeful activities are especially meaningful to older residents who are often on the receiving end of kindness from others. It gives them a way to reciprocate or play it forward. Volunteering makes the building more socially active, allowing the staff to devote more time to direct service provision. Volunteers also supplement paid staff, allowing restaurants and social spaces to have longer hours. Some able-bodied resident-volunteers accompany frailer residents to the restaurant. A noteworthy volunteer program[12] takes place at the Humanitas Deventer. In this building, students live rent free in exchange for 30 hours of volunteer work each week. They help residents by providing companionship and joining in on activities. The students bring life and excitement to the place, while the older residents impart wisdom and life lessons to the students.

FIVE: Pets, animals, and children are a source of happiness, delight, and unconditional love. Pets are encouraged through responsible policies that guide ownership. Animals including fish, birds, and domestic pets are located throughout the building. Children's day care is also a popular opportunity for volunteerism. Residents enjoy the interaction with children and employees value it as an important service for their family.

SIX: Opening building services and features to the public welcomes a broad array of visitors who engage in activities and the hospitality of the dining room and bar. Bridge clubs, art exhibits, music groups, and wedding parties are some of the groups invited to use the building. Meals, snacks, and drinks are available for sale to visitors as well as residents. Many US care settings shun the outside world, but Humanitas believes that opening the building to others makes it more approachable and less institutional. AFL buildings typically contain retail services like a beauty shop, a physical therapist, and a store for food or personal items. Reaching out to **provide caregiving services to residents in the surrounding neighborhood** is also common. They view their mission as helping all older people with problems and not just residents of their own building. AFL buildings frequently coordinate home-delivered services such as meals on wheels.

SEVEN: Designs are centered around a large multi-story atrium. Although not present in every building, many AFLs contain an atrium. They are often used as public spaces that make the building more inviting and approachable. Large activities that will not fit into a meeting room like concerts and theater performances can easily take place here. It also provides a controlled temperature setting where residents can exercise without having to venture outside the building in the winter.

DEVELOPMENT AND BUILDING CONCEPT PRINCIPLES

AFLs follow loosely structured guidelines for site selection and development. To reduce per-unit development costs and maximize program flexibility, each project has between 225 and 275 units. The unit size and price often depend on the neighborhood, with a bias toward optimizing the number of affordable units. Models include mixed uses like day care centers for children, retail stores, and health services. Most units are rented but others are offered as condominiums or cooperatives. The nonprofit Humanitas Foundation retains ownership of at least 51% of the units. Development revenues contribute to subsidies that make units affordable.

The building form is normally a mid-rise or high-rise structure. This creates a compact, elevator-supported footprint that facilitates circulation and the delivery of care services. It is quicker and easier to use an elevator to access floors vertically than to walk long horizontal distances in

Figure 8-5 **The Neptuna CS has a U-shaped configuration that wraps around a protected garden:** The garden provides a controlled view for the first floor common spaces that wrap the perimeter. The Calatrava-designed "Turning Torso" office building, located a few hundred feet away, is a dominant central feature.

low-rise buildings. Compact, well-located land parcels are expensive, so optimizing density is necessary.

AFL buildings are conceptualized as being "part of the city," not isolated from it. Many sites are located near retail centers or transportation hubs. These areas have access to a broad array of goods and services that appeal to independent older people. An AFL building also adds energy and activity to the neighborhood. Convenient public transportation makes it easy for family and friends to visit, as well as providing access to other parts of the city. The AFL model involves outreach to the surrounding neighborhood that often includes residents who have aged in place. Neighbors benefit from an AFL building if they need to move when they require more help in the future. High-density AFL buildings lend themselves to prominent landmarks. Outdoor site features include gardens and retreats that are shared with neighborhood residents.

The Continuing Care Retirement Community (CCRC) or Life Plan Community (LPC): A US Invention

The closest building type to the AFL available in the US is the Continuing Care Retirement Community, recently relabeled as a Life Plan Community (LPC) by the nonprofit housing organization Leading Age. There are still major differences between the AFL and the LPC. Where AFLs are conceptualized as a form of service-supportive housing that is accessible to all income levels, the LPC is a private, nonprofit entity usually oriented to an upper-middle-class constituency. The AFL prides itself on being open to the public and invites participation from neighborhood residents. The LPC offers more of a "country club" lifestyle focused on only the residents who live there. Finally, the LPC was created around the idea of moving individuals from an independent unit to assisted living, or to a nursing home as their physical or mental condition deteriorates. The AFL is committed to an "aging in place" philosophy that brings additional services to residents in their independent apartment. Nevertheless, the LPC is a popular US housing choice that dates back a hundred years. LPCs have evolved over time and are considered an excellent way to secure a predictable future trajectory for long-term care.

There are approximately 1900 of these housing arrangements located throughout the US.[13] They vary from high-rise models in city centers to suburban-style layouts on large-scale sites. The average community size is about 300 units but newer communities can be much larger. The NewBridge CS is featured in this book. Approximately 80% of LPCs are nonprofit and the majority are faith-based sponsorships. LPCs generally include independent living, assisted living, dementia care, skilled nursing, and home- and community-based care in separate buildings on one large site. Home care services can also be offered to residents in the surrounding neighborhood, which can help the LPC gain wider recognition while helping others.

LPC IN CONCEPT

A typical resident moves when they are in their late 70s or early 80s, and about a third to half are married. They spend on average five to nine years in an independent apartment with a range of services and amenities, including meals, cleaning, transportation, and group activities. Taking at least one meal in a community dining room is often required and included in the monthly fee. Units have full kitchens so residents can prepare meals at home if they wish. When residents become mentally or physically frail, they often move to either assisted living or nursing care, where the average age is around 88.[14] The nursing component today is often labeled a "health center" because residents also come here for minor colds and infections as well as post-acute rehabilitation stays of one to three weeks.

Forward-thinking facilities are exploring the idea of using home- and community-based services to lengthen the stay of residents in independent living and reduce the time spent in assisted living or skilled nursing. This movement toward a stronger aging-in-place philosophy is typically countered by marketing concerns. As the average age of residents in independent living increases, it can become less attractive to new, younger in-movers. The gold standard for replacement residents are active couples in their mid-70s. In fact, some facilities have discounts that target this population. They are valued because they provide leadership in various programs and uphold the community's reputation as an "active" community.

Health Care Financing

The most unpredictable financial component is the amount of time spent in the nursing home or in assisted living. This has led to three types of contracts.[15] Type A guarantees all of the costs of long-term care and is the costliest. Type B usually guarantees access but covers either a set number of days or a discounted rate for extended care. Type C is typically a fee for service with no financial support for nursing or assisted living care. Many new communities are exploring a range of financial structures, including equity-based and rental arrangements. Also "partial continuums" that contain everything except a nursing home are becoming more common because they are less financially complex. In these cases a working agreement with a nursing home in the community is normally developed in advance.

Figure 8-6 **The central park of the Akropolis AFL in Rotterdam was once a parking lot:** Parking was moved to the rear of the building and the space was transformed into a sculpture garden with water features and walking pathways. One area has a small zoo with goats, chickens, and ducks, as well as a playground for children.

The LPC attracts members who want to know where they will end up if they have dementia or need complex nursing care. In an LPC, moving to a more supportive setting is a decision made by care professionals in consultation with the resident's family. Aging in place is often a committee decision that follows norms established by the community and not ones that the resident necessarily controls.[16]

This housing choice is expensive. Most residents move from single-family houses and use their home equity as part or all of the life care fee, which can vary between $150,000 and $1 million. This fee is usually refunded in part or whole to your estate at the end of life. In addition, residents typically pay between $3,000 and $5,000 per month for services. The average unit today is a two-bedroom, between 900-1200 SF. Most units are purpose-built and can be adapted to wheelchair use. Units have full, large kitchens because the meals program usually includes only one or two meals per day bundled in the monthly fee.

Friendships Are Enhanced
One of the best aspects of the LPC is the friendship that develops among residents.[17] These are typically happy places with residents who feel well supported. It is rare to have people move out of a LPC because they feel dissatisfied. The programs and services are carefully developed in response to the needs and interests of residents. In some communities, the activity program is practically run by the residents, with the staff focused on reserving rooms and providing logistical support.

New Trends
Some of the trends in LPCs involve larger units, better access to parking and/or scooters, more sophisticated exercise programs, a more casual atmosphere, multiple dining venues, and expanded meal options. There is also continuing emphasis on technology for tracking health and wellness. Some communities have a greater interest in the arts, education, and self-discovery.[18]

Conclusions
Although few providers have experimented with the apartments for life idea in the US, most LPCs are uniquely positioned to implement this idea, albeit without the community-oriented component. Many have begun the transition by liberalizing their home services policies that help residents with impairments live longer in independent living. Others have constructed new buildings with larger units on their campus that employ "concierge" services for a range of personal care needs. As boomers insist on greater freedom and more choices in noninstitutional settings, there will be more evolution. Because the LPC is licensed to provide a range of care options, their ability to provide in-depth home health care services is facilitated.

HOW DO THE LPC AND THE APARTMENT FOR LIFE (AFL) DIFFER?

Both building types presume the older resident's health care status will require more help over time. The AFL concept deals with this dynamic circumstance by increasing home-delivered services to maintain the person's independence. It is designed to use equipment, and direct services to support the older person in their independent unit.

Instead of delivering services to the unit, the LPC relies on the idea of anticipating difficulties and then relocating the resident to a more supportive environment based on changing needs. In an LPC, moving to another setting is deemed more efficient, safer, and a better fit for the individual's needs. In that sense the system is counter to the desire of the older resident to maintain continuity by staying in their independent unit.

Another positive aspect with the AFL model is that it tests various care strategies before a move is contemplated. Housing and care is financed with different sources so moderate-income residents can participate. Delivering personal care and medical care to units in the same building saves travel time and creates efficiencies. Residents are also encouraged to be more independent and do as much as they can for themselves. The Dutch have been successful in keeping the average age of an AFL building relatively low by recruiting younger replacements.

The following seven buildings demonstrate the application of the AFL idea in different contexts.

CASE STUDY ONE: Humanitas Bergweg,
Rotterdam, the Netherlands

Architect: EGM Architecten, Dordrecht, the Netherlands

Figure 8-7 **Humanitas Bergweg was the first Apartment for Life (AFL) building:** Located in downtown Rotterdam on the site of an old hospital, the ground floor contains a grocery store. Escalators take you to a first-floor atrium that provides meals, activities, and day care for residents and people in the neighborhood.
Courtesy of EGM Architecten.

The Humanitas Bergweg AFL building was opened in April 1996.[19] Because many of the ideas were replicated in follow-up buildings, it is a useful building to scrutinize. Today's residents are still enthusiastic about the concept and the location. The average age in 2016 of 75 has stayed about the same as it was in 1996. This resulted from younger resident replacements that stabilized the growing number of the oldest-old. Of the 600 people on the waiting list, 75% are in the younger 55+ age group. However, Bergweg has also retained many older impaired residents. Fifteen of the original 250 residents from 1996 still live there, and very few have had to leave. More than 90% have died in their unit or in the dementia cluster on the roof. In 2016, 16 died and 10 moved to the dementia cluster on the top floor. They are still prepared and committed to caring for residents until the end of life.

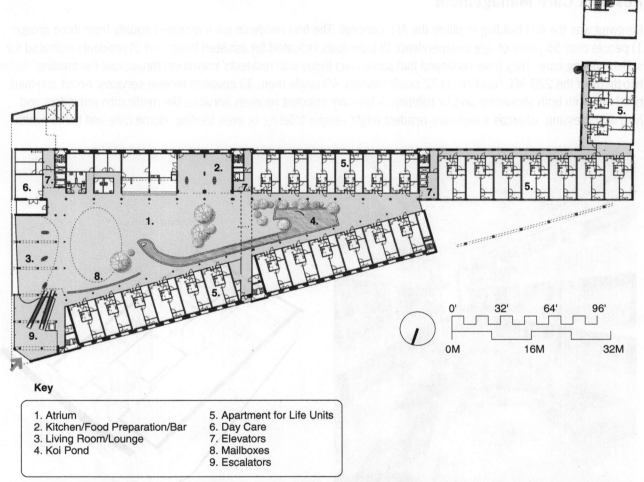

Key

1. Atrium
2. Kitchen/Food Preparation/Bar
3. Living Room/Lounge
4. Koi Pond
5. Apartment for Life Units
6. Day Care
7. Elevators
8. Mailboxes
9. Escalators

Figure 8-8 The first-floor building footprint is a triangular shape: Centrally located bridges (dotted) with access to elevators connect the north and south wings. A 150-foot koi pond near the center of the space is intertwined with a computer center, meeting rooms, mailboxes, tables and chairs, day care, and dwelling units.
Courtesy of EGM Architecten.

Building and Planning Concepts

The 195 unit AFL building with 29 units of additional dementia housing is located on an excellent site in downtown Rotterdam that was once a hospital. It is a mixed-use building with a supermarket on the ground floor and 12 stories of single-loaded housing above. The first floor has a four-story, glass-covered, nonconditioned but mechanically ventilated atrium. Movable canvas shades reduce sunlight on hot days and fans provide air movement. The atrium is triangular and is surrounded on two sides by four stories of single-loaded corridor units. The central atrium contains tables where residents and guests take meals and socialize. It resembles an enclosed shopping mall with a 150-foot-long koi pond in the center, murals, and bird sounds piped in from above. A semicircular line of mailboxes winds through one side of the atrium. Mature trees in planters demarcate smaller sitting areas. The atrium is a perfect place to socialize, take a meal, or stroll for exercise and is one of the building's strongest attributes.

Centrally placed elevators with bridges make access to units convenient for residents and staff. On the southeast side of the atrium is a bar, restaurant, and meeting rooms for activities. At the east end is a large internet café. Volunteers arrive early and stay late to man the restaurant and keep the bar open.

Resident Care Management

Bergweg was the first building to utilize the AFL concept. The first residents were recruited equally from three groups: 1) people over 55 years of age (independent); 2) individuals indicated for assisted living; and 3) residents indicated for skilled nursing care. They have continued that same ratio today with residents intermixed throughout the building. Today two-thirds of the 228 AFL residents (122 single women, 40 single men, 33 couples) receive services. About one-third need help with both showering and/or toileting. A low-care resident receives services like medication reminders and help with dressing, whereas a high-care resident might require toileting or even feeding. Home care and home health

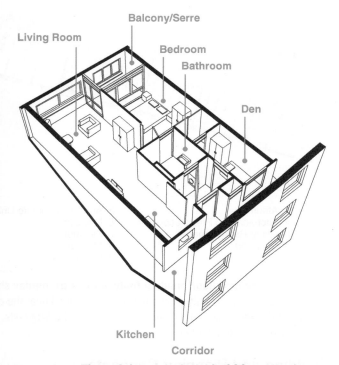

Figure 8-9 The triangular atrium creates a focal point at the narrow end: The koi pond has large, attractive fish as well as tropical and indigenous landscape materials. Canvas awnings are shown partially drawn to reduce heat absorption. Tables and chairs support a range of activities as well as games like billiards.

Figure 8-10 The unit is approximately 800 square feet: It contains a fully accessible bathroom and kitchen, as well as a separate bedroom. It also has a small den for overnight stays and an enclosed balcony. Unit access is from a light-filled single-loaded corridor that also provides additional borrowed light for the kitchen.
Courtesy of EGM Architecten.

workers visit residents in their unit on a predetermined schedule to provide services. They might visit the unit as many as three to five times a day helping with different kinds of care assistance if required. If a resident needs unscheduled or emergency help, they can order it through a call system from each unit. Services are flexible, respond to resident needs, and are expected to increase over time. The Humanitas staff include 90 full-time equivalents (FTE), including the dementia program. The workforce also contains 230 volunteers. About half come from the resident population inside the building and half from the neighborhood or from their day care program. Interestingly, 35% of the staff also volunteer.

Dwelling Units

The typical dwelling unit is 800 SF with a full kitchen, accessible bathroom, living room, bedroom, enclosed balcony, and study. The unit is flexible and can adapt to changes as a resident ages. The study is large enough to accommodate someone for an overnight stay. The bathroom is centrally located with a continuous tile floor, two doors, and a shower in the corner. It is square and large enough to accommodate a stretcher bather. The toilet has moveable grab bars that can be adjusted to take advantage of a resident's strength capacity. The unit has a full kitchen that can be modified for wheelchair use and contains a window that borrows light from the adjacent single-loaded corridor. The entry door has two panels (39 and 9 inches) that allow a bed to be rolled in and out. Finally, the French *serre* (balcony) can be opened or enclosed based on the weather and the resident's preference.

Programs and Activities

Each week approximately 20 different activities are planned in the atrium. Big activities involving a large group of residents take place twice a week. The provision of meals in the atrium is the glue that holds the lifestyle together. About 40% of residents take a meal in the restaurant, 20% have meals delivered to their unit, and the remainder cook their own meals. The atrium is open to everyone and 60 people from the neighborhood take a meal each day.

The adult day care program has expanded in the past 10 years to include eight different ethnic and cultural groups with 300 participants. Also, a children's day care program was recently added with a capacity of 60.

Figure 8-11 **The computer center and reception area has been recently expanded:** Resident volunteers work here, which is a place that is open to everyone. Humanitas strongly believes older people must have access to the internet. Murals referencing the koi pond provide an opportunity to make the space more artistically expressive. About 30% of Bergweg residents are active internet users.

Twenty-five percent of the residents in the surrounding neighborhood are over age 65 and Humanitas sponsors a home care program that serves 1500 older people in the neighborhood. About 900 get personal care services and the remainder are helped with less intensive services. A staff of more than 250 provide services to people in the neighborhood. Thirty residents have cars and 30 ride bicycles. Sixty residents use scooters for nearby trips in the neighborhood. The site has excellent access to public transit.

Dementia Services

In the beginning they remodeled individual units so they could care for residents with dementia. In 2009, Bergweg added 29 units of dementia housing in four clusters (three 7-unit and one 8-unit) to the top of the building, bringing the unit total to 224 (195 independent units + 29 dementia units). Each dementia cluster is self-contained with a shared living room, kitchen, dining area, and outdoor patio. Dementia dwelling units are small but each has a bathroom. The average age of dementia residents is 80, and the average length of stay is 2 years. Most residents who move there have late-stage dementia. About half of the current dementia population has moved from Bergweg. The others enter through their adult day care program.

Figure 8-12 Twenty-nine units of dementia housing were added to the top of the building in 2009: These units are subdivided into four small group clusters that operate separately. Each resident unit is single occupied with its own private toilet/sink and a shared bathing room. Each cluster contains an outdoor patio.

Proliferation of the Model

After 20 years the caregivers and residents of Bergweg are satisfied with the promise of the program to provide help to age in place until the end of life. By 2000, other building associations were mimicking the philosophy and approach initiated by Humanitas. Many components were replicated in buildings located in the Netherlands, Sweden, Denmark, Norway, and Australia. Although each sponsor has adjusted the building model, key elements like the home care–based support model and the commitment to aging in place are core features.

Noteworthy Features

1. First Apartment for Life Building to perfect management and service concepts.

2. Large units (800 SF) accommodate resident furniture and guest overnight stays.

3. Residents range in age from age 60 to 100.

4. The restaurant and activities are open to people in the surrounding neighborhood.

5. Residents grow older in their unit until the end of life in almost all circumstances.

6. Twenty-nine dementia units were added in 2009.

7. Personal and medical care services are delivered using a home care–style delivery model.

8. The atrium is a very effective place to meet others, take a meal, and participate in activities.

CASE STUDY TWO: Rundgraafpark, Veldhoven, the Netherlands

Architect: Inbo Architects, Amsterdam, the Netherlands

Figure 8-13 Rundgraafpark contains both subsidized and market-rate rental units as well as forty condominiums: The condominium units in the two seven-story gray buildings are combined with 113 units of rental housing. The site also contains a day care setting for 100 preschool children and a physical therapy clinic.
Courtesy of Thuis/Eindhoven and Inbo Architects.

This 153-unit Apartment for Life (AFL) atrium building, located on the outskirts of Veldhoven, was opened in 2005. It consists of 40 condo units, 113 rental apartments, and 18 dementia residents (three small group clusters of six residents each). There are approximately 225 residents and about a third are couples. The age range is from 55 to 90 and 35 residents are original in-movers.

Building Concept

The four- to five-story linear atrium is heated in the winter but ventilated naturally through the roof when the space reaches 75–78 degrees F. Residents enjoy the atrium space and use it for billiards, table tennis, and large group assemblies. Residents have created friendships through meeting one another in the atrium. An 80-car garage is located below the atrium. This site accommodates a 9,000 SF child day care center, a physical therapy clinic, and two adult day care programs with 10 participants each. The adult day care program is available to residents and neighbors. Last year four people moved to nursing homes because of a serious dementia diagnosis.

Figure 8-14 **The atrium is cooled through rooftop ventilators that open when thermostats sense overheating:** Fresh makeup air is provided by intake grills on lower floors. The top floor has a line of units facing the east, while the west side is a large clerestory window.

Activities and Services

Unlike Bergweg, there is no central restaurant for meals. Prepackaged meals arrive daily through meals-on-wheels and are distributed to residents who are "indicated" to receive them. Personal care can be "ramped up" as residents age and need more assistance. Approximately 30% of residents receive services that range from light cleaning to daily personal care visits. Fifteen percent of the residents have scooters to get around the neighborhood. Close to 80% of residents have a personal computer, tablet, or smart phone.

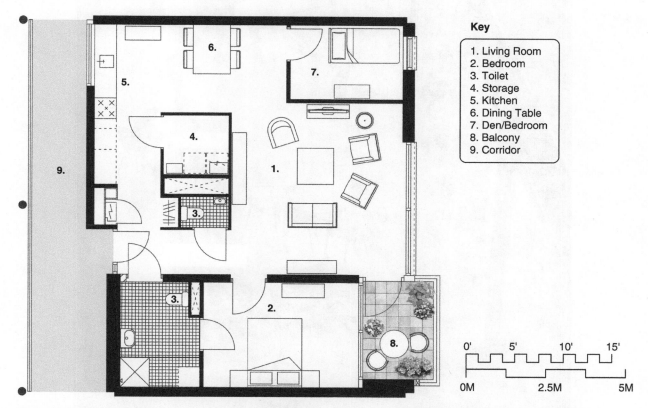

Key

1. Living Room
2. Bedroom
3. Toilet
4. Storage
5. Kitchen
6. Dining Table
7. Den/Bedroom
8. Balcony
9. Corridor

Figure 8-15 The 1100 SF Rundgraafpark dwelling unit is open and flexible: A storage room and half bath separates the living room from the kitchen while creating a small dining alcove. The kitchen has a large window that invites borrowed light from the atrium. Eliminating the second bedroom creates a larger living room.
Courtesy of Thuis/Eindhoven and Inbo Architects.

Rental and Condo Units

The size of rental units vary between 800 SF (living room and bedroom) and 1100 SF (two-bedroom) with an average size of 850 SF. About half of the rental housing is market rate and half is subsidized on a sliding scale. Rental units contain full kitchens, a large living room, a dining alcove, and a bathroom with a washer/dryer. Units open onto a single-loaded corridor that overlooks the atrium. Units receive natural light from two sides.

Two six-story buildings are condos with larger units. Like the rental units, their average age is 75 and about a third are couples. The 40 condo units range from 1000 to 2000 SF with an average size of around 1200 SF. These units also have higher-quality finishes and appliances.

Figure 8-16 **Three small group homes for people with dementia (18 people) are located on the ground floor:** Each small group cluster operates on its own. Residents who acquire dementia can move here and do not need to leave the building. Dementia residents use the atrium for group exercises.

Dementia Services

On the ground floor, open to the atrium, are three 6-unit housing clusters for people with dementia (18 total residents). Each cluster is self-contained with a separate kitchen, living room, dining room, patio, and dedicated caregivers. Both moderately impaired and severely impaired dementia residents are mixed in each cluster, with an average age of 82. If a resident requires dementia support, they can move to a small group cluster while their spouse stays in the apartment. Most dementia residents originate from the neighborhood and enter through the day care program.

Noteworthy Features

1. The atrium stimulates social exchange.
2. Larger condos and affordable rental units are mixed.
3. All units are relatively large and attract couples.
4. No meals are provided, but meals are delivered to residents who need them.
5. Early on they experimented with a telemedicine system.
6. There are three dementia clusters (18 residents total).
7. The site also has a children's day care and a physiotherapy service.

CASE STUDY THREE: La Valance, Maastricht, the Netherlands

Architect en Aan de Maas, Maastricht, the Netherlands

This 154-unit (188-resident) atrium building in Maastricht was opened in 2007.[20] It offers four types of care accommodations: 1) dementia, 2) skilled nursing, 3) service apartments, and 4) lean-to apartments. Two large polygonal, light-filled atriums are in the middle of the building.

Building Concept

On the west side are 96 single-occupied dementia units (200 SF) and 34 single-occupied nursing units (230 SF). Dementia units are clustered in two groups of eight residents each around three triangular courtyards on the ground and first floors (48 units/floor). The top floor has three group clusters (10–12) of nursing units. Most of the population is very frail, with an average length of stay of about 12 months. The length of stay has decreased because of Dutch policies that encourage older people to stay at home for as long as possible. The average age at La Valance is 82, and 72% are women. Eighty percent need help bathing and toileting, while 70% are cognitively impaired (middle to late stage). On the south side of the atrium are 24 service house units (850 SF) for couples. On the southeast edge of the site is a seven-story, 18-unit ("lean-to") mid-rise apartment building that offers independent housing with home care support.

Atriums

The landscaped winter gardens invite light into the center of the building. The living and dining rooms of the dementia and nursing clusters as well as service apartments overlook the central atrium. The three-story spaces have large trees, colorful landscape materials, and places to sit and relax. Local artists have created cheerful sculptures and music is played to animate the space. The atrium is air conditioned and ventilated in the summer. Glass-enclosed elevators provide views of the atrium.

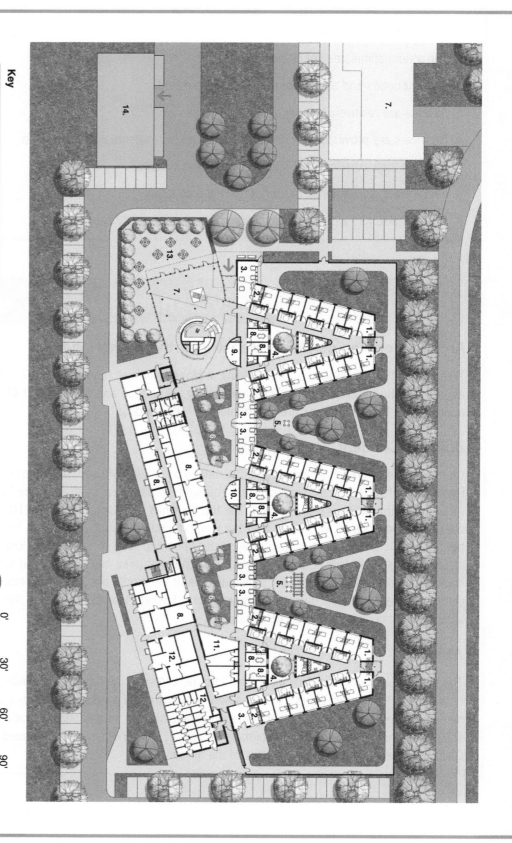

Key

1. Dementia Cluster (8 units)
2. Dementia Kitchen
3. Dementia Living/Dining Room
4. Dementia Courtyard
5. Secured Dementia Garden
6. Atrium
7. Neighborhood Restaurant

8. Offices
9. Living Room Alcove
10. Library
11. Chapel
12. Storage
13. Patio/Terrace
14. Lean to Housing

Figure 8-17 La Valance has four different types of residents: There are 96 dementia residents, 34 skilled nursing residents, 30 units for married couples, and 18 units of "lean-to housing." Dementia and nursing units are located in three-story triangular clusters on the west side of two glass-covered landscaped atriums.
Courtesy of Architecten Aan de Maas.

0'   30'   60'   90'

0M   15M   30M

Figure 8-18 **The entry to La Valance is enhanced by a dramatic two-story restaurant and an adjacent outdoor patio:** Overlooking the west side of the atrium is housing for dementia residents (first two floors) and skilled nursing residents (top floor). The entry pathway leads directly to the centrally located, landscaped atriums.

Figure 8-19 **The landscaped atriums contain trees, plants, and artwork sculptures:** The dining rooms for dementia and nursing clusters overlook the atrium. The glass roof opens to ventilate the space in the summer. Wood siding and trim is used on the inside and outside to establish a friendly, approachable residential character.

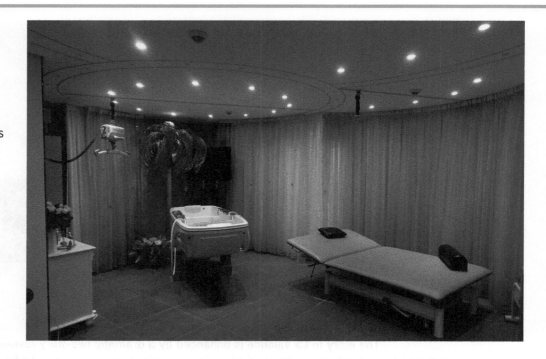

Figure 8-20 Bathing and physical therapy massage take place in a controlled environment: LED lights allow the room to be darkened and a range of soothing colors to be used as part of the bathing/therapy process. A TV monitor with relaxing visuals as well as aromatherapy are employed.

Common Spaces

Conveniently located common spaces include a library, meditation room, activity room, and beauty/manicure shop, which overlook the atrium. A two-story restaurant near the entry welcomes residents from the service house and lean-to apartments as well as family members and neighbors. A physical therapy space on an upper floor has large skylights and a Snoezelen bathing room that uses colored LED lights to enhance the mood. Although the building is predominantly brick, rough sawn 3.5" shiplap cedar siding is used both inside and outside to enhance its residential character.

Figure 8-21 The seven-story "lean-to" housing is located about 150 feet from the front door of La Valance: Residents here take home care services from La Valance and are welcome to take meals in the restaurant or prepare them in their own unit. The average age of residents here is 80–82.

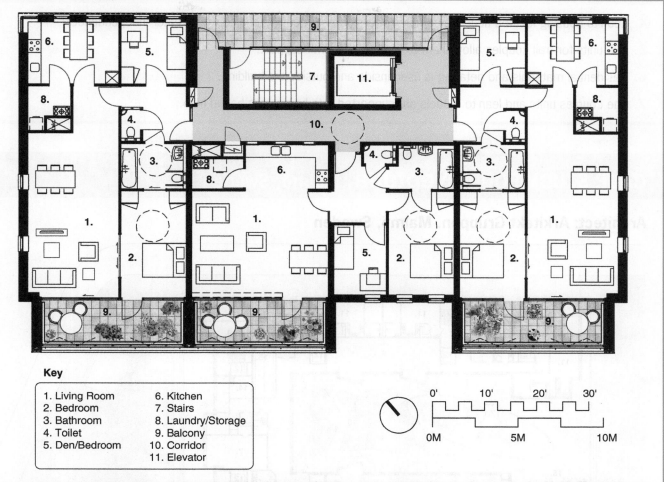

Key

1. Living Room	6. Kitchen
2. Bedroom	7. Stairs
3. Bathroom	8. Laundry/Storage
4. Toilet	9. Balcony
5. Den/Bedroom	10. Corridor
	11. Elevator

Figure 8-22 "Lean to" housing is for older residents who prefer to be located close to, but not within, the care home: The building has three large two-bedroom (1050 SF) units per floor. The bathroom contains two doors for ease of access but it lacks a stall shower. The average resident age is 85.
Courtesy of Architecten Aan de Maas.

Lean-to Housing

The "lean-to" housing is in a separate seven-story building about 50 yards from the restaurant and entry to the main building. These two-bedroom units average 1050 SF each (3 units per floor). The residents who live here are independent but could have a chronic condition or a spouse with a health care problem who needs support. Lean-to housing is popular in the Netherlands for those who like the convenience and security of being near services but would rather not be residents of a care setting.

Noteworthy Features

1. All dementia and nursing care units are single occupied (75% female) in small clusters.

2. The focus is on skilled nursing and dementia for the very frail with a yearly turnover of 50%.

3. Two atriums contain mature trees, artwork, and an operable transparent glass roof.

4. Lean-to housing located near the complex offers another housing choice with greater independence.

5. AFL units for frail couples allow them to live together with support.

6. Residential materials and detailing is used inside and outside the building.

7. The couples units and lean-to models are supported with home care based help.

CASE STUDY FOUR: Neptuna, Malmö, Sweden

Architect: Arkitekt Gruppen, Malmö, Sweden

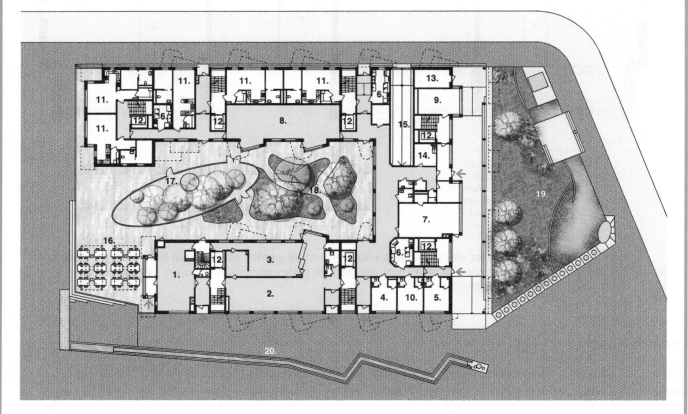

Key

1. Cafe	6. Laundry	11. Apartment	16. Outdoor Patio
2. Restaurant	7. Activity Room	12. Elevator	17. "Bubblan" Winter Garden
3. Kitchen	8. Library/Lounge	13. Trash Room	18. Garden
4. Podiatrist	9. Fitness/Gym	14. Office	19. Public Park
5. Hairdresser	10. Guest Suite	15. Garage Ramp	20. Fountain

0 20' 40' 60'
0M 10M 20M

Figure 8-23 Neptuna is a mixed-use building that contains a restaurant, a podiatrist, and a hairdresser: The 95 residential units are organized around seven separate stair towers. A centrally located garden is accessible from ground-floor resident common space. The east edge of the site has a park that contains a lagoon.
Courtesy of Arkitektgruppen I Malmö AB.

Neptuna is a five-story, 95-unit independent age-restricted housing project opened in 2005. It offers a home care–based model of service delivery for residents to age in place.[21] All of the units are one-bedroom with an average size of 550 SF. Most residents receive a partial housing subsidy, which is common practice in Sweden. It is in the Western Harbor neighborhood in Malmö, a recently redeveloped coastal promenade that features a mixture of housing and retail. The building faces the Øresund strait and is 100 yards from the famous Calatrava-designed "Turning Torso" building.

Figure 8-24 The Neptuna restaurant, bar, and terrace is designed to serve the neighborhood: The five-story building is subdivided into three horizontal zones to foreshorten and reduce its mass. The taller top floor is set back slightly and has a sloped roof form. Views are directed toward the water.

Building Concept

The building consists of seven vertical groupings with 2–4 units on each floor. Each group is wrapped around a single stair and elevator. On the ground floor each vertical cluster connects to a ring of corridors and shared spaces. This is common in Swedish multistory housing because it often facilitates cross ventilation. Neptuna's ground floor also contains a restaurant and outdoor patio on the west. These spaces are open to the public and overlook a pedestrian walkway with a view of the strait. The restaurant is open from 10:30 a.m. to 11 p.m. and regularly serves meals to a handful of residents. The site has many features including a small triangular lagoon and an adjacent park. A fountain on the south edge allows a stream of water to flow between the building and an adjacent walk street. The water flows through an open linear stone channel before ending in smaller ponds near the water's edge. Another interesting feature is a tall clear acrylic "bubblan" winter garden that contains tropical plants. This space is especially welcome during the cold and dark winters. The site is an excellent example of urban architecture with lush landscaping, engaging site features, and popular community-oriented services. The common spaces located on the ground floor include a library, laundry, fitness room, activity/meeting room, and guest suite. A retail space for a hairdresser and podiatrist that serve both residents and the neighborhood is located on the southwest corner. The top floor with a sloped roof contains a sauna and a spa. The spa and an adjacent outdoor balcony overlook the strait with a view of Copenhagen on a clear day.

Figure 8-25 The building configuration creates a secluded garden courtyard with the multistory winter garden to the right: Plant materials in the garden are local species while the winter garden has more exotic tropical plants. The unit balconies are cantilevered from the face of the building and overlook the sound.

Figure 8-26 Dwelling units that range in size from 480 to 650 SF are compact but contain large, open balconies: Doors have been removed from the bedroom, living room, and kitchen to make the units more accessible. Without doors, the units also appear larger. *Courtesy of Arkitektgruppen I Malmö AB.*

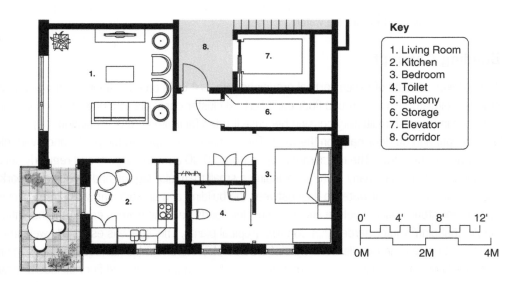

Key

1. Living Room
2. Kitchen
3. Bedroom
4. Toilet
5. Balcony
6. Storage
7. Elevator
8. Corridor

Unit Features

Units are compact, ranging from 480 to 650 SF. Each has a full kitchen, large bathroom, a medium-size bedroom, and a living room. Large cantilevered balconies have translucent fritted glass railings. Eighty percent of the units have a view of the sea and the balconies are large enough to accommodate two chairs, a table, and plants. Windows are wide with low (31") sill heights. A 36" cased opening separates the bedroom from the living room and the floor has a natural wood finish. The units are compact but the kitchens have wood cabinets, four-burner stoves, and a two-compartment sink. There is storage in the unit and the garage. The Swedish-designed bathroom system has moveable supports and a sink that can be raised or lowered.

Resident Profile

The building, open to 55+ pensioners living in Malmö, has 103 residents. The average age is 80, with an age range of between 64 and 102. Thirty-five original in-movers are still residents. There are eight couples, but two-thirds of the population are single females. About a quarter of the residents receive help with bathing and toileting and 40% have problems with memory loss. Home care workers arrive by bicycle to provide personal care services. The building helps residents age in place, but if they become extremely mentally and physically frail they move to a nearby nursing home.

Figure 8-27 **Balconies are large enough to contain plants, a large table, and several chairs and are reportedly well used:** They compensate for the slightly smaller units and 80% of them have a view of the water. The balcony has a fritted glass translucent design. *Courtesy of Arkitektgruppen I Malmö AB.*

Five residents died in 2016, and three moved because they were too frail. The garage has 32 car spaces but only 25 residents have cars. Five residents have scooters and most have bicycles.

More than 60% need a walker to get around with only 8 dependent on a wheelchair. Although the building has many frail people, it also has a core of 20–30 active residents who organize activities and events. They have an active swimming club and a walking club that meets once a week. Because there is not a full-time manager or activity director, much of the responsibility for making the building work socially is dependent on the enthusiasm of residents. One future policy change in Scandinavia is to shift more responsibility for organizing social events from staff to residents.

Noteworthy Features

1. The great location is near a promenade in a mixed-use neighborhood with retail stores.
2. Restaurant is open to everyone and integrated into the community.
3. Social housing features small but well-designed high-density units.
4. The majority of balconies have a view of the water.
5. A large enclosed winter garden is available to residents.
6. Personal care services are delivered using a home care model.

CASE STUDY FIVE: De Plussenburgh, Rotterdam, the Netherlands

Architect: Arons en Gelauff Architecten, Amsterdam, the Netherlands

This 104-unit (116-resident) project resulted from a senior housing competition that sought a contemporary architectural design for the modern tastes of an upcoming older generation.[22] Completed in 2006, the strong architectural design statement reestablished the identity of this older Rotterdam suburb. The location—next to a care center, served by a light rail station, and across from a regional shopping center—is convenient and accessible. The neighborhood is age-friendly, with ramps and wide sidewalks.

Building Concept

The unique building form links a 17-story tower with a 7-story elevated horizontal slab. Both share a wide gallery corridor where they intersect. The tower contains 48 apartments (3 per floor) and the horizontal component contains 56 apartments (8 per floor), which floats 36 feet above a large pond. The units average 900 SF. One striking aspect of the design is the use of multicolored glass panels along single-loaded corridors providing access to apartments. Two hundred shades of red, yellow, orange, and purple glass panels color the corridor throughout the day. The wide corridors have encouraged residents to move furniture here to overlook the view.

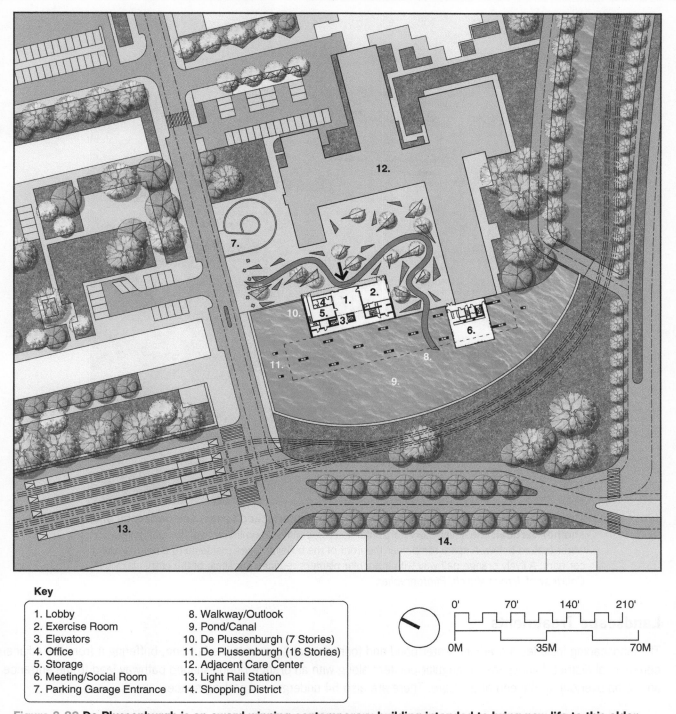

Key

1. Lobby
2. Exercise Room
3. Elevators
4. Office
5. Storage
6. Meeting/Social Room
7. Parking Garage Entrance
8. Walkway/Outlook
9. Pond/Canal
10. De Plussenburgh (7 Stories)
11. De Plussenburgh (16 Stories)
12. Adjacent Care Center
13. Light Rail Station
14. Shopping District

0'   70'   140'   210'

0M   35M   70M

Figure 8-28 **De Plussenburgh is an award-winning contemporary building intended to bring new life to this older Rotterdam neighborhood:** Located next to a retail shopping district and a regional transit hub, it is also adjacent to a nursing home that can provide help for the most frail.
Courtesy of Arons en Gelauff Architects.

Figure 8-29 **The dramatic building consists of two interlocked forms, one horizontal and another vertical:** The seven-story horizontal housing configuration floats two stories above a water feature below. A spiral ramp near the front of the building takes residents to a below-ground car park. A lively orange pathway with triangular planters reduces the scale of the entry plaza. *Courtesy of Jeroen Musch, Photographer.*

Landscape Treatments

The landscaping includes a dramatic water pond and fountain that surrounds the building, buffering it from the adjacent commercial district. Landscaped triangular planters along with an orange ribbon-shaped pathway lead to the entrance and to an overlook at the end of a bridge. There are also 54 underground parking spaces.

Common Spaces and Services

The main social space is a 2700 SF meeting room tucked under the south end of the first floor and dramatically elevated above the water pond. A glass wall overlooks the view on three sides and wraps the room. Another smaller meeting room near the two-story entry to the main building, hosts twice-weekly sessions of physiotherapy, stretching, and exercise. Adult day care for residents with dementia is available at the care center next door.

Figure 8-30a-b **A light rail transit line wraps around the building and the pond:** A community room floats above the pond and below the mass of horizontal units. It has a 270-degree wrap-around view with deep green "landscape-inspired" carpeting. Fountains with swans, and a cantilevered platform reach into the middle of the pond. The twisting balcony rail design is visually lively.

Residential Units

There are five unit types in De Plussenburgh that vary in size from 860 to 1075 SF. Most units accommodate 2 bedrooms and 1.5 bathrooms. However, many residents have chosen to eliminate the second bedroom in exchange for a larger living room. Sixteen of the 104 units are designed to accommodate three bedrooms.

The most dramatic aspect of the dwelling unit is an unencumbered 32-foot window wall that is completely free of column supports. Because the continuous window wall stretches from the floor to the ceiling, the increase in light and the panoramic view make the unit appear larger. A large 77" (2-meter) sliding pocket door separates the bedroom from the living room. When open, the full 32-foot width of the unit can be appreciated as you enter the front door.

Figure 8-31 **Two hundred shaded glass panels add interest to the single-loaded corridors from the inside and outside:** The spectacular sunsets have prompted some residents to move furniture into the wide corridors. Each unit has a horizontal glass window that provides borrowed light to the kitchen from the adjacent corridor.

A large kitchen provides space for a two-door refrigerator and a four-burner stove. The master bathroom is large and flexible with two doors that accommodate a stretcher bather. The balcony is large and unique. Horizontal and vertical undulating slabs are framed by a twisted balcony railing. The exterior appearance is in clear contrast to the surrounding boxy appearance of other neighboring structures. The useable space on the balcony however is somewhat compromised. A horizontal glass panel in the kitchen borrows daylight from the single-loaded corridor.

Resident Characteristics

The building is designed for residents to age in place with home care–delivered services. However, home care is provided through individual insurance plans that use different providers. This makes it difficult for many residents to use the adjacent care center for helping services. Currently about 40% require light services (cleaning), while 25% need more extensive help (showering, dressing, and toileting). Approximately 60% have walkers and 10% use a wheelchair. The building is purpose-built, spacious, and handicapped accessible with an

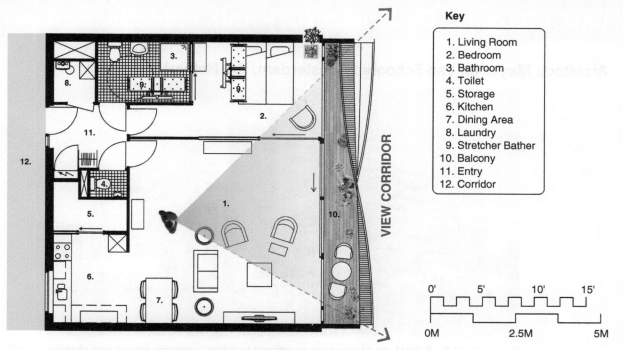

Key

1. Living Room
2. Bedroom
3. Bathroom
4. Toilet
5. Storage
6. Kitchen
7. Dining Area
8. Laundry
9. Stretcher Bather
10. Balcony
11. Entry
12. Corridor

VIEW CORRIDOR

0' 5' 10' 15'

0M 2.5M 5M

Figure 8-32 Units are adaptable to residents in wheelchairs: The bathroom with two doors can easily accommodate a stretcher bather. The 6-foot+ sliding bedroom door, when opened, reveals a 32-foot-wide panoramic view of the surrounding neighborhood from the kitchen. The one-bedroom plan can be subdivided into two bedrooms to accommodate an additional person.
Courtesy of Arons en Gelauff Architects.

active tenant organization. About a third of the residents have a car but generally they give up driving around their 80th birthday. Most residents have manual or electric bicycles and 10% have a scooter.

The age range of residents is 57 to 92, with the average currently at 80. There are 12 couples, 5 single males, and 87 single females. In 2016, 10 residents died and 8 others moved to dementia or long-term care as the building reached its 10th anniversary.

Noteworthy Features

1. Highly expressive contemporary architecture is used to attract boomers.

2. Large units are designed for residents to age in place.

3. The housing is located adjacent to a care center.

4. The building is located adjacent to a regional shopping center and tram stop.

5. The sophisticated high-rise form has great views of the city.

6. The building floats above a large water feature.

7. Personal care services are delivered using a home care model.

Architect: Meyer en Van Schooten, Amsterdam, the Netherlands

Figure 8-33 **De Kristal, an eight-story courtyard building, contains mixed-use elderly housing, retail, and civic services:** Located in the new Nesselrode District of Rotterdam near a light rail station, Humanitas provides fifty residents home care services to maintain their independence. Twenty units of housing are also available for residents with dementia.

De Kristal is a seven-story mixed-use, age-restricted (55+) building that houses 250 residents in the district of Nesselande in Rotterdam. Opened in 2008, it is sandwiched between the city and the country. Thirty retail stores located near the Kristal are arrayed along a promenade adjacent to a lake. The northern terminus of the Rotterdam metro is only 500 feet away.[23] With this rich collection of choices, residents do not need a car to lead a full and independent life.

Figure 8-34 **Single-loaded corridors access 182 low to moderate purpose-built elderly housing units:** The open courtyard has recreational facilities, plant materials, and large skylights that daylight the floor below, which contains a library, pharmacy, restaurant, and medical services. A two-story open corner visually connects the courtyard with the adjacent street.

Building Concept and Common Spaces

De Kristal contains 182 independent housing units on six floors. The average age is 75 and 40% are couples. The housing is stacked above a 110-space parking garage and a ground floor with retail and service uses. The ground floor contains retail stores, governmental offices, a restaurant, café, library, pharmacy, an outpatient clinic, a hairdresser, a community meeting space, and a performance space for children. The restaurant is an important part of the social program for Kristal and contains tables for socializing and card playing as well as a large outdoor balcony. Like Bergweg, residents also use the restaurant as a social space. Even though all units have full kitchens, between 20 and 50 residents take a meal here on a regular basis.

Figure 8-35 **The ground floor has a centrally located restaurant with tables that overlook a community information center:** This is a heavily used pedestrian pathway, which connects the help desk with the adjacent community library. Residents sit here and watch families and visitors use the library and community activities.

Residential Units

The units range in size from 650 to 1200 SF and contain 1 or 2 bedrooms with 1.5 bathrooms, a kitchen, and a storage area. Each unit is accessible from a single-loaded corridor that surrounds an open courtyard. A landscaped roof garden below has skylights that daylight the library and the restaurant on the ground floor. One hundred and seventy of the units receive sliding scale rent subsidies. The 50 residents who receive services from Humanitas have an average age of 80. Approximately 30% of this resident population are receiving a high level of support. About a third of these 50 residents are couples and half are single females. Approximately, 15% use a wheelchair to get around.

Dementia Housing

Two ten-unit resident clusters for people with severe dementia are located on the second and third floors on the east side of the courtyard. Last year 3 Kristal residents were relocated to the dementia cluster and 10 died. Residents with early stage dementia can join the day care program. Approximately 10 people use day care on a regular basis, including seven that are living in the building. There are 35 volunteers who visit and help residents.

Noteworthy Features

1. The site location is near a boardwalk with mixed-use neighborhood services.

2. The restaurant is open to the public and is used for social interaction and meals.

3. Moderate-sized social housing is adaptable for the frail.

4. The metro is nearby so few residents need cars.

5. The building is co-located in the same building with a library, community center, pharmacy, and outpatient clinic.

6. Personal and health care services are delivered using a home care style model.

CASE STUDY SEVEN: Woodlands Condo for Life Prototype, Woodlands, Texas

Architects: Perkins Eastman Architects, Pittsburgh, Pennsylvania

Figure 8-36 **This 6- and 10-story L-shaped building contains 133 dwelling units:** They range in size from 900 to 1800 SF (average of 1200 SF). The elevator core is centralized to minimize travel distances for home care workers. The units have floor-to-ceiling windows and balconies. Most services, including meals, are discretionary (not required).
Courtesy of Vlad Yeliseyev©, Perkins Eastman Architects and Sunrise Senior Living.

This Condo for Life project was proposed in the mid-2000s on a site in The Woodlands, a Houston, Texas, suburb.[24] The building, sponsored by Sunrise Senior Living, pursued the Dutch idea of an Apartment for Life in an equity-based (condo) financial format. It was not constructed but is nonetheless an instructive theoretical example. The 133-unit project was located on a site adjacent to a waterway. It was an L-shaped midrise building (6 and 10 stories) with walkable retail stores and services nearby.

Building Concept

The building used the Dutch AFL concept but adapted it to a US cultural context. The mid-rise building had a unit count of more than 130. The projected clientele in this US model was expected to be couples (40%) and singles in their mid-70s. Unlike an LPC there was no nursing home, assisted living, or dementia cluster. The presumption was that residents would age in place and be supported by intensive, peripatetic home care services. Those who needed dementia assistance would seek housing off-site. Surface and underground parking was provided for all residents.

Figure 8-37 **A swimming pool and exercise room provided options for stretching and movement therapy:** Other shared facilities included a community space for socializing, outdoor activity spaces, a dining room, and offices for assessment, monitoring, and care coordination. Residents were expected to be singles and couples in their late seventies.
Courtesy of Vlad Yeliseyev©, Perkins Eastman Architects and Sunrise Senior Living.

Unit sizes averaged 1200 SF and ranged between 900 and 1800 SF. Although never fully specified, the units were to contain dozens of features that made it easy to adapt the unit for residents as they became more frail. Shared spaces were located on a lower floor with access to an outdoor landscaped area and views of a surrounding waterway. A two-story entry created a visual connection with the lower floor. The lower level contained an exercise room, enclosed swimming pool, and activity/card room. A dining room and bistro bar was to be organized around a flexible "country club dining" format. The bar was to offer snacks and drinks for socializing. The idea was to provide flexibility for residents, allowing them to eat downstairs, in their unit, or at nearby restaurants. The personal care assistance approach was based on an agreement between the resident and a home care provider, similar to the northern European model.

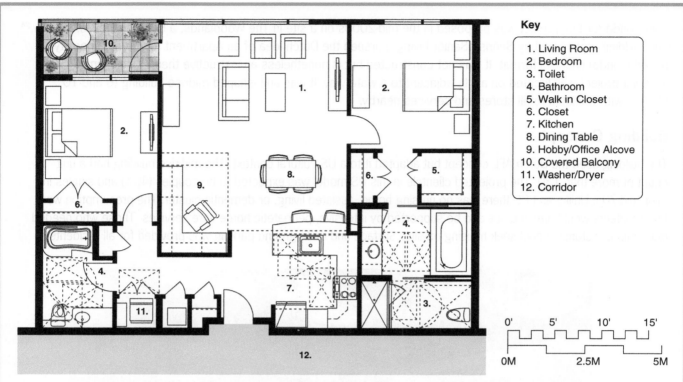

Key

1. Living Room
2. Bedroom
3. Toilet
4. Bathroom
5. Walk in Closet
6. Closet
7. Kitchen
8. Dining Table
9. Hobby/Office Alcove
10. Covered Balcony
11. Washer/Dryer
12. Corridor

Figure 8-38 This Condo for Life (CFL) dwelling unit is typical of what might be implemented in the USA: This 1350 SF two-bedroom, two-bath unit has a full kitchen, an office/hobby alcove, four-piece master bathroom, walk-in closet, and balcony. The spaces shown are large enough to easily accommodate a wheelchair, lift devices, and other equipment. *Courtesy of Perkins Eastman Architects and Sunrise Senior Living.*

Table 8-1 80 Apartment/Condo for Life Unit Features: These considerate design features can help older frail people maintain their independence. Among the most critical spaces are bathrooms and kitchens where falls often occur. Many of these ideas and products come from northern European projects designed to support people for as long as possible in independent housing.

Apartments for Life Features General Considerations

1. Easy-to-read/manipulate HVAC controls
2. Raised receptacle plugs at 1'9"
3. Switches lowered for wheelchair residents to 3'6"
4. All doors 3' wide
5. All corridors 4'0" minimum (4'6" preferred)
6. Pocket/barn doors for access and ease of use
7. Loop pulls and lever door handles that are easy to grasp and manipulate
8. Low or no thresholds; flush transitions if possible
9. Easy-to-open windows
10. Low sill heights (16" to 20")
11. Excellent sun control: drapes or external awnings
12. Cross ventilation if possible
13. Large windows (6' x 6' minimum)

14. Sound transmission of STC 50 or better
15. A 24/7 emergency generator
16. Security camera and alarm systems
17. Locked cabinet (or safe) for medications and valuables
18. Smoke and carbon monoxide detection devices
19. Five-foot turning radius in the bathroom, kitchen, and master bedroom
20. Level thresholds at front door, balcony door, bathroom, and at floor transitions
21. Switches and controls that are easy to see and glow in the dark
22. Doors that are prewired for automatic openers
23. Keyless door locks
24. Easy-to-open curtains: wands or automated
25. Numerous outlets for power or computer
26. TV/music cable for numerous rooms and two walls in the bedroom
27. Humidity controls
28. Voice-controlled switches and dimmers
29. Wood floor option (with resilient underlayment) for wheelchair access
30. Low-pile carpet or resilient floor coverings
31. Warm floors: radiant heat or baseboard heat
32. Single-lever controls
33. Wiring for two-way communication
34. Light fixtures that reduce glare from the light source (no clear filament bulbs)

Bathroom

1. Grab bars that can be added to the toilet and shower
2. Auxiliary heater or heat lamp in the bathroom
3. Lavatories at 34" with removable faces for handicapped access
4. Cabinets with a higher kick space to avoid bending over
5. Emergency call buttons with two-way communication
6. Roll-in shower (3' x 4' minimum) with the possibility of an added seat
7. Bathtub that can be easily entered and exited
8. Bathroom doors that swing out or slide
9. Medicine cabinet(s) larger and deeper than normal
10. Adjustable mirror with magnification feature
11. Shower anti-scalding device
12. Excellent high level illumination that can be reduced with a dimmer
13. Clothes hook for a towel/robe
14. Floor surfaces that are resilient and slip resistant
15. Towel rods that are stronger and can support emergency use
16. Bathroom large enough to accommodate a stretcher bather
17. Adaptable toilet height
18. Toilet paper holder on the side for access (rather than behind the commode)
19. Banjo vanity top for display and access to bath/beauty products

Kitchen

1. Full-height pantry storage
2. Two-door side-by side refrigerator
3. Possibility of increasing the light levels in work areas
4. Undercabinet lighting
5. Roll-out shelves below the counter
6. Horizontal interim shelf above the counter and below cabinets
7. Space for stool below the sink
8. Eye-level oven and/or microwave: controls in front, easy to manipulate and see
9. Hanging rack on a wall for easy access to heavy items
10. Pull-down upper cabinets

Bedroom/Living Room

1. Eye-level door peephole (residents in wheelchair) at 4'10" or glass side panel
2. Easily controlled shade devices for inside and/or outside windows
3. Good access from bed to bathroom with night lighting
4. Space for a live-in, worker, child, or grandchild overnight and during the day
5. Bedroom large enough for two single beds
6. Bedroom designed to accommodate lift devices/rails
7. Bedroom light controlled from bed
8. Internet configuration for telemedicine computer
9. Space that can be used for an office or work activities
10. Videophone to screen guests at the front door
11. Control light switch in bedroom from the bed or a control wand
12. Closet rods that can be lowered to wheelchair height

Balconies

1. Secure-feeling covered balconies sheltered from the wind
2. Low thresholds for the balcony transition
3. Wide enough balcony for furniture and plants (6' minimum depth)

Other

1. Accessible washers and dryers: front-loading stackable or side by side
2. Adequate walk-in and decentralized storage

Unit Features

The unit design was targeted toward younger-older residents. The unit design and service package was designed to match the needs of residents as they became more impaired. The 80 features listed have been shown to be useful in past examples of supportive age-restricted housing. These features include items that were planned and implemented from the beginning (5-foot-diameter wheelchair tolerances, flush transitions, etc.) as well as items that could be easily changed as residents age in place and become more frail (grab bars, pre-wiring for automatic door openers, etc.). Housing with access to in-depth services has great potential for making the lives of older people more secure and satisfying, while allowing them more choice and better noninstitutional choices.

Noteworthy Features

1. This building was to explore the AFL idea in a condo format in the US.
2. Units were to be large and targeted toward people in their mid-70s.

3. Amenities included an exercise room and enclosed swimming pool. ✗

4. It offered a discretionary (no meals required) dining program. ✗

5. The site is within walking distance of a shopping center and overlooked a scenic river. ✗

6. Personal care services were to be delivered using a home care–style model.

CASE STUDY EIGHT: NewBridge on the Charles,
Dedham, Massachusetts

Architect: Perkins Eastman Architects, Pittsburgh, Pennsylvania

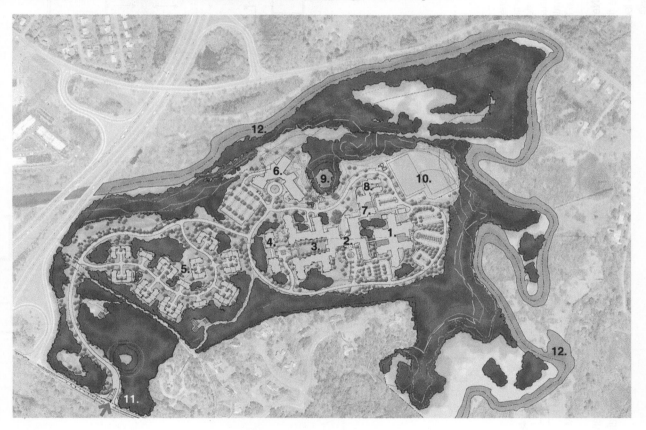

Key

1. Long-term Care Beds
2. Commons Building
3. Independent Living Apartments
4. Villas
5. Cottages
6. Rashi (K-8) School
7. Assisted Living
8. Dementia Care
9. Vernal Pool
10. Rashi School Sports Fields
11. Site Entry
12. Charles River

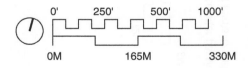

Figure 8-39 **The NewBridge Life Plan Community is located on a 162-acre site:** The varied topography and the winding path of the Charles River significantly reduced the buildable area. The hilly west side of the site was used for single-family cottages. A K-8 private school was also co-located on the campus.
Courtesy of Perkins Eastman Architects©.

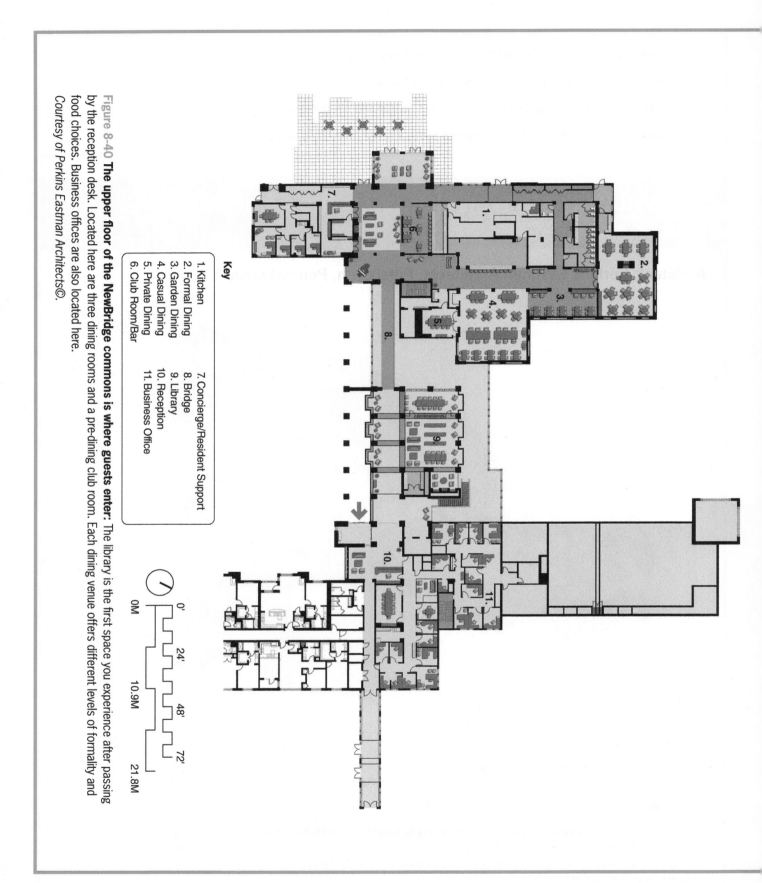

Key

1. Kitchen
2. Formal Dining
3. Garden Dining
4. Casual Dining
5. Private Dining
6. Club Room/Bar
7. Concierge/Resident Support
8. Bridge
9. Library
10. Reception
11. Business Office

Figure 8-40 The upper floor of the NewBridge commons is where guests enter: The library is the first space you experience after passing by the reception desk. Located here are three dining rooms and a pre-dining club room. Each dining venue offers different levels of formality and food choices. Business offices are also located here.
Courtesy of Perkins Eastman Architects©.

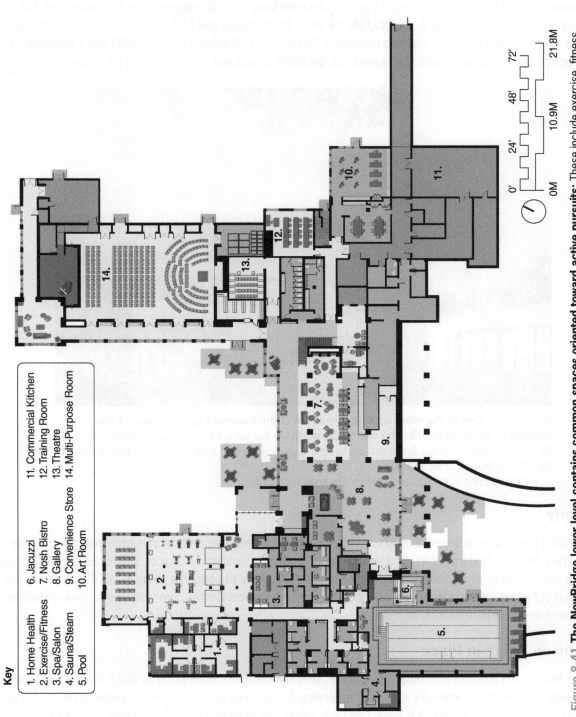

Key

1. Home Health
2. Exercise/Fitness
3. Spa/Salon
4. Sauna/Steam
5. Pool
6. Jacuzzi
7. Nosh Bistro
8. Gallery
9. Convenience Store
10. Art Room
11. Commercial Kitchen
12. Training Room
13. Theatre
14. Multi-Purpose Room

Figure 8-41 The NewBridge lower level contains common spaces oriented toward active pursuits: These include exercise, fitness, art, entertainment, and a large multipurpose room. An enclosed swimming pool and a fully equipped exercise area shares space with a casual restaurant adjacent to a two-story informal meeting space. *Courtesy of Perkins Eastman Architects©.*

NewBridge is a large Life Plan Community (LPC) outside of Boston. It opened in 2009 and is sponsored by the nonprofit Hebrew SeniorLife. It is located on a 162-acre site, of which 100 acres are developed. The community contains 594 units/beds, including 268 beds of skilled nursing, 51 units of assisted living (AL), 40 memory care (MC) units, and 235 independent dwelling units (ILU). The IL units include 24 villas, 50 cottages, and 182 apartments. The total number of residents is approximately 680. The site also contains a 450-student K–8 private school (Rashi) and a substantial two-story common facility, which was designed to be shared with the Rashi school and the surrounding community.[25]

Figure 8-42 **One of the most striking elevations is the two-story glass facade of the commons, which overlooks the site to the north:** To the left is the large multipurpose room used for special events. The top floor contains several large "townhouse" units that benefit from a view of the Charles River and the grounds.
Courtesy of Chris Cooper© and Perkins Eastman Architects.

Philosophy

The community philosophy is based around goals that include[26] 1) inclusive programming for multigenerational contact that welcomes the outside community, 2) a genuine commitment to optimizing choice, 3) a focus on small group clusters for nursing care, 4) an interest in using technology creatively to conserve energy, and 5) a commitment to wellness that optimizes independence. An alliance with Harvard Medical Center demonstrates a commitment to quality and an interest in exploring research.

Emphasis on Aging in Place

NewBridge has placed an emphasis on aging in place. Only ten residents from 2009 to 2016 have moved out of their units into assisted living, memory care, or the nursing home. They provide home care–based personal care to residents in their independent units. It is based on their needs and preferences and is offered at an additional cost. Management generally encourages residents to move once their need for care is complicated and continuous. This encourages residents to take advantage of the campus care continuum. However, the aging-in-place philosophy is very compelling and most independent residents have chosen to stay in their unit for as long as possible.[27] Because of the size of the campus, some residents have purchased scooters to get from place to place.

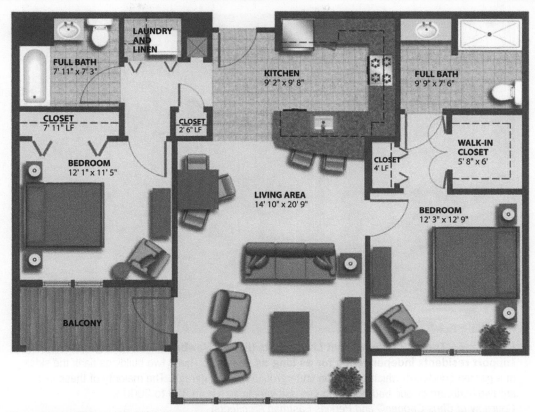

Figure 8-43 **This typical two-bedroom IL unit (1134 SF) contains two adaptable bathrooms for flexibility:** One has a walk-in shower and the other a tub. The bedrooms are on both sides of the living room, making it easier to share the unit. The elongated living room is spacious, with access to a balcony. *Courtesy of Perkins Eastman Architects©.*

Common Spaces

The common areas consist of over 80,000 SF of shared space for activities and program administration. Included are three restaurants (different price-points, food choices, and formality), a library, an arts complex, a multipurpose room, a comprehensive exercise facility, an enclosed swimming pool, a movie theater, and a convenience store. The commons building displays hundreds of pieces of original art and is an attractive setting for residents, families, staff, Rashi students, and neighbors. They are well known for their intergenerational programming, which includes tutoring as well as friendly visitations.

Residential Options

The three types of independent residential housing also provide many choices.[28] The 50 cottages include a variety of one- and two-story models as well as attached dwellings (four- to six-unit clusters) that vary in size from 1500 to 2500 SF. The Villas are three-story buildings with four units per floor. Every villa unit has two outside-facing window walls for cross ventilation and enhanced daylighting. Parking is conveniently located below grade and is accessible by elevator. Villa units vary in size from 1500 to 1800 SF.

The apartments create a four-story perimeter around a central garden. The units are sensitive to handicapped needs and are densely configured within double-loaded corridor buildings. These units vary in size from 825 to 2000 SF. Only 5% of the apartment units are one-bedroom while nearly 50% have two bedrooms and the remainder are one-bedroom with den units.

Figure 8-44 **The 182 Independent Living Units (ILU) in NewBridge are designed to support residents independently for as long as possible:** These two buildings flank the sides of a garden courtyard, which covers an underground parking garage. The majority of these units are two-bedroom or one bedroom with den and vary in size from 825 to 2000 SF.
Courtesy of Chris Cooper© and Perkins Eastman Architects.

Cost

Entrance fees vary from $600,000 to $1.3M (2017), with monthly fees that range from $3,500 to $5,500 (2017). The entrance fee is 90% refundable and the cost of a second person in a unit is $1200/month.

Resident Profile

Residents who live in independent apartments average 86 years of age and about a third are couples. It is an active community with 75% of residents serving on committees.

Long-Term Care

Assisted living (AL) and memory care (MC) are in separate buildings linked to the commons. All units in assisted living are one-bedroom apartments with the exception of two units that are two bedrooms. All memory care units are one bedroom. The unit size and configurations are consistent with the northern European emphasis on larger units.

The 18 skilled nursing clusters each contain 14 to 16 residents (268 beds). They follow the small house philosophy where residents live together and take meals in decentralized clusters. Some clusters are reserved for post-acute residents and individuals with severe memory loss. Each nursing home bedroom is outfitted with overhead lifts, of which 36 are currently in use.

Conclusions

The NewBridge community demonstrates the latest thinking about design and resident programming. The residential units embrace an "apartment for life" philosophy by offering home care–based supplementary services. As residents age in place they can move through the system of continuing care (AL/MC/SN) or stay in their own unit with help. Because NewBridge is a multiservice provider, it can provide personal and medical care at all levels. LPCs (CCRCs) are the closest equivalent to the northern European AFL. They are well positioned to provide a range of services because many of them also offer home care–type services.

Noteworthy Features

1. NewBridge, co-located with a K-8 school, emphasizes multigenerational interaction.

2. Independent units with services allow residents to age in place.

3. The nursing home uses a small house cluster philosophy.

4. The community welcomes volunteers and guests from the surrounding neighborhood.

5. Two-thirds of residents come from single-family homes and 90% are Jewish.

6. The facility has also heavily invested in energy-saving systems.

7. The building's exterior materials are authentic and residential in character.

Small Group Living Cluster Case Studies

HISTORICAL PERSPECTIVE

Near the middle of the twentieth century, the best US nursing care providers began to address the scale of the hospital-inspired nursing home. Many of these new models started by reducing double-loaded corridor configurations in preference to small group clusters of units. Instead of wheeling everyone into a dining room for 50–80 people, smaller decentralized groupings of 16 to 20 were sought out. There were more single-occupancy accommodations and a desire to humanize the nurse's station. These explorations were systematic in northern Europe but were often one-off experiments in the US. The biannual Design for Aging Competition case study books[29] shared early models for noninstitutional nursing home design approaches. These models also used changes in the physical environment as a catalyst for rethinking care delivery.

PROGRESS IN NORTHERN EUROPE

In northern Europe, especially Sweden and Denmark, the desire to create small group clusters and establish better decentralized management systems became popular after the Second World War. The growing number of older people brought attention to the problems of LTC. In these countries, LTC was financed by local governments and models were developed by local municipalities that embraced new concepts of care.[30] In the 80s and early 90s, Denmark rejected the nursing home as a viable building type. Emphasis was placed on community-based service houses that replaced hospital-like rooms with service-supported apartment units. A continuing push toward home care in the community was building momentum.

The northern Europeans (Denmark, Sweden, Finland, Norway, and the Dutch) quickly learned from one another's experiences and progress was made in establishing higher standards for both the operational and physical environment. In the mid- to late eighties it was common practice in northern Europe to 1) design housing in small clusters, 2) utilize op maat principles (customizing care), 3) eliminate the nurse's station, 4) designate primary and secondary caregivers, 5) insist on single-occupancy rooms, 6) rely on both single- and double-loaded corridors, and 7) increase the size of units from a minimum of 250 SF to 400 SF. These settings were often located in courtyard-style buildings that invited natural light while embracing views of and access to the surrounding landscape. Because the Scandinavia health care system subsidized long-term care, they made it affordable. They have always viewed LTC as a "right" and have avoided creating a financial burden on older individuals and families.

was clear that the operational and physical environment in nursing homes needed to be changed to achieve real reform. He pinpointed the environment as a major culprit, because its hospital-like appearance encouraged a care culture that resembled a hospital. He also recognized

Figure 8-45 **The NewBridge CS small house model has nursing clusters, each with 14–16 residents:** Single-occupancy rooms surround a kitchen that also operates as a nursing station. Staff were instrumental in designing the space, which is efficient for work activities but also provides places for residents to take a cup of coffee.
Courtesy of Chris Cooper© and Perkins Eastman Architects.

THE GREEN HOUSE© MODEL

In the US the first broad-based interest in these ideas occurred when Bill Thomas, with inspiration from the Pioneer network,[31] committed to the development of his successful "Green House©" nursing home prototype. His motivation for this building type resulted partly from the success of the Eden Alternative, which introduced humanizing features such as plants, pets, and children to traditional nursing home environments. His experience as the physician in charge of an upper New York State nursing home exposed him to the grim lifestyle and environment typical of a Medicaid nursing home.[32]

The Eden Alternative was relatively easy to implement and immediately improved everyday life for residents. Although very successful in making improvements, it

that nursing assistants, who were responsible for most resident care, needed a stronger voice in the creation of a happier and more homelike lifestyle. Care concepts relating to culture change such as having a dedicated care manager, cross training of workers, eliciting resident opinions/preferences, and care plans in the voice of the residents were encouraged in the Green House©.[33]

The core of the Green House© concept was the creation of a small group cluster of 10 residents living in separate dwellings. These residents were taken care of by designated universal workers who understood their personal and health care needs. Using principles and elements from the "Pattern Language"[34] such as the kitchen, the kitchen table, and the hearth, Thomas adapted iconic residential elements that defined home in the minds of residents and staff. They replaced the institutional nurse's station, dining room, and activity room.

OPERATIONAL ENVIRONMENT

The biggest operational challenge was to create a friendly social context, which led to better social interaction between residents and staff. It was generally assumed that nursing home residents suffered from a lack of control, which lead to "learned helplessness" and increased disability.[35] Residents were encouraged to help with household activities. To respect residents and reinvent these concepts, they adopted a new nomenclature. They used "elder" in place of older person or resident. Also, the head administrator was called a "guide" and a community volunteer was referred to as a "sage."

Shahbaz

To achieve better social interaction and a higher level of responsibility from the staff, a major shift was required in the way care was executed and managed. The typical hierarchy needed to be flattened and a universal worker approach was adopted. Aides were the most familiar with residents and carried out 90% of the work in a nursing home. Thomas reasoned they should receive more credit for their work and they deserved greater decision-making authority. He started by giving the aide a name, adapted from a Persian folk tale about a royal falcon. He called the new position a "shahbaz." Responsibilities included preparing food, doing laundry, providing personal care, and assisting with rehabilitation. They were required to have twice as many training hours than a typical certified nursing assistant (CNA). It was also assumed they would be closer to residents and would know them as individuals as well as patients. The shahbaz also had responsibility for monitoring guests and achieving consensus among residents about issues like food choices and activities. These decisions were discussed around the dining room table at scheduled "house meetings." Typically two shahbazim (the plural for shahbaz) worked during the day and one at night.

Clinical Support Team (CST)

The clinical support team includes physicians, registered nurses, LPNs, OTs, PTs, recreational therapists, social workers, dieticians, and speech therapists. Each of these

Figure 8-46 The 10–12 person Green House© is often designed to appear as a single-family house: In the Mt. San Antonio Gardens CS, the two 10-person buildings fit seamlessly into the context of the single-story, Arts and Crafts–style housing and the garden landscapes that connect them all together on a CCRC campus.
Courtesy of D. S. Ewing Architects, Inc.

professionals visit residents on a schedule developed in consultation with the shahbazim and dictated by resident needs. The nurse generally roams, typically covering two homes during the day and three homes at night. This team approach provides a range of therapies, treatments, and consultations which is necessary for comprehensive resident care.

Lifestyle

A rigid fixed schedule drives the efficiency of a conventional nursing home. However, giving residents as much freedom as possible over their own schedule is an important priority and makes it similar to their experience at home. Because food is prepared in the kitchen of each cluster, it is easier to use a family recipe or to prepare food consistent with individual preferences. In fact, the word "convivium" was coined to describe the happy and healthy benefits of taking a "home-cooked" meal together. The smaller-scale environment also stimulated family interaction and participation. Family members, friends, and staff often join residents at mealtimes. Social and health-related conversations with the shahbazim are fruitful because they know the residents well.

PHYSICAL ENVIRONMENT

The first building prototype in Tupelo, Mississippi, in 2004 was designed to appear as a large suburban house, consistent with tract houses in the surrounding community. These houses accommodated ten residents and contained ten bedrooms, a kitchen, a large dining table, a living room, den, spa, laundry, storage, small office alcove, and outdoor patio/balcony. The original model was programmed at 600 GSF/resident. About half the space was distributed to common and support spaces, with the other half devoted to private bedrooms and bathrooms. Interior furniture and finishes were identified through an analysis of homes from which typical residents moved.[36]

The open kitchen was larger in size and capacity than a typical residential kitchen. However, residential appliances were used to give it a friendly, noncommercial appearance. A single 10-12 person dining table accommodated all residents and the meals were served "family style" at the table rather than being individually plated and delivered from a servery.

Bedroom sizes vary, but were generally small, which made it difficult to bring bulky items like furniture. Some people brought their own bed but often the flexibility of

Figure 8-47 **All nine residents (and two staff) take meals together at a large table in the Ærtebjerghaven CS in Denmark:** Residents come early and stay after the meal for conversations and activities. The atrium in the background provides daylight and a view of the central courtyard. Candles on the table create a homey and intimate atmosphere the Danes call "hyggelig."

a hospital bed was necessary. A roll-in shower/bathroom design and an overhead rail system increased accessibility.

Construction was subject to local and state codes, so compliance was always a negotiation. Code issues were worked out in advance and involved "exceptions" to the existing code or mitigations that satisfied safety concerns. The acceptance of the Green House© model has been widespread but some states and municipalities have been less flexible, falling back on existing institutional requirements and practices.[37]

Replications of the Green House© require the payment of a franchise-type fee. This is to assure compliance with the program, features, and characteristics that are integrated into the concept. When sponsors use the model without becoming registered, they often do so to increase the number of residents per house or adjust staffing requirements. These nonofficial models are generally referred to as "small houses."

PROGRESS CONSTRUCTING THE MODEL

The Green House© movement has led to the creation of over 242 homes in 30 states (as of 10/15/17)[38] with approximately 150 additional projects under development. This reinvented LTC model provides greater autonomy, privacy, and freedom to older frail people. Although the effort is sizeable, it pales in comparison to the existing 1.4 million beds of current nursing home stock. The concept is designed to stand-alone but needs approximately 100–120 residents (10 houses) to meet expected economies of scale. Although the original model was centered on 10 residents/house it has since been liberalized to include as many as 12 residents.

Green Houses© have been a popular addition to existing retirement communities and LPCs. In these settings, existing infrastructure can allow a minimum of two to four buildings to be efficiently supported. The original Green House© prototype was sized to test its viability as a Medicaid reimbursed nursing home. Many replications have been offered for private pay markets and have grown to as much as 750 GSF per unit.[39]

RECENT RESEARCH

Studies conducted in 2003, 2009, and 2012 have sought to clarify the difference between the Green House© model and traditional nursing homes. The findings underscore the informal anecdotal and observational comments made by staff and family members since the initiation of the model. In these comparative studies improved quality of life was reported in seven quality of life domains (including privacy, dignity, meaningful activity, relationships, autonomy, food enjoyment and individuality) as well as emotional well-being.[40] Family members were more satisfied with meals, housekeeping, the general milieu, and health care. Staff reported higher job satisfaction and less job stress. Interestingly, the staff spent an increased amount of time with residents both socially (four times as much) and with direct care (23–31 more minutes/day). Although the staff time allocated was equal, the Green House© residents got far more direct attention. It is believed that the bonds forged between the shahbaz and older residents have led to dramatic improvements in quality of life and care.[41]

CASE STUDY NINE: Mount San Antonio Gardens Green House©, Claremont, California

Architects: Ewing Architects, Pasadena, California

Mount San Antonio Gardens (MtSAG) is a Continuing Care Retirement Community (CCRC) or LPC near Claremont, California. The 30-acre site dates from 1961 and has over 470 residents living in independent, assisted living, and skilled nursing beds on a richly landscaped campus. MtSAG successfully sponsored the first "Green House©" nursing home in California.[42] It took over three years of negotiation with the Office of Statewide Planning and Development (OSHPD) to resolve code compliance, operational, and construction issues because the unconventional aspects of the model were inconsistent with standard nursing home regulations and practices.

Key

1. Great Room / Living Room
2. Dining Table
3. Kitchen
4. Staff Alcove
5. Activity Room / Overnight Guest Room
6. Spa/Bather
7. Patio
8. Fireplace / TV
9. Toilet
10. Secured Gardens

0' 10' 20' 30'

0M 5M 10M

Figure 8-48 Evergreen Villas are the first Green House© nursing homes in California: They utilize a 10-unit cluster plan with generous common areas. Two outdoor patios are created on the north and south sides of this building. Their placement on a CCRC campus allows them access to a range of campus amenities.
Courtesy of D. S. Ewing Architects, Inc.

Building Concept

In 2013, MtSAG constructed two 10-person Green Houses© on the eastern edge of their campus. The infrastructure of the CCRC made it economically feasible to support two single-story buildings at 7000 SF each. The outside perimeter of the building is clad in horizontal wood siding, creating continuity with the campus. The landscape contains lush and mature sustainable plant materials.

Operational Considerations

The shahbaz takes overall responsibility for cooking meals, cleaning, doing laundry, and providing personal care assistance and rehabilitation. Their placement on a CCRC campus makes it easier to offer additional activities and

Figure 8-49 **An Arts and Crafts motif is used with stained horizontal wood siding and gray/black trim:** The materials and detailing are residential in character. Surrounding landscape materials are lush but sustainable. Note the spaced siding that secures the patio. The building fits the general character of cottages located on the campus.

services. Some staff feel the work is more demanding in the Green House©, but personal relationships with residents compensate for the extra work. Each house has two shahbazim during the day and one at night. Physical therapy takes place in the activity room, the resident's room, or a larger physical therapy space on campus. Records are kept electronically and thus are available anywhere at any time.

Common Space

Ten bedrooms form a U- shaped configuration surrounding a 14-foot cathedral ceiling that resembles a lodge. This is where the living room, fireplace, and dining table are located. A large symbolic fireplace located in the center of the building separates the dining table from the living room. The living room has a dozen soft seats anchored by a television. The floor material is a medium tone stained wood and the ceiling is cedar planking. The wood and granite materials used on most surfaces are residential in character. Surrounding the central space are clerestory windows that invite light from the south, north, and west. Two outdoor patios on the north and south sides of the building provide views and access to the outside. The south patio connects to the kitchen and facilitates outdoor dining. An administrative alcove located adjacent to the north patio provides security for the patio, which is surrounded by a 6-foot wood fence. Service spaces include a laundry, hair care alcove, activity room, and therapy tub and are on the east end of the plan.

Kitchen and Dining

An open kitchen provides additional space for an eat-in area for residents, which is popular for coffee and snacks. Emotionally distraught or difficult residents can also take meals here. The large dining room table accommodates 14 people. Family, friends, and staff are also invited to take meals together following the convivium concept

Figure 8-50 **An open-beam ceiling gives the house a "lodge" appearance:** A stone fireplace separates the living and dining areas. Post-and-beam architecture with exposed roof rafters and hardwood floors reinforce its residential character. Clerestory windows invite light from above. The kitchen and patio are visible in the background.
Courtesy of D. S. Ewing Architects, Inc.

of sharing food and fellowship. The kitchen area is devoted to food preparation, storage, and dishwashing. A separate scullery reduces kitchen noise but can also isolate the staff from the rest of the building.

Resident Bedrooms

Like most Green House© designs, resident rooms are single occupied with a private bathroom and vary in size from 295 to 315 SF. Tall windows allow natural light to enter each unit. Resident doors are 42" wide and are handsome, solid-core, carved wood doors with a unique tree design. There are four portable lifts for residents. Unit entry doors have two-way hinges that allow them to open into or out of the room. Medications are stored in a locked compartment in each resident's room.

Resident Characteristics

Residents are an eclectic group of individuals. About 70% have some form of cognitive impairment and 50% are in wheelchairs. Seventy-five percent are female and the average age is 85. They have also attracted private pay residents from outside the CCRC.

Figure 8-51 **The kitchen alcove is adjacent to an outdoor patio, an enclosed scullery, and the dining room table:** An accordion fire door partition allows the kitchen to be open but still smoke and fire protected. Counters in the kitchen give it eat-in capability for snacks or small family gatherings. *Courtesy of D. S. Ewing Architects, Inc.*

Noteworthy Features

1. This was the first Green House© constructed in California.

2. Each of the two buildings serves a group of 10 residents.

3. The interior design has a "lodge-like" residential appearance.

4. The building is certified Silver LEED.

5. The CCRC infrastructure allowed two buildings to be economically feasible.

6. Service and activity enhancements are available on the CCRC campus.

CASE STUDY TEN: Leonard Florence Center for Living, Chelsea, Massachusetts

Architect: DiMella Shaffer Architects, Boston, Massachusetts

The Leonard Florence Center for Living in Chelsea, Massachusetts, opened in 2010 as the first "urban" Green House©. The six-story, compact building is located on a two-acre site. Earlier Green House© models were primarily single-story wood buildings planned as separate houses. Previous Green House© projects rarely allocated any shared space for group activities that served all residents. The Leonard Florence Center contains two 10-resident clusters on each of five residential floors (a total of 100 residents). Each residential floor has elevator access to resident-oriented shared spaces on the ground floor level.[43]

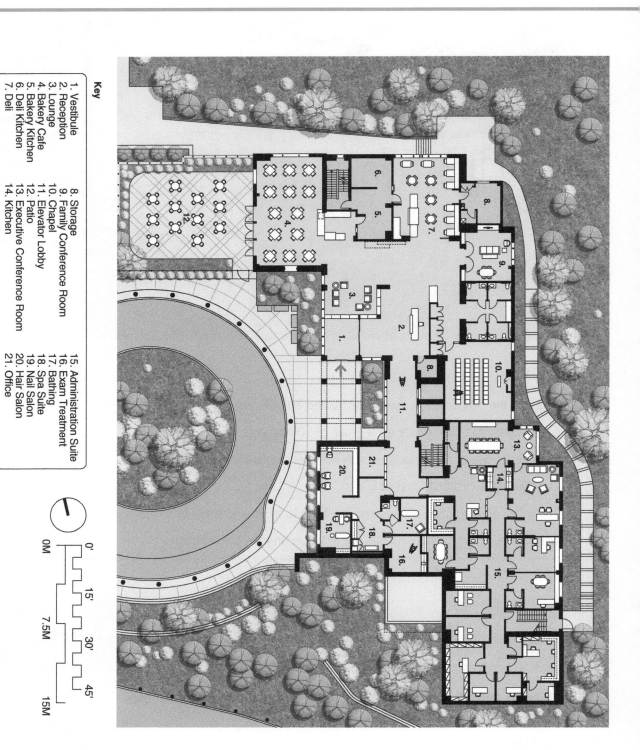

Key

1. Vestibule
2. Reception
3. Lounge
4. Bakery Cafe
5. Bakery Kitchen
6. Deli Kitchen
7. Deli

8. Storage
9. Family Conference Room
10. Chapel
11. Elevator Lobby
12. Patio
13. Executive Conference Room
14. Kitchen

15. Administration Suite
16. Exam Treatment
17. Bathing
18. Spa Suite
19. Nail Salon
20. Hair Salon
21. Office

Figure 8-52 The ground floor contains shared spaces for residents and guests, as well as administrative offices: A chapel, cafe, library, patio, and reception is located here, as well as a spa, hair salon, and exam/treatment room. This space is intended as common space for the 100 residents in the 10 Green Houses© clusters in the building. *Courtesy of DiMella Shaffer Architects.*

0M   7.5M   15M
0'   15'   30'   45'

Figure 8-53 **The brick six-story building is designed to resemble a residential building with large windows and spacious balconies:** A sheltering porte cochere welcomes visitors. Outdoors patio spaces are also available here for residents as well as people from the neighborhood. *Courtesy of Robert Benson Photography.*

Common Spaces

Located on the ground floor is a café, kosher deli, meditation space, spa (haircut, massage, and whirlpool bath), and library/family room. These destinations are designed for residents as well as family members and friends. The centralized elevator is a short distance to these destinations, making them relatively easy to visit with a walker or wheelchair. An outdoor patio overlooking a garden on the ground floor is popular in the summer. The steel frame building is faced with brick to make it appear residential in character.

Operations

Each Green House© uses two shahbazim during the day and one at night. The shahbaz takes responsibility for cooking, laundry, and providing personal care assistance. However, at Leonard Florence, housekeeping is managed by a separate group of staff. One nurse supports two Green Houses© on a 24/7 basis. Specialists (such as physicians, OT, PT, and social workers) come to each house when needed. Because of the intimate scale of the setting, they have been successful in developing events with family members. The busiest time is late afternoon, when the shahbaz must carefully plan and prioritize tasks.

As in most Green House© settings, the meals are prepared in each house based on the preferences of residents. They customize the lifestyle of each resident by providing them freedom to spend the day based on their own schedule and not on one established by the staff.

Figure 8-54 **The bakery café on the ground floor is where residents and families can visit and enjoy time in another place away from their small group cluster:** This space resembles a neighborhood coffee shop. The stacking of unit clusters above a common meeting space floor in this urban Green House© creates more choices for families and caregivers. *Courtesy of Robert Benson Photography.*

Unit Clusters

Each unit cluster has bedrooms that surround a centrally located shared space, which includes the kitchen, living room, and dining room table (with 12 seats). These common spaces are configured in an open plan arrangement. Meals are made to order and menus are designed collaboratively with residents. Each 10-room cluster has a distinctive "front door" that opens from the elevator lobby. Back of the house spaces behind the elevator core and located between the two "houses" contain an office, storage, and laundry. The open modern kitchen conceals the equipment used for health care monitoring, which is located here. A "den" in the corner away from the main space is used by visiting families or for meetings that require privacy. On the west facing side of the common space is an enclosed balcony that can be ventilated in the summer.

Two houses for people with ALS (Lou Gehrig's disease; age 30–40), and one each for multiple sclerosis (age 40–60), Parkinson's, and short-term rehabilitation take advantage of the flexibility of this model. Located as separate small groups, they hire especially trained staff to serve residents with different challenges. The ALS residences are wired to use the most advanced computer-based technology and to give residents (especially those in wheelchairs) enhanced independence.

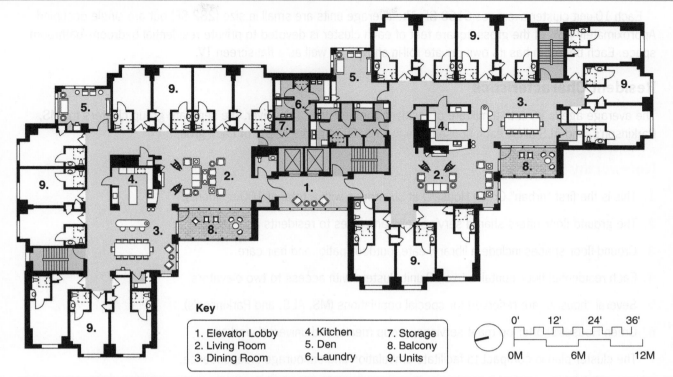

Key

1. Elevator Lobby	4. Kitchen	7. Storage
2. Living Room	5. Den	8. Balcony
3. Dining Room	6. Laundry	9. Units

0' 12' 24' 36'

0M 6M 12M

Figure 8-55 A typical floor contains two L-shaped 10-unit resident clusters: The shared spaces in each cluster include a living room, dining table, kitchen, den, and balcony. Each house operates independently. Shared between the two houses are two elevators, a laundry, utility space, and a storage area.
Courtesy of DiMella Shaffer Architects.

Figure 8-56 The dining table, open kitchen, and den portrayed in this picture represent the scale and residential style of the cluster: Wood floors, residential light fixtures, and residential-scaled furniture establish a noninstitutional character. Large windows and a large balcony provide access to outdoor spaces in each cluster. *Courtesy of Robert Benson Photography.*

Each 10-unit cluster averages 6160 SF. The average units are small in size (282 SF) but are single occupied. Approximately 46% of the gross square feet of each cluster is devoted to private residential bedroom/bathroom space. Each bedroom has its own private roll-in shower as well as a flat-screen TV.

Resident Characteristics

The average age is 86 with a mixture of resident competencies. However, the separate group clusters for MS, Parkinson's, and ALS allow each house to be custom fitted to the needs of each group.

Noteworthy Features

1. This is the first "urban" Green House© at six stories with a total of 100 residents.

2. The ground floor offers shared services and amenities to residents and visitors.

3. Ground-floor spaces include a library, café, outdoor patio, and hair care.

4. Each residential floor contains two 10-unit clusters with access to two elevators.

5. Several "houses" are reserved for special populations (MS, ALS, and Parkinson's).

6. Green Houses© offer op maat services, group meals, and universal workers.

7. The cluster plan is compact to facilitate ambulation and encourage independence.

CASE STUDY ELEVEN: The New Jewish Lifecare Manhattan Living Center, Manhattan, New York

Architect: Perkins Eastman Architects, New York, New York

This high-rise Green House© long-term care setting anticipates construction in 2018 on 97th street between Amsterdam and Columbus Avenues on the Upper West Side of Manhattan.[44] Like the Leonard Florence case study, this is a multistory Green House©. However, this building is much taller and is located in a dense urban area of the city.

Building Concept

The building is 20 stories with residential units above and an entry, shared spaces, and administration offices on the lowest two floors. Eleven floors will be devoted to nursing home accommodations using two back-to-back Green House© clusters of 12 residents each. There will be 22 total clusters with 264 residents. The building will also contain six floors of post-acute rehabilitation for 150 additional residents, for a grand total of 414 residents. The typical post-acute floor will contain 25 single-occupancy units surrounding a core of administrative and common spaces on each floor. Residents in post-acute care will have the option of taking a meal in a group setting or in their room. A dedicated physical therapy space will also be located on each post-acute floor.

Figure 8-57 **The 20-story Manhattan Lifecare building is located on the Upper West Side of Manhattan:** In addition to Green House© clusters it also contains six floors of post-acute rehabilitation. The building contains two therapy gardens with one located on the roof. The lower two floors have office space, clinical services, and shared common space.
Courtesy of LiFang Vision Technology Company, Ltd.© and Perkins Eastman Architects.

Common Spaces

The ground floor will be devoted to an entry for residents, staff, and service vehicles, as well as an 8700 SF garden. There will also be a 4000 SF rooftop therapy garden. The second floor will share facilities and activities with the Green House© and post-acute residents, as well as people from the surrounding neighborhood. This floor has a large multipurpose room, chapel, cafe, library, beauty shop, spa, and meeting rooms. These shared spaces will be accessible from the residential floors above and are likely to host visitors, friends and family.

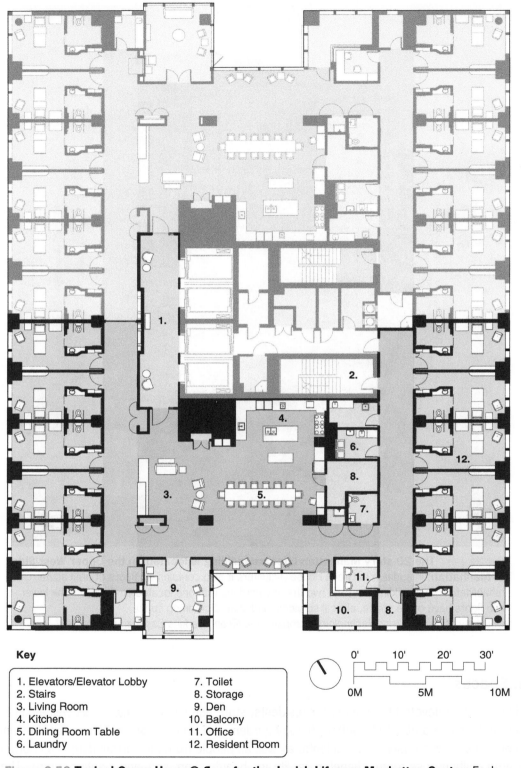

Key

1. Elevators/Elevator Lobby
2. Stairs
3. Living Room
4. Kitchen
5. Dining Room Table
6. Laundry
7. Toilet
8. Storage
9. Den
10. Balcony
11. Office
12. Resident Room

0' 10' 20' 30'
0M 5M 10M

Figure 8-58 Typical Green House© floor for the Jewish Lifecare Manhattan Center: Each floor contains two 12-person Green House© clusters that share a bank of four elevators. There are 22 Green House© clusters (11 floors) in the building (264 units/residents). The 12 units in each cluster are for single-occupancy residents.
Courtesy of Perkins Eastman Architects©.

Figure 8-59 Each Green House© cluster has an identical stacked plan: The shared spaces include a living room, kitchen, dining room table (which seats 12 residents and 2 staff), a balcony, den, and laundry. The open centralized plan with built-in casework makes it easy for residents to navigate. Finishes and fixtures are residential in character.
Courtesy of LiFang Vision Technology Company, Ltd.© and Perkins Eastman Architects.

Another special second floor program of the Jewish Home is its Geriatric Career Development Program (GCD). This program is a rigorous career training and college preparation course targeted toward high school students who seek careers in senior services and geriatric care. The students provide companionship, activities, and clinical care for residents.

Green House© Cluster

Each Green House© cluster will contain 12 residents (two more than most early Green Houses©). The clusters will serve a mixed population of physically and cognitively impaired residents. Two floors will contain a kosher meat unit cluster paired with a kosher dairy unit cluster. Dwelling units will be approximately 245 SF and single occupied with ceiling heights of 10 feet. Each residential unit will be outfitted with a ceiling-mounted electric lift designed to move residents from the bed to either a shower chair or wheelchair. Each unit has its own dedicated roll-in shower, toilet, and lavatory.

Each cluster contains the following shared spaces: a kitchen, living room, dining room table for 14 (12 residents and 2 staff), den, laundry, activity space, and an outdoor terrace. As in all Green House© projects, a decentralized, universal worker-style management team (shahbazim) will take ownership of the house and will foster close resident and caregiver relationships. As part of that philosophy, op maat programming will give residents as much freedom as possible to live a life based on their own wishes.

The Green House© model radically reduces the distance between the resident's room and the dining table and activity space, so residents have shorter walking distances. Food is expected to be prepared in each Green House© kitchen based on menu planning initiated by the shahbazim and served family-style.

Figure 8-60 **Dwelling units are relatively small but single occupied:** They measure 245 SF and have 10-foot ceiling heights. The windows are large with low sill heights but only 2 out of 12 have corner windows. Ceiling-mounted lifts will allow residents to be moved safely. The bathrooms include three fixtures (lavatory, toilet, and shower). *Courtesy of LiFang Vision Technology Company, Ltd.© and Perkins Eastman Architects.*

Resident Characteristics

Although the building has not received residents yet, the population is anticipated to be like other Green House© buildings. They expect residents to have an average age of 81–86. About half are expected to have cognitive impairments and they anticipate an average length of stay of three years. They are prepared to serve very frail residents through the end of life and will welcome private pay as well as Medicaid recipients. They expect it will attract people from the surrounding neighborhood as well as elsewhere in Manhattan.

Noteworthy Features

1. It will be located on 97th street on the Upper West Side of Manhattan in a 20-story tower.

2. It will offer rehab and nursing care on separate floors.

3. Green Houses© will offer op maat services, group meals, and universal workers.

4. Each Green House© floor will have two clusters of 12 residents (24 single-occupied units).

5. The building will offer services to the neighborhood on the ground and first floors.

6. Gardens on the ground floor and roof will be open to residents.

7. The Geriatric Career Development Program will offer internships for students.

CASE STUDY TWELVE: Hogeweyk Dementia Village, Weesp, the Netherlands

Architects: Molenaar and Bol and Van Dillen Architects, Weesp, the Netherlands
Landscape Architects: Niek Roozen, Landscape Architects, Weesp, the Netherlands
Planners: Dementia Village Advisors and Architects, BH Vught, the Netherlands

Figure 8-61 **The southeast elevation uses a layer of trees and turf between the façade and the street to soften its appearance:** This outer perimeter of the village contains few doors or sidewalks. A variety of brick materials and colors are used with differing fenestration patterns to create a residential look.

The Hogeweyk Dementia Village, which opened in December 2009, is a unique care setting that has attracted worldwide attention. Located on a four-acre site in the town of Weesp (17,000 population), it provides autonomy and freedom to a severely cognitively impaired resident population. The village houses 152 residents in 23 small group homes of six to seven people. The one- and two-story brick building looks residential from the street. Seven different courtyards are woven together by wide sidewalks with an internally focused plan. The complex is secure with an entry vestibule on the south edge of the site. Once past the secure entry, everyone is free to walk to different destinations and activities on-site. This allows residents freedom of movement outside their dwelling unit and promotes walking without the fear of getting lost or being injured by traffic.

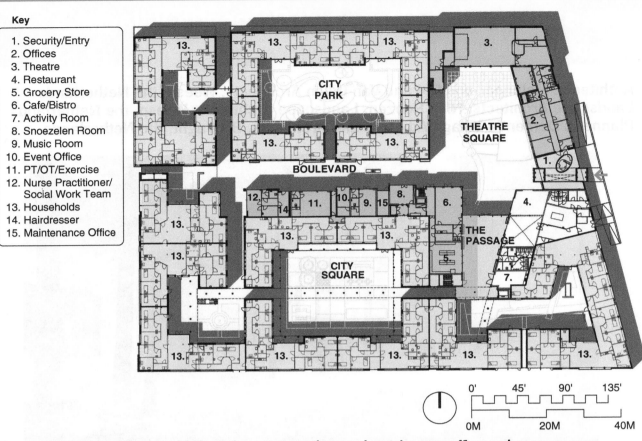

Key

1. Security/Entry
2. Offices
3. Theatre
4. Restaurant
5. Grocery Store
6. Cafe/Bistro
7. Activity Room
8. Snoezelen Room
9. Music Room
10. Event Office
11. PT/OT/Exercise
12. Nurse Practitioner/ Social Work Team
13. Households
14. Hairdresser
15. Maintenance Office

Figure 8-62 The central boulevard is the main east-west pathway and contains many offices and common space destinations: "The Passage" is a covered and enclosed space where the restaurant, main activity room, and grocery store are located. "Theater Square" is an outdoor civic courtyard with a fountain, which is also adjacent to the performance space/auditorium. *Courtesy of Molenaar and Bol and Van Dillon (MBVDA) Architects and Dementia Village Advisors.*

Building and Planning Concepts

A looped pathway connects housing clusters with places to sit, relax, exercise, and carry out activities. The courtyards can be subdivided into three large plazas, and four smaller squares and gardens. After passing through a secure lobby you enter into a civic "**Theater Square**" with whimsical sculptures, a pond, and a fountain. Straight ahead is the boulevard and to the left is an enclosed multistory passage where the restaurant, bistro, and supermarket are located. The theater square is a courtyard where events can be held without disturbing the rest of the village.

The enclosed "**Passage**" is two stories in height and supports a range of planned and unprogrammed activities in a protected space. The supermarket, bistro bar, activity room, and restaurant here form an agglomeration of activity.

The "**Boulevard**" runs from the entry to the west edge of the site. It provides a linear way-finding element in contrast to the looped pathway system. It resembles a walk street in a small village and shares similarities to Disneyland, which has a looped pathway and a linear entry axis that keeps children from becoming lost. The boulevard includes a doctor's office, physical therapy space, beauty/barber, music room, Snoezelen therapy space, and maintenance office. In conventional nursing homes some of these spaces would be treated as back-of-the-house spaces. Here they contribute to activity and engagement. The main "**City Park**" with a pond in the center is surrounded by four L-shaped "homey lifestyle" residential clusters. Looped pathways here lead to all four unit entries.

Figure 8-63 **Stores and services along the boulevard resemble the main commercial street of any small Dutch town:** They have moved counseling and maintenance offices to these visible locations, as well as shared community spaces, like the restaurant, physiotherapy, and the bistro. These active places add to the liveliness of the boulevard.

The **"City Square"** is a paved urban space with large mature trees—like you might expect in a city. This is where a group of "urban lifestyle" houses are located. A bridge on the upper floor creates a continuous pathway. The ubiquitous sidewalk with park benches and shade is designed to **encourage walking** for exercise—something that is known to be beneficial to memory-impaired residents. Many walkways are covered so residents can also walk regardless of weather.[45]

The two-floor public elevator is called automatically when you stand in front of the door. When it arrives and you enter, the door closes and takes you to the top floor without having to push a button. It is helpful to residents who might not know to push the button.

Landscaping

The village uses many different local plant materials. This gives various sectors a unique appearance while using familiar local trees for continuity. **Mature trees** are specified to give it an established look. The landscape is lush with water used judiciously in courtyards. The **Pavement** of different colors, patterns, and materials adds individuality. Sidewalks and pathways have streetlights, street signs, and benches. Corners of courtyards are entry points to houses. They use special planting, tables, chairs, bird feeders, and birdbaths to make them easier to recognize.

Lifestyle Clusters

Creating lifestyle clusters allows Hogeweyk to have people with similar backgrounds live together as friends. They believe sharing the same interests, habits, values, preferences, ways of living, and point of view motivates friendships

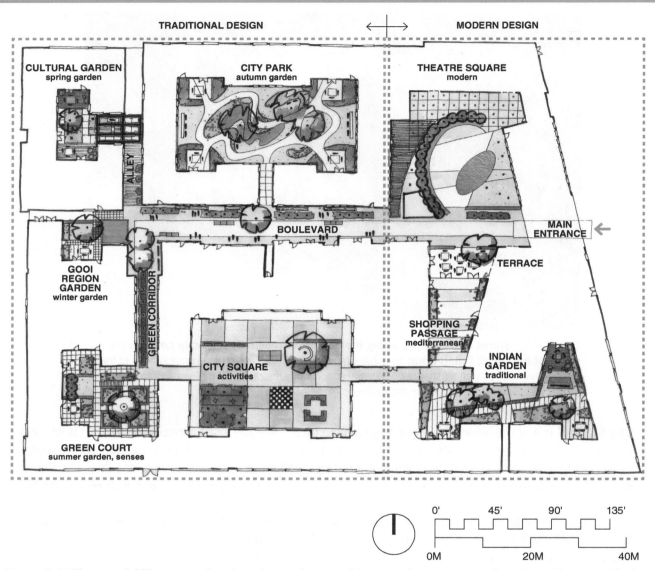

Figure 8-64 **Hogeweyk Village contains three large plazas and four smaller squares and gardens:** These are linked together through a looped pedestrian sidewalk that connects each small residential group cluster with common spaces and services. The landscaping is rich and varied with native plants, water features, and places to sit, relax, and recharge. *Courtesy of Niek Roozen Landscape Architects.*

and social exchange. Looking for continuity and maximizing cooperation and friendliness is the goal. In doing so, food, traditions, and rituals can be customized for each group. Friends that share the same interests can maintain past pursuits. Each lifestyle cluster is different. Some people read the paper and others feel strongly about having a pet.[46]

Seven Lifestyle Groups

1. **Traditional (Craftsman):** The identity of this group comes from having a traditional profession or managing a small business. Residents are traditional, hardworking, early-to-bed and early-to-rise individuals.

2. **City (Urban):** This "urbanized" group has spent their lives in the city. Many come from Amsterdam and are outgoing and informal.

3. **Het Goois (Aristocracy):** These residents believe manners, etiquette, and appearance are important. The term comes from an upper-middle-class neighborhood where residents have formal, timeless values and have often had servants.

4. **Cultural (Arts and Culture):** Art and culture is appreciated by this group, many of whom are international travelers. The unit interiors are colorful and food choices are adventuresome.

5. **Christian:** These residents practice the Christian religion, which for them is an important part of daily life.

6. **Indonesian (Colonial):** Indonesia was a former colony of the Netherlands and many people moved to the Netherlands when independence was declared. Traditional Indonesian culture determines their daily routines. They are interested in nature, spirituality, and Indonesian food.

7. **Homey:** These residents believe that caring for family and the household is important, and domestic tasks and tradition are meaningful. The focus is on housekeeping, family, and the simple life.

Figure 8-65 Residents often accompany caregivers to the on-site grocery store, where they buy groceries for their lifestyle group: The selected food is used to prepare meals, often with recipes familiar to residents. Homes are grouped into seven different lifestyles, which offer activities and food choices based on past experience.
Courtesy of Vivium care group | De Hogeweyk.

To arrive at a best lifestyle fit, residents and their families complete a 70-question survey to match them with an appropriate lifestyle affiliation. They can be placed on two waiting lists if the scores are similar. There are approximately three houses for each lifestyle with seven waiting lists.

The unit plan and interior design is custom fitted to each lifestyle. This includes furniture, accessories, artwork, colors, and fabrics, as well as tablecloths and flatware. Staff with input from residents and families, make most of the decisions about decor. The "cultural" group, for example, has the liveliest colors, while the "homey" group is the most subdued with unpretentious accessories.

Figure 8-66 **Group homes are furnished to match the interior design finishes and treatments of different lifestyles:** This living room is from an "urban" lifestyle group. Colors, fabrics, artwork, wall coverings, and furniture styles were identified through interviews with residents and family members, as well as site visits to their homes.
Courtesy of Vivium care group I De Hogeweyk.

The design of each group home reflects corresponding lifestyle patterns. The "Indonesian" group has a large central kitchen combined with their living room. The "goois" cluster places emphasis on an entry space with a locked front door and doorbell. The "homey" group uses the door from the patio to enter the house though the living room. House locations are matched to the village context. For example, "urban" houses are located around the main square and "homey" houses around the park pond.

All residents at Hogeweyk have a severe dementia diagnosis. The average length of stay is about 2.5 years and one-third to half of the resident population turns over yearly. The average resident age is around 84.

Activities

The village is interested in matching the individual interests of residents to the various activities available. There are approximately 20 weekly activities and club meetings offered to all residents. These include small group events as well as large celebrations, like the food festival or flower show. Large events are staged in the theater or the middle of the passage. Smaller ones take place in meeting rooms. The idea is to give all residents access to the activities they enjoy. For example, a member of the "urban" lifestyle group can share her passion about flower arranging or Mozart with residents from any other lifestyle group. So even though they live in clusters with people of similar backgrounds they can share their passion for specific activities with any of the other 151 residents.

Each house makes a daily trip to the supermarket bringing a resident to help them shop. They expect residents to visit the restaurant in the passage at least once a week. They have a Snoezelen bed with 10–12 regular users. This therapy is used with the most agitated residents or those who have difficulty speaking and communicating.

Some residents leave the building for off-site activities like swimming or dinners at local restaurants. Hogeweyk is also very interested in inviting outsiders to visit the building. They believe activities with other private or civic groups give the building a stronger community identity.

Figure 8-67 **The crafts room is one of several common spaces that support the activities program at Hogeweyk:** A music room, Snoezelen room, bistro, and theater are also available for a range of weekly clubs. The passage (enclosed arcade) and the theater square (courtyard) are often used to stage larger events.

Dwelling Unit Features

Each house has an L-shape configuration with two short corridors located on both sides of a central entry space. Although every house is unique, they share many of the same basic features. Each house has six bedrooms (a 172 SF space for a bed and a sink), two shared bathrooms, a living room, kitchen, terrace, and a small staff space. Thirteen of the 23 houses have one larger double-occupancy bedroom (215 SF) to accommodate residents who prefer the companionship of another person. They believe smaller bedrooms encourage residents to spend time together in shared spaces. Although most people have their own bedroom, three bedrooms share a bathroom. Individual private bathrooms would have been convenient and would likely be pursued in follow-up projects.

In general, most houses have large windows and receive light from two sides. Medications are usually stored in each kitchen, and one corner of the living room normally operates as a staff office with a computer. To satisfy residents' habits, there is one smoking room for each lifestyle group (seven in total).

Philosophy of Care

Hogeweyk embraces many philosophical ideals, including independence, autonomy, security, and self-esteem. They believe residents live a safe and happy life.[47] The village is designed to replicate the normal life of someone from the community. They live their lives as before with full independence and within the confines of the secured setting. Residents see themselves in what appears to be a familiar and normal surrounding, which also reduces anxiety and fear.[48] Family and friends regret most the inability to verbally communicate. Because so many residents still enjoy music, they find this to be a very effective way to communicate with those who can no longer speak. Holding hands (touching) also compensates for the lack of communication and demonstrates emotional support. The Hogeweyk philosophy focuses on eating, drinking, and being happy.

Figure 8-68 **The village is designed to have an inward focus toward courtyards and gardens:** This is the "city square," which contains "urban" lifestyle clusters. The hardscape plaza contains trees, sitting areas, and activities that are familiar to residents from larger cities. Colorful, mature, and indigenous plant materials are located here.

Staffing and Management

They believe residents should make as many decisions as possible. Residents are encouraged to help prepare meals, do laundry, shop for food, and help one another. Caregivers direct activity rather than lead it. Each house is encouraged to understand their uniqueness and their special lifestyle attributes. Staff must be trained to prepare meals consistent with that lifestyle. Every resident has a designated staff member who knows them well.[49] The staff dress in street clothes, have special dementia training, and are a stable work force with low turnover. Resident populations are mixed in terms of ability, although most are severely cognitively impaired. Approximately five hours of direct care each day is provided to each resident. They use an op maat approach to customize care so residents operate on their own schedule. Although they have not conducted formal research on their caregiving approach, they have observed informally that residents take fewer medications, are happier, eat better, and live longer.[50]

Families are welcome at any time and can stay as late as they want. In the "Indonesian" house, family members often volunteer to prepare meals. Hogeweyk is committed to working with families. If families want more magazines, fresh flowers, or special treats, they try hard to accommodate them. Hogeweyk also has 120 volunteers of all ages.

There are four roving social workers involved in dealing with emotionally distraught "difficult residents." Because agitation is common, staff are trained to calm residents and defuse problems. Residents can be physically aggressive and verbally abusive. Social workers live in the "resident's reality" as much as possible. One of the worse things is to correct a resident. Listening to a resident's story helps them to make sense of their situation. Just talking to residents often allows them to forget what is upsetting them.

Figure 8-69 **The main restaurant at Hogeweyk is elegant:** It contains a covered and enclosed dining area in the passage as well as tables outside that overlook Theater Square. Everyone is welcome, including residents and their family members. Hogeweyk also encourages residents to visit restaurants in the surrounding community.

The original Hogeweyk building was first constructed on this site in 1993. The old building was a traditional concrete-frame four-story nursing home. They used a similar lifestyle approach, placing three slightly larger groups on each floor, but the old design hampered their effectiveness.

Although the actual cost of care is $8,000/month, no one pays more than $3,600/month. The cost to residents is calculated on a sliding scale based on income and partly subsidized by the government.

Noteworthy Features

1. Hogeweyk is a secured village for 152 residents that allows everyone to walk freely.

2. There are 23 small group homes of six to seven residents each.

3. Residents are clustered into seven lifestyle groups that match their backgrounds and interests.

4. Lifestyle attributes embrace food, interior design, and resident interests.

5. Universal workers at each house prepare food and provide care.

6. Residents from all seven lifestyles are invited to participate in 20+ weekly clubs and activities.

7. Seven courtyards with connecting sidewalks facilitate walking throughout the village.

Architect: Schmidt Hammer Lassen Architects, Arhus, Denmark

Figure 8-70 **Ærtebjerghaven consists of five small group cluster buildings, each with nine residents:** Each one-story buildings has a sloped ceiling and a central courtyard for daylighting. A long bar building contains administrative offices and serves to connect three of the five clusters. All connecting corridors are enclosed.
Courtesy of Schmidt/Hammer/Lassen Architects.

Ærtebjerghaven consists of five small one-story group clusters of nine residents each, located in Odense, Denmark. The 6500 SF buildings are connected by enclosed conditioned corridors on a multiacre suburban site. The entry building located in the center of the site contains administrative offices, staff facilities, and a therapy room. Fifty residents live here including five couples that live together. Most need extensive nursing care. About 35% are in wheelchairs. Each building cluster has its own dedicated staff and operates with decentralized authority to create five unique environments. Each house has a mixed competency population. However, 80% of residents have dementia, and nearly half of these are severely impaired. The house design is modern in style but uses residential materials.

Building Concept

A compact, centrally focused cluster, known as an "Osmund" plan, minimizes corridors by having all units open to a central common space. A transparent glass courtyard in the middle of the plan surrounded with tall glass walls daylights the darkest part of the building. The courtyard is open to air and heavily planted. It provides an intimate view of a garden that attracts birds and wildlife. Mesh shades suspended on wire supports control the amount of sunlight (and heat) that enters the courtyard.

Key

1. Dining Table	7. Shared Patio
2. Activity Alcove	8. Laundry
3. Courtyard/Atrium	9. Computer Alcove/Office
4. Kitchen/Servery	10. Storage
5. Living Room	11. Staff Toilet
6. Covered Porch	12. Corridor

Figure 8-71 This "Osmund" plan is a compact configuration designed to minimize corridor lengths: Each cluster contains six shared common spaces including a dining room, activity area, living room, two patios, and an atrium/courtyard. The ceiling heights in the central portion of the plan vary from 10 to 14 feet. *Courtesy of Schmidt/Hammer/Lassen Architects.*

Figure 8-72 **The courtyard provides excellent natural light and an attractive controlled view in the center of the plan:** The living room is in the foreground and the activity table is in the background. Note the change in ceiling height and the canvas shades that can be pulled over the atrium on a hot sunny day.

Two doors to the courtyard allow residents and staff access. Each interior common area contains a living room, dining room, activity table, and kitchen. Food is prepared in each house based on a menu negotiated with residents. The kitchen is in a separate room adjacent to the dining table. Breakfast and lunch are prepared here from scratch, while dinner is delivered from a central kitchen, warmed and served. Two outdoor patios (one covered and one open) are in perimeter alcoves that are configured to avoid unpleasant breezes. The biggest outdoor space has a large table and barbecue equipment for outdoor dining.

Unit Features

The compact residential unit measures approximately 410 net SF but includes many features, such as a small tea kitchen, a table, living room furniture, a separate bedroom, and a large European style roll-in bathroom. The tea kitchen has a refrigerator, a counter, and several cabinets (one with a lock for valuables and medications). A double pocket door (two meters in width) is ingeniously used to create privacy for the bedroom. If a sense of spaciousness is required, the sliding doors can be left open. All rooms have overhead ceiling track rails and 13 rooms are outfitted with hydraulic lifts. The lift mechanism can transfer residents from their bed to either a shower/geriatric chair or a wheelchair.

A shower/geriatric chair can be rolled into the shower or over the top of the commode, avoiding the need for a transfer. A 43" pocket door to the bathroom slides out of the way. Large, wall-to-wall windows with 22" sill heights and 80" header heights make the living room and bedroom appear larger. The use of an oak wood floor also gives the unit a cozy residential feeling. The bathroom has fixtures placed on three separate walls to provide a large central space for maneuvering. The lavatory can be moved up and down, as well as side to side to accommodate those with limitations. Each unit has a small private patio accessible from the living room.

Figure 8-73 The shared living room is located adjacent to a partially covered patio: This space receives natural light from a full height window wall and the adjacent central courtyard. The higher ceiling height makes the room appear spacious but the furniture is residential in scale and type.

Figure 8-74 The kitchen for food preparation and finishing is located adjacent to the dining room table: Breakfast and lunch are prepared in this room, while the dinner meal is delivered and plated here. In this house the dining table is parallel with the courtyard to optimize natural light and view.

Resident Characteristics and Care Philosophy

Opened in June 2005, the residents range in age from 70 to 99 with an average age of 87. There are 5 couples, 3 men, and 37 women and all of them are frail. In the last 5 years, they have implemented a computer-based health care tracking system called Sekoia.

Figure 8-75 Each 410 SF dwelling unit is single occupied with a separate bedroom: It is large enough to accommodate a small living room, a patio, a small table, and a tea kitchen alcove. Sliding doors facilitate movement. The compact bathroom has a continuous tile floor and a flexible lavatory that can be moved in four directions.
Courtesy of Schmidt/Hammer/ Lassen Architects.

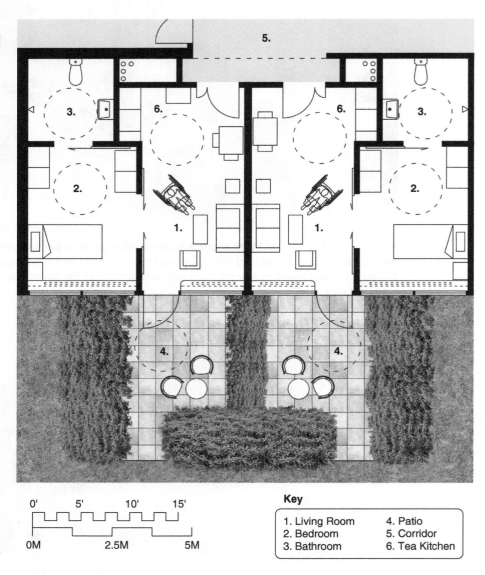

Key

1. Living Room	4. Patio
2. Bedroom	5. Corridor
3. Bathroom	6. Tea Kitchen

The smaller, intimate size of the cluster and the friendly disposition of the staff have encouraged family visitation and participation. The dining room table accommodates nine/ten residents and up to three staff members. Due to the frailty level of residents, staff monitors dining, especially for the 25% who require eating assistance. Staff is also welcome to take their meals with residents. In Danish nursing homes, staff turnover is minimal–estimated at 50% over the last 10 years. During the last five years, sicker and more cognitively impaired residents have moved into the building.

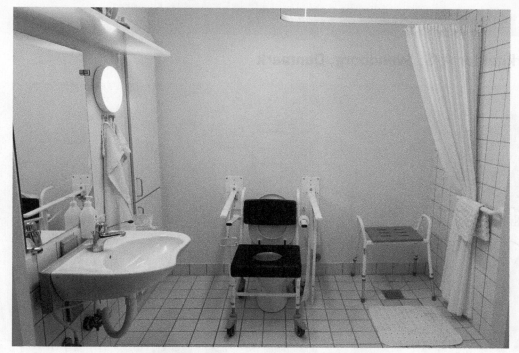

Figure 8-76 **The simple bathroom plan is compact and accessible:** Fixtures are located on three walls, opening the center (with a 5-foot diameter turnaround) for shower chair manipulation. Residents are moved by lift from the bed to a chair, which rolls over the commode and can be used for showering.

Staff prefers the decentralized management philosophy and the fact that each house can be operated in a slightly different way based on staff input and resident preferences. Residents here are actively involved in programs to help others. The building is popular, with a waiting list that typically requires a year for admission even though the turnover is 40% a year.

Noteworthy Features

1. An "Osmund Plan" directly connects resident rooms to shared common space.

2. Units at 410 SF are compact but have a separate living room and bedroom.

3. Each of the five clusters (45 units total) operates separately on its own schedule.

4. A European-style bathroom with a continuous tile floor facilitates transfers and mobility.

5. A large courtyard surrounded by glass allows light to enter the center of the building.

6. Lifts are available in each unit to help residents maintain their independence.

7. Residents are a mixture of the physically and cognitively frail.

C & W Arkitekter A/S, Svendborg, Denmark

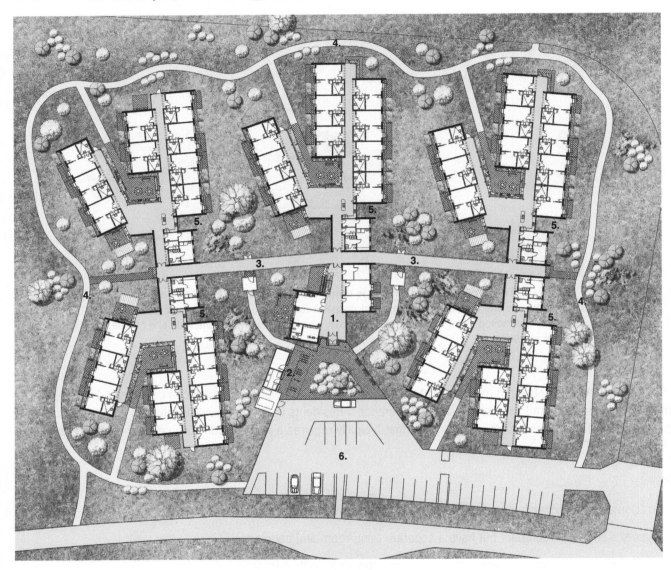

Key

1. Main Lobby, Office/Staff
2. Bicycle/Storage
3. Enclosed Corridor
4. Outdoor Looped Walking Pathway
5. Cluster Houses
6. Parking

Figure 8-77 Herluf-Trolle consists of five small group clusters with nine to ten residents each: Each one-story cluster is connected to the building entry via enclosed corridors. The entry area contains office spaces, meeting rooms, and staff support rooms. An external pathway for exercise surrounds the site.
Courtesy of C&W Arkitekter A/S.

Herluf Trolle is a 47-unit nursing home opened in 2005. It is subdivided into five smaller 6500 SF one-story houses on a multi-acre suburban site. Three houses have 9 units and two houses have 10 units. The one-story building is red brick with a band of clerestory windows above. The clerestory is topped by a thin-cantilevered roof that provides shade control. The entry building at the center of the site contains administrative offices and staff facilities. Eight-foot-wide conditioned glass corridors connect the five houses. A walking club of 10 residents uses a looped trail that surrounds the outer perimeter of the site.

Figure 8-78 **The single-story Herluf Trolle entry has a dynamic angled approach:** A tall flat roof floats over rooms and corridors allowing clerestory light to enter corridors and common spaces. The combination of brick and wood exterior cladding along with lush landscaping contributes to its residential character.

Building Concept

Each unit cluster is a similar shape that combines a large 750 SF, 12-foot-high common space with a V-shaped corridor configuration that leads to resident units. The three activity spaces within this large room are a living area that seats 8, a dining room table that seats 12, and an open kitchen that encourages resident participation in meal preparation. Clerestory windows surround the space near the ceiling bringing in natural light.

A tall window wall overlooks a protected exterior courtyard in the center of the plan. It is protected from breezes and is used for outdoor activities. Each cluster has furnished and organized their patio in a different way. Some use it as a garden, while others have located a table with barbecue equipment here.

Two residential corridors emanate from the common space. One has three units along a single-loaded corridor and the second has six units in a double-loaded configuration. Clerestory windows above 9 feet allow light to enter the corridor from both sides. Alcoves carved into the corridor walls provide space for artwork and furniture that personalize each unit entry. A room at the entry of each of the five building clusters is designated for laundry, food storage, and "back of the house" functions.

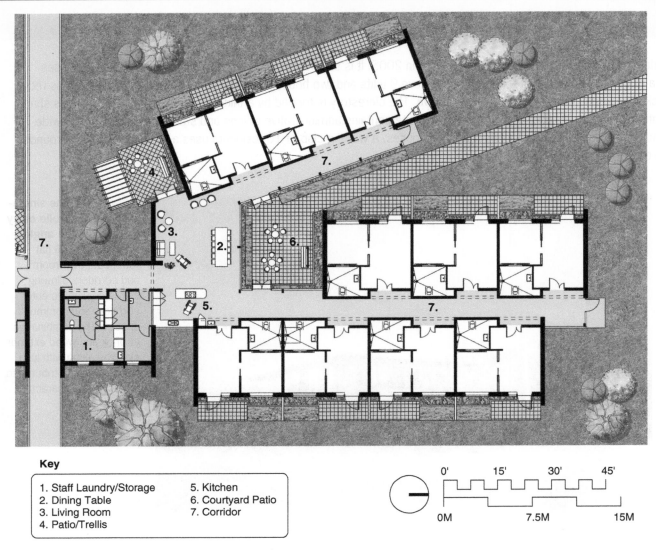

Key

1. Staff Laundry/Storage
2. Dining Table
3. Living Room
4. Patio/Trellis
5. Kitchen
6. Courtyard Patio
7. Corridor

0'   15'   30'   45'

0M   7.5M   15M

Figure 8-79 Each residential cluster has a central shared space and two corridors that connect to units: Common spaces include a dining room table, a living room, an open kitchen, a protected courtyard, and an outdoor trellis. The nine units are linked via single- and double-loaded corridors.
Courtesy of C&W Arkitekter A/S.

Unit Features

At 415 SF, the units are relatively large and single occupied. Each contains a bedroom, bathroom, living room, patio, and tea kitchen with a table. An oak floor adds residential character. The door between the bedroom and living room is a 45" pocket door that can be opened or closed depending on the resident's need for privacy. A two-way rolling track is installed in every bedroom. When required, an electric lift component is added. Because residents are older and heavier, 35% of the units have installed the lift component. Only one staff member is necessary to make the lift transfer, which helps prevent back injuries, a major cause of disability claims. The lift system allows residents to be moved from their bed to a wheelchair so they can navigate throughout the building. Or they can be lifted into a lighter, less bulky shower chair and rolled into the bathroom, which has a continuous tile floor. This portable shower/ geriatric chair fits over the commode and can also be used for showering. A lavatory placed on the wall can be raised,

Figure 8-80 **The L-shaped food preparation space in Herluf Trolle is tucked into one corner of the open plan:** The freestanding cooking island can be lowered or raised to encourage resident participation. This large open-plan space with clerestory windows around the perimeter also accommodates the living room and dining room table.

lowered, or moved to one side. The fixture layout on all three walls maximizes flexibility, providing additional space for showering. A pair of barn doors located between the bathroom and bedroom opens to 40" wide.

A large glass window and patio door located on the living room side of the unit introduces copious amounts of light. Patio spaces are large and are popular with residents who plant flowers or bring outdoor furniture. Nonintuitive window and door locks are used to discourage dementia residents from opening the door and windows without assistance. The Danish constitution does not allow the staff to lock exterior doors so they must use other methods to insure safety. Residents who are an elopement challenge are outfitted with GPS monitoring devices. Furthermore, there is a buried perimeter security system that can alert management if a resident wanders away from the site. Small RFID chips sewn into resident clothing activate this system.

Figure 8-81 **One large room contains the kitchen (far end), dining table, and living room area:** The space is used for activities, meals and dining throughout the day. The dining/activity table is parallel to a tall window wall that overlooks a well-protected patio, which is used for gardening, picnics, and barbecues.

Resident Characteristics and Care Philosophy

The average age of residents is 84.5, with an age range of 60 to 95. Residents with dementia and physical impairments are intermixed, which is typical in Danish nursing homes. Residents move in for a variety of reasons. Some suffer a stroke or acquire dementia. For others spousal conflicts are an issue or their house is too small to accommodate equipment. Herluf Trolle has 1 couple, 12 single males, and 34 single females. About 85% have been diagnosed with dementia and 35% use wheelchairs. Although the vast majority has

dementia, 90% are able to use an emergency call pendant, which allows them to have voice contact with the staff. Approximately 70% are incontinent and 17% need feeding assistance. In the last year 17 residents died (36% turnover).

Each cluster prepares an individual menu based on resident preferences. A cooking island floats in the room with a large overhead hood. To encourage resident participation in food preparation, the counter is adjustable from 26" to 48". Thus, a resident seated in a wheelchair or someone who chooses to stand can both

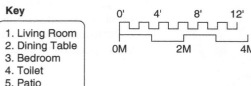

Key

1. Living Room
2. Dining Table
3. Bedroom
4. Toilet
5. Patio
6. Corridor

0'   4'   8'   12'

0M   2M   4M

Figure 8-82 **The 415 SF dwelling unit is relatively large and single occupied:** It contains a bedroom, a small living room, a full bathroom, a tea kitchen, and a patio. The European-style bathroom contains fixtures on three walls. Each entry has a corridor alcove where residents can display or store personal items.
Courtesy of C&W Arkitekter A/S.

Figure 8-83 **Electric lifts on a rolling gantry facilitate safe transfer from the bed to a shower chair or wheelchair:** The shower chair can be rolled into the bathroom (under the shower or over the toilet). A wheelchair allows a disabled resident access to the rest of their unit and the common spaces in the building.

be accommodated. Food is ordered twice a week from a local grocer for breakfast and lunch. Prepared food for the evening meal is available from a central kitchen.

They encourage op maat (customized resident schedules) and designated care providers are permanently assigned to each resident to encourage good communication and social exchange. The small clusters are family friendly and residents have a voice in management policies and menu selection. The kitchen table is a popular place where residents and staff take meals as well as carry out activities. The plan is compact and encourages residents to walk, but units are separated from the shared common space.

Noteworthy Features

1. The 415 SF units are single occupied with a separate living room and bedroom.

2. The five group clusters base their schedules on resident preferences.

3. They offer op maat services, group "family style" meals, and universal workers.

4. Tall ceilings and a clerestory surround allow light to enter from above.

5. A Y-shaped resident unit corridor plan connects units to a large common space.

6. A mentally and physically frail population is intermixed.

Smaller-scale Assisted Living Buildings (25 to 40 Units) and Other Options

These last seven case studies represent different building types that illustrate several different housing options for the oldest-old. These eclectic examples suggest influences, possibilities, and organizational approaches. Some embrace philosophies with social and design-related impacts on residents like the Vigs Ängar, while others deal with small settings that embrace ideas about residential scale and rural character such as the Ulrika service house and the Irismarken nursing home. A hospice, a co-housing project, a vacation village, and a dementia care floor in an assisted living building are used to illustrate other building design approaches for residents with special needs or different preferences for group living. There are literally hundreds of different building types and combinations that could be illustrated in this section but this sampling of popular building types can illuminate and influence our thinking.

CASE STUDY FIFTEEN: Vigs Ängar Assisted Living
Köpingebro, Sweden

Architect: Husberg Arkitektkontor, Brantevik, Sweden

Vigs Ängar is a one-story, 32-unit assisted living building located in Köpingebro a south coast Swedish town near Ystad. It has two major courtyards; one is primarily landscaped and the other is a mixture of hard and soft surfaces.[51] The building is subdivided into two smaller 12-unit clusters of assisted living and one 8-unit secured dementia cluster. The looped circulation system contains single- and double-loaded corridors that add density and provide views of the two courtyards for daylight and orientation purposes. The courtyards use mature trees, flowing water, and ground

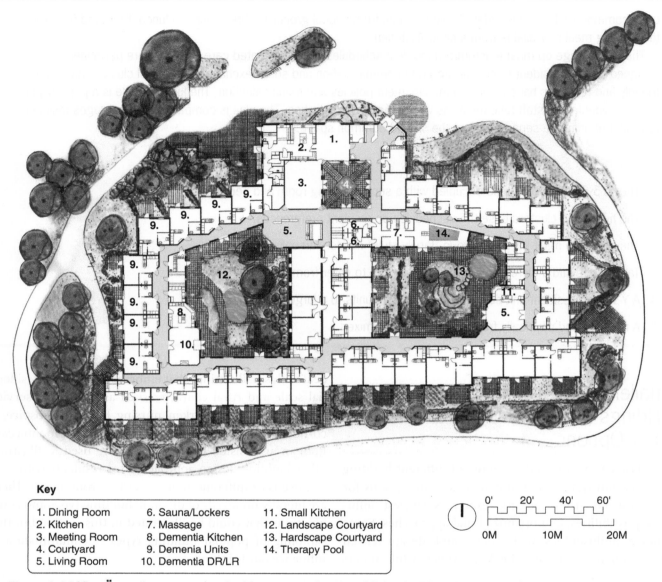

Key

1. Dining Room	6. Sauna/Lockers	11. Small Kitchen
2. Kitchen	7. Massage	12. Landscape Courtyard
3. Meeting Room	8. Dementia Kitchen	13. Hardscape Courtyard
4. Courtyard	9. Demenia Units	14. Therapy Pool
5. Living Room	10. Dementia DR/LR	

0' 20' 40' 60'

0M 10M 20M

Figure 8-84 Vigs Ängar is a one-story double-courtyard assisted living building: It consists of two 12-unit assisted living clusters with one 8-unit dementia cluster. The looped circulation system combines single- and double-loaded corridors. Following an anthroposophic architecture style, one courtyard is primarily landscaped and the other primarily paved. *Courtesy of Lillemor Husberg.*

cover to create views from units and the corridor. They believe everything "contributes to life" and therefore the design details matter and support the lifestyle and philosophy of living. Daylight, landscape, and water are highly valued elements.

The design is heavily influenced by the philosophy of Rudolph Steiner. The style, known as anthroposophic architecture, is well suited to housing for older people. Many characteristics typify this style but it appeals to the senses using natural materials, subtle color differences, and views of the grounds. Large windows mounted high and low invite light and connect the interior with the sky and the landscape. The building is clad with wood siding and stained a light reddish yellow.

Figure 8-85 **This courtyard contains a combination of paving, landscape, and a water feature:** The one-story scale, the gray wood cladding and the casual patio furniture create an inviting space. An earthen berm near the center of the courtyard subdivides the space into smaller, more intimate sitting areas. *Courtesy of Lillemor Husberg.*

Building Concept

Circulation weaves among the common spaces, including the courtyards, café/kitchen, therapy pool, and meeting room.[52] Lounges are often located in corners to give them dynamic views of courtyards. Inside corners are canted 45 degrees to improve views and facilitate wheelchair maneuvering. Double-loaded corridors receive natural light from clerestory windows. Colder colors are used in corridors and warmer colors in common spaces.

Large Meeting Room

A large square room is used to host events including a weekly exercise program that involves deep breathing. The room has a high ceiling with a few clerestory windows and a large round window. The volume at the top of the room is larger than at the base. The meeting room is linked to the entry courtyard, which provides daylight and access to the outside.

Anthroposophic Features

Various aspects of the Steiner philosophy show respect for individual and artistic thinking.[53] Large windows stretch from the ground plane to the ceiling and wrap around the perimeter to create winter garden spaces. Corner windows create panoramic views and capture different daylight conditions. Wood is used extensively for floors, exterior cladding, and items you touch like handrails, counters, and furniture. Simple light fixtures made from canvas and wood are used as pendant and sconce fixtures throughout the building. Glass mullions in doors and windows take on an uplifting shape splitting large sections of glass into smaller triangular and polygonal fields. Larger rooms are rectilinear but have walls that lean outward at the top with sloped ceilings. Pastel colors with subtle color differences are used for walls and ceilings. Three wood-burning fireplaces are positioned throughout the building. A pool, tub, and massage room is designed to reduce stress and create a quiet place for relaxation. Residents are also encouraged to keep dogs and cats as pets.

Figure 8-86 Meeting rooms with tall ceilings are used for stretching and deep breathing exercises in concert with the Rudolph Steiner philosophy of anthroposophy: Emphasis is placed on natural materials including wood for cladding, floors, and handrails. Windows are often placed high in a room and light fixtures are covered with canvas to soften their brightness. These rooms are shaped with angled corners and sloped walls that create a room geometry that is wider at the top of the room than at the base.

Figure 8-87 The 45-degree clipped corner of this courtyard is a shared lounge that overlooks the outdoors: The canvas light fixtures, the use of earth tones, the view of a paved outdoor area, and the operable windows give the space a connection to, as well as protection from, the outdoors.

Dementia Cluster

A small, secured dementia cluster for eight people is designed to embrace the anthroposophic aesthetic with wood floors, fabric light fixtures, a fireplace, a greenhouse-style window, and easy access to the courtyard. An informal "farmer's kitchen" with a central island and good views of the courtyard encourages dementia residents to participate in chopping vegetables for dinner. The kitchen island can be lowered for wheelchair participants.

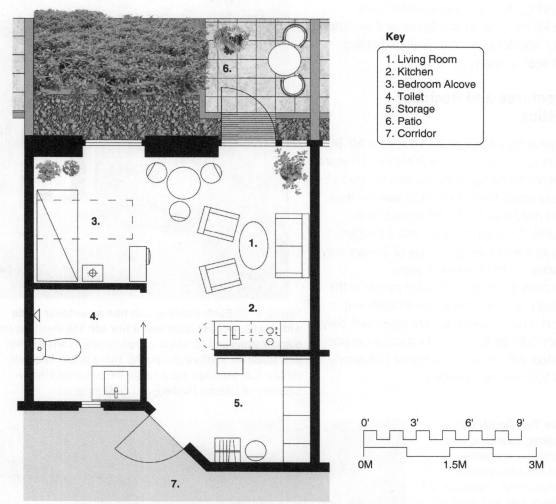

Key

1. Living Room
2. Kitchen
3. Bedroom Alcove
4. Toilet
5. Storage
6. Patio
7. Corridor

0'   3'   6'   9'

0M   1.5M   3M

Figure 8-88 The 400 SF dwelling unit contains a full kitchen, bed alcove, storage room, and patio: The compact galley kitchen contains a wood butcher-block counter and the bathroom has a continuous tile floor. The ceiling slopes from 8 feet at the outside perimeter to 12 feet near the entry to the unit. *Courtesy of Lillemor Husberg.*

Landscape Treatments

Lush plant materials are an important feature that contribute to its relaxed atmosphere. The two main courtyards are designed for residents to spend time outside when it is pleasant. Three units have patios that open onto one courtyard while the other patios surround the building's exterior perimeter. Every residential unit has access to a private patio that connects to a walking path surrounding the building.

Unit Designs

Single-occupancy dwelling units vary between 350 and 400 SF. There are also four larger 600 SF units designated for couples. Typically, a unit contains a living room, bathroom, bed alcove, entry space, storage room, and outdoor patio. The unit has a small galley kitchen with a refrigerator and a two-burner range. The end of the kitchen counter can flip up or down and is adjustable for wheelchair access. A sloped ceiling makes the unit appear larger.

Program Features and Resident Characteristics

The average age at Vigs Ängar is 86.5 (range is 60–98). The building was opened in 1995 but in the last 10 years has attracted more dementia residents. About a third of the residents use wheelchairs, a third can walk on their own, and a third need a walker to get around. There are 8 single males, 22 single females, and 2 couples (34 total). With an average length of stay of 3 years they lose approximately 10 residents each year.

They also provide services to 20 older people in the surrounding neighborhood through home health and meals on wheels. Four to five neighbors take lunch daily in the café. They sell various oils and massage creams that are consistent with the anthroposophic philosophy of stress reduction and aromatherapy.

Figure 8-89 **Each dwelling unit has an outdoor patio with a wide access door and a low sill:** The emphasis on outdoor views and access is complimented by small patios with space for furniture and plants. These patios frequently contain side plantings and a hedge for additional privacy. *Courtesy of Lillemor Husberg and Frida Rungren.*

Figure 8-90 **The Vigs Ängar pool is used for stretching, exercise, and relaxation:** The pool is considered an important part of the anthroposophic lifestyle, which also involves massage and aromatherapy. South light and views of the courtyard are facilitated by large glass window walls.
Courtesy of Lillemor Husberg.

Therapy Pool and Bath

The pool is open to residents as well as people from the community. It is used for relaxation, as well as stretching exercises. The bathtub is used by 26 residents twice a month. They believe the tub and pool help residents relax and thus have less need for medications and fewer sleep disturbances.

Noteworthy Features

1. It uses anthroposophic architecture to create a residential, natural setting.

2. Three courtyards offer views, outdoor access, and daylight to rooms and corridors.

3. Those with dementia and the physically frail are served in separate clusters.

4. Unit designs have large windows and access to a private patio.

5. Single- and double-loaded corridors weave the units and courtyards together.

6. Water, plants, and animals are an important part of the lifestyle.

7. Emphasis is on water and aromatherapy.

CASE STUDY SIXTEEN: Ulrika Eleonora Service House, Louviisa, Finland

Architect: L&M Sievänen Architects Ltd., Espoo, Finland

Ulrika is a small group home located in Louviisa, a rural coastal town near Helsinki. The building, opened in 2002 has 32 residents in single-occupancy units within four group clusters. There are two clusters for people with dementia (7 and 8 residents) and two for nursing residents (8 and 9 residents). They are in two single-story L-shaped buildings, where each wing shelters a small group cluster.[54]

Building Concept

Each configuration creates an outdoor patio where the two legs meet. The courtyard faces south with a view toward the town. Finland is known for its colorful wood architecture and it has been used here on the inside and outside, to give the building its residential character. The use of horizontal wood detailing is reminiscent of the work of Alvar Aalto. The building is sited on a hilly outcropping with a distinctive standing seam metal roof.

Common Spaces

The living and dining room furniture is scaled to resemble a large rural farmhouse with a galley kitchen on one side. Cabinets are stained wood and the kitchen dishwasher and oven are raised 12" for ease of access. Bold colors and horizontal wood panels differentiate the living, dining, and kitchen spaces. Even the sauna and laundry have wood ceilings. Residents sunbathe and eat outside in good weather. A porch partially shelters the area with a translucent roof. The corridor emphasizes distinctive unit entries by using translucent glass in side panels next to the door.

Key

1. Nursing Clusters (17 Units Total)
2. Dementia Clusters (15 Units Total)
3. Living Room
4. Kitchen
5. Dining Area
6. Patio
7. Courtyard & Garden
8. Back of House

0'   15'   30'   45'

0M   7.5M   15M

Figure 8-91 Ulrika Eleonora features two L-shaped wings wrapped around outdoor patios: This small town service house has 32 units that are subdivided into four clusters (two for dementia and two for skilled nursing). The rooms are single occupied and the groups of 7–9 residents are adjacent to a kitchen, dining, and living room. *Courtesy of L&M Sievänen Architects Ltd.*

Unit Design

Units are approximately 260 to 280 SF. A corner window allows residents to see outside while in bed. Residents bring their own furniture; however, some highly impaired individuals require hospital beds that can be raised or lowered. Units have high ceilings that slope from 8' to 12'. The nursing units have a sink and refrigerator with built-in shelving.

Figure 8-92 **The building's bright yellow wood siding fits into the surrounding neighborhood:** Located on a hill and nestled into the surrounding forest, it has commanding views of the surrounding hillside. Corner windows with low sill heights invite light into the units.
Courtesy of L&M Sievänen Architects Ltd.

Figure 8-93 **There are separate distinct entries to the dementia and nursing home components of Ulrika Eleonora:** The identity and special character of the building is reflected in its distinctive design. The influence of the modernist architect Alvar Aalto can be sensed in the bright pastel colors and the use of wood cladding.
Courtesy of L&M Sievänen Architects Ltd.

Figure 8-94 **Viewed from below, the building wraps around a central courtyard:** The sloped zinc roof, the indigenous colors that match adjacent residential housing, and the horizontal wood slats that define the corners add a modernist but residential touch to the building facade. *Courtesy of L&M Sievänen Architects Ltd.*

Resident Characteristics

Dementia residents spend most of their time in the common space, while nursing residents spend more time in their rooms. The average age of residents is 87. Seventeen residents have wheelchairs distributed 75% in the nursing wing and 20% in dementia. About 60% of residents have a dementia diagnosis.

Noteworthy Features

1. Its small scale and use of color allow the buildings to fit the surrounding context.

2. The two L-shaped buildings create courtyards with easy access to outdoors.

3. Four small clusters (two in dementia and two in nursing) fit nicely around a dining room table.

4. Both dementia and the physically frail are served in separate clusters.

5. Residential treatments and detailing create a friendly noninstitutional appearance.

6. Units are small but low corner windows bring in light and provide views from the bed.

CASE STUDY SEVENTEEN: Irismarken Nursing Center, Virum, Denmark

Architect: Rubow Arkitekter, Copenhagen, Denmark

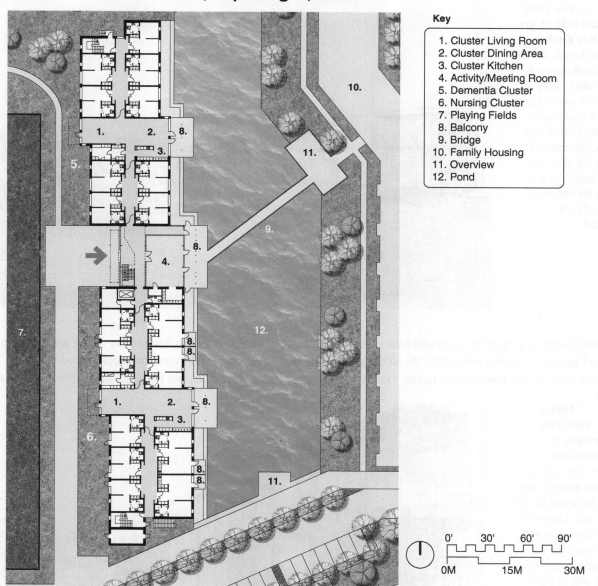

Key

1. Cluster Living Room
2. Cluster Dining Area
3. Cluster Kitchen
4. Activity/Meeting Room
5. Dementia Cluster
6. Nursing Cluster
7. Playing Fields
8. Balcony
9. Bridge
10. Family Housing
11. Overview
12. Pond

Figure 8-95 Irismarken is a thin two-story nursing home flanked by a lake and sports field on opposite sides: It contains 36 units split into four clusters of nine residents each (two dementia and two skilled nursing). Each cluster is subdivided with common space for a living room, dining room table, kitchen, and two balconies. *Courtesy of Rubow Arkitekter.*

Irismarken is a 36-unit two-story nursing and dementia care building opened in 2010 located in the Virumgaard neighborhood of Copenhagen. It is part of a larger development that includes three additional housing complexes. Irismarken is a thin, elegant building sandwiched between a picturesque pond on the east and an active playing field on the west. The pond is home to ducks and frogs and the field is used regularly by sport teams.

Building Concept

Units along both sides of the building have views. Located in the middle is an entry with an open stair and a large sloped, two-story meeting room for staff training and special resident activities. There is also a pedestrian bridge on the east that connects Irismarken to a regional kitchen on the other side of the pond.

Figure 8-96 **The pond on the east side of the building has ducks and frogs:** Large shared balconies that overlook the water are located at the center of each cluster. Materials include white stucco, black steel trim, and a zinc-colored roof. Offsets in the plan and attached balconies add variety to the massing. *Courtesy of Lars Bo Lindblad.*

Residents live in four clusters, each with nine units. At the center of each cluster is a living room, dining area, kitchen, and shared balcony. The nine units (420 SF) on the ground and first floors on the north are for people with dementia. They do not have private balconies or patios. However, the cluster has a shared balcony (or patio) facing the east and west.

Figure 8-97 **Large "clip-on" balconies create access to nature:** Balconies extend the view, add a substantive amenity, and increase the visual interest of the facade. Lower-floor balconies are wider and cantilever over the water. All four unit clusters have balconies and/or patios (on both sides) that link to common shared spaces. *Courtesy of Lars Bo Lindblad.*

The south portion of the building is intended for skilled nursing residents and has two unit sizes. Four units on each floor (8 total) with eastern lakeside views are designed for couples and have a separate bedroom and a full kitchen (650 SF). These have large balconies that cantilever over the water. The 10 units on the west side (five on the ground and five on the first floor) are 450 SF. The ground floor units on the west side have small patios, while the second floor units do not have balconies. Each nursing cluster on the south has a centrally located living room, dining room, kitchen, and shared balconies (east and west) on each floor. This shared space is where meals are served and activities are carried out. Living room seating is on the west side and a large table for meals and activities is on the east side. The kitchen is centrally located within an alcove.

Figure 8-98 **Dining tables overlook the pond with direct access to the balcony:** The common space cuts through the center of the plan, making light and view available in both directions. The lower 20 inches of the window glass is fritted to make the edge feel more secure.

Common Features and Services

A light breakfast is available in the morning and open-face sandwiches with soup are served in the evening. At noontime a warm meal from the main kitchen is delivered. The computer system is shared among the nurses, the assistant nurses, and the care staff. Everyone can read what is written about each resident but only the nurses can comment on meds and communicate directly with doctors.

Danish care facilities have a strong emphasis on exercise and physiotherapy. A group of six to seven residents walk for exercise every week. Families and volunteers also walk with residents. Physical therapy equipment is available in public corridors to encourage use. They are exploring new ideas including a special bathing chair, lighting that leads from the bed to the bathroom at night, a WanderGuard system, and mats installed at the side of the bed to monitor movement at night.

Figure 8-99

A multipurpose room for group meetings, near the center of the building, is adjacent to the main entry: A bridge connects Irismarken with the central kitchen and additional activity and support spaces on the other side of the pond. This one-story sloped ceiling space is located between the dementia and skilled nursing clusters.

Unit Design

The couples' units have a full kitchen, while smaller units have only a tea kitchen (cabinets and a sink). Residents in the smaller units often bring in a refrigerator and/or microwave. A bed is provided but residents bring in the rest of the furniture, including their favorite light fixture.

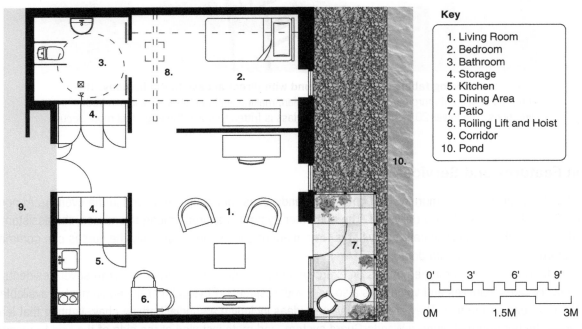

Key

1. Living Room
2. Bedroom
3. Bathroom
4. Storage
5. Kitchen
6. Dining Area
7. Patio
8. Roiling Lift and Hoist
9. Corridor
10. Pond

Figure 8-100 Units for couples that measure 650 square feet are large: Eight larger units are located in skilled nursing with balconies that overlook the lake. They feature a full kitchen and a rolling lift to move residents. Flexibility and the perception of space is enhanced by using a cased opening between the living room and bedroom. *Courtesy of Rubow Arkitekter.*

There is no door that separates the bedroom from the living room. The cased opening is 48" wide and adds flexibility. Bathroom fixtures are located on three walls in a room with a continuous tile floor. Bathroom doors are double sliders. The floors are wood grain and look residential and the ceiling heights are 10 feet. The windows in the bedroom are narrow but are eight feet in height. The mullion is low enough to view outside from the bed.

Resident Issues and Characteristics

The 36 units with 8 couples' units can theoretically support 44 residents, but because there are only two couples, the total population today is 38. There are 3 single males and 31 single females. This is a very frail population, with an average age of 87 and an age range between 70 and 97. About half use a wheelchair to get around and about 20% are dependent on the ceiling-mounted lift. The remainder use a walker or cane to ambulate. Almost everyone has some help with toileting and bathing. They help 10 people with eating but currently have no residents with a gastric tube. Ten residents have no indication of dementia, but the remainder (28 residents) are split between severe and medium-level memory impairment. Four people use a GPS tracker provided by a city agency. Ten residents self-manage incontinence but need reminders. Last year 10 people died (25% turnover). Only five people have no family. The remainder are evenly split between those who see their family more than once a week and those who see them once a month.

Figure 8-101 **Units contain a space for a separate bedroom and living room:** Enough space is available in the living room to comfortably place a couch, a table, and breakfront, which can be filled with meaningful possessions. Large windows enhance the light entering the unit with a view of the play field below.

Noteworthy Features

1. The building is located between a pond and play field with active views on both sides.

2. The thin building has good light penetration with offset corridors to mitigate its perceived length.

3. There are two dementia clusters (north) and two nursing clusters (south) with 9 residents each.

4. All residents share a common meeting room in the center of the building.

5. Each cluster has a dining and living room, a kitchen, and two balconies (or patios).

6. Eight units in the nursing clusters (out of 18) are for couples (650 SF).

7. Residents are encouraged to participate in physical therapy and to walk for exercise.

Architects: Mithūn Architects, Seattle, Washington

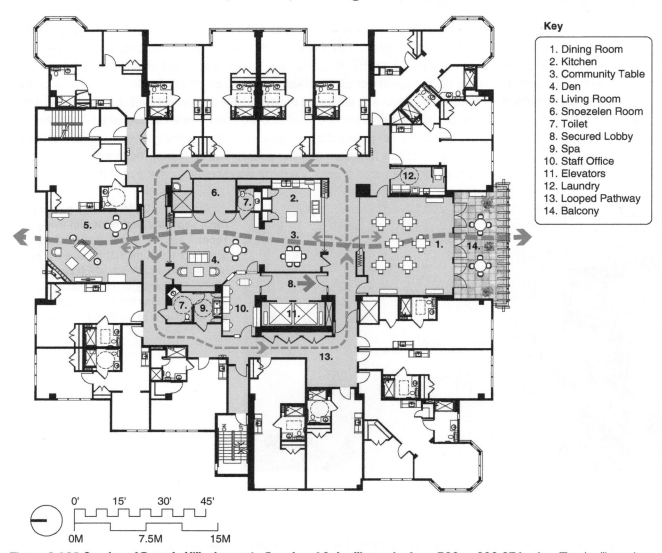

Key

1. Dining Room
2. Kitchen
3. Community Table
4. Den
5. Living Room
6. Snoezelen Room
7. Toilet
8. Secured Lobby
9. Spa
10. Staff Office
11. Elevators
12. Laundry
13. Looped Pathway
14. Balcony

Figure 8-102 Sunrise of Beverly Hills dementia floor has 16 dwelling units from 500 to 800 SF in size: The dwelling units surround the perimeter of the square building with shared spaces creating a north/south axis in the middle of the building that receives daylight and natural ventilation from both sides (green ribbon). A looped circulation pathway (red) keeps residents from getting lost. *Courtesy of Mithūn Architects and Sunrise Senior Living.*

This five-story, 80-unit assisted living building was opened in the "golden triangle" of Beverly Hills in 2005. The dementia care cluster, located on the fourth floor, contains 16 dwelling units. Three unit types range in size from 500 SF (single) to 800 SF (one bedroom). Residents at the beginning stages of the disease typically live in assisted living. Later as the disease progresses to a medium or severe stage, they typically move to a smaller secured dementia unit. This building design is often referred to as a "home within a home." The dementia unit operates independently, hiring dementia trained staff and offering features that support this population.

Figure 8-103 **Sunrise is a five-story urban building:** The fourth floor is the secured dementia cluster with a south-facing terrace. The ground floor has patio seating adjacent to the street that opens onto the dining and living rooms. Wide and tall windows some with clerestories, flood dwelling units with natural light.
Courtesy of Sunrise Senior Living.

Building Concept

This dementia cluster is characterized by relatively large units, a looped pathway for unit access, and a series of shared common spaces in the center of the plan.

These spaces arrayed in an open plan, support various activities including an outdoor patio, dining room, kitchen table, activity/den, living room, and a Snoezelen room (for sensory stimulation and quiet retreat). The floor is secured at the elevator lobby with a key code monitored by a staff office on the north side of the elevator lobby. A window and door between the elevator lobby and the office allow visitors to make contact with the staff. A spa/bather, laundry room, and toilets are arrayed along the looped corridor.

This sponsor is known for their interest in Dutch ideas and concepts. They are committed to the Dutch op maat philosophy of scheduling the resident's day around their needs and interests rather than dictating meal times and bathing around the staff's schedule. They also have adopted a system of "designated caregivers" that pairs residents with specific individuals who know them well and can cater to their interests, needs, and preferences. When you enter the floor, wall-mounted photos identify the staff by name to facilitate communication with visitors and family members.

(a)   (b)

Figure 8-104a-b **The dementia floor dining room has access to a south-facing patio for light and ventilation:** Residents can take a meal outside or relax during the day. Dining room tables vary in size and residents are served restaurant style. Place settings feature contrasting colors for easy recognition.

Common Spaces

The large-size units and generous common space mean that residents have a choice to stay in their units or spend time together in common spaces. These areas are for various activities and are visible and accessible. This allows residents to see one another and identify activities that might be of interest. The dementia unit, which utilizes the entire fourth floor, has a south-facing balcony terrace and two elevators that connect to the ground floor. Dementia residents are encouraged to take walks in the pedestrian-friendly Beverly Hills commercial district with staff members, volunteers, or relatives. The surrounding neighborhood is relatively flat, with interesting window shopping opportunities.

A large table is integrated with the kitchen, and is a popular place for residents to start their morning with coffee or to socialize during the day. The close proximity to the secured entry allows residents to greet visitors as they enter and exit the floor. Food prepared in the first-floor kitchen is brought to the floor in bulk containers, plated, and served in the dining room.

Figure 8-105 **A living room is on the north end of the central axis:** Flexible soft furniture in small group clusters allow several activities to take place at the same time in this room. This room is accessible from the looped circulation pathway.
Courtesy of Martha Child Interiors and Jerry Staley Photography.

Resident Units and Characteristics

The memory care unit allows assisted living residents whose dementia diagnosis has progressed to benefit from the programs and services available here. In addition to being large (by dementia standards), the rooms also have tall 9' ceilings, low 24" sill heights, and tall 6' windows. Two of the larger units have a four-piece bathroom that includes an easy-access tub. The looped circulation pathway makes it easy for residents to find their way to the major shared spaces and avoid getting lost. If they walk far enough they will encounter all four shared spaces and return to their own unit entry door.

Residents average 80 years of age. Only about 20% need a wheelchair to get around and the majority of residents are classified with severe dementia.

Noteworthy Features

1. The "Home within a home" memory care cluster is on the fourth floor of an assisted living building.

2. The Beverly Hills central location facilitates walking, window shopping, and exercise.

3. The looped circulation plan minimizes confusion by directly connecting units to shared spaces.

4. The central open plan allows residents to see and sample most ongoing activities.

5. The three dwelling unit types are large, with spacious windows that have low sill heights.

6. The unit operates on a Dutch op maat schedule with designated caregivers.

Architects: Tegnestuen Vandkunsten, Kobenhaven, Denmark

Figure 8-106 **Egebakken has 29 units along four streets with a commons building inserted between two of the streets:** Located on a 6-acre site, it is sandwiched between an oak forest on the north side and Lake Esrum on the south. The units are attached but have periodic breaks to facilitate walking pathways.
Courtesy of Oakhill (Egebakken) and Tegnestuen Vandkunsten.

Egebakken, also known as Oakhill, is an equity-based co-housing project with 29 one-story units.[55] Opened in 2005, it is in the small town of Nobedo, 28 miles north of Copenhagen. The 6-acre site has a view of Lake Esrum toward the south (the largest lake in Denmark) and is adjacent to a mature oak forest used for walking and exercise. The subdivision plan is simple and consists of four streets with linear attached units parallel to each street. A 1600 SF common building, named the "telescope" because of its unusual shape, is located at the entrance to the site, within easy walking distance of the residences.

Figure 8-107 **A 1600 SF common building greets you at the entry to the site:** A kitchen, library, exercise equipment, tables, and soft seating are available for shared community events. The forest preserve has walking trails that connect to the north edge of the site.

Although co-housing does not provide personal care assistance for residents, the Danish home care system makes it possible for older frail people to age in place in their unit by providing them home care assistance (including personal care as well as health care). This is more effective in a context where established informal friendships between residents often provide supplemental care and social opportunities. Policy makers believe strong friendship networks will be necessary to supplement formal services provided by all care systems in the future.

Figure 8-108 **The front of the unit accommodates an entry, carport, and laundry room:** Stained gray larch siding, a zinc standing seam shed roof, and a matching gray-brown brick are the exterior materials. Clerestory windows light the utility room and highly placed punched windows provide light for the kitchen and living room.

Unit Design

A simple but uniform massing vocabulary is shared throughout the housing. The main volume is an extruded trapezoidal shape that measures 35' to 50' in length and accommodates shared spaces. The roof slopes from 14'6" to 11'. Clerestory windows strategically placed on the highest walls allow light to filter into spaces below. This space is subdivided based on the interests and needs of each resident. Some have created a large kitchen, dining area, living room, and den. Others have an open plan with glass partitions that demarcate separate rooms.

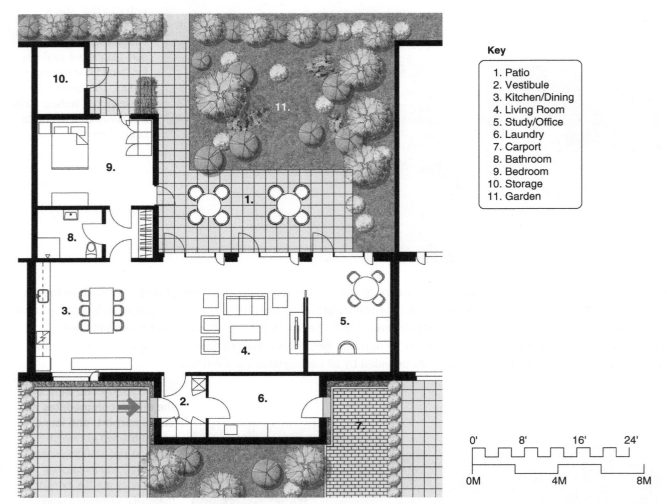

Key

1. Patio
2. Vestibule
3. Kitchen/Dining
4. Living Room
5. Study/Office
6. Laundry
7. Carport
8. Bathroom
9. Bedroom
10. Storage
11. Garden

Figure 8-109 **The 1450 SF L-shaped unit consists of an extruded shared space and a bedroom wing:** A private outdoor patio and garden is created at the rear of the parcel. The building is placed close to the street with a carport, entry, and utility space. *Courtesy of Oakhill (Egebakken) and Tegnestuen Vandkunsten.*

Each dwelling is an L-shaped configuration with bathrooms and bedrooms forming a shorter perpendicular leg in the rear overlooking a garden. Bathrooms are modern and adaptable and bedrooms have lower, intimately scaled ceilings. Four units are 1000 SF, 16 units are 1250 SF, and 9 units are 1450 SF. "Clip on" additions to the large volume include a winter garden, storage space, and extra bedrooms and bathrooms.

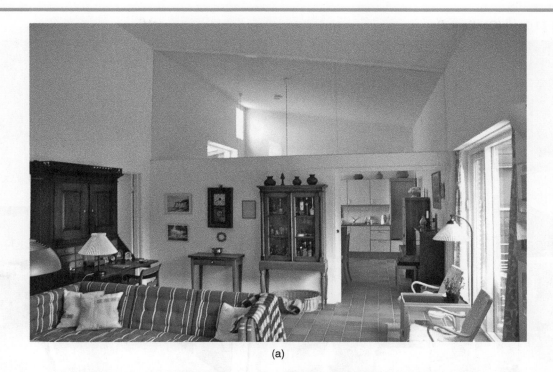

(a)

(b)

Figure 8-110a–d The long trapezoidal open plan has flexibility and can be subdivided: The tall wall is 14'6" and the shorter wall is 11'. High windows are placed on both sides. This illustrates four layouts that contain an office, a display case for antiquities, a study, a corner kitchen, a kitchen table, and a living room area.

Figure 8-110a–d **(Continued)**

(c)

(d)

The houses are compact but are planned on a generous site with plenty of open space. The palette of materials include 1) dark brown clinker brick, 2) a gray Siberian larch siding, and 3) a zinc roof. The site has an extensive sidewalk system and trails that lead into the adjacent forest. Large grasscrete areas parallel to the street provide additional parking when needed.

Residents and Philosophy

Oakhill consists of like-minded people in the same stage of life. They are mostly active empty nesters. Residents are especially interested in neighbors who value individual freedom but also desire to be part of a close community of friends and colleagues. This approach characterizes many new co-housing projects where residents have numerous competing affiliations. Of the 53 residents in the 29 houses, 80% are couples (25 couples and 4 single females) and 40% are still working. The age range is 53 to 80, with an average age of between 65 and 70. Although relatively young, they are all committed to the idea of aging in place cooperatively.

Services and Activities

The common house is the hub of social life for Oakhill. The unusually shaped building has window walls on the south and north. The south entrance with a ceiling height of 8' expands to nearly 20' on the north end, which overlooks the adjacent forest. Each unit allocated 55 SF to create the 1600 SF shared building, which has a kitchen, library, reading space, tables for snacks, and a multipurpose open area. Activities include bridge, billiards, table tennis, a reading circle, lectures, concerts, wine tasting, and gymnastics. The common building accommodates everyone for a monthly dinner. A committee of five coordinates the use of the common house. All activities are based on the initiative of residents themselves. Everyone pays dues for operation and maintenance of the common facilities, but participation in activities is voluntary.

Noteworthy Features

1. The owner-occupied co-housing project is located north of Copenhagen in Nobedo.

2. It is adjacent to an oak forest with trails and overlooks the largest lake in Denmark.

3. Units are well designed from a kit of parts with customized flexibility.

4. The common house accommodates meals, exercise, meetings, and socializing.

5. Danish home care service delivery makes it possible for residents to age in place.

6. Co-housing is common in Denmark and facilitates informal support networks between residents.

CASE STUDY TWENTY: Willson Hospice, Albany, Georgia

Architects: Perkins and Will, Architects, Atlanta, Georgia

Hospice environments for end-of-life care are often superior to nursing home settings. In addition to having smaller size unit clusters, they are also more family centered. They frequently embrace nature and provide spaces for meaningful activities and behaviors. Environments are often residential in character with staff that are kind and supportive. The Willson Hospice is an exemplar in almost all categories.[56]

Opened in 2010, it is part of a larger caregiver network that includes home care workers. They serve more than 150 people a month in southern Georgia. The residential units at Willson are targeted toward families seeking respite and residents with complex care requirements or no family support.

Building and Site Context

The building, located on 14 acres of a large 210-acre rural preserve, connects the residents, visitors, and staff with this extraordinary natural landscape. This regional amenity is open to everyone in the surrounding area. It is an award-winning Audubon sanctuary with continuous pathways that weave human activity with the local ecology of birds, deer, and plants. Tranquility gardens and patios serve each of three residential clusters with shade protected outdoor spaces. The site contains walking trails, observation platforms, and gardens, which range from intimate to park-like in scale.

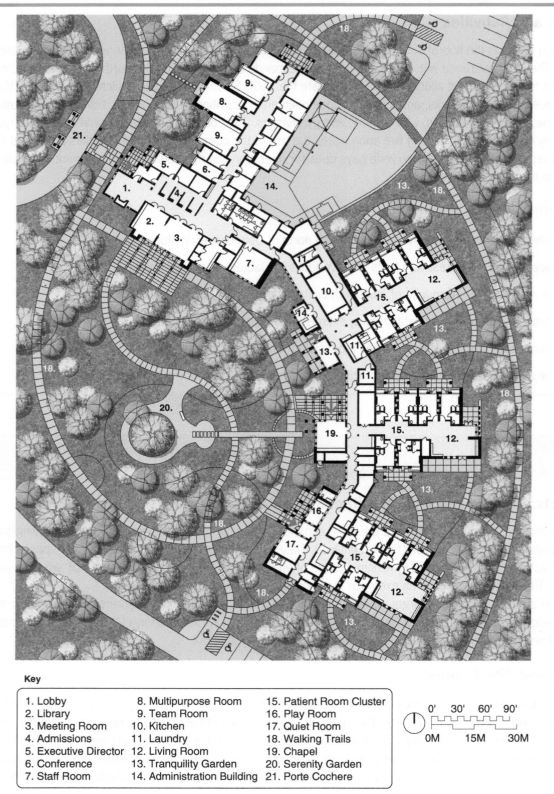

Key

1. Lobby	8. Multipurpose Room	15. Patient Room Cluster
2. Library	9. Team Room	16. Play Room
3. Meeting Room	10. Kitchen	17. Quiet Room
4. Admissions	11. Laundry	18. Walking Trails
5. Executive Director	12. Living Room	19. Chapel
6. Conference	13. Tranquility Garden	20. Serenity Garden
7. Staff Room	14. Administration Building	21. Porte Cochere

Figure 8-111 The Willson Hospice is located on a 14-acre site and is part of a wildlife sanctuary: It consists of three six-unit residential clusters connected by a curved corridor to a main entry building. Each unit shares access to a nearby living room. Dedicated rooms for worship and children's play are shared with families. *Courtesy of Perkins+Will.*

The administrative building located near the entrance to the site welcomes visitors and provides staff with office space, meeting areas, and a library. Residential units are clustered in three buildings and connected via a curved enclosed corridor. Along the corridor from the administration building to each cluster are rooms for music/contemplation, children's play, family food preparation, and worship.[57]

Residential Clusters

Each cluster has six dwelling units and an 800 SF family room, with wooden tables, soft seating, a reading inglenook, and a children's play space. With large windows, beautiful views of the surrounding landscape, and access to outdoor gardens, it is located close to resident rooms. The use of natural wood, cork, and stone makes the interiors familiar, inviting, and authentic.

Resident Rooms

The small single-occupancy residential units measure 250 SF. During the planning process a full-size mock-up of a resident room was used to test the placement of

Figure 8-114 **Each cluster has a pavilion-like living room with soft seating, tables, and play spaces:** The use of heavy timber framing in conjunction with glass panels creates excellent daylighting. The 800 SF room has a variety of small spaces and alcoves for a range of different activities. *Courtesy of Jim Roof Creative.*

furniture and equipment. Reading lamps attached to the bed allow it to be moved throughout the room and even outside on the private patio. Residents take their meals here with an over-the-bed table.

Corner windows with views of the surrounding landscape are outfitted with blackout curtains to facilitate sleep. Specially designed wide window seats are large enough to accommodate the 90% of visitors who spend the night. Shelves are available to personalize the place with photos and memorable objects. However, the average length of stay, which varies from 3 to 5 days, doesn't lend itself to a high level of personalization. They are currently exploring the addition of a long-stay cluster that could shelter participants for 6 months, the maximum stay allowed under Medicare.

Residents and Programs

Activities are customized based on their energy level and interests. Most participants are bedbound or wheelchair bound and often experience physical discomfort. More than 75 volunteers read, talk, share their pets, or walk in the gardens with residents. Because of the short end-of-life stay, family members are often present. One reason individuals come here is to spend the time they have left with family members. Facilities like the shared kitchen, chapel, and kids play space allow families to spend time with their loved ones.

The hospice is a powerful model to examine because of its emphasis on living the remaining days of a person's life in a meaningful, positive way. There is much to be admired about how the setting is conceptualized around consequential and joyful resident needs and experiences. It makes you ponder why this caregiving approach hasn't been extended to nursing homes. Even though the emotional commitments of staff are intense, they have an extremely low 5% annual turnover rate. Willson is open to all income groups but finds that, because of its primarily cancer-oriented older clientele (80% are over 65), most participants are covered under Medicare.

Figure 8-115 **Although small, the units are rich in materials, textures, and features:** A wide and deep window seat is available for overnight stays. The resident bed is flexible and can be moved throughout the room as well as outside through a wide door. Thick curtains can be drawn to darken the room when needed.
Courtesy of Jim Roof Creative.

Noteworthy Features

1. Willson is adjacent to a beautifully landscaped Audubon park with walking pathways.

2. It has 18 units in three residential clusters that each contain a shared living room.

3. The living room is used primarily for reading and socializing.

4. Each single unit has access to a private patio with a bed that can be moved.

5. An oversized window seat/bed serves the overnight stay needs of friends or family.

6. Residential materials like wood and stone give it a noninstitutional character.

7. Activities rely on volunteers who are creative, accommodating, and kind.

CASE STUDY TWENTY-ONE: Musholm Bugt Feriecenter, Korsør, Denmark

Architects: AART Architects, Aarhus, Denmark

The Danes love their summers, and a cherished memory of summertime is going to the beach. Dozens of vacation villages dot the periphery of Denmark's three island land masses. The concept of a vacation is a standard offering of nursing homes and service houses in Scandinavia during the summer. Unlike US resorts, where a few units are set aside for the handicapped, Denmark has dedicated resorts with the latest accessibility equipment. They are not just for older people, but welcome a range of ages and disabilities.[58]

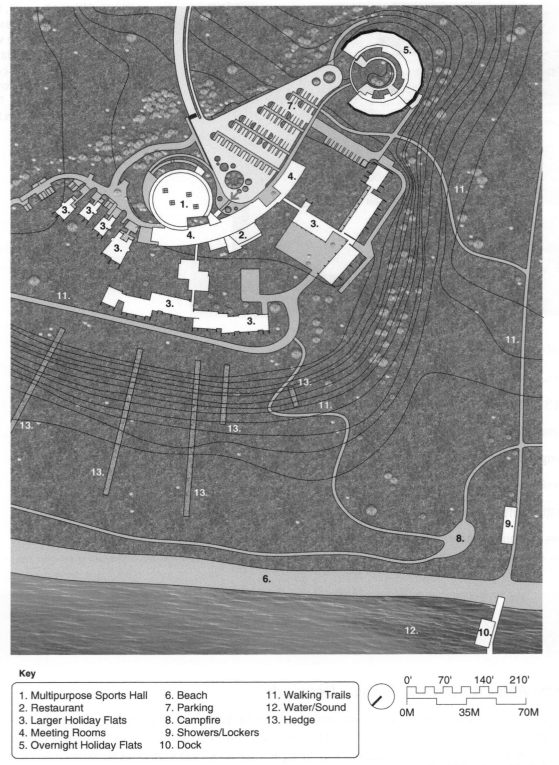

Key

1. Multipurpose Sports Hall
2. Restaurant
3. Larger Holiday Flats
4. Meeting Rooms
5. Overnight Holiday Flats

6. Beach
7. Parking
8. Campfire
9. Showers/Lockers
10. Dock

11. Walking Trails
12. Water/Sound
13. Hedge

0' 70' 140' 210'
0M 35M 70M

Figure 8-116 Vacation villages for the disabled are common in Denmark: The 172 units at Musholm are designed to be used by handicapped and frail people. A beach, a dock, and a network of walking paths, as well as a restaurant and recreational activities, are available here for all ages.
Courtesy of AART Architects.

Figure 8-117 Musholm combines four important themes—art, architecture, ecology, and accessibility: The site is located within 500 feet of the water's edge and overlooks the Great Belt Bridge. The site is a natural, non-manicured landscape with units that contain 14-foot skylights with commissioned artistic murals.
Courtesy of Jens Markus Lindhe, Photographer and AART Architects.

Building Concept

Musholm has an extraordinary site 500 meters from the beach with a long view of Musholm Bay, the Great Belt Bridge, and the sound between Funen and Zealand. The focus is on accessibility, art, architecture, and ecology. Sixteen of the bathrooms have 14-foot tall skylights with commissioned artistic murals. A recent addition added a large round building that can be used as a lecture space, concert hall, or sports venue. There are lots of active outdoor sports for families and older people, including bonfires, ball games, swings, sandboxes, fishing, nature interpretation, and walks. The exterior cladding materials are cedar and concrete, which blend seamlessly into the natural landscape.

Figure 8-118 A restaurant with a sloped wood ceiling is open to guests: Although many of the accommodations include their own food preparation space, some of the hotel-type suites rely on a centrally located dining room, which is sited to overlook the grounds and the water.

Accommodations

The village dates from 1996 and includes a total of 172 beds subdivided into 33 houses/units and 24 hotel-type suites. The accommodations vary from 325 SF to 2500 SF. The average size is approximately 475 SF. Most units are designed to accommodate groups of 4 to 10 people, including handicapped guests in wheelchairs. Some units have full kitchens, while the suites are smaller and similar to hotel rooms. The prime constituency is families with disabled children or older relatives. The rooms are outfitted with special features such as overhead lift devices, beds with side rails, keyless locks, handicapped-style bathroom fixtures, and electronically controlled curtains. They cater to group housing arrangements like service houses, nursing homes, and housing for the developmentally disabled.

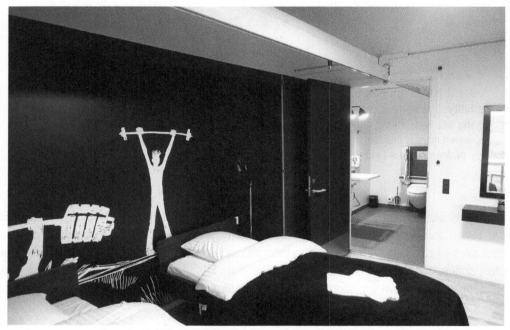

Figure 8-119 **Units for 3–7 day stays have a range of handicapped features:** Ceiling lifts move guests from their beds to the adjacent bathroom. The bathroom contains a European continuous tile floor, a cantilevered moveable sink, a toilet with built-in grab bars, a roll-in shower, and a continuous clerestory window.

Noteworthy Features

1. The Musholm vacation village is sponsored by the Muscular Dystrophy Association.

2. The village showcases art and architecture in a setting for the disabled.

3. It is located near the Zealand coast and has a pier with a range of activities.

4. Vacation groups of residents and caregivers stay 3 to 5 days during good weather.

Endnotes

1 Andersson, J.E. (2014), Residents Are at the Center of Good Architecture for Dementia Housing: A Historical Perspective, Power-point lecture, https://www.divaportal.org/smash/get/diva2:775831/FULLTEXT01.pdf (accessed 10/7/17).

2 Fich, M., Mortensen, P.D., and Zahle, K. (1995), *Old People's Houses: An Architectural Guide to Housing for the Elderly in Greater Copenhagen*, Kunstakademiets Arkitektskole, Copenhagen.

3 Rosenfeld, L.P., and Chapman, W. (2006), *Home Design in an Aging World*, Fairchild Books, New York.

4 Regnier, V. (1994), *Assisted Living Housing for the Elderly: Design Innovations from the United States and Europe*, John Wiley & Sons, Hoboken NJ.

5 Mens, N., and Wagenaar, C. (2010), *Health Care Architecture in the Netherlands*, Nai Publishers, Rotterdam.

6 Humanitas/Over(view) (2017), http://www.stichtinghumanitas.nl/home/homepage/over-humanitas (accessed 10/7/17).

7 Although rewritten, reorganized, and reformatted; much of the "AFL Eight Core Components and Characteristics" was paraphrased from the writings and presentations of Hans Becker as represented in *Levenskunst op Leeftijd* (2006), Eburon Academic Press, Delft.

8 Peterson, C., Maier, S., and Seligman, M. (1995), *Learned Helplessness: A Theory for the Age of Personal Control*, Oxford University Press, New York.

9 Becker, H. (n.d.), The Humanitas Foundation in a Nutshell, http://artandaging.net/kaken/append1humanitasnutshell.htm (accessed 10/7/17).

10 Becker, H. (2006), *Levenskunst op Leeftijd*, Eburon Academic Press, Delft.

11 Becker, H. (2012), *A Taste of Good Living: The Senior Citizen's Restaurant*, Euburon Academic Press, Delft.

12 Reed, C. (2015), Dutch Nursing Home Offers Rent-free Housing to Students, PBS Newshour (April 5), http://www.pbs.org/newshour/rundown/dutch-retirement-home-offers-rent-free-housing-students-one-condition (accessed 10/17/17).

13 Zarem, J. (2010), *Today's Continuing Care Retirement Community*, American Association of Homes and Services for the Aging (AASHA), Washington DC.

14 Ibid.

15 AARP, Caregiving Resource Center (2010), About Continuing Care Retirement Communities, http://www.aarp.org/relationships/caregiving-resource-center/info-09-2010/ho_continuing_care_retirement_communities.html (accessed 10/7/17).

16 US Government Accountability Office (2010), Older Americans: Continuing Care Retirement Communities Can Provide Benefits but Not Without Some Risks, http://www.gao.gov/products/GAO-10-611 (accessed 7/10/17).

17 Wasik, J. (2016), The Everything-in-One Promise of a Continuing Care Community, *New York Times*, (February 26), https://www.nytimes.com/2016/02/27/your-money/the-everything-in-one-promise-of-a-continuing-care-community.html (accessed 10/26/17).

18 Zarem, *Today's Continuing Care Retirement Community*.

19 Regnier, V. (2002), *Design for Assisted Living: Guidelines for Housing the Physically and Mentally Frail*, John Wiley & Sons, Hoboken NJ.

20 Mens, N., and Wagenaar, C. (2010), *Health Care Architecture in the Netherlands*, Nai Publishers, Rotterdam.

21 Anderzhon, J., Hughes, D., Judd, S., Kiyota, E., and Wijnties, M. (2012), *Design for Aging: International Case Studies of Building and Program*, John Wiley & Sons, Hoboken, NJ.

22 Mens and Wagenaar, *Health Care Architecture in the Netherlands*.

23 Ibid.

24 AIA Design for Aging Knowledge Community (2008), *Design for Aging Review*, 9th ed., Images Publishing Group, Australia.

25 Perkins Eastman (2013), *Senior Living*, 2nd ed., John Wiley & Sons, Hoboken, NJ.

26 AIA Design for Aging Knowledge Community (2011), *Design for Aging Review*, 10th ed. Images Publishing Group, Australia.

27 Jewish Community Housing for the Elderly Blog (2012), Humanitas in Rotterdam Offers Extension of the JCHE Model (May 2), http://www.jche.org/insight-reader/items/humanitas-in-rotterdam-offers-extension-of-jche-model-397.shtml (accessed 10/26/17).

28 NewBridge on the Charles: Hebrew Senior Life (2017), Welcome to NewBridge on the Charles, http://www.hebrewseniorlife.org/newbridge (accessed 10/7/17).

29 American Institute for Architects (1997), *Design for Aging Review, 1996-7 Review*, AIA Press, Washington DC.

30 Fich, M., Mortensen, P.D., and Zahle, K. (1995), *Old People's Houses: An Architectural Guide to Housing for the Elderly in Greater Copenhagen*, Kunstakademiets Arkitektskole, Copenhagen.

31 Pioneer Network (2017), Pioneers in Culture Change and Person-Directed Care, https://www.pioneernetwork.net/about-us/overview/ (accessed 10/7/17).

32 Thomas, W. (1996), *Life Worth Living: How Someone You Love Can Still Enjoy Life in a Nursing Home*, VanderWyk and Burnham, Acton, MA.

33 Thomas, W. (2007), *What Are Older People For?* VanderWyk and Burnham, Acton, MA.

34 Alexander, C., Ishikawa, S., and Silverstein, M. (1977), *A Pattern Language: Towns, Buildings, Construction*, Oxford University Press, New York.

35 Brawley, E. (2006), *Design Innovations for Aging and Alzheimer's*, John Wiley & Sons, Hoboken, NJ.

36 Thomas, *What Are Older People For?*

37 Anderzhon et al., *Design for Aging.*

38 The Green House Project (2017), http://www.thegreenhouseproject.org (accessed 10/15/17).

39 AIA Design for Aging Knowledge Community (2011), *Design for Aging Review: 10th Edition*, Images Publishing Group, Australia, 158–63.

40 Guide Book for Transforming Long-term Care, (2010), http://blog.thegreenhouseproject.org/wp-content/uploads/2011/12/THE-GREEN-HOUSE-Project-Guide-Book_April_100413.pdf (includes research outcomes 2003 and 2009), (accessed 10/15/17).

41 Rabig, J., Thomas, W., Kane, R., Cutler, L., and McAlilly, S. (2006), Radical Redesign of Nursing Homes: Applying the Green House Concept in Tupelo, Mississippi, *Gerontologist.* (46)4, 533–539.

42 Mt San Antonio Gardens (2016), Evergreen Villas: A Revolutionary Alternative to Traditional Skilled Nursing Care, http://www.msagardens.org/evergreen-villas/, (accessed 10/15/17).

43 Anderzhon et al., *Design for Aging,*

44 The New Jewish Home: The Living Center of Manhattan (2017), A Green House Grows in Manhattan, http://jewishhome.org/innovation/the-living-center-greenhouse/, (accessed 10/15/17).

45 Mens, N., and Wagenaar, C. (2010), *Health Care Architecture in the Netherlands*, Nai Publishers, Rotterdam.

46 Anderzhon et al. *Design for Aging.*

47 Planos, J. (2014), The Dutch Village Where Everyone Has Dementia, *Atlantic*, (Nov 14), http://www.theatlantic.com/health/archive/2014/11/the-dutch-village-where-everyone-has-dementia/382195/ (accessed 10/15/17).

48 Tagliabue, J. (2012), Taking on Dementia with the Experiences of Normal Life, *New York Times* (April 24), http://www.nytimes.com/2012/04/25/world/europe/netherlands-hogewey-offers-normal-life-to-dementia-patients.html?_r=0 (accessed 10/15/17).

49 Glass, A. (2014), Innovative Seniors Housing and Care Models: What We Can Learn from the Netherlands, *Senior Housing and Care Journal*, 22(1), 74–81.

50 CNN's World's Untold Stories (2013), Dementia Village, video (July 30), https://www.youtube.com/watch?v=LwiOBlyWpko (accessed 10/15/17).

51 Husberg, L., and Ovesen, L. (2007), *Gammal Och Fri (Om Vigs Angar)*, Vigs Angar, Simrishamn, SW.

52 Feddersen, E., and Ludtke, I. (2009), *A Design Manual: Living for the Elderly*, Birkhauser Verlag AG, Basel, Switzerland, 206–7.

53 Coates, G. (1997), *Erik Asmussen, Architect*, Byggforlaget, Stockholm.

54 Feddersen, E., and Ludtke, I. (2009), *A Design Manual: Living for the Elderly*, Birkhauser Verlag AG, Basel, Switzerland, 210–13.

55 Egebakken: An active community of friends (n.d), http://egebakken.dk/english.aspx (accessed 10/10/17).

56 AIA Design for Aging Center (2012), *Design for Aging Review*, 11th ed., Images Publishing Group, Australia, 58–67.

57 Perkins+Will (2017), Willson Hospice House, Albany, Georgia, http://perkinswill.com/work/willson hosp-hospice-house.html (accessed 10/15/17).

58 Musholm: Ferie, Sport and Conference (2017), http://www.musholm.dk (accessed 10/15/17).

CHAPTER NINE

Programs that Encourage Staying at Home with Service Assistance

PURPOSE-BUILT age-restricted housing that provides help and assistance to the frail, like the examples outlined in Chapter 8, work for many because they provide support at the margin of need. But for individuals with families who are able to help or older people who insist on staying at home for as long as possible, there are many more programs today than were available five years ago. The following briefly describes nine programs that have sought to provide an alternative to conventional group living arrangements. These programs make physical modifications to the environment, deliver personal care and transportation assistance to the home, or involve strategies that make it easier for family members to lend a helping hand. These types of programs are multiplying and are becoming more effective through high-tech communications innovations.

One: Home Modification Programs

Physical home modifications allow older people to age in place with greater safety and accessibility. This is especially important for individuals who are wheelchair bound.

Home modifications are important but need to be considered in conjunction with service assistance to be truly comprehensive. Getting the environment right is important but it is only half of the solution.

THREE LEVELS OF INTERVENTION

There are generally three scales that define home modifications[1]:

1. **Changes to the building**

2. **Installation of special equipment and furnishings**

3. **Changing behaviors**

Changes to the Building

These are disruptive, expensive, and are often treated as a last resort. They include items like replacing the tub with a shower, creating an accessible door to the bathroom, or adding a ramp to replace stairs in front of the house.

Figure 9-1 **Two-story homes like this one in Los Angeles constructed 75 years ago are difficult to adapt:** The bedrooms are on the top floor, the ground floor is constructed on three levels, the bathroom doors are narrow, and kitchen storage requires a step stool or stooping to access.

Installation of Special Equipment and Furnishings

These items typically have a high benefit/cost ratio. Adding grab bars in the shower and handrails next to the commode are relatively simple projects. Using offset hinges on narrow doors or a curtain in place of a door is another example. These solutions utilize adaptive adjustments or furniture replacements to facilitate aging in place.

Changing Behaviors

These are the easiest and least expensive changes, but are disruptive to daily habits and lifestyle. Examples of this might include transforming a ground-floor living room to a bedroom to avoid climbing stairs or taking a sponge bath in place of a tub bath.

The following list[2] rank orders the six most popular home modifications that older people make to their dwellings.

1. **Handrails/grab bars: 2 million**

2. **Widened doors: 756K**

3. **Ramps: 736K**

4. **Bathrooms, access: 713K**

5. **Kitchens, access: 544K**

6. **Lever handles: 495K**

Findings from remodeling studies show income and housing tenure impact the amount of money spent on minor or major modifications. Given the high costs associated with nursing home care, it is surprising so few people commit to minor changes that increase safety and accessibility.[3] When adding shower grab bars and handrails around the toilet, the cost is much less than a one-week nursing home stay. Falling and injuring yourself is the biggest risk that well-placed modifications can prevent or minimize. A well-designed or adapted dwelling unit can allow you to maintain continuity with very little disruption. Dozens of home modification and safety lists are available on the internet.[4] Also, many public agencies and private organizations conduct assessment reviews listing items that should be modified or could cause future problems.

Home modification lists usually detail hazards in the home. Two important items are 1) slipping and tripping hazards (cords, throw rugs, stairs, clutter, wet bathroom floors) and 2) increasing illumination levels (kitchen, bathroom, living rooms, corridors). A third concern is a lack of handrails, grab bars, or features that increase safety in the environment.

Figure 9-2 **Many kitchens have upper and lower cabinets that are either too high or too low to conveniently access:** Using a step stool or stooping is difficult and can be dangerous. Storage options like a pantry cabinet or roll-out drawers for undercounter storage can make an older kitchen more elder-friendly.

Figure 9-3 **Retrofitting a house for wheelchair accessibility is often challenging:** In this modest Los Angeles neighborhood, the retrofitted ramp appears to be too steep. Making adjustments that solve the problem of access are difficult to accomplish given existing parameters. Retrofitting this house would likely uncover other challenges with wheelchair tolerances.

WHEELCHAIR ADAPTATIONS

These are necessary adjustments when planning the environment for wheelchair access and use. They include steps that limit wheelchair accessibility, thresholds that are hard to navigate, door openings that are too narrow, reach capacity limitations in the kitchen, and transfer difficulties in the bathroom. One of the most troubling problems in the bathroom is the presence of a combination tub and shower. This fixture is common in post–World War II housing. Fortunately, a combination tub and shower can be replaced with an accessible shower in a way that avoids major replumbing costs. New tubs with doors are also available, but they can be more costly.

SAFETY AND MANIPULATION ADJUSTMENTS

The two most common problems are safety (falls) and the manipulation of door handles, faucets, stove controls, and heavy kitchen items (arthritis). In the kitchen, adding pantry storage or increasing lateral access for heavy items is often doable. Roll-out shelves and portable counters can be explored without huge expenditures. It is important to be prudent and to examine ways of simplifying your life.

This might mean reducing kitchen items or finding a decentralized storage space for rarely used objects.

There are dozens of books with creative approaches to the redesign of kitchens, bathrooms, and site access. Also, many "easy living" internet retailers have devices that can be helpful for individuals with specific needs. Furthermore, the home repair and remodeling industry today is aware of the special needs of older people and how to make environments more accessible. However, most major changes can take as long as 4 to 8 weeks to complete and require substantial expenditures that may not add to the value of the house. At this stage, moving into a better-suited dwelling unit becomes a viable alternative. Middle-age and older home buying customers today are more frequent, and thus the market is sensitized to their needs. Often new houses meet accessibility considerations or can be easily retrofitted with minor modifications when required.

Two: Danish Home Care System

The amazing Scandinavian housing and home care–based support system provides personal and health care services for people in their own homes as well as in purpose-built

Figure 9-4 A virtual home care visit involves a Skype-like connection with the recipient at their dwelling unit: Other screens display the client's medical record and appointment schedule, as well as allowing for internet searches. This relatively new technology in Denmark is preferred by some clients because contacts are shorter but more frequent.

housing. They are committed to affordable health care as well as affordable nursing care. Regardless of income, older people have access to subsidized LTC through nursing homes, services houses, and home-based visits.

Helping older people through comprehensive home care–based services started after World War II in Denmark. The late 1950s saw the first public initiatives focused on helping older people maintain independence outside of institutions. Nursing home construction was expanded in the '70s and '80s to serve the growing elderly population. However, in 1987 a moratorium on new nursing home construction was followed by a stronger commitment to a home-based care system designed to help older people age in place. This approach challenged the older person to do as much as they could for themselves to avoid a more passive institutional placement. Home care–based services have proven to be less expensive and are preferred by most older people.

CONTINUING IMPROVEMENTS

The 1980s led to multidimensional assessments that focused on what could be done to help older people maintain independence. This process identified nursing home placement criteria as well as the use of enhanced rehabilitation therapy to achieve a better life. Doctors, nurses, and social workers assessed physical problems as well as the older person's social life. An individual program involving exercise and activity was created to help each older person achieve a better life. Even today, almost all frail residents go through this screening, which emphasizes how they can help themselves. The program is carried out with equipment and trainers at community-based centers or at the older person's home. Although costly, the assumption is that it pays off in better health and less time spent in a costly institution or hospital.[5]

Figure 9-5 **Danish home care workers typically visit clients using electric cars in first-ring suburbs:** This allows them to move quickly from one location to the next and is much faster in an emergency. Electric bicycles are also replacing regular ones, because trip lengths are growing and care workers are aging.

HOME CARE PROGRAM OPERATION

Funded by the local municipality, the home care program is organized at the neighborhood level. Caregivers in urban areas use bicycles or electric cars to make home visits. Although today, electric bicycles are becoming more popular as caregivers grow older and the territories increase in size. In sparsely populated areas like Jutland with greater distances, advanced telemedicine technology is increasingly common. What makes the program successful is the focus on individual needs, as well as the peripatetic delivery system. Home care consists of three principal workers: nurses, assistant nurses, and helpers (personal caregivers) who work together in teams. Helpers typically receive 14 months of training, while assistant nurses get 26 months and nurses receive 42 months.

Older people are paired with the same care team at least two-thirds of the time. This allows the team to know a client's specific habits, interests, and problems. Visits are scheduled when needed, meaning once a week or as much as eight times a day. Typically, home care workers meet as a group in the morning and then again at noon. Their day ends around 3:30 to 4 p.m. Every week the team takes 30 minutes to discuss client-related problems.

Helpers use smart phones, but nurses use tablets to add notes to client electronic records, which are shared with colleagues, doctors, and specialists. To avoid redundancy, nurses are the only ones who communicate with doctors and are authorized to change medications. In rural districts, electronic image transmission is common.

HOME CARE VISITS

Home visits last around 30–45 minutes but can vary from 20 minutes to an hour. Mornings consist of one-hour visits where they get the resident 1) out of bed, 2) showered, 3) toileted, 4) morning medications, 4) breakfast, and 5) lunch (which is stored in the refrigerator for later). They also schedule night visits and specify special equipment, including items such as a dialysis machine, respirator, IV, or a gastric tube. About half of the clients have a pendant or wristwatch emergency call button. When staff receive an alert at night, they respond by phone and when necessary send someone to the resident's home. If they make more than 8 visits a day and/or spend more than 3 hours a day providing services, they consider the possibility of an institutional placement. That decision is made in consultation with the older person, the doctor, the nurse, and the family.

Family members are involved, even though the system is designed to work without their direct assistance. Recently there has been a strong focus on how family, friends, and neighbors can be of direct assistance. It is estimated that between 15% and 20% of older clients do not have families or have unresponsive family members.

VIRTUAL HOME CARE

To improve the system and reduce costs, Danes are experimenting with virtual home care visits. Although started as demonstration projects, they will be fully implemented in 2018. Clients are provided a computer-based tablet to communicate with a monitor located in a nearby home care office.

Figure 9-6 **The Netherlands is transitioning between electronic and paper records:** This home care worker's tablet contains her schedule of assignments for the day. It also has information about this client's medications, his history of conditions, and other pertinent information that can help her to monitor his health more effectively.

Video communication appointments are usually 5–7 minutes in length and are scheduled at specific times and days by the older person. Most clients select the morning (7:30–9:30 a.m.). Typical calls involve discussion about how they are feeling and an inspection of their current medications. Clients can ask questions or request more assistance. The older person likes the predictable nature of the call and prefers the shorter, more frequent interactions. Home nursing visits, for efficiency purposes, are scheduled during a 3- to 5-hour window, which can disrupt the older person's schedule. A traditional personal care (non-medical) home visit takes 20–30 minutes, so twice as many Skype visits can be completed in the same time. The priority themes in the conversation are usually food, medications, and happiness/mood.

A typical call is made from the home care office by a helper who follows the call on three computer monitors. One monitor displays the health record of the resident with a schedule of appointments. The second monitor has emails and a search system to research diseases, underlying causes, and symptoms. The third monitor transmits the video image of the client. If the caregiver fails to make contact, a neighbor or relative is called. If no one responds, the caregiver can visit the apartment and gain access with a lockbox key on the premises.

The camera and portability of a tablet allow clients to show an infected finger or the inside of the refrigerator. They foresee the possibility of linking the tablet to a portable robotic stand that can move throughout the apartment. The Danes seem

committed to making this system work more effectively as demand grows and the number of visits increase.

This technique is particularly effective with early dementia (MCI) residents who must be directed or reminded. They are often missing structure, and a call provides more focus and less distraction than a home visit. However, nurses value direct contact with the older person, which they believe provides better information about health status.

CONCLUSION

This system or aspects of this system in the US would provide a dramatic improvement to the current situation. By keeping older people in their own homes and helping them to maintain their competency at an optimum level, the Danes are able to avoid institutionalization for everyone except the frailest individuals with debilitating cognitive limitations.

Three: PACE (Program for All-inclusive Care for the Elderly)

PACE is the oldest and perhaps the best known of the community-based managed care programs operating in the US. It is a very effective alternative to placement in a nursing home for the frailest-frail. Its target criteria for participants are 1) people over age 55 living in a PACE service area, 2) state certification as needing skilled nursing care, and 3) ability to live safely in the community with the help of PACE.

Figure 9-7 The Brandman PACE Center is located in a newly remodeled building on the Los Angeles Jewish Home for the Aging campus in Reseda, California: The entry vestibule to this 12,000 SF building greets and secures the 190 participants. The program mixes clinical services within a social atmosphere.

There are approximately 122 PACE programs operating 233 PACE Centers in 31 states serving around 40,000 people. The objective of the program is to help older frail people live as independently as possible in the community. The program does this through a process of 1) patient assessment, 2) comprehensive care planning, 3) communication and coordination between service providers, and 4) promoting patient engagement in health care.[6]

PACE involves a multidisciplinary team of physicians, nurse practitioners, nurses, social workers, therapists, van drivers, and aides. These individuals work with participants to achieve improved health status, a higher quality of life, lower mortality, increased choice, and greater confidence in dealing with the problems of aging.

PROGRAM COMPONENTS

A typical program includes a day care facility with activities, recreation, and clinical help. Drivers provide transportation to a PACE center usually three times a week. They also provide transportation needed to live independently and to access health care appointments. They coordinate the efforts of individual specialists and combine payments from Medicare, Medicaid, and private pay into a single rate.

Participants are similar to nursing home residents. The average age is around 80 (three-quarters of them are over age 75), 75% are female, about half suffer from dementia, and they average 7.9 medical conditions. Ninety percent live in the community (many of them alone) and are visited frequently by home care and home health workers. Program sizes vary, but the average (in 2013) was slightly fewer than 300 participants. The average center includes a health clinic with an on-site physician and nurse practitioner, physical and occupational therapy facilities, and a common room for social and recreational activities.

One requirement is to provide care services for the same cost or less than what someone would be charged in a nursing home. Participants, because they are carefully managed, cost 10–15% less than comparable nursing home residents.[7] Research studies show they have better self-rated health and preventive care, as well as fewer unmet needs and less depression than comparable nursing home populations.

The program goals are to promote longevity, optimize functioning, and provide palliative care. Different strategies are used depending on each patient's needs. PACE has the flexibility to solve problems by going beyond the highly structured system for reimbursement when a necessary service is

Figure 9-8 **Participants are involved in activities, converse with others, and see specialists who can help them with challenges:** The focus is on keeping individuals active and engaged while facilitating independence in their own home. One of the most valuable side effects of membership in PACE are the social bonds created between participants.

required. Because they know how their participants live, they can make home modifications to avoid hazards. For example, they can upgrade door locks to reduce the need for anxiety medications. The care management approach explores the antecedents associated with health problems. PACE is different from simple case management and referral because it examines and manages all the participant's care needs.

PROGRAM HISTORY

The program evolved from a program for frail Asian-Americans in San Francisco. On-Lok Senior Health Services, initiated in 1971, eventually grew to include housing, adult

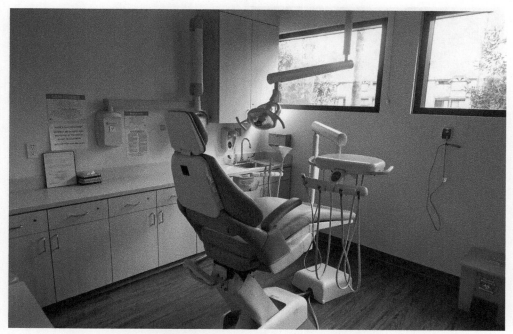

Figure 9-9 **The PACE screening process involves a multidimensional examination of health, lifestyle, and independence concerns:** The purpose is to pinpoint the services and supports needed for each PACE member to live independently in the community. The PACE staff includes physicians, social workers, gero-psychologists, dentists, and physical therapists. They even have a dental chair available for examinations and procedures.

day health, a social day care center, and complete medical and social support for nursing home eligible older people. In the 1990s, with help from the Robert Wood Johnson Foundation, the John Hartford Foundation, and the Retirement Research Foundation, a replication effort was mounted that led to establishing 11 PACE organizations in 9 states. These sites received Medicare and Medicaid waivers as full payment for the services they provided.[8]

PACE also explored programs in rural areas. In 2006, 15 grantees were provided seed funding to establish models for rural defused populations. PACE utilized telehealth technology, including Personal Care Response (PERS), fall detection, and remote monitoring. PACE offers community care options to help people stay in their own homes for as long as possible. Another aspect of the program involves working with family members to train and sensitize them to important health considerations.

BRANDMAN CENTER FOR SENIOR CARE

In 2013, the Los Angeles Jewish Home in Reseda, California, opened a PACE program with 190 participants. The individuals in this program have an average age of 78, 61% are female, and half have a dementia diagnosis. About 20% live alone and 40% are living with family in the community. The remainder live in independent senior housing, assisted living, or board and care homes. About 5% have no family involvement. About a quarter use a wheelchair and 65% use a cane or walker to get around.[9]

Program, Services, and Facilities

The program is split into morning and afternoon sessions and most participants average two sessions a week. Seven vans shuttle residents from their home to the center. The program mixes clinical appointments with social activities. Their multiservice staff includes nurses, a dentist, doctor, pharmacist, physical therapist, podiatrist, and neuropsychologist. One strength is the breadth of their assessment and treatment team. The 12,000 SF building contains a space for group activities and several smaller rooms for group and individual therapy. There is a shower, warming kitchen, reception area, laundry space, quiet room, exam rooms, outdoor terrace, and a triage space with two hospital beds. They are open five days a week and coordinate home care visits from the center.

Figure 9-10 **One of the most important components is the van transportation system that picks up clients from their homes and delivers them to the center and back:** The center accommodates two back-to-back (2–2.5 hr.) shifts. The average age of participants is 78 and about half of them have a dementia diagnosis.

Most participants are dual eligibles (Medical/Medicare) but there is also flexibility to serve private pay participants on a sliding scale. The intake process starts with a multidisciplinary assessment from eight staff members, which creates a baseline and treatment plan. Residents must shift their care to center physicians, but can leave the program at any time.

Four: Home– and Community– Based Care: The 1915c and 1115 Waiver Programs and Long-term Care Insurance

1915c WAIVER PROGRAM

In the US, the Medicaid 1915c program has been very successful in helping older people and other dependent populations avoid institutionalization by providing personal and medical care services to live independently in the community. There are over 300 programs implemented in 47 states. Since 1995, the funding for home- and community-based care as a percentage of the total LTC and Support Services (LTCSS) budget has increased from 18% to 51%,[10] while expenditures for institutions have decreased from 82% to 49%. Today most funding is devoted to keeping people out of institutions. The waiver program is targeted toward both the aged and the developmentally disabled, but half of those covered are older people.[11]

The program (like PACE described earlier) requires that older people live independently in the community at a cost that does not exceed the cost of institutionalization.[12] The people served by this program are "dual eligibles" who quality for both Medicaid that covers LTC and Medicare that covers direct medical expenses. Waiver program members are a high-need and high-cost population with minimal family support who are considered in danger of institutionalization.

SECTION 1115 WAIVER PROGRAM

Other demonstration programs funded under Section 1115 like the LA Care Health Plan have promulgated a more integrated approach linking the older person to basic medical care, emergency services, and LTC supportive

Figure 9-11 **Waiver programs have been devised to keep individuals out of skilled nursing homes:** They are targeted toward dual eligibles who qualify for both Medicaid and Medicare. In addition to direct services, these programs also provide access to exercise and social exchange, which helps older people stay independent longer.

services. The presumption in this demonstration program is more than just helping people avoid institutionalization. There are major expenditures when older people must be readmitted to hospitals through emergency rooms. Providing higher-quality preventive care and better coordination of ancillary services helps those at risk live a more independent, healthy life. These demonstration programs generally have five-year terms from which outcomes are researched to uncover opportunities for improvement. The focus on the most indigent and frail populations has not been that helpful to older people who have income and/or assets that disqualify them from Medicaid. Unfortunately, the major cutbacks proposed in post-Obamacare health care proposals could have devastating impacts on these dual eligible programs.

LONG-TERM CARE INSURANCE AND PRIVATE SECTOR PROGRAMS

One of the best options to offset the potential cost of financing private home care is long-term care insurance. According to the America Association of Long-Term Care Insurance, 264,000 receive long-term care insurance

benefits. About half of the recipients use it for home care and most recipients (63.7%) are over the age of 80.[13] Approximately 8.1 million people are covered by some form of LTC insurance. But as with many insurance products, most participants made the decision to participate earlier in life when fees were more affordable.

Individuals with incomes and assets that keep them from qualifying for Medicaid must look to the private sector for solutions. Private home care agencies are evolving in their sophistication, but still struggle with age-old problems. Chapter 11 outlines how new technology is bringing better information and assistance to individuals in the community. The approaches being tested include 1) wearable devices that monitor health indicators, 2) training and education that encourage better health-related behaviors, 3) the electronic transfer of health care warnings through Telehealth communication systems, 4) the provision of professional advice when it is needed (just-in-time), 5) response to emergency situations, and 6) the organization of support for chronic conditions (including home health care visits). Systems are rapidly evolving that use smart phone technology to deliver knowledge and provide help.

Figure 9-12 In urban environments, transportation is a major concern for the oldest-old: The frail have a very difficult time using conventional public transportation to and from destinations like a doctor's office. Paratransit options can be arranged by service coordinators and are a key component to a comprehensive system.

At $20–25/hour, often with three-hour minimum time periods, private home care services can be difficult for many older people to afford. Comparing these expenses with the ongoing costs of assisted living may make it easier to see the potential savings available through home care. Scandinavian home care services provide excellent affordable care; however, they are financed by government entitlement programs.

Less commonly, some US age-restricted housing providers offer home care services on an as-needed basis coordinated through an on-site manager. Housing owners cannot dictate that residents use a particular service and they have a responsibility to other residents to maintain a secure environment. Additional complications can occur when home care workers are not employed by an agency or must meet project-initiated security requirements.

Hybrid arrangements that layer home care services with apartment-style living are likely to be more popular in the future so these issues will need to be clarified. This approach is more common in Life Plan Communities (LPCs) but often the sponsor controls the choice of home care workers to maintain tighter security.

Five: Beacon Hill Village (BHV)

In 2002, a group of older people in the historic Beacon Hill neighborhood of Boston created an organization to help them age in place in this picturesque but less age-friendly neighborhood. Beacon Hill contains mostly turn-of-the-century red brick 3- to 5-story walk-up apartments. The neighborhood contains about 13,000 people, 14% of which are over age 60.

Beacon Hill Village (BHV) is a "virtual village" that helps older people live independently using a three-prong approach.[14] First, BHV identifies services that are needed by older neighborhood residents. These range from personal care to roof repair as well as ongoing needs like transportation. BHV negotiates discounts and oversees repair work to make certain it's done properly. Second, they offer several healthy living programs centered on members. These include exercise classes, bike riding, walking clubs, and tai chi, as well as lectures. To minimize costs, activities take place in existing nearby facilities (like a local library or senior center) in the neighborhood. Third, other programs are targeted toward the cultural arts, education, and

Figure 9-13 **The first "village" was devised by a group of older volunteers in the not-so-age-friendly Boston neighborhood of Beacon Hill:** These individuals were seeking to facilitate access to transportation, home care, and home maintenance. The system they established was unique and quickly became a national model.

travel. These provide the "social glue" that connects members and often leads to substantive friendships. They also recruit volunteers to help, some of whom come from their membership.

DRIVEN BY A DESIRE TO MAINTAIN INDEPENDENCE

They believe many members can successfully live in their apartments until the end of life if they have help. Members want and need supportive services and home repairs/modifications to age in place. However, the most significant aspect of village membership has been the social connections that have evolved with the program. These give older members, many of whom are living alone, a way to engage with others.[15]

The BHV community concierge is the broker, consolidator, and connector of services. This component of the program is popular with members as well as relatives and family, especially those who live some distance away. Having an advocate in the community is valuable for everyone. Typically, a third of residents are heavy users of village activities and services while a third are rarely involved. Less engaged members benefit from knowing help is there when they need it. BHV has attracted a large waiting list of 800 people that are "not quite ready yet" to commit to

regular membership. Recruiting new and replacement members is an ongoing challenge. Typically, membership fees pay only 50–60% of the operating budget. The remaining funding comes from charitable contributions.

Tapping synergistic volunteers is an important aspect of the program. Transportation for grocery trips, services to support aging in place, and technology support are popular and growing. The organization today serves 400 members that range in age from 50 to 97 (average age of 74). About 40% are couples with a large single female segment. In general, a typical BHV constituent is middle class with a medium income. Most do not qualify for moderate income housing nor are they wealthy enough to buy into a Life Plan Community (LPC).

VILLAGE TO VILLAGE NETWORK

By its example, Beacon Hill Village has spawned 200 separate villages throughout the US, with 150 under development in 45 states.[16] A national organization called the Village to Village Network (VtVN) was established in 2012 to provide technical assistance to create new villages. Each village has a slightly different organizational and management structure, but they all share the desire to bring people together and help them stay independent in the community.

Figure 9-14 **One approach they pioneered was to "borrow" space from local agencies like senior centers and businesses for program activities:** In doing so they took advantage of excess space in libraries, churches, and parks for organized events involving their membership. This movement has become an amazingly successful grassroots effort.

One common theme is their "grassroots" character, which is led by and for older adults in the community. Some villages work under formal service agencies, but their attractiveness is centered on how they involve older people to help others help themselves. Newer villages are highly dependent on volunteer support. The Capital Hill Village in Washington, DC, reports that 80% of its calls are fielded by volunteers.

The VtVN allows each village to learn from the experiences of others and to test new ideas that achieve higher utility and value. Typical villages in the US have a similar profile to the Beacon Hill constituency. Members range in age, but 87% are over the age of 65 and 23% are over the age of 85. In a study conducted in 2016 of 115 villages, the average village size was 146 members. The latest survey shows 36% are from urban areas, 35% from suburban areas, 13% from rural places, and 16% serve a mixed setting.[17]

These "virtual villages" have become effective community-based support groups for "aging in place." Because

Figure 9-15 **More than 200 replications of the original Beacon Hill Village have taken place:** Although most programs are targeted toward older constituents, intergenerational programming has also been popular. This park with a shaded pavilion near a children's playground would be a perfect venue for such a program.

they are designed by and for the people who use them, they are different from organizations that manage care facilities or a typical public agency. Their commitment to help one another stay independent in the community has tapped a deep and powerful motivation. It also seems well suited to boomers who desire more control over the future.

Six: Age-Friendly Cities

In 2005, the World Health Organization (WHO) developed guidelines for Age-Friendly Cities. The founding principles included 1) combating ageism, 2) enabling autonomy, and 3) supporting the concept of healthy aging in all policies and at all levels. This international effort was piloted with data from 33 cities in 22 countries. In 2007, a publication identified eight topic areas where efforts were to be focused. This development of topic areas and needed reforms brought a commitment to share information and recruit other countries and municipalities to join the effort. Today the program operates in 287 cities and communities in 33 countries, affecting 113 million people.[18]

The eight topic areas are 1) transportation, 2) housing, 3) social participation, 4) respect and social inclusion, 5) civic participation and employment, 6) communication and information, 7) community support and health services, and 8) outdoor spaces and buildings. Since

inception, additional emphases have been added, including affordability, design quality, personnel training, adaptability/accessibility, safety, intergenerational exchange, technology friendliness, and service availability.

Today's efforts also include more emphasis on nutrition and fitness. Other enhanced areas of interest include health care that addresses chronic conditions, the needs of the older-old, LTC at home, and safety.[19] Volunteering, community service, and political action have also grown in importance in numerous age-friendly communities.

STRONGER EMPHASIS ON VOLUNTEERING

The movement has become a catalyst for focusing efforts in communities today. One universal problem is the shortage of funding to attack large and overwhelming problems. During the global recession, this was especially evident. This has challenged the movement to be more political and more cooperative. One interesting aspect of the movement is how it has evolved differently in different places. The emphasis on local action has allowed solutions to specific problems to be identified, while community engagement has given local contributors a sense of control and achievement. The movement is inclusive and optimistic, making it endearing and enduring. Furthermore, associations with academic institutions and powerful membership

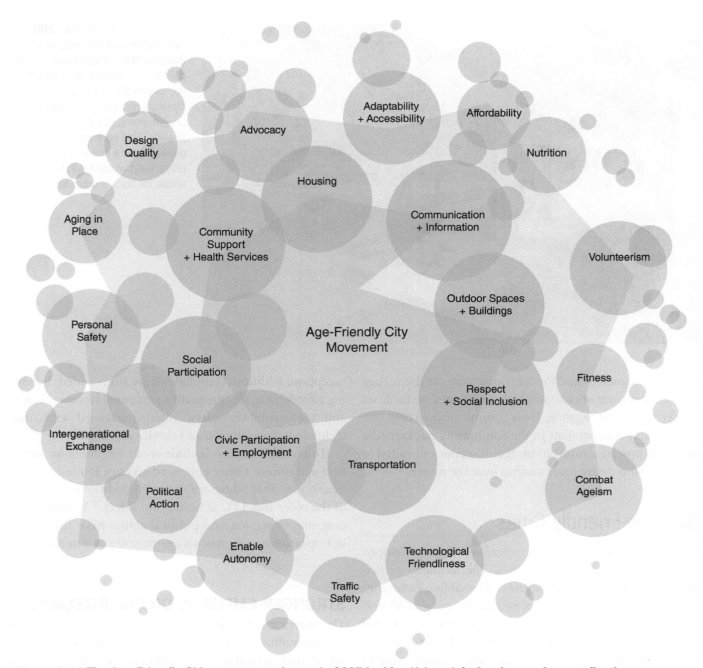

Figure 9-16 **The Age-Friendly Cities movement began in 2007 by identifying eight focal areas for coordination, program development, and advocacy:** Since then, other topics have been added, including service provision for the oldest-old. One major emphasis has been on making the city a safer and more supportive environment for all populations.

organizations like AARP have provided legitimacy and enhanced the communication of principles and the intended impacts to a broader audience.[20]

The direct participation, interest, and enthusiasm of older people has propelled these programs forward. Significant efforts have focused on helping people age in place, as well as calling on government, nonprofit, and proprietary organizations to support this goal. Better transportation systems, higher-quality sidewalks, and better-equipped parks are benefits that accrue to all ages and income groups. This universal approach to making improvements for the greater good has credited the

Figure 9-17 **This international movement is being implemented at a grassroots level in many participating municipalities:** One broadly shared emphasis has been on parks and fitness activities. The logic is that existing amenities need upgrading and that parks are inherently multigenerational but could be especially beneficial to the oldest-old population.

movement with being broad-based. Sidewalk improvements and better intersections for pedestrians help everyone live a safer life, but especially older people and children.

AGE-FRIENDLY IMPROVEMENTS HELP EVERYONE

In some places like New York City, research has led to action plans that enlist the interests of various agencies. There, 59 initiatives were identified that made the city more age-friendly. Reports published in 2011 and 2013 outlined the progress made on these goals as well what still needed to be accomplished.[21]

Some action items like an examination of traffic conflicts revealed that four times as many people over the age of 65 were killed in pedestrian accidents as those under 65. Twenty-five of the most dangerous intersections in the city were mapped and safety solutions implemented. After the changes were made, fatalities decreased an average of 20% and some areas saw pedestrian injury decreases of 40% to 60%. This has since become an ongoing program called Safe Streets for Seniors.[22]

Age-friendly cities continue to help older people, especially in municipalities where specific funding for age-related programs is less available. Making it easier to age in place appears to benefit everyone.

Seven: Accessory Dwelling Units (ADU)

The housing concept labeled a "granny flat," "mother-in-law suite," or "accessory apartment" has been around for at least 70 years. Garage remodels to accommodate an additional family member were common before World War II. Dating from the early 1920s, these accessory dwellings predated subdivision standards, which later often forbid them.

Around 1970, a formal discussion evolved about how to best accommodate an older relative in a dwelling unit that could be constructed within or adjacent to a single-family house. Unfortunately, this socially motivated idea violated zoning codes in many cities. Few appeal mechanisms and standards were developed for these structures and very few US cities embraced the concept with enthusiasm.

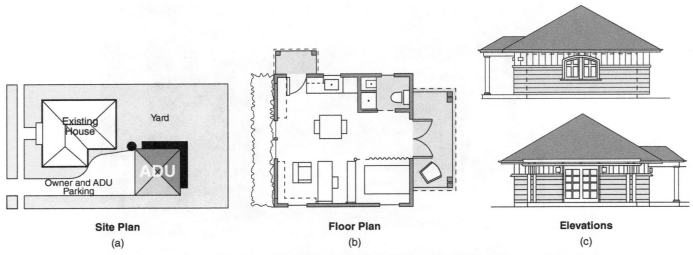

Site Plan	Floor Plan	Elevations
(a)	(b)	(c)

Figure 9-18a–c Advocating for accessory dwellings in mature neighborhoods for older people makes tremendous sense from a planning perspective: It is a popular strategy in the UK and Canada that has achieved substantial success. In the US, it has been less successful. But the city of Santa Cruz, California, has been on the forefront by advocating planning standards for this housing type. *Source: City of Santa Cruz.*

CONCEPT IS SUCCESSFUL IN OTHER COUNTRIES

Although development has languished in the US, countries like Canada, Britain, and Australia have created standards that encourage accessory dwelling development. One early legal question was "Who could live there?" Provided that it was a family member, most planning commissions obliged. But when that person moved out or died, there was ambiguity about the future. About 10 to 15 years ago, city planners began to explore how to increase the density of first-ring suburbs. Adding ADUs increased density and added affordable housing stock. This approach also added density with little environmental impact. Some planners even characterized the impact as "invisible density." The "tiny house" craze gave it an additional boast as millennials and younger people saw the ADU as a way to live in an affordable but private dwelling in a middle-class neighborhood.

Meanwhile, thousands of units were developed in places like Vancouver, Canada, and London, England, demonstrating its enhanced social and economic benefits. In Vancouver an amazing 35% of the current housing stock contains an ADU, compared to less than 1% in Seattle, Washington, and Portland, Oregon.[23] The success of the Canadian program is attributed to low regulatory barriers and the strength of the real estate market.

Today cities like Santa Cruz, California, and Portland are developing standards for planning and construction that allow site placement, building massing, and design aesthetics to be addressed. The motivation is often to accommodate a friend or an adult child or provide additional income to the homeowner. These dwellings have grown from places for grandparents to live, to addressing the community's goal for affordable housing. Design studios in the architecture programs at UCLA (City LAB)[24] and UC Berkeley[25] have studied the issue and arrived at compelling arguments for broader-based implementation.

FOUR BASIC TYPES OF ADUs

There appear to be four common types of ADUs: 1) a suite detached at grade, 2) a suite attached at grade, 3) a basement suite, and 4) a garage apartment (often constructed above the garage). The garage and basement units can create accessibility conflicts, so most designs intended for older people are at grade level. Although construction costs vary based on location and site placement, most ADUs cost around $100,000 ($90–$110/SF). Depending on the market, they often rent for between $850 and $1,000 a month. They normally include a small kitchen, a bathroom, a living room, and a sleeping alcove that range in size from 400 to 700 SF.[26] Although ordinances vary, it is not uncommon for parking or impact fees to be waived by municipalities that are encouraging ADU construction. Santa Cruz states in its ordinance that only 7% of its citizens can afford the cost of a single-family house in the city so ADUs help solve a major housing affordability problem.[27]

Eight: GenSmart House and Next Gen House

PARDEE HOMES, PASADENA, CALIFORNIA, AND LENNAR HOMES, ORANGE COUNTY, CALIFORNIA

Multigenerational housing is not a new concept in the US. Fourteen percent of the current population, nearly 16.5 million people, live in this housing type. What is new is the interest homebuilders like Lennar (Next Gen)[28] and Pardee (GenSmart)[29] have in developing housing prototypes that are custom fit to this lifestyle choice. Lennar is credited as the first to commercialize this idea. Their survey research showed half of respondents wanted a way to accommodate their elderly parents in their next home. Lennar has plans to construct its Next Gen prototype in 200 of its communities throughout the US. It has become popular because it allows extended families to live together. A key attribute appears to be the ability to provide privacy and togetherness under one roof.

A 3- to 4-bedroom house today is about 2500 SF, compared to 50 years ago when the average house was 1500 SF. The smallest size Next Gen model combines a 1500–1600 SF house with an 800–900 SF conjoined suite.[30] But most of the combined Next Gen models are approximately a third larger than the average newly constructed house today. The small attached Next Gen suite usually contains a living room, bedroom, and a full bathroom. The entry kitchenette and stackable washer/dryer closet are placed in a corner of the living room. There are dozens of plans for the larger conjoined models based on the circumstances and desires of buyers. Depending on site location and housing size, prices range from $200,000 to $1M. The largest is the "superhome," which at 4100 SF has 7 bedrooms and 4.5 bathrooms.

BROAD APPEAL

These housing prototypes benefit extended family living in numerous ways. Market interest is driven by 1) boomerang children, 2) boomer preferences to downsize, 3) the traditional living patterns of immigrants and minority families (especially Asian and Latino), and 4) the opportunity to save money by splitting housing costs with several family members. A strong resale market and the fact that this attached unit can be transformed for other uses has also encouraged development. The smaller suite could serve as a space for a nanny, a home office, a room for overnight guests, or even an internet vacation rental.

When used for an older family member, there are many important features that increase its utility and popularity. First, the concept is particularly appealing for grandparents who want to spend more time with their extended family but also want their own privacy. Second, for older people who are starting to experience difficulties or are security conscious, being near family members is reassuring. Third, the first-floor unit is handicap accessible and contains no stairs. Fourth, the unit has its own separate front door with an internal connection to the shared living room and kitchen space of the larger house. The occupant can come and go without disturbing anyone else. Fifth, it is economical compared to the cost of two separate units (initial price, utilities, real estate taxes, and upkeep).[31] Living together can typically save as much as $1000–$1500 a month. Because the suite is separate, it has its own outdoor space and its own decor. Compared to the traditional "casita," a popular model choice in active adult housing, the Next Gen or GenSmart suite is larger and has more features.

LIMITATIONS

The downsides are minimal. Zoning and building codes often restrict a single-family house from having two kitchens, which is typically enforced by allowing only one oven. The Next Gen and GenSmart suite has a sink, refrigerator, cabinets, and a microwave. Installing an oven is relatively easy to do but could violate local building codes. The modern and commodious kitchen in the main house can accommodate several people working together and the large dining space here can easily seat everyone for a combined family meal. The kitchen design is comparable to upscale layouts specified in large homes today with granite counters and stainless steel appliances. For many extended families, the option of taking meals together is generally considered a major benefit.

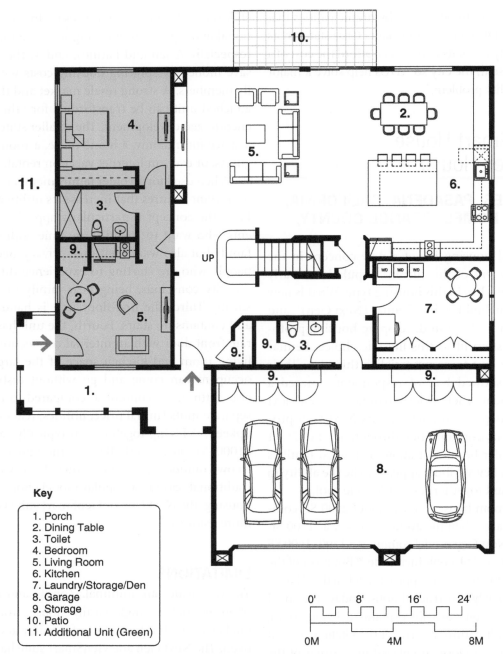

Key

1. Porch
2. Dining Table
3. Toilet
4. Bedroom
5. Living Room
6. Kitchen
7. Laundry/Storage/Den
8. Garage
9. Storage
10. Patio
11. Additional Unit (Green)

Figure 9-19 Housing developers have been exploring a range of housing types for extended families: These are popular with larger families who seek to live together as well as older family members who would like to live close to their children. The GenSmart plan shows a two-story dwelling that combines a 1000 SF accessory unit on the ground floor with a larger 1500 SF family accommodation.
Courtesy of Pardee Homes and Bassenian Lagoni.

Depending on size, the bigger house is either one or two stories with the conjoined suite on the ground floor. Building one single, large, combined house is also economical because additional square footage is minimal when it is added to a conventional two- to four-bedroom house plan.[32]

This represents a very American approach by buying a house that solves the problem, rather than trying to make do with an existing situation that is fraught with difficulties and shortcomings. Younger Americans typically move when they need more space or can leverage their home investment. This housing design is a very practical solution that also facilitates aging in place.

Nine: Naturally Occurring Retirement Communities (NORC's)

The concept behind a NORC is simple but powerful. Older people move less frequently than younger people, often finding themselves aging alongside neighbors they have known for years. Over time, these concentrations of older people can account for as much as half of the resident population of an older rental building or a post–World War II neighborhood. This concentration of older people can create a community of age peers who can share personal care services. Although estimates vary, between 17% and 30% of older people live in a NORC building or neighborhood. This phenomenon, identified by Michael Hunt in the mid-1980s, suggested how these settings could be used for shared services and informal helping networks. NORCS are considered 1) buildings where the majority of residents are over age 60, having aged in place, 2) neighborhoods of single-family or duplex houses with a majority of constituents over age 60, and 3) rural areas with lower population densities that have high concentrations of people over age 60.[33]

PENN SOUTH WAS THE FIRST NORC

The first official NORC service program was initiated in 1985 in New York City's Penn South housing development,[34] a cooperative of 2820 units in ten 22-story high-rise buildings that first opened in 1962. It contained a well-integrated social community, which made it easier to initiate an aging-in-place program. The Jewish Federation of New York City assembled private resources to support the concept. The success of the program led to follow-up funding from New York City and New York State through the NORC SSP (Supportive Services Program).

Previously more than 50 NORC-SPP programs in 25 states served approximately 50,000 participants. Follow-up projects were tailored to local conditions and opportunities with the idea of helping residents stay independent

Figure 9-20 **Park La Brea towers is the best known NORC in southern California:** This post–World War II development is comprised of 13 ten-story towers. By the late eighties many residents had aged in place when the Jewish Federation devised a plan to provide them with supplemental care. Interest in the project waned as general interest in NORCs decreased.

Figure 9-21 **Massive single-family housing developments after World War II catered to veterans:** Many families moved into suburban dwelling units like this one during the 1950s and stayed there until they were old and frail. These are referred to as NORC neighborhoods. They are like NORC multifamily buildings but in a suburban, single-family context.

through the provision of social and health-related services. NORC projects tapped local resources and networked with other direct service providers. The core services included 1) case management assistance, 2) health care management, 3) education and recreational activities, and 4) volunteer opportunities. Each program had different supplementary services that ranged from transportation to adult day care.

NORCs created a socially cohesive community by encouraging participants to volunteer and thus created a precursor to the Village Movement. One major difference between the two programs was the source of organizational support. NORCs were an initiative of the Jewish Federations of North America (JFNA), while the Village movement is a consumer-based grassroots movement.

US PROGRAMS LOST FUNDING SUPPORT WHILE OTHER INTERNATIONAL PROGRAMS FLOURISHED

Defunding of Title IV of the Older Americans Act reduced federal support and limited public support for the NORC initiative. As of 2012, only 29 of the original programs were left. In contrast, the JDC-ESHEL program in Israel used the same organizing principles and has continued to be very successful. Their growth and stability was the

result of a steady source of public funding that allowed the older frail to stay in their homes.[35] The inability of NORC-SSP programs to provide direct services like home care as well as sophisticated health monitoring, as demonstrated in the PACE program, also meant participants had little access to health care for chronic conditions. Nonetheless, NORCS still represent an extremely efficient way of helping people stay independent.

OTHER APPROACHES TO RETROFIT EXISTING HOUSING

In Portugal, a rapidly aging southern European country, there have been proposals to remodel existing mid-rise buildings to serve as housing with services. The work of Antonio Carvalho[36] capitalizes on the existing prototypical design of five- to seven-story family housing in Lisbon. His approach has been to remodel each floor into a small group cluster. Depending on the space available, food preparation could occur within each cluster or could be centralized on a ground or first floor with other shared uses. This approach could be targeted toward neighborhoods with high concentrations of the oldest-old. It is far less disruptive than replacing existing housing with purpose-built new construction.

Endnotes

1 Fall Prevention Center of Excellence, USC Leonard David School of Gerontology (2017), Basics of Fall Prevention, http://stopfalls.org/what-is-fall-prevention/fp-basics (accessed 10/2/17).

2 USC Leonard Davis School of Gerontology, Home Modification Resources (n.d.), Home Modifications Among Households with Physical Activity Limitations, http://www.homemods.org/resources/pages/hudmarket.shtml (accessed 10/15/17).

3 Golant, S. (2015), *Aging in the Right Place*, Health Professionals Press, Baltimore, 132.

4 USC Leonard Davis School of Gerontology, Home Modification Resources (n.d.), Home Modifications Among Households with Physical Activity Limitations, http://www.homemods.org/resources/pages/hudmarket.shtml (accessed 10/15/17).

5 Raffel, N., and Raffel, M. (1987), Elderly Care: Similarities and Solutions in Denmark and the United States, *Public Health Report,* 102(5), 494–500.

6 National PACE Association (2017), Find a Pace Program in Your Neighborhood, http://www.npaonline.org/pace-you/find-pace-program-your-neighborhood (accessed 10/15/17).

7 Medicare.gov, PACE (2017), https://www.medicare.gov/your-medicare-costs/help-paying-costs/pace/pace.html (accessed 10/15/17).

8 National PACE Association (2017), Understanding the PACE Model of Care, http://www.npaonline.org/start-pace-program/understanding-pace-model-care (accessed 10/15/17).

9 Brandman Centers for Senior Care (2017), Healthcare Solutions for Frail Seniors, http://brandmanseniorcare.org (accessed 10/15/17).

10 Medicaid.gov, Long Term Services and Supports (2016), 2014 Medicaid Spending, https://www.medicaid.gov/medicaid-chip-program-information/by-topics/long-term-services-and-supports/downloads/ltss-expenditures-fy2013.pdf (accessed 9/1/16).

11 Henry J Kaiser Family Foundation (2016), Medicaid Home and Community-based Services Programs: 2013 Data Update, http://kff.org/medicaid/report/medicaid-home-and-community-based-services-programs-2013-data-update (accessed 10/15/17).

12 Arc (2014), *The 2014 Federal Home and Community-Based Services Regulation: What You Need to Know*, Arc of the United States, Washington DC.

13 American Association for Long-Term Care Insurance (2017), Long-Term Care Insurance Facts—Statistics, http://www.aaltci.org/long-term-care-insurance/learning-center/fast-facts.php (accessed 10/21/17).

14 Beacon Hill Village (2017), Welcome to Beacon Hill Village, http://www.beaconhillvillage.org (accessed 10/15/17).

15 AARP (2014), Beacon Hill Village: A Livable Community, 6-minute video, http://assets.aarp.org/external_sites/caregiving/multimedia/CG_BeaconHill.html (accessed 10/15/17).

16 Village to Village Network (2017), http://vtvnetwork.org/content.aspx?page_id=22&club_id=691012&module_id=248579 (accessed 10/15/17).

17 Graham, C., Scharlach, A., Nicholson, R., and O'Brien, C. (2016), National Survey of US Villages, UCB Center for the Advanced Study of Aging Services, Berkeley, CA.

18 World Health Organization (2017), Ageing and the Life-course, WHO Global Network for Age-friendly Cities and Communities, http://www.who.int/ageing/projects/age_friendly_cities_network/en (accessed 10/15/17).

19 HUFFPOST (2017), Age-Friendly Cities, http://www.huffingtonpost.com/news/age-friendly-cities (accessed 10/15/17).

20 AARP Livable Communities (2017), AARP Network of Age-Friendly Communities: An Introduction, http://www.aarp.org/livable-communities/network-age-friendly-communities/info-2014/an-introduction.html (accessed 10/15/17).

21 Age-Friendly NYC (2017), Current Priorities, http://nyam.org/age-friendly-nyc/about (accessed 10/15/17).

22 New York City DOT (2017), Pedestrians: Safe Streets for Seniors, http://www.nyc.gov/html/dot/html/pedestrians/safeseniors.shtml (accessed 10/15/17).

23 Sightline Institute (2017), Why Vancouver Trounces the Rest of Cascadia in Building ADUs, http://www.sightline.org/2016/02/17/why-vancouver-trounces-the-rest-of-cascadia-in-building-adus/?gclid=CPC67pSYh8wCFUKUfgodV5sJMw (accessed 10/15/17).

24 UCLA CityLAB (2017), Backyard Homes, http://citylabtest.aud.ucla.edu/projects/backyard-homes (accessed 10/15/17).

25 UC Berkeley Environmental Design, Frameworks (2011), Studying the Benefits of Accessory Dwelling Units, https://frameworks.ced.berkeley.edu/2011/accessory-dwelling-units (accessed 10/15/17).

26 Accessory Dwellings (2017), Accessory Dwelling Units: What They Are and Why People Build Them, https://accessorydwellings.org/what-adus-are-and-why-people-build-them (accessed 10/15/17).

27 City of Santa Cruz (2017), Accessory Dwelling Unit Development Program, http://www.cityofsantacruz.com/departments/planning-and-community-development/programs/accessory-dwelling-unit-development-program (accessed 10/15/17).

28 Lennar (2017), Next Gen: The Home within a Home, http://nextgen.lennar.com (accessed 10/15/17).

29 Pardee Homes (2017), GenSmart: Amazing Guest Rooms, https://www.pardeehomes.com/trends-and-design/gensmart-suites-make-ah-mazing-guest-rooms (accessed 10/15/17).

30 NewHomeSource (2017), Multigenerational Homes: Multigenerational Living Is Back, https://www.newhomesource.com/resourcecenter/articles/multigenerational-living-is-back-with-a-new-twist (accessed 10/15/17).

31 NewHomeSource (2017), Lennar's NextGen Home-within-a Home Provides Multigenerational Living, https://www.newhomesource.com/resourcecenter/articles/lennars-nextgen-home-within-a-home-provides-solutions-for-multigenerational-living (accessed 10/15/17).

32 Olick, D., CNBC Realty Check (2016), Under One Roof: Multigenerational Housing Big for Builders, http://www.cnbc.com/2016/02/08/under-one-roof-multigenerational-housing-big-for-builders.html (accessed 10/15/17).

33 New York City Office of Aging (2015), NORC Blueprint: A Guide to Community Action, "What is a NORC?" http://www.norcblueprint.org/norc (accessed 10/15/17).

34 Penn South (2017), Living in a Cooperative Community, https://www.pennsouth.coop/cooperative-living.html (accessed 10/15/17).

35 Next Avenue (2012), NORC's Some of the Best Retirement Communities Occur Naturally, http://www.nextavenue.org/norcs-some-best-retirement-communities-occur-naturally (accessed 10/15/17).

36 Carvalho, A. (2013), Habitação para idosos em Lisboa: de colectiva a assistida. O caso de Alvalade (Housing for the elderly in Lisbon: from multifamily housing to assisted living. The Alvalade case study), PhD thesis, Instituto Superior Técnico da Universidade Técnica de Lisboa.

CHAPTER TEN

Therapeutic Use of Outdoor Spaces and Plant Materials

THE landscape matters to everyone, including older people. We have known this intuitively for hundreds of years, but in the last 40 years we have gathered convincing empirical evidence. In 500 BC, the Persians created gardens for sensory purposes by combining beauty, fragrance, flowing water, and cooling temperatures.[1]

How Does the Landscape Make a Difference?

Today it is not uncommon to find buildings in high-density cities like Singapore draped in landscape 6 to 15 stories above the street.[2] One of the Lufthansa Senator Lounges in the Frankfurt Airport has a life-size, back-lighted wall mural of a German forest that is approximately 60 feet wide and 15 feet tall. Padded recliners adjacent to the mural provide a place for travelers to read or relax. We also know that prisoners in detention facilities, office workers, young minorities in public housing, and people in health care settings are all adversely affected when they are denied visual access to natural landscape views.[3, 4, 5, 6] Since the landmark work of Roger Ulrich[7] in the mid-eighties, a great deal of evidence-based research

has been conducted to understand this phenomenon. Some theories claim the connection with landscape is innate and appears as a survival response. Other studies have shown deep and powerful connections to mental health and physical well-being.[8] Research conducted in health care facilities often use physiological measures (stress hormones in the blood, blood pressure, pulse) to gauge impact.

Biophilia

E.O. Wilson,[9] an environmental biologist, was one of the first contemporary scholars to write about the benefits of outdoor spaces. He believed that humans had a deep-seated desire to affiliate with and otherwise respond positively to nature. From a design perspective, Stephen Kellert[10] has provided a framework for defining how the experience of nature can be translated into environmental settings. His work "emphasizes the necessity of maintaining, enhancing and restoring the beneficial experiences of nature in the built environment." He identifies 12 features of the natural environment: 1) color, 2) water, 3) air, 4) sunlight, 5) plants, 6) animals, 7) natural materials,

Figure 10-1 The Senator Lounge in the Frankfurt Airport features a backlighted mural of a forest: Located at the end of the lounge and separated by a partial wall, it includes recliners oriented toward the screen. The purpose is to provide a quiet and relaxing place for travelers to unwind.

8) views and vistas, 9) facade greening, 10) geology and landscape, 11) habitats and eco-systems, and 12) fire. He also identifies 60 other elements and attributes that define a universe of impacts.

Ulrich has identified four major therapeutic benefits of biophilia: 1) sense of control, 2) exposure to nature, 3) encouraging exercise, and 4) promoting social exchange.[11] Ulrich's research with Craig Zimring has laid the foundation for many of the issues identified as environmental stressors in health care settings.[12] The category of "ecological health," which includes gardens, views of nature, landscape-themed artwork, soothing music, nature sounds, and soothing colors has maintained prominence as a major influence on health and well-being. Ulrich found that "viewing nature" reliably produced stress reductions within a 3- to 5-minute period. In other work, he demonstrated how scenes from nature could reduce pain perception. The more engrossing the nature-induced distraction, especially those that mixed sound with images, the greater the pain alleviation.

In long-term care, where chronic conditions are more common, benefits appear to be profound with the physically and cognitively frail. Susan Rodeik[13] has

systematically examined impacts and effects of gardens and landscapes on assisted living and dementia residents.

Physical Health Benefits

Because older frail people experience difficulty with ambulation but need to stay mobile, some of the most powerful benefits come from walking for exercise. This can take place inside, but many buildings are not designed to encourage residents to walk. They either do not have enough space or lack seating for residents to periodically rest and recharge. Going outside, depending on the season and climate, is often a much better alternative. Exercise can have positive physical benefits such as strengthening agility, gait, and posture. It can help reduce the losses in bone density and muscle mass, which result from sedentary behavior. Likewise, it can support balance control and mitigate high levels of stress and anxiety. Many chronic conditions can be aided by exercise, including arthritis, heart disease, cognitive function, and Type 2 diabetes.[14]

Figure 10-2 **Large mature trees provide a picturesque feature in any landscape:** In addition to the beautiful branching pattern of this live oak, it offers shade, a contrasting scale element, and a place for relaxation. Trees also communicate a sense of timelessness and a connection to nature.

Figure 10-3 **A partially enclosed atrium at the Champalimaud Centre for the Unknown in Lisbon, Portugal, has aesthetic and therapeutic purposes:** Patients undergoing chemotherapy view the garden from the inside or undergo therapy in adjacent outdoor spaces. Balconies and terraces that overlook the garden in this multistory building serve patients, doctors, and researchers.

Mental Health Benefits

Spending time outside can improve mood and lessen agitation and aggression. Access to sunlight and high levels of artificial light have been shown to reduce depression as well as Seasonal Affective Disorder (SAD). Because sunlight is brighter than any artificial light it is especially effective. For those with trouble sleeping or prone to depression, sunlight can reset circadian rhythms and result in higher levels of vitamin D. Studies from health care settings demonstrate that natural environments have major impacts on stress reduction.[15] These are so powerful that many hospitals prescribe nature videos or use virtual reality simulations[16] for patients convalescing from surgeries.

The option of going outside offers choices including social exchange or privacy and solitude. When you live in a group environment where meals are taken together and activities are often jointly offered, getting away even from your friends is welcomed periodically.

BENEFITS FOR PEOPLE WITH DEMENTIA

People with cognitive impairments clearly show benefits from having contact with the outdoors. Dementia robs the individual of memory, learning, judgment, and the ability to fully understand what is happening to them. Frustration and misunderstanding often lead to agitation and aggressive behavior. Emotional outbursts and aggressive, demeaning rhetoric can be difficult for the staff and other residents to tolerate. Medications are frequently used to control these outbursts but their most common side effect is drowsiness and inactivity.

Figure 10-4 This UK dementia garden has places to sit, pathways for walking, a gentle flowing fountain, and planter boxes for resident gardens: Secured gardens are especially attractive to the families of dementia residents. The right mix of furniture can also help residents and visitors think about how these spaces can be activated.

However, people with moderate dementia are often ambulatory and accustomed to walking and being physically active. Going outside to exercise is a very natural and appropriate way to respond, but takes time and patience on the part of the staff. Residents can experience hallucinations, depression, delusions, pacing, wandering, and sleep disorders. Studies have shown that for people with dementia, spending time outdoors decreases agitation and aggressive behaviors, improves sleep, adjusts hormone imbalance, and stimulates vitamin D production.[17] Benefits from better sleep patterns and lower agitation save money and aggravation by reducing staff time and the use of sedative-type medications. Other therapeutic strategies focus on security, stimulation, companionship, and building on existing strengths. Dementia affects each individual in a unique way, making it complicated to treat but fascinating to study. It is gratifying to know that outdoor exposure has positive benefits for almost all cognitively impaired individuals. Because contact with nature is so effective, spending time outside is crucial. Most dedicated dementia clusters have a secured outdoor area, but many are designed to be used only with staff supervision, which eliminates the ability of residents to access these spaces at will. Engaging residents in activities they have experienced earlier in life, such as feeding birds and watering plants, can also provide an enhanced sense of purpose.

Design Considerations for Gardens and Outdoor Spaces

Designing outdoor spaces for people with physical frailty and dementia requires careful attention to detail as well as common sense. Rodiek and Schwartz[18] discovered that one of the major impediments was high thresholds at exit doorways. They also found exit doors were often too heavy and thus difficult for residents to manipulate by themselves. Other common shortcomings were inadequate seating and sun protection. Criticisms from staff and families about "low interest" landscapes involved plants with little variety in terms of color, type, and size. Also criticized were settings that contained too much hardscape (paved area) in proportion to softscape (plants and ground cover). A good percentage of softscape is 60–75%, depending on the nature of the garden and if assembly uses are anticipated. Sidewalks that are 5 feet in width allow two people to walk side by side without taking up too much space. Both hardscape and softscape are important. The beauty, color, and lushness of a garden are mood enhancing, while paving is necessary to encourage walking and exercise.

VARIETY AND STIMULATION

The best gardens are stimulating but not overpowering. Plant choices should embrace differences in height, color,

(a)

(b)

texture, fragrance, and touch. The garden should have natural background sounds (for example, birds, insects, squirrels, flowing water, and wind). These should be integrated with interesting places to sit, engaging activities, and objects to see. Making the garden area more in scale and character with a typical backyard garden can make it familiar and endearing. It is important to be well maintained and coordinated with the growing season. Plants like succulents, vegetables, or herbs can define specific planting beds, while vertical trellises, hedges, and closely

Design Considerations for Gardens and Outdoor Spaces **257** spaced trees can provide a sense of three-dimensional enclosure. Water is a sacred element that can create a quiet spiritual mood or a lively attractive display and is necessary to attract animal life. A well-designed garden uses foreground and background planting as well as raised beds to make it easier to see, touch, and smell different plants.

INSIDE LOOKING OUT

Keep in mind that more residents will be looking at the garden from the inside than from the outside, especially in the winter. Some older people are sensitive to breezes as well as hot or cold temperatures due to their inability to regulate body temperature. Also, remember that Ulrich's research was about visual connection and not necessarily direct experience. Views to the garden should start with big windows and low sill heights. This optimizes the view for a person sitting at a dining room table as well as for someone lying in bed. Designing the inside building edge to accommodate a chair or a built-in window seat can optimize the view. Bringing plants, birds, scenery, and wildlife to the building edge creates an animated scene. Bird feeders, temperature gauges, and water features can be easily viewed from the inside. Views of attractive outdoor sitting areas can motivate residents to go outside, while placing outdoor features too far away from the security of the building edge may result in less use. When given the choice, residents often prefer to sit near a door at the building's edge rather than in the middle of the garden.

An active area that is often overlooked is the entrance to the building. It is a favorite place to sit and watch the activity of entering and exiting the building. Also, visitors frequently form their first impression of the place at this point. Decorations that celebrate holidays, along with changes in seasonal planting, are seen by the greatest number of visitors when placed here. Winter gardens, atriums, solariums, and conservatories can be used as dramatic entry or sitting areas adjacent to a living room or dining room space.

FAMILY SUPPORT AND SOCIAL USE

The outdoor landscape should be a retreat as well as a place for families to celebrate a birthday, holiday, or anniversary.

Figure 10-6 **A narrow sitting area outside of the Beverly Hills CS dining room takes in activity along the adjacent street and sidewalk:** Located on the south, it receives plenty of sun. Plant materials growing along an elevated trellis with umbrella tables below provide shade and a comfortable place to "people watch."

Families generally appreciate outdoor areas because they provide privacy. On sunny days they can lighten everyone's mood while providing a place to sit, eat, and relax. Tables and chairs that accommodate 5 to 8 people provide flexibility. Even when empty, furniture suggests places that accommodate conversation and relaxation. The same thing can be said for children's play equipment. When located an appropriate distance from the building so residents are not disturbed, it sends a message to families that everyone, even children, are welcome. Family members often feel that walking for exercise in the fresh air is a refreshing change of pace. The scenery can stimulate different topics of conversation as well as memories. When a building is located close to a shopping center, children's day care, or a park, these places can be convenient nearby destinations. Special events and barbecues that draw larger crowds can be staged outside or under a tent on the grounds. Using outdoor space this way is also cost effective. Night lighting can look attractive and may make it more attractive to sit outdoors after the sun sets. Sometimes in the summer, outdoor spaces are too warm during the day but are perfect in the evening because of re-radiation from surrounding hard surfaces. Heating elements are often used on porches to extend their use during cool days in the fall and spring.

FURNITURE

Outdoor seating should be sturdy and well-constructed for the type of climate anticipated. Generally individual chairs that are easy to reposition are the most effective. Chairs with relatively high seats and armrests are easier to exit. Padded furniture on a resilient frame is the best choice for construction, and wood is less likely to overheat in the sun than metal. Rocking chairs and gliders are popular because the gentle motion is often soothing, with pleasant associations. However, they may be hard to enter or exit.

GARDENS FOR NURTURING

One of the most commonly shared activities for older people is to tend a garden or nurture plants. Because this often serves a lifelong interest, it bodes well for its popularity later in life. However, as a person ages their ability to participate in gardening is often limited. The oldest-old must be careful about too much sun exposure on thinning skin, which can easily be damaged. Wearing a hat can reduce susceptibility to temperature and humidity swings, and placing foam around the handles of garden tools can make them easier to manipulate for those with arthritis.[19]

Common features include raised planting beds, a convenient water source, and a supply of potting soil. For serious gardeners, a small shed or greenhouse can be used to store supplies and protect plants from high and low temperatures. It is also important to have stable chairs and tables. Low

Figure 10-7 **Lightweight chairs like this one from the Vigs Ängar CS courtyard have armrests and can be easily repositioned to take advantage of views and sun access:** Wood is a resilient material that does not absorb heat and can be outfitted with a padded seat for comfort and to increase the seat height.
Courtesy of Lillemor Husberg.

fences are useful in keeping out animals and other intruders. Vegetables, spices, and flowers are favorite summer plants that can produce food as well as create beauty.

In Europe, allotment gardens located adjacent to public parks are very popular. When well maintained, a resident garden can be attractive, but toward the end of the growing season it can appear shabby. Selecting a location with good sun access but relatively low overall visibility is often prudent. The oldest-old are often too impaired to actively participate in gardening but still enjoy the vicarious pleasures of watching others tend plants or walking through a garden. Gentle ramped surfaces, frequent benches, raised planting beds, and handrails are important considerate features.

Figure 10-8 **This orange grove is adjacent to a resident garden near an assisted living building in southern California:** These trees are appreciated because they are well maintained, symbolize southern California, and can be harvested by residents and their families. The decomposed granite base (compared with pavement) reduces problems with residents slipping on fruit when it falls to the ground.

Dementia Gardens

Landscape spaces for people with dementia are like those for the physically frail with a few exceptions. People with dementia benefit more from access to outdoors because they often live in confined settings. Physically, many have the ability to ambulate and enjoy walking freely outside or within the building. Elopement is a concern, especially in the beginning, when residents first move to a secured environment. Many spry residents are tempted to escape through open windows or by climbing a low-perimeter garden fence. For this reason, fences should be 6 to 8 feet in height and difficult to climb. A solid or thick landscape-covered surface should be used when a fence overlooks a busy street or sidewalk. Some fence designs stop at 6 feet with a more open trellis design above that height. This can result in a more attractive residentially scaled fence that is still an effective barrier. There are benefits to using

Figure 10-9 **Walking is the easiest and most popular form of exercise:** A path around the perimeter of a building is a good place to start. In this assisted living building in the UK, a separate walking pathway within a secured area is available for residents with memory loss.

courtyards for a dementia garden, as demonstrated in the Vigs Ängar and De Hogeweyk case studies, because they can facilitate staff monitoring. Toxic plants should be eliminated. Also plants that drop seedpods or fruit may cause a slipping hazard and can be equally dangerous. Specifying fruit trees, for example, often requires a location away from paved surfaces or more vigilant maintenance.

Because staff are the "gatekeepers," they must feel comfortable with the visibility of the garden from the inside of the building. The grounds should be configured to avoid blind spots and landscape planting arranged so their height and mass does not block visibility. Large windows from public spaces that take in a full view are important safety considerations. If surveillance is compromised, the staff will lock doors and the garden will be made inaccessible.

Staff concentrate on personal caregiving and are often less available to walk residents individually. This is a job well suited to volunteers, family members, or even less-impaired residents living in the dementia cluster. Walking groups are popular and there is evidence they are more effective when organized in the morning.[20] The garden should have a walking pathway, preferably of a looped design. A "figure eight" plan can offer a short and long route as well as adding variety. The pathway should be designed to eventually return to the place where it started. A "dead end" design can confuse some residents who might not know how to turn around or find their way back. Spaces adjacent to the inside and outside of an exit door are also important. An inside entry can be configured to display hats, boots, coats, and rain gear. This makes it easier to protect residents when they exit during inclement weather. An outdoor sheltered porch should be available near the exit door so residents can sit in a protected area. There are many theories that direct the placement of landmarks for orientation purposes.[21] These work for some residents but not all. Generally having an open view of the garden, like the open plan of an interior space, makes it easier for residents to contemplate where they are going and how to return. Using familiar objects like barbecues, garden sheds, mailboxes, and vegetable gardens as visual mnemonic devices can be helpful. It is useful to know what residents use in their own homes as a point of departure for designating features that could become familiar. In some gardens, basketball hoops have been used to encourage upper body strength-building. The view of landscape and the opportunity to experience it has significant therapeutic value.

Figure 10-10 **The Swedes love the outdoors, which is why every nursing and dementia unit has an outdoor patio:** In the Vigs Ängar CS a paved garden area with a table and chairs is located a few steps away from every unit. Here, residents can host friends and family members, as well as enjoy the sun. *Courtesy of Lillemor Husberg.*

European Atrium Buildings

One of the most interesting and popular building forms in northern Europe is atrium-style purpose-built housing for older people. The mild summer and cold, windy winter factor into its popularity. However, a second strong influence is its socially conducive and landscape-friendly qualities. It also works well because its central shared space is often used for exercise in the winter. The light-filled atrium sandwiched between two rows of dwelling units allows sunlight to enter each unit from both the atrium and the exterior sides of the building. The single-loaded corridors serving units on both sides of the atrium create views and introduce sunlight, encouraging residents to sit outside their unit and overlook the atrium.

(a)

(b)

(c)

(d)

Figure 10-11a–d Atriums work well for housing older people in northern Europe: They create a sheltered space in the winter where residents can exercise. They also are popular places to socialize and pursue activities. Hard floor (concrete) and soft floor (soil) atriums are the two most common treatments. Most atriums are naturally ventilated.

Clockwise from upper left: Kuuselan Palvelukoti, Tampere, Finland; Egely, Ballerup, Denmark; Reinaldhuis, Haarlem, The Netherlands, and Rundgraafpark, Veldhoven, The Netherlands.

Atrium buildings can be classified depending on the design and nature of the atrium space. In some buildings the atrium is conditioned (heated and cooled) and treated like a huge lobby. This is familiar in atrium-style hotels and office buildings in the US. Northern European atrium buildings used for housing seem more intent on creating a comfortable but not necessarily fully conditioned atrium space. This strategy protects residents from strong cold winds in the winter, which can discourage them from going outside. It also benefits from solar gain, which along with supplemental heat can raise the temperature, making it only a few degrees cooler than a typical dwelling unit in the winter. These buildings are rarely air conditioned in the summer but benefit from ventilation equipment that expels naturally rising hot air through the roof. Overheating in the summer triggers ventilation fans and openable glass panels. Some also use canvas or fabric scrims to block direct sunlight to reduce heat. These atrium spaces can be very warm during extremely hot days, but at night are comfortable because they cool off after sunset. Through much of the year the atrium requires very little supplementation. Humidity in northern Europe is relatively low so it doesn't compromise comfort in the mid-summer. Because the walls supporting the sides of the atrium are structural, they are rather easy and inexpensive to enclose. Fire and smoke suppression systems are also necessary but are often not that complicated or costly.

PLANT MATERIAL USE

How plant materials have been arrayed on the ground plane varies among building designs. In general, plant materials are used to create a relaxed milieu and to introduce the psychological and therapeutic benefits discussed earlier. In an atrium, plants are better protected and may experience a longer lifespan, like they could in a greenhouse. In these controlled settings, birds, fish, and other caged wildlife can also be introduced to give the atrium additional life and variety. On upper floors, plant materials can screen the balcony edge, open views or afford additional privacy.

In some buildings, the atrium floor is a solid concrete lid above another ground floor use. In this condition, trees and plant materials are placed in containers or in shallow raised earthen berms above the slab.

When the atrium floor is soil, the base provides the opportunity for relatively large plants and trees to be placed (like the La Valance CS). These designs create atriums that are more like gardens, which use plants and landscape features to add delight. A 50/50 or 40/60 split of hard surface to soft landscape is common. Hard surface materials are often planned for large and small scale activity purposes. A simple 3 × 3 matrix of atrium types might involve a hard, semi-hard, and soft soil floor treatment on the X-X axis with a fully conditioned, partially conditioned, or unconditioned atrium space on the Y-Y axis.

Figure 10-12 **This winter garden/atrium in a Dutch housing project is created by stretching the facade that covers a single-loaded corridor to enclose an additional garden space:** The heavy planting in combination with a sizable paved area is used as a retreat for residents and a special events space for the neighborhood.

QUALITIES OF ATRIUM BUILDINGS

Transparent roof treatments often involve clear glass panels in scissors-like formations that facilitate run-off and allow some portion of the glass enclosure to be opened for ventilation. Other treatments include flat louvers that can pivot or skylights on tracks that can slide to one side. When big enough, large sliding horizontal skylights used on a flat roof can change the character of the space from an atrium to a courtyard.

Atrium spaces have many compelling qualities. The atrium roof is often clear glass, which allows shadow patterns from mullions to be cast on walls and floors. The visible sky can change color and intensity, giving the atrium remarkable dynamic variety. Cloud patterns, sunrises, sunsets, starlight, and moonlight all offer unique nuances. Even the sound of rain and the ability to sense it from a protected space is a special experience. The natural sunlight that filters through a roof to the ground plane has a captivating quality. The full spectrum color of natural light is more vivid and beautiful than artificial light. Because much of northern Europe is in the extreme northern latitudes, they experience fewer hours of daylight in the winter. They value natural light and take advantage of it as much as possible. In the summer, daylight is abundant and is appreciated even more.

A key benefit of an atrium is the opportunity it provides for protected exercise all year long. Older people, especially in the winter, are cautious about their safety. Cold winds, snow, slippery surfaces, and the discomfort of going outside all discourage residents from walking for exercise in the winter, as well as in the late fall and early spring. Walking clubs are often popular and when the weather doesn't cooperate, a group of residents can walk around the atrium for exercise and feel secure. Even in the winter, temperatures in the atrium are moderate. Some buildings with smaller atriums set them aside for specific activities such as exercise and muscle strengthening. These centrally located spaces provide residents with a visible reminder of how important physical fitness is to longevity and health.

SOCIAL AND PSYCHOLOGICAL QUALITIES

Shared atrium spaces are often friendly places because people know one another and feel secure. The openness of the space and its central placement makes it a perfect place for social encounters. Small tables with chairs accommodate conversations among 2 to 4 people. Larger discussion groups like a reading circle or a card-playing group can also easily adapt to these spaces. Activities that need flexible space like table tennis, billiards, and exercise often benefit from an open space. Larger group events can be staged with the cascading single-loaded corridors above, providing additional viewing platforms for events. Large atriums can invite neighbors to events like a farmer's market or a thrift shop sale, which benefits everyone. Several atriums use the Dutch and Danish ritual of morning and afternoon coffee to generate activity and invite residents from the neighborhood. Residents can participate directly or they can watch the activity and enjoy it vicariously.

Figure 10-13 **This Dutch two-story enclosed street provides a protected route from dwelling units to a main common building:** This is especially useful in the winter because of cold wind gusts from the North Sea. The space is not conditioned but has ventilators to reduce overheating in the summer.

The setting is informal enough to recruit passers-by or curious onlookers. When large plants and trees fill the atrium and subdivide spaces into smaller intimate places, they often add an element of serenity.

Wide corridors adjacent to units make it easy for residents on each floor to meet one another informally. Sitting areas can be designed into the open corridor like in the Akropolis AFL in Rotterdam, where an outward 18" bulge in the corridor edge accommodates a chair and table. Floor-bound friendships are easier to make when there is an excuse for saying hi to a neighbor.

ENCLOSED STREET

One of the simplest approaches is to create an enclosed street. These are often one- or two-story spaces that are approximately 10–18 feet in width. They can be intimate and simple and often have directionality leading to a common community space at one end of the "street." These spaces are friendly with windows and doors that connect dwelling units to the corridor. If the shared corridor is wide enough it can accommodate a small table with a few chairs and can become a place where residents socialize with one another. Plants can be trained along walls on both sides of the corridor, softening the space. Wall and floor surfaces are usually exterior materials, like brick and concrete tile. The second story of a two-story building usually has a narrow walkway that floats in the center of the space, allowing light to filter down on both sides to the floor below. This kind of light- and plant-filled space is a great replacement for a dark and dingy double-loaded corridor.

CONCLUSIONS

Popular atriums in northern Europe have been shown to be beneficial in many ways. Their use should be explored further in the US, especially in Frost Belt areas, where the temperate climate available inside the atrium can encourage social exchange and exercise in the winter.

Endnotes

1 Detweiler, M., Sharma, T., Detweiler, J., et al. (2012), What is the Evidence to Support the Use of Therapeutic Gardens for the Elderly? *Psychiatry Investigation*, 9(2), 100–110, https://www.ncbi.nlm.nih.gov/pmc/articles/PMC3372556/pdf/pi-9-100.pdf (accessed 10/15/17).

2 Williams, F. (2016), This Is Your Brain on Nature, *National Geographic*, 229(1) 50–51.

3 Kuo, F.E., and Sullivan, W.C. (2001), Environment and Crime in the Inner City: Does Vegetation Reduce Crime? *Environment and Behavior* 33(3), 343–67.

4 Moore, E. (1981–82), A Prison Environment's Effect on Health and Care Services Demands, *Journal of Environmental Systems*, 11, 17–34.

5 Rodiek, S., and Schwartz, B. (eds.) (2007), *Outdoor Environments for People with Dementia*, Haworth Press, Binghamton, NY.

6 Largo-Wight, E., Chen, W., Dodd, V., and Weiler, R. (2011), Healthy Workplaces: The Effects of Nature Contact at Work on Employee Stress and Health, *Public Health Reports*, 126 (Suppl 1) 124–130.

7 Ulrich, R. (1984), View Through a Window May Influence Recovery from Surgery, *Science*, 224, 420–21.

8 Marcus, C.C., and Sachs, N. (2014), *Therapeutic Landscapes: An Evidence-Based Approach to Designing Healing Gardens and Restorative Outdoor Spaces*, John Wiley & Sons, Hoboken, NJ.

9 Wilson, E.O. (1984), *Biophilia: The Human Bond with Other Species*, Harvard University Press, Cambridge, MA.

10 Kellert, S., Heerwagen, J., and Mador, M. (2008), *Biophilic Design: The Theory, Science and Practice of Bringing Buildings to Life,* John Wiley & Sons, Hoboken, NJ.

11 Marcus and Sachs, *Therapeutic Landscapes*.

12 Ulrich, R., Zimring, C., Zhu, X., et al. (2008), A Review of the Research Literature on Evidence-Based Healthcare Design, *Health Environments Research and Design*, 1(3), 61–125.

13 Rodiek, S. (2002), Influence of an Outdoor Garden on Mood and Stress in Older Persons, *Journal of Therapeutic Horticulture*, 13, 13–21.

14 Marcus and Sachs, *Therapeutic Landscapes*.

15 Sternberg, E. (2009), *Healing Spaces: The Science of Place and Well Being*, Harvard University Press, Cambridge, MA.

16 Westervelt, A. (2015), Virtual Reality as a Therapy Tool, *Wall Street Journal*, June 26, http://www.wsj.com/articles/virtual-reality-as-a-therapy-tool-1443260202 (accessed 10/15/17).

17 Sternberg, *Healing Spaces*.

18 Rodiek and Schwartz, *Outdoor Environments for People with Dementia*.

19 Victoria State Government, Better Health Channel (2017), Gardening for Older People, https://www.betterhealth.vic.gov.au/health/healthyliving/gardening-for-older-people (accessed 10/15/17).

20 Louvering, M.J., Cott, C.A., Wells, D.L., et al. (2002), A Study of a Secure Garden in the Care of People with Alzheimer's Disease, *Canadian Journal on Aging*, 21(3), 417–27.

21 Zeisel, J. (2007), Creating a Therapeutic Garden That Works for People Living with Alzheimer's, in *Outdoor Environments for People with Dementia* (eds. S. Rodiek and B. Schwarz), Haworth Press, Binghamton, NY.

CHAPTER ELEVEN

How Will Technology Help People Stay Independent and Avoid Institutionalization?

THERE are many technologies on the horizon creating possibilities for the oldest-old who seek additional support to stay independent. The internet and cloud computing make much of this possible today. Previous technological innovations like Personal Response Systems (PERS) are being combined with newer technologies that enhance communication and information availability. Developments in internet-based services and devices are facilitating communication and making it easier to stay at home with connections to people and services who can help achieve that goal. Some of the most intriguing possibilities involve technological applications for fall prevention and the use of communications technology to direct personal care support for the frail. These devices will provide an opportunity to stay at home with technological assistance rather than move to an environment with services like assisted living. This chapter contains a range of topics where new technologies have the promise to radically reorder the status quo, creating efficiencies and opportunities that enhance independence and facilitate aging in place.

Transportation Is a Major Barrier Today

A remarkable 55% of men 85+ drive[1] and when they can't they typically rely on friends and relatives to drive them to important destinations. Even with older driver training tutorials, like the web-based AARP program, older people can reach a point when driving a car is hazardous both to themselves and to others. Older drivers typically have trouble seeing, hearing, and reacting. Furthermore, people with dementia often experience deterioration in driving skills without being aware of it.

Online rideshare companies have offered an attractive alternative to driving your own vehicle and retirees can benefit from this both as consumers and as providers. Older drivers have been shown to be highly valued by online services. Retirees with Medicare coverage often do not need health care benefits and retirement gives them the flexibility to work when they want. Uber reports that older drivers (55+) are dependable and highly rated by consumers and make up 25% of current drivers. The addition

Figure 11-1 **Taxicabs have traditionally been one of the most common forms of nonfamily transportation for the oldest-old:** With the advent of internet ride sharing companies in metropolitan areas, using an automobile to get around is even more affordable. In the future, driverless vehicles may further increase access and affordability for older people and the handicapped.

of an "accessible" transportation choice in the Uber smart phone menu also demonstrates their interest in serving this potential market. Furthermore, the increase in popularity of "shared ridership" at a lower price point may appeal to older retirees, who are likely to be making discretionary trips with fewer time constraints. However, to participate in this new world, older people will need to sharpen their computer skills.

Internet Service Utilization

Widespread use of computer-assisted devices is increasing dramatically with the emergence of the boomer cohort. Boomers are more familiar with these technologies and have greater potential to be active tech-adaptors. However, the technological savvy of the current 65-and-older population lags far behind younger cohorts. While 84% of all Americans use the internet, only 58% of the 65+ population use it. In 2015, 64% of all Americans owned a smart phone, but only 27% of the 65+ population had one. However, 54% (twice the percentage of the 65+ users) in the 50–64 cohort use them.

The two major barriers are **financial ability** and **technical knowledge.** Because the smart phone and the tablet have become popular portal devices for the older population to connect to the internet, it is particularly important to provide access to knowledge about how to finance and use these devices. Big shifts in smart phone

Figure 11-2 **An issue that threatens the independence of the oldest-old is their lack of knowledge about the internet and smart phones/tablets:** In the Humanitas Bergweg AFL, equipment and assistance is available to help residents and older people in the community stay current with new technologies. Home care programs here and abroad are increasingly using smart devices to monitor clients and schedule services.

usage will be necessary in the oldest cohorts for this technology to be effective. The other advantage is that it will enhance communication with younger family members.

In the last decade, along with the emergence of online rideshare services, new startups are bringing goods and services to the home. These online service providers make it possible to avoid driving and allow older people to receive groceries and pharmaceuticals, make home repairs, clean the house, or get medical advice about themselves or their pets without leaving the house. These types of services have actually been around for decades, but the internet has created better access and given them renewed relevance.

Home-Delivered Services

Today, online grocery services are vigorously competing with fixed stores located in the community. Both online grocery and food delivery services have identified older consumers as a growing market. Along with easier transportation access, these services solve a lot of logistical problems for older people in cities and suburbs. Driving can be dangerous and hauling groceries is an additional hassle for someone with debilitating arthritis. Traditionally older people are not early adaptors but necessity may provide the incentive to be more adventuresome. They can benefit in many ways. Companies like online vacation rental services have simplified access to underutilized resources that can be shared with a broader market. Given the amount of "underutilized" space in the housing stock occupied by older people, this could be a significant financial benefit.

The growth potential of the shared economy has entrepreneurs thinking about how to apply this model to home care. In 2015, venture capital sources heavily invested in private home care startups (**Honor, HomeHero,** and **Hometeam**[2]). Some of these programs are starting with less sophisticated communications technology, but are poised to adapt new advanced systems as the market grows and matures. Computer-based home care assistance has been evolving in public systems in northern Europe, but the home care business in the US has been primarily private pay based and is limited by cost and availability. Today older people are much more open to staying home with peripatetic help.

Programs like **PACE** (Program for All Inclusive Care for the Elderly) and **CBCS** (Community-Based Care Systems) have sought to weave together health care monitoring with home care service and therapy, allowing the

Figure 11-3 PERS devices that allow residents to call for help have been around for decades: Today, these devices are being linked to more sophisticated response systems. In addition to emergency response, new services such as professional advice and real-time monitoring are available. In the future, wearable devices will likely be programmed to anticipate potential problems.

older person to stay at home and avoid a nursing home placement. The main market for these providers has been low-income "dual eligibles" who qualify for expanded Medicare and Medicaid services, thus reducing the cost burden.

The steady advance of **PERS** into the domains of health monitoring and video communication demonstrate the future of these services. **Great Call,**[3] a relatively new company in the 30-year-old emergency response business, has developed systems that facilitate family communication through **video chat.** They have options for conversations with health care professionals and an urgent call response system that establishes two-way communication in the event of a fall or emergency. The latter is similar to the OnStar calling system available for cars. These added services include important capabilities and are expanding devices to be more proactive.

Another direction is the use of **wearable devices** that monitor fitness activities, global position, and health care indicators, such as weight, heart rate, and sleep patterns. More than a half dozen companies (**Fitbit, Garmin, Vivosmart, Jawbone, UP2, etc.**)[4] are merchandizing these types of wearable fitness devices. They are evolving and may soon anticipate falls by monitoring changes in gait or balance control, perhaps through insoles located in shoes. This device could provide proactive advice to avoid a serious fall before it occurs or to pinpoint a medication adherence problem before it becomes critical.

Figure 11-4 Large corporations are testing new technologies and designs to make it easier for older people to carry out everyday tasks independently: The desire is to combine knowledge of human anatomy with better products and designed environments. These approaches will usher in more sophisticated helping technology in the decades ahead.

Today, these "wearables" appear to be more popular with technology-savvy younger cohorts but it is predicted that by 2019, 20% of the 65+ will also be using them.[5] Paired with emergency response technology, it can be a great way of monitoring movement activity and communicating the result to the person or their family.

Advances in artificial intelligence and connectivity will make access to other devices more informative. These will generate a huge amount of information that will one day be used for predictive models. Systems that utilize **GPS** and **RIFD** technology can now monitor the location of Alzheimer's wanderers to reduce anxiety for caregivers and families. Electronic "geo-fences" have sometimes been used to give dementia residents freedom with security. A device like this is in use at the Ærtebjerghaven CS.

Services like **NEST**, in addition to being a proactive security system, have the capability of internet messaging as well as access to the Internet of Things. They become more useful than a traditional security system by allowing remote access to energy management devices like a thermostat, locking system, or lighting controls. The next chapter will be to tie the system into an Artificial Intelligence (AI) platform, making it more independent and consistent with your past experiences and future activity patterns. Examples of advanced and financially affordable AI are the **Amazon Echo, OK Google,** and the **Apple Siri.** Through the voice-controlled Alexa program, the Echo continues to expand its capabilities. You can order **Domino's** pizza, **Spotify** music, and **Uber** transportation. The open platform design for most of these devices invites developers to create useful apps, which will continue to increase its utility as the popularity of the device grows. The devices are also affordable and user friendly. Its greatest future promise will likely be coordinating services. However, it needs to be connected to the internet and today it has limited appeal to the 75+ market, but this will likely change over time.

Typically, early adapters of Echo and Nest are upper-middle-class, well-educated young people in their 30s and 40s. These technologies may eventually come from this group of "children" to assure them their parents are safe and secure. The flexible communications platform makes it easy to replace a granny cam or any other remote monitoring device. Tie-ins with medication-dispensing equipment and reports from mobile caregivers can also increase the utility of these devices.

Figure 11-5 **PARO, the baby seal, has demonstrated its ability to calm individuals with dementia:** These "comfort devices" are more common today as toymakers assess the other end of the age spectrum for new applications. This approach is controversial. Some critics argue these devices contribute to a lack of meaningful human contact but research has found them to be effective.

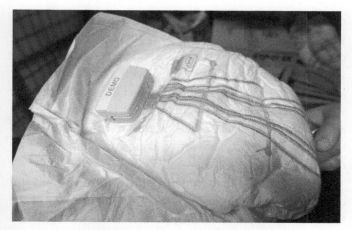

Figure 11-6 **Incontinence is a major LTC issue but today adult diapers have made this serious challenge manageable:** The cost of products and the labor, however, remains substantial. This three-day diaper system is used to arrive at a more predictable toileting schedule.

Driverless Cars

These were a "futurist" dream only a few years ago before Google became serious in testing the potential for mass implementation. Today, after two million miles of test-driving, 5 states have legalized them and 15 are considering it.[6] There are many compelling arguments for implementing the program, ranging from better traffic management to a reduction in the number of needed parking spaces. There is also the potential to save thousands of lives and prevent even more injuries from accidents. Although difficult to establish, most estimates place savings close to a trillion dollars a year. Timelines vary but most industry experts believe it will be a reality between 2020 and 2030. Most car companies applaud the idea and are working to make the transition as seamless as possible. Today's new cars contain intelligent safety features embedded in the car's operating system, including accident avoidance technology. Cars today are extremely reliable and advances in smart phone and AI technology will make them even safer in the future. The driverless car, unless held up by legal or cultural concerns, is likely to be inevitable.

Older, younger, and handicapped people will be among the major beneficiaries of the increase in mobility and potential cost savings. The most difficult family discussion is telling older family members they must give up driving. These transportation advances will make those conversations much easier.

Social Robots

It is a short jump from Alexa to social or affect-oriented robots, classified as devices with communications capabilities. They use AI but have the capability of mixing human-like learning to program themselves.[7] In contrast, functional robots have electro-mechanical capabilities along with the ability to communicate. Social robots appear to be on the cusp of broader distribution as helping devices for the elderly. True robots with brain and brawn are probably still a decade or more away. Most social robots that have been devised are mobile, interactive, and multidimensional. They are partly your therapist, partly your companion, and partly your servant. They have the capability of being more friendly and personal than **Siri** or **Alexa**. Using an avatar or screen with a human-like face allows it to smile and to provide facial gestures that are welcoming. Because the aging market is narrow, the first applications of devices such as this have been oriented toward a broader constituency, like use as a family helper or a personal assistant.

The **Robotbase Personal Robot**[8] can move around and communicates like a personal assistant. It has many of the same AI capabilities as the Apple **Siri**. In fact, critics have called it a "**Siri** on a stick." Prototypes are being tested and software is continually being developed. It is treated as a platform rather than a product, which opens it to a broader group of application developers. Advertisements describe it as a personal family robot capable of telling stories, playing music, turning on lights, locking doors, storing recipes, and making and receiving calls. It learns about your needs and interests and becomes more useful over time. It is composed of an avatar (Maya), can move around and is remotely controlled. The preliminary cost of the device is around $2,000. There are some interesting capabilities associated with the device as a companion for people with mild to moderate dementia. With the appropriate programming, it could suggest songs or learn how to communicate with people struggling with dementia. These devices often focus on people with memory loss because they are often very active and often respond positively to encouragement, yet they need direction. With some added advancements they could take walks with older individuals.

The **Giraffplus**[9] is an application being tested by individuals with mild cognitive impairment (MCI) in Europe. This mobile device can follow you around the house and provide reminders to do tasks like exercise or take medications. It is user directed and allows you to make and receive calls. You can be connected to your doctor and it measures and reports your blood pressure, weight, and blood sugar. This device has been tested in Western Europe with a small number of subjects in their own homes. Other social robots at various stages of development include the **Pepper**, **NAO**, **Jibo**, and **Buddy**.[10, 11] Some are desktop models while others have mobile capability. These examples are still under development and have limited capabilities.

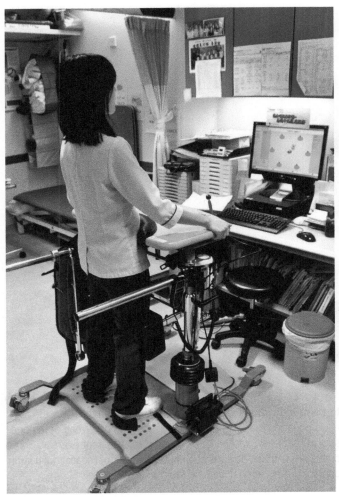

Figure 11-7 Equipment like this has been used diagnostically to measure gait and balance difficulties in the laboratory: In the future sensors in your shoes may be able to diagnose movement problems in real time while providing feedback about how to correct your stance before you trip or fall.

Another collection of devices often referred to as "comfort toys" mimic the behaviors of animals. The best-known and -researched toy in the last decade is **Paro**.[12] This Japanese toy robot looks like a soft, fur-covered baby seal. It has five sensors that allow it to respond to your voice or to your touch. First introduced in 1993, it has been primarily used to calm and comfort people with dementia. Research has shown that it reduces stress, enhances mood, and mitigates loneliness. The cost of the device (around $5,000) has kept it from being broadly distributed. The **companion robotic cat** by Hasbro is a recent less expensive option.[13] Introduced in 2016, this robotic toy costs slightly less than $100. It is not as sophisticated

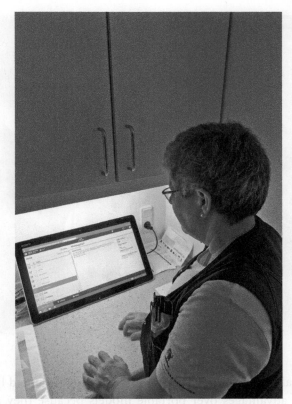

Figure 11-8 Computers are now omnipresent in most care settings: They are a comprehensive source of information about the needs and problems of residents and are becoming increasingly common in resident rooms for convenience and privacy. Although very useful, they do not replace individual caregivers who take responsibility for monitoring specific individuals.

as **Paro** but still responds to petting by turning over and by purring. It responds to your touch by encouraging you to pet it more. Its eyes close after a few minutes to extend battery life. These devices are not meant to substitute for family members, but the hope is that future models will continue to provide more positive feedback.

With the advent of sophisticated artificial intelligence capabilities, devices will become more personal and therapeutic. There is legitimate concern about the future of AI applications. Experts believe that AI will easily benefit society in the short run. But as soon as 2050, the blending of human and machine intelligence could bring us closer to "singularity," which would make it difficult to control. In response, entrepreneurs like Elon Musk are working toward devices that can be implanted in the brain to harness computer-based knowledge.

His company Neuralinks hopes initial efforts will help to control the side effects of diseases like Parkinsons.[14]

Functional Electro-mechanical Robots

Robots with electro-mechanical capabilities are familiar from movies, such as C3PO and R2D2 from *Star Wars* (1977). They have been around for decades, starting with the clunky ones as seen in *The Day the Earth Stood Still* (1951), and continue today in dark dramas like *iRobot* (2004) and *Ex Machina* (2015) or even comedies like *Robot and Frank* (2012). Autonomous helping robots with the capability of mimicking human movement and intelligence are probably at least 10 to 20 years away. There is controversy surrounding devices that threaten to replace human beings, as there is concern they will take over jobs in the future. A recent large-scale threat is "self-driving" long-haul trucks. Some estimates predict that more than a third of US jobs will be at "high risk" for automation by the early 2030s.[15] Industrial robots that carry out repetitive tasks are becoming increasingly common in manufacturing. Predictions peg the worldwide number at 52,000 in 2017. **Boston Dynamics,**[16] which has received numerous government defense contracts, has developed four-legged animal-like robotic devices for toting heavy loads over rugged terrain. The US military has strongly supported the development of robotic devices for defusing bombs and other warfare applications.

Japan is focused on the service demands of their large aging population, and therefore has an emphasis on robots targeted toward helping the elderly. Honda and Toyota have substantial research programs. The **ASIMO**[17] (Advanced Step in Innovation Mobility) represents Honda's 30-year investment in robotic research. This functional robot is 4 feet in height (eye level for a seated human) and weighs about 110 pounds. It walks at a rate of 4 miles/hour and can do various tasks, including opening a bottle, pouring a drink, kicking a ball, walking up and down stairs, and dancing. It is not capable of performing any personal care tasks, but future research is targeted toward these possibilities. **ASIMO** is an experimental prototype that can be leased for $150,000/month. Production models with practical applications appear to be years away. Early experiments like the nursebot, which was designed to deliver medications, seem crude in comparison to newer social

Figure 11-9 **Scooters are becoming more common as residents chose to replace cars with these safer, smaller-scale vehicles:** In northern Europe the government subsidizes the cost of scooters to encourage their use. They are a safe and efficient form of personal transportation, which is primarily used for local shopping and personal business destinations.

and mechanical models. Models that have taken advantage of artificial intelligence are also more user-friendly. The problem of directing devices to carry out useful work is a major challenge to the industry.

The **Robear**[18] is a Japanese transfer device that has been designed to resemble a smiling bear. It is a mobile device that can lift and carry a person between two outstretched arms. It has been anthropomorphized to look like an affectionate, friendly animal. This strategy could be applied to overhead lift devices, which might make them more whimsical and friendly, especially for people with dementia.

Transfer and Lifting Devices

The antecedent for robotic devices that assist in moving and transferring older people are lift devices. In the UK, Canada, Australia, and northern Europe they are relatively common because of concerns about workplace injuries. They are becoming more popular in the US as residents become frailer and more overweight. These devices increase employee retention and productivity, allowing middle-aged caregivers to avoid injury. Lift devices can either be built-in and connected to ceiling-mounted supports (like a rolling crane) or they can be self-contained mobile devices that are rolled into a room

to make the transfer. The crane-like ceiling-mounted lifts have advantages over portable models because they are always available but they are often more expensive. They are permanently stored near the ceiling of the room and are less bulky. Portable lifts are large and difficult to navigate because they require a lot of space. They are often stored in a separate room and are shared between residents, which can limit their availability.

Most northern European settings use a gantry-style ceiling-mounted unit that can move freely in two directions.[19] This provides lift flexibility by not requiring the older person to be moved from a single discrete location. The rolling gantry can be installed near the ceiling and attached to the wall, which bears the weight and partially disguises it. Other devices are suspended on steel columns that bear the weight of the assembly on an adjacent wall or floor. These portable models avoid attachment to the ceiling and can be assembled over a bed when needed. They utilize a similar electric lift motor and are often used in private apartments and houses.

A two-person manual lift requires caregivers to twist their body as they lift and move a resident. In addition to requiring two people, caregivers can injure themselves more easily or even drop the resident. Because a ceiling lift is convenient and easy to operate, they are more likely to be utilized on a regular basis. As they become more

Figure 11-10 **Ceiling-mounted electric lifts are commonly available to move residents in most northern Europe LTC settings:** Unfortunately, in the US this option is less common. The result for caregivers is that they are far more likely to sustain a debilitating back injury, especially when they lift and twist while transferring someone.

common, costs will likely drop. A gantry-style rolling crane attached to the wall can be less than $5,000, with the hydraulic lift motor varying from $2,500 to $5,000. Most northern European nursing homes and US Green House© models use a version of this technology. Safety standards for the movement and transfer of older people need to be updated. When compared to the cost of injury or the costs associated with disability compensation, they are good investments that generally pay for themselves.

Integrated lift devices are also very common for bathers and bathtubs. Usually a chair guided by a robotic arm is lowered outside the tub. It swivels to facilitate entry, lifts the person over the edge of the tub, and lowers them into the water. These devices are more popular in places like the UK, where regulations support cultural preferences for a bath over a shower. In the US, the extra time required to provide a bath can minimize its use. These lift devices can also frighten some people with dementia, which has led US providers to rely more on showers than bathtubs. Without lifting hardware, getting into and out of a conventional bathtub is both difficult and dangerous for older people with limited upper body strength. Tubs with doors are more popular, but often require the older person to be ambulatory.[20]

Exoskeletons

Research on exoskeletons has been centered either on helping people walk again or on providing additional strength to carry out tasks. Exoskeletons in industry and military application often consist of a metal framework of arms and legs that you can climb into like a uniform. These applications focus on lifting and moving heavy objects without causing harm to the operator. It resembles a mechanical body suit with electric motors that provide freedom of movement. The suit is controlled by the user; like a conventional car, it does not operate on its own. The devices manufactured today, like the **HULC** (Human Universal Load Carrier), the **Power Loader,** and the **XOS 2,**[21] can typically lift and manipulate 100 pounds in each arm. Military applications allow weapons to be easily carried and manipulated. In industry, they can be used to assemble large-scale components, move heavy loads, or navigate through the fragments of a collapsed building after an earthquake. They amplify the strength and force of the user, allowing them to combine the strength of a machine with the accuracy of a human operator. Exoskeletons have the potential, like lift devices, to allow a trained caregiver or family member to move a very frail older person. Before this can be fully implemented, issues like grip strength and safety need greater refinement.

Another application is as a rehabilitation therapy tool. Soldiers who have lost limbs or the control of arms and legs use these devices to relearn how to walk and move their arms. Independent exoskeleton devices like the **ReWalk** or **Ekso GT** can help people without lower body strength to walk upright with crutches. It exercises muscles and can possibly regenerate nerve circuits.

Figure 11-11 **One impressive aspect of the Danish home care system is how data and scheduling is tracked by experienced professionals:** Most information is available on computers, which are used to reschedule appointments and track trends and the progress of chronic problems. Morning and afternoon meetings with caregivers provide the opportunity to share experiences and help older residents stay independent in their own dwelling unit in the community.

Larger-scale rehabilitation devices like the **Lokomat**[22] utilize a treadmill to provide immediate feedback. This device is operating in over 400 installations throughout the world, providing user feedback about gait and balance control. The **MIT-Manus**[23] works on upper body limbs to overcome stroke damage by providing visual feedback as you carry out a manipulation regimen. Both devices utilize exoskeleton concepts for rehabilitation. Honda has developed a **Walking Assist Device**[24] that supports body weight and reduces load on the legs and knees. It is especially helpful when ascending or descending stairs. Motors lift the leg higher to lengthen a person's stride, making it easier to walk further and faster. These devices have a clinical appearance and a substantial price tag, which will need to be resolved for wider distribution.

The **AXO suit**[25] is an experimental exoskeleton designed to help the elderly remain active. It was created by a European university-industry research group. Like other exoskeletons, motors provide a power boost of up to 30 to 50% to supplement existing strength capacity. It is intended for errands, exercise, and activities that contribute to quality of life and independence rather than a prosthetic for everyday life. It is referred to as a tool rather than a robotic device. Advances in artificial intelligence and sensing create the potential to measure problems and ameliorate them by educating users about how to avoid falls in the future. These devices could also be designed to mitigate the severity of injuries due to a fall.

Protective Clothing

Another emerging area of study is the use of fabrics and materials to absorb the energy of a fall, thus reducing injury. A look at any of the "adaptive aging" websites[26] exposes a large collection of products designed to make life easier and safer for older people. Fall mitigation, which is a very important aspect of healthy aging, offers hard helmets, bulky hip protectors, and other devices that safeguard the older person from falls but ignore style and body image. Fashion and protective clothing designers operate in different orbits. Combining them requires a melding of design and engineering. Recently, scientists have produced materials intended to absorb the energy of a fall. One product, called **Armourgel**,[27] is thin and extremely resilient. It can easily be attached to the outside of an undergarment. Although it awaits commercial distribution, it has the potential with the right design to be attractive to the older consumer.

Along with functional and personal robots, exoskeletons and advanced energy-absorbing fabrics have the potential to provide help, support, and protection that can keep older people independent and active.

Scooters (Personal Operating Vehicles) and Mobility Aides

Mobility aides from the world of scooters and wheelchairs are exploring the future of personal mobility. These products are reinventing creative transportation alternatives for older people. The most popular "mobility scooter" is the **Amigo**,[28] which was introduced in the 1960s as "a friendly wheelchair." With the advent of electric cars and the widespread use of scooters in malls and grocery stores, they appear to be gaining broader acceptance. Scooters are very flexible and can operate indoors and outdoors. In the US, three- and four-wheel scooters qualify for 80% coverage

Figure 11-12 **Lately we have experienced tremendous growth in artificial intelligence:** Devices like OK Google, Amazon Echo, and Apple's Siri are increasingly being considered as potential helping devices for families, children, and the aged. It is likely that in the next 5–7 years we will see focused AI applications for the oldest-old.

under Medicare and can cost as little as $2,000. However, the qualifications for this benefit are stringent and only the most frail can meet them. In northern Europe and the UK, liberal policies have been implemented to get older people to abandon their cars for safer sidewalk-restricted personal vehicles. These policies hope to encourage greater mobility as well as safety. Scooters reduce traffic, minimize parking conflicts, and increase the mobility of the older people. Most sidewalk-restricted scooters travel at 4 mph, while higher-speed Class C vehicles are allowed on roads and highways. The "age-friendly initiative" introduced in Chapter 9 encourages increased mobility options for older people, including scooters. These devices help older people maintain their independence in the community. In Europe, higher density mixed-use development patterns with convenient stores and services make this type of transportation solution very effective.

Power wheelchairs are also available under Medicare, but it is difficult to qualify for them. Because they are expensive, the demand for market-rate models is low. Innovation in the wheelchair industry has suffered from

problems of affordability. The **Smart Chair**[29] is a cross between a scooter and a wheelchair. It is priced similarly to the Amigo, with a weight of 50 pounds, a speed of 5 mph, and a range of 15 miles. It is collapsible and can be stored in a trunk or checked as luggage on an airplane. The most sophisticated Segway-inspired wheelchair was the **iBot,** which had a production price of $25,000. Its inability to qualify for Medicare or Veterans Administration subsidies forced production to end in 2009. This product was a step forward in mobility but was unable to secure a market. Ten students at the ETH in Zurich created a prototype called the **Scalevo** that uses Segwey-like technology. Like the iBot, it has the capability of going up stairs (backwards) and raising the seat/platform to normal eye height. The **Ogo**[30] is a wheelchair that borrows physics principles from the Segway. It moves faster and is maneuverable in off-road conditions.

Virtual Reality

New virtual reality programs are priced for a mass market at a fraction of their cost in the past. **Google Cardboard** adapts to a smart phone for only $15–20. Devices like **Oculus Rift**, contain improvements in optics and image clarity, which have made them more effective and more realistic. These changes in affordability and quality have led them to predict sales of 500 million devices by 2025. The broad-based distribution of this product will also attract applications of this technology to a range of topics, including health care and the aged.

Most health care applications have dealt with professional training and clinical treatments. This tool has great promise in surgical training and remote applications. It has also been used to treat phobias and psychological problems that respond to immersion therapy. Phobias like the fear of flying or claustrophobia can benefit from this type of safe but realistic exposure to fearful experiences, as can PTSD and autism.

Older people with limited mobility can use this technology to have a fuller and more stimulating life.[31] Programs being developed by **Rendever** can take a shut-in to a unique architectural setting or a seaside venue where the outcome can be both stimulation and relaxation. VR experiences can take a wheelchair-bound person through a field of flowers or up the side of a mountain in a highly realistic way. **DEEP**, an Oculus Rift application, centers on relaxation, pain management, and meditation. New applications under development make exercise more stimulating and engaging. Future therapies for stroke rehabilitation and dementia treatment are also experimenting with virtual reality applications. Today, hospitals are using VR for postsurgical exposure to green spaces and landscapes, in an effort to increase the pace of postsurgical convalescence. Treatments for chronic conditions have even greater potential to increase comfort, reduce pain, and control stress.

Replaceable Body Parts

One common approach to disability brought about by aging has been the replacement or repair of body parts. It is common today to replace hips and knees as well as to perform cochlear implants and lens replacements for cataracts. These are routine, simple procedures with a high success rate. Recent refinements have involved the use of 3D printing technologies to reproduce the exact configurations of the titanium joint in hip replacements. There are a lot of individual differences in the size and shape of the pelvis, which can be anticipated with a custom appliance. The better the fit, the more comfortable and successful the procedure will be.

Once you move from mechanical replacements to body organs, two big issues emerge. First, you require a human donor, and second, the nature of body chemistry is to reject the organ unless immunosuppressant drugs are employed. Today the number of people waiting for organs far outpaces the donor pool. For example, thousands of people die each year waiting for a kidney transplant.[32]

Because of technological advances, new organs are being grown or manufactured in the laboratory using a recipient's own cells. Three-dimensional printing techniques first create a framework or scaffolding for replacement organs. Replacements are then seeded with human cells from the organ recipient to avoid rejection. Although this technology is still at the experimental stage, it is probably within 10 years of being available for widespread application. Organs such as skin, kidneys, the liver, and the pancreas are likely candidates for this type of organ replacement. Hearts and lungs are also on the list, as are

brain cells for stroke victims and muscle and bone tissue. CRISPR technologies associated with gene editing are also allowing us to avoid the traditional problem of rejection as well. Older people have body parts that essentially wear out, so being able to replace them makes tremendous sense, especially for the oldest-old.

DNA-based Medicines and Therapies

We are on the cusp of a revolution in medical care where genomics is being combined with personalized aging. The fine-tuning of genetic knowledge can be used to predict the impacts various medications and therapies have on each unique individual. There is no "one size fits all" when it comes to growing older. As Pinchas Cohen[33] has stated, "No matter how closely related we are, no two people experience the aging process in the same way." This approach, which uses personalized aging to arrive at **"personalized medicine,"** has proven to be effective in treating various cancers. We have known for decades that prescribed medications react differently in every individual. With a better picture of the unique disposition of the 25,000 genes that define each person and the use of big data analyses to sort out various patterns, we have the capability to match the most effective medications to specific individual genetic profiles.

Genetically sensitive medicine provides the opportunity to anticipate problems that are likely to occur. Knowing this, we can alter our lifestyle and our food choices as well as medication regimens in anticipation of aging challenges. Some chronic problems like Type 2 diabetes and pain management could greatly benefit from this genetically based knowledge. Wellness apps in the future may also monitor your body's response to medications and lifestyle choices. Bringing this advice to the person on a real-time basis with predictable outcomes is likely to be a powerful incentive for healthy living.

This strategy also includes matching our genetic profile to food choices (often called **nutrigenomics**[34]) and our own personal exercise regimen. Although there is good evidence that a sedentary lifestyle and obesity lead to a shorter life, making choices that are informed by our genetic profile can help maintain better health and a longer life. This extends the personalized aging model by considering culture, environment, and personal experience. It also focuses on nutrition and exercise, which are important influences that affect well-being and longevity.

To implement these approaches, it may take 7 to 10 years to reach a point when genetic analysis is inexpensive enough for widespread application. Still the potential for disease avoidance and the promulgation of healthy aging are important topics that deserve the research support necessary to achieve this goal.

CONCLUSIONS

Although difficult to implement, simple changes in the system of providing medical advice for chronic conditions is clearly needed. The ability to connect with the individual and their unique health circumstance may be the missing link. The combination of individual genetic and lifestyle knowledge filtered through a source of artificial intelligence that knows your health history with continuous updates from a mobile health device could be a game changer. It has the potential to deliver very accurate advice about your current health situation that can guide better future choices.

Endnotes

1 Foley, D., Heimovitz, H., Guralnik, J., and Brock, D. (2002), Driving Expectancy of Persons Aged 70 Years and Older in the United States, *American Journal of Public Health*, 92(8), 1284-89, https://www.ncbi .nlm.nih.gov/pmc/articles/PMC1447231 (accessed 10/22/17).

2 Glatter, R. (2015), A Startup Poised to Disrupt In-Home Senior Care, Forbes, September 25, https:// www.forbes.com/sites/robertglatter/2015/09/25/ a-start-up-poised-to-disrupt-in-home-senior-care/#7d3e46ff6536 (accessed 10/22/17).

3 GreatCall (2017), We Make It Easy for You to Stay Active, Mobile and Independent, https://www.greatcall .com/family-caregivingsolutions?gclid=CIuQo6z pi8wCFcdhfgodCFUB_Q&gclsrc=aw.ds (accessed 10/22/17).

4 Stables, J. (2017), Top Ten Fitness Trackers, Wareable, https://www.wareable.com/fitness-trackers/the-best-fitness-tracker (accessed 10/22/17).

5 Freier, A. (2015), The Future Is Wearable: US Wearables Market Set to Double by 2018, Business of Apps, http://www.businessofapps.com/the-future-is-wearable-us-wearables-market-set-to-double-by-2018 (accessed 10/22/17).

6 Weiner, G., and Smith B. (2017), Automated Driving: Legislative and Regulatory Action, CIS, http://www .cyberlaw.stanford.edu/wiki/index.php/Automated_ Driving:_Legislative_and_Regulatory_Action (accessed 10/22/17).

7 Aron, J. (2014), Computer with Human-like Learning Will Program Itself, New Scientist, https:// www.newscientist.com/article/mg22429932-200-computer-with-human-like-learning-will-program-itself (accessed 10/22/17).

8 PSFK (2017), Personal Robot Assistant Seeks a Loving Home, http://www.psfk.com/2015/01/personal-robot-assistant-home.html (accessed 10/22/17).

9 Turk, V. (2014), Robots Are Caring for Elderly People in Europe, Motherboard, http://motherboard .vice.com/read/robots-are-caring-for-elderly-people-in-europe (accessed 10/22/17).

10 Soft Bank Robotics (2017), Robots: Who Is Pepper? https://www.aldebaran.com/en/cool-robots/pepper (accessed 10/22/17).

11 Soft Bank Robotics (2017), Robots: NAO, https:// www.aldebaran.com/en/cool-robots/pepper (accessed 10/22/17).

12 PARO Therapeutic Robot (2014), http://www.parorobots .com (accessed 10/22/17).

13 Tan, A.M. (2015), Hasbro's New Robotic Cats Are "Companion Pets" for the Elderly, Mashable, http:// mashable.com/2015/11/19/hasbro-companion-pets/#LeyFkdSBWuqn (accessed 10/22/17).

14 Winkler, R. (2017), Elon Musk Launches Neuralink to Connect Brains with Computers, *Wall Street Journal* (March 27), https://www.wsj.com/articles/ elon-musk-launches-neuralink-to-connect-brains-with-computers1490642652 (accessed 10/22/17).

15 Masunga, S. (2017), Robots Could Take Over 38% of US Jobs Within About 15 Years, Report Says, *Los Angeles Times* (March 24), http://www.latimes.com/ business/la-fi-pwc-robotics-jobs-20170324-story.html (accessed 10/22/17).

16 Boston Dynamics (2017), Boston Dynamics: Changing Your Ideas About What Robots Can Do, https://www.bostondynamics.com/robots (accessed 10/22/17).

17 Watson, M. (2014), Honda's ASIMO: The Penalty Taking, Bar Tending Robot, Auto Express video, https://www.youtube.com/watch?v=QdQL11uWWcI (accessed 10/22/17).

18 Moon, M. (2015), Robear Is a Robot Bear that Can Care for the Elderly, https://www.engadget.com/2015/02/26/robear-japan-caregiver (accessed 10/22/17).

19 Tollos (n.d.), Why Use a Ceiling Lift? http://www.themedical.com/index.php/products/safe-patient-handling/electric-patient-ceiling-lifts/why-use-a-ceiling-lift (accessed 10/22/17).

20 Consumer Affairs (2017), Compare Reviews for Walk-in Bathtubs, https://www.consumeraffairs.com/homeowners/walk-in-bathtubs/# (accessed 10/22/17).

21 Bowdler, N. (2014), Rise of the Human Exoskeletons, BBC News, http://www.bbc.com/news/technology-26418358 (accessed 10/22/17).

22 Shirley Ryan Ability Lab (2017), Lokomat Gait Training, https://www.sralab.org/services/lokomat (accessed 10/22/17).

23 MIT Manus Robotic Rehabilitation Project (2012), https://www.youtube.com/watch?v=EN5_24biEWU (accessed 10/22/17).

24 Honda (2017), Walking Assist: Supporting People with Weakened Leg Muscles to Walk, http://world.honda.com/Walking-Assist (accessed 10/22/17).

25 AXOSUIT (2017), Welcome to Axo Suit, http://www.axo-suit.eu (accessed 10/22/17).

26 Easier Living: Everyday Independence (2017), Cushioned Clothing, http://www.easierliving.com/cushioned-clothing/default.aspx (accessed 10/22/17).

27 Queen Elizabeth Prize for Engineering (2017), Armourgel: Reducing the Danger of Falls Through Smart Materials, http://qeprize.org/createthefuture/armourgel-reducing-danger-falls-smart-materials (accessed 10/23/17).

28 Amigo (2017), Amigo TravelMate: Folding Travel POV/Scooter, http://www.myamigo.com/support/customize/218-travelmate-5 (accessed 10/23/17).

29 SmartChair (2017), The World's Best Innovative Electric Chair, https://kdsmartchair.com (accessed 10/23/17).

30 Ogo Technology (2017), Grab Life by the Wheels, https://ogotechnology.wordpress.com/page/2 (accessed 10/22/17).

31 Williams, R.W. (2017), How Virtual Reality Helps Older People, Next Avenue, https://www.forbes.com/sites/nextavenue/2017/03/14/how-virtual-reality-helps-older adults/#339e071c44e2 (accessed 10/22/17).

32 Cole, D. (2013), Repairing and Replacing Body Parts, What's Next? *National Geographic,* http://news.nationalgeographic.com/news/2012/13/130415-replacement-body-parts-longevity-medicine-health-science/, (accessed 10/22/17).

33 Pinchas, P. (2014), Personalized Aging: One Size Doesn't Fit All, in *The Upside of Aging: How Long Life Is Changing the World of Health, Work, Innovation, Policy and Purpose* (ed. P. Irving), John Wiley & Sons, Hoboken, NJ.

34 Lewis-Hall, F. (2014), The Bold New World of Healthy Aging, in *The Upside of Aging: How Long Life Is Changing the World of Health, Work, Innovation, Policy and Purpose* (ed. P. Irving), John Wiley & Sons, Hoboken NJ.

CHAPTER TWELVE

Primary Themes, Takeaways, and Conclusions

The US and the World Will Experience a Much Older Population

■ There will be more 85+, 95+, and 100+ year-old people in the future due to an increase in longevity and diminishing fertility.

■ The increasing proportion of Latino elders may shift our thinking toward home care and away from institutionalization. New models of institutional or community care may evolve to better include the family.

■ The biggest gains in the oldest-old throughout the world will be in the "less developed" countries.

■ China will have the fastest-growing aging population in the next 20 years due to the dearth of children born during the "single child" era. India will follow and along with Japan, will influence our thinking about long-term care models.

■ Will the new oldest-old be healthier or more impaired? What will be their health span vs. their longevity?

■ Will we experience more "compressed morbidity"? (i.e. a healthier and more active population near the end of life)?

■ Disability in the older population has lately been decreasing, but will obesity increase chronic impairment and reduce longevity?

Home Care Models and Integrated Health Care Models Are Needed

■ How can we best help older people "age in place" in independent or purpose-built housing with home delivered services?

■ There should be more programs in the US like the home care–supported models in northern Europe, which maintain the oldest-old in independent housing for as long as possible.

■ The PACE and the MCBC programs for dual eligibles (Medicaid and Medicare) help low-income frail people stay at home with medications, exercise, social support, and dental care. Combining home care with day care visits two or three times/week can effectively monitor health care and chronic conditions. PACE-type programs emphasize everyday care and health maintenance in place of diagnosing acute conditions and pursuing illusive cures.

■ Programs (like PACE) that provide ongoing comprehensive assessments and support should be subsidized on a sliding scale for those who do not qualify for Medicaid because of income.

■ "Aging in place" is often aging in isolation and leads to loneliness and depression. Living in independent housing with services available, like an Apartment for Life, provides meaningful opportunities for social exchange, friendship development, and reciprocal helping.

■ Living in an older two-story house in the suburbs may be dysfunctional. Supportive and accessible housing choices should be considered, even if it requires moving.

■ Families often invite an older relative to move in and to help them maintain their independence for as long as possible.

Assisted Living (AL) Is a Viable Alternative but Comes with Restrictions in the US

■ Assisted living is an improvement over skilled nursing and can delay or eliminate placement in an institution.

■ Even the best AL is somewhat institutional. Your daily life is constantly monitored by staff members with access to your apartment.

■ Although less expensive than skilled nursing care, AL is still unaffordable for many people and is rarely subsidized.

■ Because many services are provided, including meals and personal care, residents can be "oversupported" and can lose the initiative to do things for themselves.

■ Social programs that engage residents and create opportunities for fellowship and friendship formation are beneficial aspects of AL.

■ Unlike northern Europe, many US states limit the amount of medically related help provided in AL. Sponsors often cannot provide direct medical assistance like dressing wounds, providing insulin, or monitoring equipment. If residents need this type of help they often must either move in with relatives or to a nursing home.

■ Smaller residential group homes in the community are also a useful alternative. However, they may not be as professionally managed as a larger AL residence.

The Apartment for Life (AFL) Model Provides Personal and Medical Care in Independent Housing

■ This Dutch senior housing type combines independent age-restricted housing with medical and personal care provided through a home care delivery system.

■ The basic philosophy is to provide supportive services to older residents, allowing them to age in place and reach the end of life in their own independent unit. This avoids a last-minute move to assisted living, a skilled nursing facility, or a hospice.

■ The AFL builds on the modern idea that health care can be delivered to your own independent dwelling rather than requiring you to relocate to an institutional setting. Communications technology has facilitated this model by allowing home health, personal care, and emergency help to be summoned or scheduled when needed.

■ Severely demented residents who cannot safely maintain their independence are an exception. They are encouraged to move to small group homes (clusters of 6–12 residents) located within or adjacent to the AFL housing. Utilizing adult day care, a cognitively impaired AFL resident can often stay in their independent unit for a longer period of time.

■ The AFL philosophy encourages social interaction, an active lifestyle, and access to services when needed. Residents are encouraged to do as much as they can for themselves and help others through volunteerism.

■ AFLs are very social environments that use public spaces and restaurants to foster new friendships and informal helping relationships. They also invite family and friends to be part of a resident's everyday life.

■ The AFL is a similar model to the Continuing Care Retirement Community (CCRC) or Life Plan Community (LPC) in the US. Except residents need not move from their housing unit when they become frail. Also, the building is open to residents in the surrounding community, and provides adult day care and home care services to people in the neighborhood.

■ AFL units are offered as apartments or condominiums. Apartments are generally smaller and range from 700 to 1000 SF. These units are larger than AL or skilled nursing environments and allow residents to surround themselves with meaningful furnishings and memory-stimulating accessories. The larger unit size allows residents to accommodate additional equipment and have space for overnight stays.

■ AFL buildings have great potential for implementation in the US and should be more widely available. They can be made more affordable than assisted living, which often requires residents to take services for tasks they can do on their own.

Small Group Housing Clusters for the Extremely Mentally and Physically Frail Is Likely to Continue, Even with Other Options Available

■ Although policy makers in northern Europe have attempted to stop the growth of nursing homes, this building type is necessary for individuals with an advanced diagnosis of dementia or for those who have become extremely frail as they age.

■ Northern European LTC pioneered small clusters of (less than a dozen residents) in nursing environments nearly 40 years ago. Typically, five to seven clusters are located in separate buildings or in a single building on separate floors. Each cluster is treated as a self contained independent household.

■ Small decentralized households have been shown to be more effective than traditional nursing homes. The Green House© is the US exemplar that follows these criteria. Urban models augment small residential clusters with shared spaces for various activities.

■ In the last 15 years only about 2500 Green House© units have been created, which will not begin to satisfy future needs.

■ Northern European nursing homes are typically single occupied. Danish nursing homes, which average 400–500 SF, allow residents to bring in furniture and personalize

their unit. Units often accommodate a bed alcove, living room furniture, and a small table. They also provide access to private patios/balconies that connect residents with nature.

■ The Green House© and northern European clusters are managed as individual households with food choices, activities, and policies that are consistent with the preferences of residents.

■ Compared to traditional US nursing homes, small group clusters appear friendlier, with more interaction between residents, staff, and family members.

Most Existing US Nursing Homes Are of Poor Quality and Need to Be Phased Out or Upgraded

■ Many traditional nursing homes in the US are of poor construction quality. The median building age is 36 years and the standards utilized for construction often rely on institutional building and finishing materials. In northern Europe, the nursing home stock is owned and operated by the local municipality and costs are covered by single-payer insurance programs. A sense of civic pride advocates for modernization and improvements.

■ In the US, the caregiving atmosphere is also problematic. The majority of facilities are supported by Medicaid payments and sponsors report these reimbursements are too low to justify expenditures for improvements.

■ Given the lack of competition among US facilities and the low expectations of consumers, there have been few incentives to motivate improvement. After World War II, nursing homes in the US and northern Europe were comparable. But over the last 70 years, the northern Europeans have steadily increased quality by enlarging rooms, mandating single occupancy, and decentralizing care in small group clusters.

■ US facilities are often compared to prisons for their institutional character and lifeless, depressing appearance. Scheduling the day around a resident's needs and preferences is rarely considered. This is a standard feature in northern European homes that employ op matt programming.

- In addition to their uninspired appearance, the majority of US nursing homes have small, double-occupied (side-by-side) beds that share a toilet and lavatory. There is not enough space for personal furniture, so residents must settle for photographs and artwork mounted to walls. Even small accessories are often difficult to accommodate. Most bathing occurs in a large shared institutional shower room. To minimize the distance between the nurse's station and each resident's room, double-loaded corridors are commonly used. To minimize costs, food service generally takes place in a single large room where all residents are fed.

- Most buildings avoid the use of carpeting, so surfaces are hard and noisy even at night. HVAC systems are low quality and rarely employ the newest ventilation technology to evacuate unpleasant odors.

- Narrow operating margins leave little time for social contact. US nursing homes are usually not happy places with satisfied employees. Affect is in short supply and the compensation levels for most employees is minimal. Turnover rates can be as much as 100% in a year. Therefore the assignment of care workers to a particular resident (designated caregiver) is rare, and thus staff members often have little knowledge about a resident's history, interests, or preferences.

- Most residents have families who visit periodically, some every day. But the places are not physically inviting and often the staff view family and friends as additional burdens rather than welcome guests.

- The work of a nurse's aide requires physical exertion and residents are often uncooperative, confused, and temperamental. Today's residents are frequently obese and difficult to move, often requiring a "two-person lift." Portable or fixed lifts are required in Europe, but are rare in the US. US employees often suffer from workplace back injuries that can lead to disability.

- Given the 18–30 month average length of stay of residents, the time spent in the setting is not temporary. Still, even hospice environments with shorter end-of-life placements appear to be better environments in which to live.

- Despite their negative appearance and character, nursing homes are expensive, especially if you do not qualify for Medicaid. Market rates range by region but a single occupancy room in 2015 averaged $250 a day.

How Can We Help Those with Dementia Live a More Satisfying and Meaningful Life?

- Individuals with severe cognitive impairments are the most vulnerable aging population. Even with good family support, it is a challenge to keep them at home as the disease progresses. A nursing home placement is often the final step for the most severely impaired.

- We need better models for people with dementia that deliver care in a more humane way. Larger dwelling units, better trained workers, small group clusters, access to the outdoors, and a family-friendly operating philosophy are important. Innovative settings like the Hogeweyk Dementia Village and small group cluster models like the Green House© deserve replication.

- Depending on the individual, people with dementia can live as long as 10 years with the disease as it steadily reduces their cognitive ability. Current medications only slow progression at the beginning stages, and sometimes it is at the cost of organ damage. Even though medications and high-tech interventions can support people with early stages in the community, severely cognitively impaired individuals often require heavy care in secured environments. Although major strides in the treatment of dementia have occurred, there is no cure in the foreseeable future. Early detection may help plan for the onset of the disease, but today most are simply counseled to stay as mentally and physically active as possible.

- The onset of the disease is unique and depends on how the brain has been affected. Previous behavioral characteristics of the individual also play a role. Understanding how the disease progresses can inform individual therapies and responses.

- Improvements in devices that track individuals or programs that provide redirection can increase safety, autonomy, and enhance freedom.

- Many therapies focus on activities that provide immediate sensory satisfaction, like hand massage. Snoezelen therapies have been employed in northern Europe to facilitate communication with those who have lost their ability to speak.

- In northern Europe over the last ten years, the percentage of severely cognitively impaired residents has rapidly risen. Because those with severe dementia cannot stay at home by themselves, they must live with a spouse, a family member, or in a nursing home.

- Dementia is a major public health crisis and requires a concerted government effort to fight. It is a disease that will affect the US and the rest of the world even more in the near future.

Baby Boomers Have High Expectations for Quality Long-term Care Services but Lack the Means to Purchase Them

- Ten thousand baby boomers (born between 1946 and 1964) turn 65 each day. As they age, more are pondering how to deal with memory loss and acute episodes like a stroke. Approximately 70% of the 65+ cohort will eventually need some form of LTC. Unfortunately, many believe that this often-quoted 70% doesn't apply to them.

- A third of the baby boomer population has very little, if any, savings set aside for retirement, not to mention long-term care. This is especially true for older women. They not only live longer, but their reliance on a joint family retirement income places them at risk when a spouse dies and their income is reduced. Also, they often spend money on long-term care for their spouse, leaving themselves with fewer financial resources at the end of their life.

- Many baby boomers believe falsely that Medicare or Medicaid pays for all long-term care expenses or it will be likely do so in the future. Boomers have unrealistically high expectations for quality and are often naïve about access and affordability. The recent political reaction against Medicaid expansion indicates how difficult it will be to expand long-term care coverage in the future.

- There is little hope the quality of Medicaid-funded nursing homes will be significantly improved in the next decade. There is no concerted national or state-level effort to remodel or upgrade them. Doing so would require a huge investment. Baby boomers who have placed family members in a nursing home know them well enough to fear them.

- Long-term care insurance pays for both in-home care and nursing home stays. However, less than 25% of the over-65 population have this protection.

- Systems that support older people in their own homes are gaining momentum. Investors see an opportunity to employ new communication technologies and hourly workers to solve the problem.

- A higher percentage of boomers are working longer and retiring later to compensate for a shortfall in their retirement income and contingency funds for care needs. Often they are not capable of working longer and many have access to only part-time low-paying jobs.

- Many people believe their family will care for them at home as in previous generations. However, "sandwich" obligations to children and dispersed family settlement patterns continue to make this more difficult. The falling fertility rate has also reduced the number of offspring, with more older people in nursing homes who have no close family members.

- LTC is likely to take place first at home with supplemental assistance from home care agencies. But, as baby boomers age, need more help, or have more care needs, they may find it necessary to rely on a nursing home. This is especially true if they have a dementia diagnosis.

Supporting Friendships and Increasing Affect Make Places to Live Happier

- The oldest-old often have limited social circles because they outlive their close friends.

- It is important to make nursing homes joyful and happy places. Age-restricted independent housing for younger older people has a reputation for creating a social environment with active residents who share similar interests.

- Upbeat housing and service models like Apartments for Life emphasize living life to the fullest.

- "Hospice" or palliative care environments are often better than nursing homes because they emphasize living the last few days/weeks/months of life in a positive, joy-filled way.

- Programs that emphasize the arts, education, and intergenerational exchange can also nurture positive feelings.

- Dogs, cats, pets, plants, and children can create positive, unique, and memorable experiences. The use of these features, pioneered by efforts like the Eden Alternative, are effective in adding life and joy to nursing home environments.

- Making family and friends feel welcome encourages them to visit and continue to be part of a resident's life.

- Older people, especially those in institutions, often "act out" because they are depressed, unhappy, or frustrated. In response, caregivers rely on chemical controls that suppress bad behavior at the price of confusing residents or leaving them unresponsive.

How Will Advances in Technology Make a Difference?

- Advances in artificial intelligence can make future social robots valuable companions. Devices can be programmed with knowledge that is of interest to individuals, as well as information targeted toward beneficial outcomes. Widespread implementation is likely to be within 5–7 years.

- Experimental rudimentary robotics and AI have helped those with mild cognitive impairment by cueing them away from danger and engaging them in exercise activities.

- Robotic devices that can help older people carry out instrumental tasks are a decade or more away. They may first be employed to relieve the physical burden of moving and lifting family members.

- Self-driving cars could solve transportation problems in rural and low-density suburban environments where access is a serious problem. This developing technology may be widely available in less than 5–7 years. Their presence will also greatly improve accessibility, safety, and mobility in all environments.

- Wearable devices will continue to be employed to monitor health and increase walking safety and fall prevention.

- Better access to scheduled personal care help, emergency response, and advice/training will reduce the burden of aging in place. Replacing 24/7 human monitoring with devices that sense or anticipate problems will make it easier and safer to live independently in age-restricted housing or at home.

- Replacement organs and body parts are likely to help us live longer by upgrading a worn-out pancreas or replacing bones and lung tissue. Even harnessing the body's ability to self-correct will soon find its way into DNA editing protocols like CRISPR.

- The advent of new technology will solve age-old problems, reframe assumptions about the future, and very likely create new challenges for everyone.

An Emphasis on Exercise and Connections to Outdoor Spaces

- Exercise is still the miracle elixir for those who contemplate a long and healthy life. Research has found value in all forms of exercise, including regimens that strengthen muscles, facilitate stretching, and encourage aerobics.

- The northern Europeans (especially the Danes) heavily encourage movement therapies. Most European service housing mixes traditional exercise with physical therapy regimens. Also, supplemental programs for strength building and aerobic exercise are often prescribed as an individual becomes more impaired. Danes feel an obligation to stay fit and independent.

- The use of a wearable device can encourage stretch goals for walking and movement exercise. These can also facilitate friendly competition with family and friends.

- Many nursing homes do not encourage residents to walk to the dining room, and instead move them in a wheelchair to save time. This short-term thinking gradually erodes the competency and motivation of the older person.

- Exposure to outdoor space generates a calming response as well as, reducing anxiety and depression. Outdoor spaces visible from the inside encourage residents to explore gardens and walking pathways. This is especially helpful for people with dementia, where exercise and exposure to the outdoors can reduce stress, enhance relaxation, and encourage movement.

- Windows with low sill heights and high header heights connect the inside to the outside. Visible and accessible patio spaces encourage outdoor space use.

More Comprehensive Approaches at the City and Neighborhood Scale

■ The "Age-Friendly City" program helps older frail people live independently by creating a more supportive urban infrastructure. This is one of the best overall strategies to help an older urban population live a long and healthy life.

■ The program centers on 8 topics that benefit older people as well as other age groups. For example, calming and directing street traffic to create a safer pedestrian environment helps all age groups.

■ This approach harnesses the power of older volunteers to advocate for a better, more accessible city. It centers on using existing resources to make the urban environment a better place for families and older people.

■ Programming for older people in the community includes exercise classes, library programs, and courses at local community colleges. Parks often provide excellent access to activities and exercise.

■ Programs, like those implemented through the Village movement, employ volunteers to support seniors in their quest to age in place.

■ Age-friendly community surveys show that programs for older people rarely focus on technology, public health, intellectual stimulation, and social media.

■ Friendships and informal helping relationships from models like co-housing can encourage people to help one another.

Conclusions

It is always tempting to wonder where we will be in 20–25 years. In 2040 I will be 93 and, if I am still alive, I will likely be living the dilemmas described in this book.

I have been writing about this topic for the last 30 years, and have studied the aging population and related housing—domestic and abroad—for the last 45 years. I have experienced the growth of conventional nursing homes, the emergence of assisted living as an alternative, and the trend toward cluster design in nursing homes.

I have watched the growth in dementia and have felt the frustration of my scientific colleagues who have sought an elusive cure. I have also watched as European systems have done an excellent job keeping frail people independent while their facilities have filled with dementia residents. With the advent of PACE (which I have known from the beginning of the On-Loc prototype), I have also watched new programs creatively combine housing and services. As our aging population has grown in size and average age, it is clear that we need to carefully and quickly find better solutions to help everyone stay independent.

LTC has been redefining itself, and more home care approaches seem inevitable and logical, especially with the proliferation of new technology. I hope these alternatives will evolve quickly in the US. Alternatives such as assisted living have been clearly targeted to the more affluent population of older people. Their piecemeal approach, which limits medical care, is shortsighted. Northern European nursing homes have larger single occupancy units in small clusters. They have also managed to deliver more private, high quality medical services in a better environment than we have in the US.

Progress has been slow, but there are models we can advocate for and approaches that are well worth expanding. We need a commitment to a better future. A great start would be to replicate the success of northern European models—like the Apartment or Condo for Life. We need to commit more resources, demand better affordable accommodations, and raise our expectations for providing care in humanistic ways.

There are certainly dark storm clouds on the horizon. If the number of the older-old expands at the predicted rate, our current system will be overwhelmed. We see China struggling with the problem by proposing bigger and more autonomous institutions rather than reinventing a new family-based system of care. Northern Europeans, with the highest-quality systems, are struggling with fewer resources. How the Europeans solve their current problems will also suggest directions for the US. Europeans are operating today with percentages of the 65+ populations that are higher than the US. However, our aging population is steadily moving in their direction and will be approaching them by 2040.

I look forward, with optimism and trepidation, and hope that some of what I have discussed in this book will help stimulate the discussion of what we need to do next.

Index

Note: Page references in *italics* refer to figures and photos.

A

Accessibility, 10, 47, 54, 55, 57–58, *58*, 65, 69, 86–87, 161, *225*, 229, *231*, *244*, 286

Accessory dwelling units (ADU), 245–247, *246*

Activities of Daily Living (ADLs), 17–18, 42–43, 45, 49, 73, 94–96, *95–97*. *See also* Long-term care (LTC)

Adaptability, 6–7, 54–55, 65–66, *66*, *244*

Adult day care, xxiii, 37, *38*, 49, *98*, 115, *116*, 123, 126, 250, 282

Ærtebjerghaven (CS 13), 40, *41*, 47, 83, *160*, 184–189, *184–189*

AFL. *See* Apartment for Life (AFL); Apartment for Life (AFL) case studies

Age Friendly, 29, 138, 243–245, *244*, 287

Aging in place, *xxi*, 1–5, 9, 29, 115, 118–119, 124, 154, 230, *244*, 249, 282. *See also* Home-based service assistance

Amazon, 270, *277*

Amigo, 66, 276–277, 280

Anthroposophic Architecture, 106, 111, 196–201, *196*, *198*, *200*, *262c*

Apartment for Life (AFL), 113–157

  core concepts and components of, xxii–xxiii, xvi–xvii, *xxi*, 57–58, 65, 111–114, 120–126, 147–157, 282–283

  dwelling unit design, 85–87, *86–88*

  general considerations for, *148–150*

  Humanitas style of, 113–120

Armourgel, 276

Arthritis, xxvi, *15*, 17, 19–20, 43, 232, 254, 259

Artificial intelligence (AI) devices for homes, 270–273, 276, *277*

Artwork, *65*, 70, 73–74, 84, *105*, 115, *131*, 133, *180*, 254, 284

ASIMO (Advanced Step in Innovation Mobility), 273–274

Assisted living (AL), xx, xxii, xxiv, 1, 3, 5, *19*, 22, 33, 37–38, *38*, 43–47, 58, *71*, *75*, 85–86, 93, 99, 104, 111, 118, 122, 147, 195–201, *196*, 210–214, *210–213*, 237, 240, *260*, 282, 287. *See also* Apartment for Life (AFL); Building case studies; Design ideas and concepts; Long-term care (LTC); Outdoor spaces and plants

Atriums, *xxi*, 7, 62, *63*, *65*, *67*, 78, *79*, 84, 117, 129, *131*, 133, 258, 261–265, *262–264*

Autonomy, 1, 53–54, 91, 161, 175, 243–244, *284*

B

Baby boomers, 30, 285

Balance control, xxvi, 20–21, 66, *67*, 72, 100, 269

Balconies, 64, 84, 86, *87*, *136*, *137*, 146, 150, *167*, *205*, *206*, *207*, *208*, 283

Bathroom design, 20, 29, 43, 66, 71, 74, 76, 86–87, *88*, 112, *122*, 123–124, 137, 142, *143*, 145, 149–150, *155*, 164, *174*, 181, 186, *189*, *194*, 207, 213, 216, *225–226*, 229, *230*, 232, 246–247

Beacon Hill Village (BHV), 240–243, *241–243*

Becker, Hans, xvi, 99, 104, *105*, 113, 116

Bergweg Humanitas (CS 1), *xxi*, *79*, 87, *98*, *99*, 101, 115, *120–124*, 120–125, 145, *268*

Biophilia, 253–254, *254*

Building case studies, 111–228
  Apartment for Life (AFL), 113–157 (*See also*
    Apartment for Life (AFL) case studies)
  European history of home-care serviced
    buildings, 111–113
  smaller-scale assisted living case studies, xxiii,
    195–226 (*See also* Smaller-scale assisted
    living case studies)
  small group living clusters, xxiii, 157–195
    (*See also* Small group living cluster case studies)

C

Caregiving and management practices, xix-xxiii,
    xxv, xxvii, 3, 41–44, 53–55, 57, 83, 91–111,
    117, 222, 283
  accommodating independence with,
    53–55, 91–93, *92*
  Activities of Daily Living (ADLs) and, 18,
    94–96, *95–97*
  avoiding institutional lifestyle, 106–107, *107*
  dining rooms/nutrition, *18, 19,* 101–104, *103,* 116,
    123–124, 128–129, *131, 145,* 147, 157, 160,
    163, *165,* 168, *169, 173, 183,* 186, *187,* 191,
    193, 206–207, *207,* 211, *212, 225, 258*
  primary/secondary/designated caregivers, 93–94, *94*
  quality of life issues and, 42–43, *99,* 99, 104–106,
    105, 107–, *109,*161, 236, 276
  treating staff with respect, 54, 55, 109–110,
    110, 283–284
Carson, Dan, 78
Carvalho, Antonio, 250
Certified Nursing Assistants (CNAs), 44
Children, 9, 18, 21, 25–26, *26,* 31, 33, 48–49, 65, 71,
    74–76, 97, 105, 107–109, *108,* 114, 116–117,
    119, 123, *125,* 145, 158, 221, 226, *243,*
    258–259, 285–286
Choice, xix, xxii, xxvii, 1, 10, 37–52, 53–54, 81,
    102–104, 114, 154–155, *168, 179,* 212, 240,
    247, 278, 282–283

Clinical support teams (CST), 159–160
Cohen, Pinchas, 101, 278
Co-housing projects, *5,* 48, 111, 195, 214–219,
    214–218, 287
Comfort (first-order concept), *14,* 45–46, 53,
    54–55, 64, 70, 71, *71,* 76, 222, *259,* 263
Community table design (100% corner), 76–78,
    77, 78, 210
Compression of morbidity, 31
Continuing Care Retirement Community (CCRC),
    4, 5, 6, 38, 84–85, 111, 118–120. *See also*
    Apartment for Life (AFL)
Control (first-order concept), xxi, 2, 40, 42, 45, 53,
    54, 96, *99,* 107, 114, 159, 254
Convivium, 105, 160, 163
Courtyards, *xxv,* 60, *61, 110,* 129, 175–178, *176, 178,*
    182, 182, 195, *196,* 197, 261

D

Danish home care system, 93, 215, *232–234,*
    232–235, *276*
Daylight and skylight, *41,* 42, 62, 68–69, *68,* 132,
    142, *144,* 145, 155, *160,* 184, *184,* 195–197,
    210, 222, 225, *225,* 264
Dementia
  activities for, 17, *39,* 42–45, *75,* 83, *83,* 93, *95, 96,*
    102, 128, *128,* 235–238, *238,* 267, *271,* 272–275
  AFL core concepts for, xxiii, 118, 147
  effect on housing issues, 8
  at home vs. facilities, 5, 49, 84, *107*
  independence and, 21–22, 93, 270, 272–273
  outdoor spaces and plants for, *xxv,* 48, 58, 60–61,
    67, *72,* 254–256, *256,* 260–261, *260, 261*
  overview, 31, 37, *39,* 66, 97, 108–109, 111, 113,
    115, 118–119, 123–124, 126, 129, 140, 143–
    144, 146–147, 184, 195, 235, 283–287
  special design considerations for, *xxiv,* 16,
    21, 38, 44, 69, 71–74, *72–74,* 84, 86, 121, *124,*
    130–131, 144, 175–183, *175–183,* 193–194,

196, 199–200, *202–203*, 204–206, 208–209,
208, 210–213, *210–213*, 275, 278
See also individual case studies
Demographics and living arrangements, 25–35
aging population growth in US vs. other
countries, 26–31, *27, 28, 30*
ethnicity and, 33
family support and, 33, 47
gender and, *32*, 32–33
impacts of demographic growth, *31*, 31–32
income and, 32–34
longevity, xxv, 19, 25–26, 32–34, 55, 281
mortality and fertility, world population, xxv,
25–26, *26, 27*, 29, 49, 281
Denmark. *See* Danish home care system;
Northern Europe
Design ideas and concepts, 57–88
for dwelling units, 83–87, *84–88*
interior design and impact on senses, 46, 65, *70*,
70–72, *71*, 179–180, *180*, 261
refining design attributes and considerations,
64–74, *64–73*
See also Outdoor spaces and plants; *individual
case studies*
Designated Caregiver, 93, *94*, 211, 213, 284
Dignity (first-order concept), 40, 43, 45, 53, 54,
109, 114, 161
DNA-based medicines/therapies, 2, 104,
278–279, 286
Driverless cars, 3, 271
Dutch Apartment/Condo for Life (AFL) model. *See*
Apartment for Life (AFL)
Dwelling units, xx, *xxii*, 43, 83–87, *84–88*, 111–113,
123–124, *136, 146, 174*, 200, *210*, 222, 245–249,
261, *264*, 265. *See also individual case studies*

E

Echo (Amazon), 270, *277*
Eden Alternative, 107, 158, 286

Egebakken Co-Housing (CS 19), 214–219,
214–218
Enclosed street design, *264*, 265
Environmental docility hypothesis, *14*, 54–55
Europe, aging population growth in, 28–29. *See also*
Northern Europe
Exercise
atrium design for, 62, *63, 117*, 122, *128*, 261,
262, 264–265
avoiding falls and, 20–21, *20*, 272
caregiving and, 96, 233
in northern Europe, xx, 100, 207,
outdoor spaces for, *48*, 60, *67, 72*, 73, 108, *109,
110*, 116, 239–240, 254–256, 260–261,
260,
overview xxvi, *xxvi, 4*, 8–10, *10*, 29, 42, 140, *147,
153*, 155, 197, *198*, 275–276, 278–279,
281, 286–287
as second-order concept, 53, 54, 55
for upper-body arm muscles, *101*
walking for, 66–67, *96, 116*, 176–177, 190, *198*,
214, *215*, 258,
water resistance, *8, 200–201*
Exoskeletons, 275–276

F

Falls, avoiding, xxvi, 17, 19–21, *67*, 71–72,
148, 269, 276
Familiarity (second-order concept), 54, 55
Family and friends
design ideas for, 74–76, *75*, 78, *79*, 83, 86, 167,
171, 195, 209, 211, 219, 221–222
gender of family caregivers, 25, *32*, 32–34, 48,
114–116, 119
helping, xix, 2–9, 18, 21, 23, 29, 42, 92, 94–97, 102,
104–106, 132, 163, *165*, 182, 188, 234,
237–238, 241, 245, 247
functional purpose, 268–273, 275, 276
kitchens for hospice visitors, 47

moving closer to, 9
outdoor space, 57, 67, 73, 181, *183*, *258*, *261*
visitors to AFLs, 117, 282–286
welcoming, 54, 55, 58–59, 64, 107–109, 160–161,
    179, *180*, 229
Fences, 60, 259–261, 270
"Figure eight" or looped pathways, *48*, 60, 73, 176,
    178, 191, 195, *196*, *210*, 211–213, *213*, 261,
First-order concepts for housing the frail, 53, 54
Frank Lloyd Wright, 69, 72
Functional electro-mechanical robots, 66,
    271, 273–274
Functional purpose (second-order concept), 54
Furniture. 1, 3–4, 10, 15, 17, 42, *44*, 46, *69*, 70,
    70–71, 71–72, *73*, 73–74, 83–86, 104, 115,
    142, 150, 160, *169*, 179–180, *187*, 191, *197*,
    200, 201–202, 208, 222, 258, *259*, 259,
    283–284. *See* Design ideas and concepts;
    Outdoor spaces and plants

G

Gawande, Atul, xx, xxx–xxxi
GenSmart House, 247–249, *248*
Geriatric Career Development Program, 173–174
Green House model, xvi, xxi, xxiii, 40–43, 47, 64, 73,
    96, 102, *103*, 105, 109, 111, 158–159, *159*,
    161–174, *162–170*, *162–169*, *171–174*, 275,
    283–284. *See also* Small group living cluster
    case studies
GPS Monitoring, 193, 209, 270

H

Happiness and joy, as goal, 42, 48, 55, 101, 104–105,
    105, 114–116, 235
Herluf Trolle (CS 14), *xxv*, 40, 83, 87, 190–195,
    190–194
Hogeweyk Dementia Village (CS 12), xxv, 22, 60, 70,
    73, 75, *83*, 86, *96*, 101, *102*, *107*, 175–183,
    175–183, 284

Hoglund, David, xix
Home care-based services,
    home- and community-based care, xx, *xxii*, xxiii,
        xxv, 229–252, 91–94, *92*, 111, 124, 135, 154,
        157, 232–234, *234*, 238–240, *238–240*
    long-term care options, *46*, 47–49,
    overview, 1–6, 281–282
    See also Workforce
Home-like appearance (second-order concept), 54–55
Home modification programs, 2–3, *16*, 229–232,
    230–231
Home within a Home, 210, 213
Howell, Sandra, 81
Hospice models, (LTC), 37, 44–47, 59, 65, 195,
    219–223, *220–223*, 282, 284–285
House meetings, *97*, 159

I

Incontinence, 42–43, 71, *271*
Independence, xv, xvi, xx, 10, 13–24, 29, 42–43,
    65–66, 100, 107, *112*, *144*, 148–150, 181, 233,
    236, *237*, 241, 267–268, 282
    as AFL core concept, 114
    caregiving and management practices
        for, 91–93, *92*
    chronic conditions and disability, 17–18, 276–277
    chronic disease and risk factors, 18–22, *20*, *21*
    as first-order concept, 53, 54, 55
    Lawton's Environment-Press Model, *14*
    range of aging changes and, 13
    sensory modality changes, 13–17, *15–19*
Individuality (first-order concept), 42, 53, 54
Injuries, management of, 9–10, *10*, 21, 42, 99, 109,
    245, *275*, 271, 274, 267
Interstitial space design, 60–62, *62*
Instrumental Activities of Daily Living (ADLs), 18
Internet service utilization, 8, 122, *123*, 130, 150,
    232, *232*, 241, 267–270, *268*
Irismarken (CS 17), xxiv, 68, 78, *93*, 195, 205–209,
    205–209

K

Kahn, Robert, 9
Kellert, Stephen, 253–254
Kitchen residential design, *3, 7,* 47, *49,* 65,
72–73, *74,* 76, 84, 86–87, 95, 112, 115,
118–119, *122,* 123–124, 127–128, *136,* 137,
142–143, 145, 148–150, *148, 188,* 194, 197,
199–200, 216–219, 226, 230, *231,* 232, 237,
246–247, *248*
Kitchen commercial design, 10, 72–73, *77,* 83,
95, 100, *107,* 145, *145, 152, 158,* 160,
162, 163–165, *165, 166, 168–169, 172–173,*
173, 180–181, 186, *187,* 191–192, *193,*
195, *196,* 199, 201, *202, 205,* 206–207, *208,*
210, 211–212, *212, 215, 220,* 222,
225, 237, *270*
Kristal, De, (CS 6), *2, 74,* 84, *84,* 97, *100, 103,*
144–146, *144–145*

L

Labor Force Participation Rate, 33
La Valance (CS 3), *18,* 48, *59, 63,* 65, *78, 103,*
129–134, *130–133,* 263
Landscape. *See* Outdoor spaces and plants
Lawton, M. P., xx, 13, *14,* 54
"Lean-to" housing example, 133, *133*
Learned Helplessness, 13, 114, 159
Lennar Homes, Orange County,
California, 247
Leonard Florence Center for Living (CS 10),
165–170, *166–169*
Life Plan Community (LPC), xxii, 5, *6, 64, 67,* 70,
84–85, 118–119, 151–157, *151–156, 158,* 282.
See also Continuing Care Retirement
Communities (CCRC)
Lighting, 10, 14, *16, 17,* 21, 59, 64, 66, 68–70, *68,* 87,
105–106, 150, 207, 259, 270
Longevity. *See* Demographics and living
arrangements

M

Long-term care (LTC), 37–51
activities for residents, overview, *39, 40, 43–45, 47,
48,* 101, 254
alternatives to, 22, 37, *104, 113*
assisted living settings, 43–45
checklist for, *42*
defined, xx, 37
future of, 49, 287
insurance, 239–240, 285,
overview, 47, 156, 118, *151–152,* 156–158
See also Demographics and living arrangements;
*individual case studies; individual types of
living arrangements*

M

Martha Child, xx, *19,* 44, *61, 62, 71, 80, 213*
Medicaid, xx, xxiv, 2, 8, 33, 38, 44–45, 49, 161, 174,
236–239, 269, 281, 283–285
Mobility, xxvi, 9, 13, 19, *46,* 48, 78, *268,* 271, *274,*
276–277, 286
transportation issues, *2,* 3, 5–6, 9, 58, 117–118,
229, 236, *238, 240,* 240–241, 243–244, *244,*
267–271, *268, 274,* 276–277, 286
Mortality rates. *See* Demographics and living
arrangements
Moving, of household, 4–9
Mount San Antonio Gardens Green House (CS 9),
64, *103, 159,* 161–165, *162–165*
Muscle strength, 19–21, *101,* 275–276
Musholm Bugt Feriecenter (CS 21), 223–226,
224–226
Music and music therapy, 16, *39,* 59, 73, 83,
101–102, *102,* 109, 115, 129, 176, 181,
221, 254

N

National Shared Housing Resource Center, 7
Naturally occurring retirement communities
(NORC), xxiv, 249–250, *250*

Neighborhood, 59–64, 97–99
    aging in place and, xxiii, *2*, 3, 29
    design ideas, 43, *79*, *143*
    serving the neighborhood, xxiii, 54, *92*, 97–99,
        98, 100, 112, 117, *120*, *167–168*, 171, 200,
        234, 250, *263*, 264, 282
    site issues, and outdoor space, *78*, 113, 117–118,
        127, 135, *135*, 138, *143*, 146, 157, 212,
        234, *241*, 287
    qualities, 57–63, *58*, 66–67, 123–124, 128, *139*,
        174, *203*, 231, 240, *246*, 249, *250*
Neptuna (CS 4), *58*, *59*, *68*, 97, *117*, 134–138,
    134–137, *257*
Nest, 270
Neutra, Richard, 58
NewBridge on the Charles (CS 8), *6*, *64*, *70*,
    151–157, *151–156*, *158*
New Jewish Lifecare Manhattan Living Center
    (CS 11), 170–174, *171–174*
Next Gen House, 247–249, *248*
1915c waiver programs (home- and community-
    based care), xxiv, 8, 238–239, *238–239*
Northern Europe
    nursing home changes in, 40
    progress of small group living
    clusters in, 157–158
    See also individual case studies
Nursing homes
    alternatives to, 40, 44–47, *239*, 275
    changes made to, in Northern Europe, 40–41,
        41, 95, 43, 233
    checklist for, *42*
    Danish Nursing Homes, 83, 85, *97*, 100, 184–189,
        184–189, 190–195, *190–194*, 205–209,
        205–209, 223, 226
    facts and figures about, 5, 10, 33, 37–41,
        111–112, 161, *162*
    Medicaid and traditional, 2, 38, 64, 239
    problems of, xix-xxii, xxiv, 8, 20–22, 38–39, *40*, 78,
        104, 106–109, *106*, 114, 158, 176, 222, 283–287

Nutrition, xxvi, 9–10, *10*, 19, 101–104, *103–104*, 116,
    243, *244*, 278

O

Observation, design for, 78–80, *79*, *80*
Oldest-old population
    defined, xx, xxii–xiii, xxv, 2, 17, 19–22, 26, 28–29,
        31–33, 40, 53, 57–58, 111, 121, 195, *240*, *244*,
        245, 250, 281, 285
    meeting needs of, 1–11, 259
100% corner/community table design, 76–78, *77*, *78*, 210
Open plan, *xxi*, *19*, 69–70, *69*, 73, 168, 211,
    216–218, 261
Op maat (customization) programs, 40, 93–94, *93*,
    102, 114, 157, 173–174, 182, 211
Osmund Plan, 184, *185*, 189
Outdoor spaces and plants, 253–266
    biophilia and, 253–254, *254*
    dementia gardens, *256*, 260–261, *260*, *261*
    design considerations for, 42, 57–62, *58–59*,
        61–63, *72*, 75, 96, 110, *169*, 243, *244*
    European atrium buildings, 261–265, *262–264*
    health benefits from, *67*, 253–256, *255*, 257–259, 286
    overview, *79*, *80*, 85–86, 286
    shade control, 69, 219

P

PACE (Program for All-inclusive Care for the
    Elderly), xxiv, *xxvi*, 37, 48, 235–238, *235–238*,
    250, 269, 281, 287
Pardee Homes, Pasadena, California, 247
PARO (social robot), 108, *271*, 272–273
Pastalan, Lee, 78
Personalization
    personal environment, 46, 83–84, *84–85*, 222
    primary, secondary, designated caregivers and
        computers, 93–94, *93–94*, 107
    as second-order concept, 54–55

Personal Emergency Response Systems (PERS), 87, 267, 269, *269*

Pets, *45*, 47, 71, 107–108, *109*, 116, 158, 197, 222, 269, 286

Physical environment, defined, 54

Plussenburgh, De (CS 5), *17*, *86*, 138–143, *139–143*

Potential Support Ratio, 33

Predictability (first-order concept), 53, 54

Primary path design, 81–82, *81–82*

Privacy (first-order concept), xxi, 39, 42, 47, 53, 54, 84, 102, 161, 168, 186, 192, *200*, 247, 255, 258, 263, *273*

Protective clothing, 276

Purposeful activity, *47*, 54, 55, 101

R

Rendever, 277–278

Replaceable body parts, 278

Retreat space, 80–81, *80*, 211, 258, *263*

Rideshare companies, 267–268

Robear, 274

Rowe, John, 9

Rundgraafpark (CS 2), *7*, *20*, 84, *87*, *108*, *116*, 125–129, *125–128*, *262*

S

Safety
of assisted living vs. residential care settings, 43, 72, 160–161, 193, 261, 264, 275
necessity of safety and home care services, xxvi, 1, *2*, 6–8, 10, 16, 21, 87, 229–230, 232, 243, *244*, 245, 271, 277, 284, 286
as second-order concept, 54, 55

Sarcopenia, 19

Scooters, 58, *58*, 66, 69, 119, 124, 127, 138, 154, *274*, 276–277

Seasonal Affective Disorder, 255

Second-order concepts for housing the frail, 53–55

Section 115 waiver programs (home- and community-based care), xxiv, 8, 237–239, *239*

Sensors (electronic), *272*

Sensory modality change, 13–18, *15–19*

Sensory stimulation (second-order concept), 54, 253

Service House Models, xxiv, 85, 112–114, *112–113*, 129, 132, 157, 195, 201–204, *202–204*, 223, 226, *257*

Shahbazim, 159–160, 163, 167, 173

Smaller-scale assisted living case studies, 195–226
overview, 111, 195
See also individual case studies

Small group living cluster case studies, 157–195
operational environment, 159–160
overview, 111, 283
physical environment, 160–161,
progress in Northern Europe, 157–158
recent research, 161
See also individual case studies

Small Houses. *See* Green House model

Smit, Jacques, xx, 83

Snoezelen therapies, *39*, 42, 73, 132, 176, 180, *181*, *210*, 211, 284

Social connection, 74–82, *244*, 281–282, 284–287
in active adult communities, 8–9
in AFLs, *104*, 119
atrium design for, *xxi*, 62, *63*, *116*, 264–265, *262*
caregiving and management practices for, *20*, 101–104, *102–103*, 138, 195, *235*, 236–237
courtyards, 60, *61*
design ideas and concepts for, 46, 70, *74*, 74–83, *77–85*, *97*, *111–112*, 114–116, *116*, 140, 145, *145*, *147*, 178, 212, 219, 246, 249–250, 255, 258, *258*,
as first-order concept, 53–55
importance of, 9–10, *10*, 15, 20, 64–66, 159–160, 241, 243,
overview, 241, 285–286
peer interaction, 8–9
research, 161, 254,

Social robots, 108, 271–274, *271*, 286
Steiner, Rudolph, 106, 196–198, *198*
Stimulation, 211, 256–257, 287
   as AFL component, 116, 117
   plants, pets, kids, and creative arts for,
        107–109, *108*, *109*
   as second-order concept, 54–55
Street (enclosed) design, *264*, 265
Strength capacity, 19–21, 67, 123, 276
Sunlight, 3, *41*, 47, 60, 62, *65*, 68–69, *68*, 73, 121,
        142, 144–145, 155, 160, 184, 195–197, 201,
        210, 222, 253, 255, 261, 263–264
Sunrise of Beverly Hills Dementia Cluster (CS 18),
        210–213, *210–213*, 258
Supportiveness (second-order concept), 54–55
Supra-personal environment, defined, 54

T

Technology, xv, xxv, 267–280, 286
   artificial intelligence devices, 239, 270–273, *277*
   Danish home care system, 232–235, *232–234*, *276*
   DNA-based medicines and therapies, 278–279
   driverless cars, 271
   electronic safety systems, 7–8, 239
   exoskeletons, 275–276
   home-delivered services, 115, 168, *234*, 241, 267,
        269–271, *269*, *270*, 275–276
   monitoring with, 119, 237, 268, *273*, *274*
   nutrigenomics, 101, 278–279
   protective clothing, 276
   for record keeping, *94*
   replaceable body parts, 278
   robots, 108, 271–273, *271*,
   scooters and mobility aides, *274*, 276–277
   sensors, 243, *272*
   on-line ridership, 267–268, *268*, 271
   virtual reality, 277–278

Thomas, William, xx, 96, 158, 159
Trading Ages simulation exercise, *15*
Transfer and lifting devices, 100, *101*, 109, 148,
        150, 174, 186, 192, *194*, *220*, 232, 274–275,
        275, 286
Transportation
   mobility and, 9
   technology and, 267–268, *268*, 271
   See also Home-based service assistance
Triangulation, 82–83, *83*

U

Ulrich, Roger, 253–254, 258
Ulrika Eleonora Service House (CS 16), *66*, *68*, 195,
        201–204, *202–204*
Universal Design (UD), 54, 65–66, *66*, *88*, 113
Unpredictability of aging, 1–2
Use it or Lose it, 99–100, *99*

V

Vigs Ängar Assisted Living (CS 15), 195–201,
        196–200, *259*, *261*
Village to Village Network, xxiv, 240–243
Virtual home care, 234
Virtual reality, 255, 277–278
Volunteers, 75, *79*, *98*, 101, 113–116, *115*, 122–123,
        146, 182, 207, 212, 222–223, 241–245,
        241, 261, 287

W

Waiver programs (home- and community-based
        care), xxiv, 8, 238–239, *238–240*
Walking. *See* Exercise
Wealth span, 2
Wearable Devices, 239, *269*, 286

Wellness
   caregiving and management for, 104–106, *105*,
      119, 154, 278, 287
   as second-order concept, 54–55
Wheelchairs, *49*, 54, 69, 72, 86, *143*, 164, 168, 184,
      194, 200, 204, 226, 276–277
Willson Hospice (CS 20), 46, 59, 219–223, *220–223*
Windows, *19*, 42, 47, 58, *62*, 64–66, 68–69, *68*, 72,
      85, 106, 109, 137, *137*, *146*, 148, 150,
      163–164, *164*, *167*, *169*, *174*, 181, 186, 191–193,
      193, 196–198, *198*, *203*, 209, *209*, *211*, 213,
      215, 216, *217*, *221*, 222, 258, 260–261,
      265, 286
Wintergardens and Greenhouse-type spaces,
      58, *59*, 60, 73, 129, *134*, *136*, 138, 197,
      199, 216, *257*, 258–259,
      263, *263*
Woodlands Condo for Life Prototype (CS 7), 65, 84,
      146–151, *146–148*

Workforce
   in assisted living vs. residential care settings, 43, 44
   Certified Nursing Assistants (CNAs), 44
   as extended family, 114
   in hospice, 46
   in nursing homes, 40
   respect for staff, 54, 55, 109–110, *110*
   in small group living clusters, 159–160
   See also Home-based service assistance

Y

YES Culture, 114

Z

Zeisel, John, 53, 79
Zimring, Craig, 254

Workforce
in assisted living vs. residential care settings, 43, 44
Certified Nursing Assistants (CNAs), 11
as extended family, 114
in hospices, 40
in nursing homes, 40
respect for staff, 51-55, 109-110, 110
in small group living clusters, 159-170
see also Home-based services

Y

YMCA clubs, 114

Z

Zabol, John, 79
Zoning, Greg, 154

Wilson
Caregiving and management for, 104, 104, 105,
119, 151, 154, 159
second-order change, 51-52
Wheelchairs, 49, 54, 67, 72, 94, 101, 104, 168, 186,
190, 200, 201, 226, 230, 252
Wilson, Margaret (case), 36, 50, 119-131, 220-221
Windows, 18, 32, 37, 64, 68, 72,
82, 104, 109, 133, 132, bee, 163-164, 167, 169, 174, 181, 186, 191,
193, 196-198, 302, 309, 309, 311, 312,
313, 314, 317, 323, 324, 338, 340, 261, 267,
286
Wintergardens and Greenhouse type spaces,
56, 59, 66, 94, 177, 179, 136, 138, 197,
199, 216-217, 256-256, 261, 262,
Worthlessness, feelings of (by homes per C.5.?), 65, 84,
146-151, 148-148